Piracy and Law in the Ottoman Mediterranean

Piracy and Law in the Ottoman Mediterranean

Joshua M. White

STANFORD UNIVERSITY PRESS
STANFORD, CALIFORNIA

Stanford University Press
Stanford, California

Printed and bound by CPI Group (UK) Ltd, Croydon, CR0 4YY

Library of Congress Cataloging-in-Publication Data

Names: White, Joshua M., 1981– author.

Title: Piracy and Law in the Ottoman Mediterranean / Joshua M. White.

Description: Stanford, California : Stanford University Press, 2017. | Includes bibliographical references and index.

Identifiers: LCCN 2017005043 | ISBN 9781503602526 (cloth : alk. paper) | ISBN 9781503603929 (epub)

Subjects: LCSH: Piracy—Law and legislation—Turkey—History. | Piracy—Law and legislation—Mediterranean Region—History. | Piracy—Turkey—History. | Piracy—Mediterranean Region—History. | Piracy (International law)—Mediterranean Region—History. | Turkey—History—Ottoman Empire, 1288–1918.

Classification: LCC KKX4395 .W55 2017 | DDC 345.56/0264—dc23
LC record available at https://lccn.loc.gov/2017005043

Typeset by Newgen in Sabon-Roman

For my parents

Contents

Preface

In March 2011, the Libyan dictator Muammar Qaddafi warned a French journalist that, if his regime fell, "There will be Islamic jihad in front of you in the Mediterranean . . . there will be acts of piracy here, at your doors, 50 km from your borders. [Osama] bin Laden's people will come to impose ransoms on land and sea. We will return to the time of Barbarossa, of pirates, of Ottomans imposing ransoms on ships."[1] As Qaddafi's remarks make clear, the legacy of piracy lives on in the historical memory of the Mediterranean. His reference to Tripoli's past as a hub of corsairing—effectively state-sponsored piracy—spoke directly to interpretations of Mediterranean history that view piracy within the frame of a perpetual holy war between Islam and Christianity, with the Muslim corsairs of North Africa lined up against those of Catholic Malta and Livorno. Qaddafi conjured the image of the North African pirate as scourge of Christendom and, drawing an analogy with al-Qaeda, constructed a genealogy of violence that made contemporary terrorism its latest incarnation.

The subsequent chaos in Libya may have made Qaddafi's desperate warning appear prescient, but if he was correct that economically marginalized, strategically located weak states are ideal breeding grounds for piracy, his understanding of the history of Mediterranean maritime violence was fundamentally flawed.[2] Although the famous corsair admiral Hayreddin Barbarossa (d. 1543), the "Red Beard" Qaddafi referred to, and his acolytes were instrumental in the extension of Ottoman sovereignty to Algiers, Tunis, and Tripoli over the course of the sixteenth century, the Ottoman central government exercised little control in those places during the seventeenth-century halcyon days of Mediterranean piracy. Nor were religious motivations paramount, although the rhetoric of holy war was omnipresent in the early modern Mediterranean. In the 1620s, as fleets from North Africa were staging raids as far away as Iceland, they were also sacking Ottoman Mediterranean ports and attacking Ottoman shipping, casting a dark shadow on their holy warrior credentials. The North African corsairs—most of them European "renegades," or converts—were hardly alone in their predations. A whole host of Christian and Muslim pirates terrorized the Ottoman Mediterranean between the 1570s and the first decades of the eighteenth century. The Ottomans were not simply perpetrators or enthusiastic supporters of piratical violence as they have usually been portrayed, but rather its most prominent victims.

This book, the first on Mediterranean piracy to make extensive use of a wide range of Ottoman sources, tells some of those victims' stories. It traces the causes and consequences of the early modern Ottoman Mediterranean's pervasive piracy and follows the individuals, institutions, laws, and customs involved in sorting out the personal, legal, and diplomatic predicaments pirates left behind. From the realm of high diplomacy to the provincial courtroom, it addresses the Ottoman experience of and response to piracy in Ottoman waters.

Law is what defines piracy, distinguishing it from the legitimate violence of war, and law is what makes it legible to the historian. Piracy generated paper trails that crisscrossed the seas, often for years after an attack, as rulers and diplomats sought redress, owners the return of stolen property, and captives their freedom. The legal lens makes a fuller spectrum of piracy visible. It brings the considerable effects of piracy on Ottoman foreign and domestic policy and on Ottoman legal theory and practice into relief.

Where was the line between acceptable and illegal raiding, and who had the right to set it? Debates surrounding this question had a dramatic impact on the Ottoman center's relationship with its overseas provinces, in particular driving a wedge between Istanbul and North Africa in the seventeenth century. What made the eastern half of the Mediterranean "Ottoman" after the 1570s, this book argues, was not so much Ottoman control of the land nor Ottoman mastery of the sea—which was ephemeral—but the fact that it was an Ottoman legal space. Over the course of the seventeenth century, the challenge of piracy helped define its contours.

Scholars' overreliance on European-language sources and myopic focus on the major corsairing operations have obscured the diversity of Mediterranean piracy and its far-reaching effects on the Ottomans. The so-called Barbary Corsairs and their Catholic counterparts have received ample attention, the former more so than the latter. Much of the scholarship is based exclusively on European documentary evidence, especially captivity narratives and diplomatic correspondence.[3] Studies focusing on various national groups of Europeans in North African captivity abound, but the stories of Ottoman-subject captives and victims of piracy have rarely been told.[4]

The fact that nearly every study of piracy and captivity in the early modern Mediterranean has focused on the activities of the parallel organized raiding enterprises based out of North Africa, Malta, or Livorno is unsurprising. The institutional support these corsairs received increased the political, diplomatic, and military significance of their activities and, crucially, increased the quantities of source material available to the modern historian. Whereas the Maltese left behind archives, the local pirate operating out of a small frigate on the Anatolian coast left none. But that focus conceals the chaotic and ambiguous reality of the Ottoman Mediterranean and the wider range of local and long-distance piratical actors it hosted.

What is more, the neglect of Ottoman sources has resulted in the near-total absence of Ottoman administrative and legal institutions and their representatives from the historiography of Mediterranean piracy. The Ottomans, if mentioned at all, are presented as complicit, impotent, or simply absent. The Ottoman Empire, sovereign in fully half of the Mediterranean, has been almost completely left out of the story. By reinserting the Ottomans, this book offers a revised appraisal of the shape and impact of maritime violence in the early modern Mediterranean.

To reconstruct the Ottoman experience of and response to piracy in the late sixteenth and seventeenth centuries, this book draws on research in archives and libraries in Istanbul, Venice, Crete, London, and Paris across a wide range of sources, including Ottoman administrative documents, European ambassadorial dispatches, Ottoman court registers, manuscript collections of Islamic legal opinions, Ottoman chronicles, and captivity narratives. For granting access and fulfilling my many requests, I am grateful to the librarians, archivists, and staffs of the Prime Ministry's Ottoman Archives, the Süleymaniye Library, and the Islamic Research Center (İSAM) in Istanbul; the State Archives of Venice; the UK National Archives in Kew (London); the Vikelaia Municipal Library in Heraklion, Crete; and the National Library of France in Paris. My thanks go as well to the staffs of the Hatcher Library at the University of Michigan, the Alderman Library at the University of Virginia, and the Butler Library at Columbia University, and to Chris Gist at the UVA Scholars' Lab for his help with the map.

Over the years spent researching and writing this book, I benefited from the generous support of many institutions, mentors, colleagues, and friends. It is a great pleasure to finally acknowledge them here. I thank first my mentors. Rudi Lindner is a true mensch—humane, patient, generous with his time, and endlessly supportive—and the model I try to emulate as a teacher and a scholar. I will always be grateful to him for his kindness and good humor. Gottfried Hagen, to employ the old cliché, has forgotten more than I will ever know. He inadvertently spurred me toward this project and, later, pointed me in directions I never would have thought to look; his influence is on every page. John V. A. Fine and Diane Owen Hughes kindly shared their wisdom with me and offered valuable comments on an earlier version of the manuscript. Leslie Peirce has been an inspiration and a friend to me and this project for many years now. Elizabeth Thompson gave me a wonderful opportunity and has helped me make the most of it.

Many thanks go to the colleagues and friends who read and commented on the manuscript. The book you have before you is far better thanks to the efforts of Emrah Safa Gürkan, Will Smiley, Molly Greene, and Judith Tucker. Ananda Burra, Zoe Griffith, Sharon Kinoshita, Erin Lambert, and Michael Talbot offered invaluable feedback on individual chapters. Needless to say, the errors of fact or interpretation that remain are entirely my own.

For helping facilitate my research across many countries and more trips, for giving generously of their knowledge and often their hospitality, I thank Guy Burak, Antonis Hadjikyriacou, Colin Heywood, Wolfgang Kaiser, Alexandros Katsigiannis, Elias Kolovos, Tijana Krstić, Hayri Gökşin Özkoray, Natalie Rothman, Marinos Sariyannis, Nur Sobers-Khan, Katerina Stathi, Yannis Spyropoulos, and Nicolas Vatin. For moral support and welcome distractions over the years of research and writing, I thank my friends and fellow travelers, especially Richard Antaramian, Sheree Brown, Ian Campbell, Lale Can, Alison DeSimone, Matt Ellis, Kelly Ferneding, Tobias Graf, David Gutman, Piotr Kosicki, Vjeran Kursar, James Meyer, Nevila Pahumi, Emily Price, Will Smiley, and Eric and Rachel Snead.

The research and writing of this book were supported with generous fellowships and grants from the American Council of Learned Societies (ACLS), the American Research Institute in Turkey (ARIT), the Council of American Overseas Research Centers, the US Department of Education's Fulbright-Hays Program, the Mellon Foundation, the National Endowment for the Humanities, the University of Michigan, and the University of Virginia.

ARIT, in the beautiful Bosphorus-side neighborhood of Arnavutköy, was my home in Istanbul for more than two years and the place where this project first took shape. I thank Tony Greenwood and Gülden Güneri for making ARIT a warm and hospitable environment. I am grateful to my colleagues in and beyond the Department of History at the University of Virginia for their encouragement and the robust trade in ideas. I especially want to thank Paul Halliday, Paul Kershaw, Erin Lambert, Erik Linstrum, Amanda Philips, Ahmed al-Rahim, Jonah Schulhofer-Wohl, Robert Stolz, Melissa Thomas-Hunt, and Elizabeth Thompson (now at American University). This book was completed during a yearlong residency at the Heyman Center for the Humanities at Columbia University under the auspices of the ACLS; I thank the staff and fellows for making it a genial place to write and my New York friends and my aunt for keeping me from spending too much time there. Kate Wahl, editor-in-chief at Stanford University Press (SUP), guided this book to press with breathtaking efficiency. I am indebted to her and the entire SUP staff.

Above all, I thank my family: my parents, Perrin White and Marjorie Boeck; my brother, Ben, and his wife, Matan; my nephew, Noah; my aunt, Marjorie White; and my late grandparents. My mother is the source of my curiosity and my wanderlust. With her as my inspiration, it is little surprise that I indulge both for a living. My father has immersed himself in every aspect of my work from the beginning. My most dependable editor, he has read every page of this book multiple times and saved you, the reader, from some of my worst prolix tendencies. My parents' boundless support made all things possible. This book is for them.

Note on Place-Names, Transliteration, and Dates

Where cities and geographical features have well-known names in English, I have used these. For example, Salonica, rather than Thessaloniki or Selanik. In other instances, I have preferred to use names current in the period under study, usually the Ottoman ones. Alternate names and the present-day place name are given at first mention, as in Avlonya (Valona, present-day Vlorë in Albania).

A modified Modern Turkish orthography is used for transliterating Ottoman Turkish. Turkish words that are well known in English, like "pasha," are used instead of *paşa*. Others are italicized throughout. Words and phrases that are of Arabic origin, when they appear in an Ottoman Turkish context, are rendered according to Modern Turkish orthographical conventions (e.g., *darülislam*); although this and similar terms are already definite, I still employ the English definite article where appropriate for clarity and consistency. All translations are mine unless otherwise noted.

Dates in the body are given according to the Gregorian calendar. References in the notes preserve documents' original dates. For Ottoman documents, this means the Islamic lunar (*hijri*) calendar. Months are abbreviated as follows: Muharrem M, Safer S, Rebiyülevvel RA, Rebiyülahir R, Cemaziülevvel CA, Cemaziülahir C, Receb B, Şaban Ş, Ramazan N, Şevval L, Zilkade ZA, Zilhicce Z. Ottoman documents sometimes eschew precise numerical dates in favor of the following terms, which have been reproduced as they appear: Gurre (the first of the month), Evail (between the first and tenth), Evasıt (between the eleventh and the twentieth), Evahir (between the twenty-first and the thirtieth), and Selh (the last day of the month). The Venetian calendar year began on March

1; when there is a discrepancy between the Venetian and Gregorian dates, the date is marked "m.v." (*more Veneto*). For example, February 3, 1625, m.v., would be February 3, 1626. English documents often give both Old Style (Julian) and New Style (Gregorian) dates, separated by a slash, as in November 11/21, 1606; otherwise, Old Style dates, which are ten days behind the Gregorian date, are indicated (OS) as necessary.

Mytilene
Izmir
Chios
Euboea
Kuşadası
Samos
Andros
Paros
Naxos
Kos
Ios
Milos
Santorini
0
150 KM
Venice
Livorno
Dubrovnik
Nova
Rumeli
Edime
Istanbul
Rome
Draç
Salonica
Naples
Avlonya
Volos
Anatolia
Iskenderun
Aleppo
Corfu
Izmir
Lefkada
Kuşadası
Silifke
Cephalonia
Morea
Messina
Zante
Rhodes
Cyprus
Tripoli
Baf
Modon
Koron
Sicily
Tunis
Crete
Candia
Malta
Damietta
Alexandria
Tripoli
Cairo
Egypt
0
125
250
500 Kilometers

Piracy and Law in the Ottoman Mediterranean

Introduction

On September 13, 1614, a group of men gathered in the Ottoman court of the seaside district of Galata. Situated across the Golden Horn from Istanbul proper, Galata was the maritime nerve center of the Ottoman Empire. Housing extensive port facilities, warehouses, and associated industry, as well as the Ottoman Imperial Arsenal, it was home to a diverse population of Christians, Jews, and Muslims. It played host to seamen and merchants hailing from England to India and to the European ambassadors to the Sublime Porte. The court of Galata, convened in the home of its judge (*kadi*), was open to all of these, whether Ottoman subject or foreigner, free or enslaved, Muslim or non-Muslim, permanent resident or brief sojourner. On that Saturday, the Ottoman judge, his scribe, and the court witnesses had assembled to hear the suit lodged by Ali bin Yusuf of Jerba against a Venetian merchant named Nicolo, who had come to the Ottoman capital to trade.

In his complaint, Ali stated that eight years earlier, his son Süleyman, a ship captain (*reis*), had sailed to the Greek port of Volos on the western Aegean mainland, where he had loaded a cargo of wheat on his saïque, a medium-size vessel commonly used for trade within the Ottoman Mediterranean. Süleyman Reis's wheat was intended for the markets of the perpetually hungry city of Istanbul, but he had not traveled far from Volos before he was intercepted by a galleon captained by the defendant, Nicolo. Süleyman's saïque was no match for the Venetian's large, heavily armed broadside sailing ship. In the ensuing melee, Süleyman Reis and five of his sailors were killed. One survivor from the initial assault, a certain Mehmed bin Abdüsselam, was handed off to one of Nicolo's crew members for execution, but he managed to escape and eventually made his way back to Istanbul. Eight years later, he was present in that Galata courtroom with Ali bin Yusuf; it was he who had informed Ali of his son's fate and the identity of his alleged killer. Nicolo, Ali reiterated, had murdered his son and five others and had made off with his son's ship, its cargo, and all of the crew's personal property. Now he demanded that Nicolo pay the price for his crimes as the law required. He wanted restitution. And he wanted blood.[1]

Ali was effectively accusing Nicolo of piracy. It could be nothing else. Venice and the Ottoman Empire had been at peace since 1573, so no Venetian would have had license to attack an Ottoman merchant vessel. To those "individuals who despoil others through privately exercised force and without urgent reasons to do so," the Dutch jurist Hugo Grotius wrote in 1605, "we give the name 'pirates' when their activities take place upon the sea."[2] Grotius's definition of the pirate not only fit in Nicolo's case, it matched the Ottoman understanding of sea robbery as well. But Nicolo was identified in the court not as a pirate but as a merchant by profession. If he sidelined in piracy, he did so opportunistically. As was so often the case in the early modern Mediterranean, defining a pirate was a question not so much of who or what, but *when*.

Slaving was common in the early modern Mediterranean and helped meet the demand for servile labor on all sides of the sea. Muslims targeted Christians and Christians targeted Muslims for sale in distant markets. But in the eastern half of the Mediterranean the line between legal and illegal raiding was not simply religious. Due to the provisions of the Ottoman-Venetian treaty that prohibited the enslavement of either side's subjects and Venice's assiduous efforts to stay on the Ottomans' good side, Nicolo would have faced execution by Venetian authorities were he caught with Ottoman captives. For the Venetian part-time pirate preying on Ottoman shipping, it was far too dangerous to take prisoners and risk leaving witnesses, even though it meant sacrificing the significant sums that could otherwise be had from their sale or ransom. It was self-preservation that motivated the Venetian galleon captain to execute the crew of Süleyman's ship. Dead men, after all, tell no tales.

Indeed, despite the fact that at least one got away that day in 1606, a single eyewitness was one short of the two required to meet the evidentiary standards of the Ottoman courts. After Nicolo denied the accusations leveled against him, claiming that he had been in Alexandria at the time of the attack, Ali was asked to provide the court with additional evidence. Unable to produce another witness to rebut Nicolo's denial, he requested a continuance to procure more evidence. This was duly granted by the court, but no subsequent entry appears in the surviving registers from Galata.[3] Nicolo did not wait around to see if Ali could produce new evidence against him. He had probably weighed anchor before the ink from the scribe's pen was dry.

This book is about piracy, but it is not about pirates. Rather, it is about the administrators, diplomats, jurists, and, above all, the victims—those who had to contend most with the consequences of maritime violence. For roughly a century and a half, beginning with the conclusion of the Ottoman-Venetian war for Cyprus in 1573 and continuing into the eighteenth century, the eastern half of the Mediterranean was gripped by a plague of piracy. The unchecked activities of pirates and corsairs—the particularly Mediterranean species of privateer who raided the enemy religious other with the license of a sovereign—routinely affected both Ottoman and European subjects, resulting in frequent domestic and interstate legal disputes over ships, cargo, and captives. Pirates churned up a sea of paper in their wake: letters, petitions, court documents, legal opinions, ambassadorial reports, travel accounts, captivity narratives, and vast numbers of decrees attest to their impact on lives and livelihoods throughout the Ottoman Mediterranean world.

The appellation "Ottoman Mediterranean" has long been used by scholars to describe the eastern half of the Mediterranean basin. By 1574, the mainland coasts from Venice's Adriatic frontier to the borders of Morocco formally acknowledged the authority of the sultan in Istanbul, as did all the major islands east of Sicily except Crete, until 1669, when it too joined the fold. Sometimes the term has been deployed with additional implications, for instance, that the defining feature of the seventeenth-century Ottoman Mediterranean was its reunified Greek Orthodox ecumene.[4] This book argues that what made the eastern half of the basin the "Ottoman Mediterranean" was that it was a unified legal space.

Imagine a line emerging from the southeastern Adriatic seaboard that cuts south through the narrow entrance—a pirate gauntlet in this period—of that formerly Venetian lake and across the Ionian Sea before curving gently toward the Egyptian coastline, terminating to the west of its ports. Such a line encompasses the waters of the Levant, the southern shores of Anatolia and Cyprus, the tesserae of the Aegean's archipelagic mosaic and its rugged mainland coast. What this line excludes are the North African port cities of Tripoli, Tunis, and, farthest west, Algiers.

The borders of the Ottoman Mediterranean were dictated by the legal institutional limits of Istanbul's reach within the greater empire and were thus decoupled from Ottoman sovereignty. Istanbul did not appoint judges in North Africa as it did for the rest of the Ottoman Mediterranean, and the North Africans followed the opinions of their own jurists above those of the Ottomans' chief jurist in Istanbul, whose opinions were supposed to have the force of law throughout the empire.[5] By the late sixteenth century, the North African port cities hardly respected the diplomatic agreements Istanbul concluded with foreign powers; by the 1620s, they were openly pursuing their own foreign policies. Unbridgeable differences over what constituted legal raiding contributed to North Africa's placement outside the bounds of the Ottoman Mediterranean.

This book tells the story of the emergence of the Ottoman Mediterranean legal space and the role piracy played in shaping it. By 1670, we can speak of an Ottoman Mediterranean defined not so much by Ottoman political control of the islands and coasts or naval supremacy in the waters in between, but by the reach of Ottoman law as it was formulated by the empire's chief jurists and applied by its centrally appointed judges. The book's six chapters chart the Ottoman experience of piracy within this space and detail the Ottoman response to it, which came primarily in the spheres of law, diplomacy, and administration. The reasons for this, and for the absence of a robust military response, lie in the Ottomans' long and complicated history with private naval contractors and the confluence of a variety of political and military challenges in the late sixteenth and early seventeenth centuries.

The activities of corsairs and naval irregulars, some loosely affiliated with the Ottoman state, played an important role in the warfare of the early modern Mediterranean. In the Western Mediterranean, the fall of Nasrid Granada in 1492 to the combined forces of Aragon and Castile and the subsequent Iberian invasions of North Africa triggered a corsair war. North African rulers welcomed both Iberian Muslim refugees and adventurers from the Eastern Mediterranean and gave them license to raid Spanish ships and shores in exchange for a share of the booty. The Ottoman Empire was soon pulled into the conflict in North Africa, and Ottoman adventurers like the Barbarossa brothers and their acolytes were instrumental in realizing the littoral's incorporation into the empire over the course of the sixteenth century.[6]

After shunting aside the local Muslim dynasts who had recently employed them, these corsairs became foreign usurpers only marginally more welcome to the local populations than the Spanish whom they had expelled from Algiers and whose vigorous efforts at expansion they continued to fight on land and sea. Oruç Barbarossa thus turned to Istanbul, seeking the legitimacy that Ottoman sovereignty would bestow on his rule. Sultan Selim I's conquest of the Mamluk Sultanate in 1517 brought Syria, Egypt, and the Hijaz under his authority, making the Ottoman sultans Protectors of the Holy Cities of Mecca and Medina and reuniting the north and south of the Eastern Mediterranean for the first time in nearly a millennium. As the preeminent dynasty in the Islamic world, the

Ottomans were the perfect patrons: rich, powerful, respected, and distant. And so, in 1519, Algiers joined the Ottoman fold by request rather than conquest. It was at first a paper acquisition that cost Istanbul little and gained it less, but it inextricably drew the empire into North African affairs. The brewing imperial conflict with the Habsburg dynasty, the Ottomans' bête noire in both Central Europe and the Mediterranean thanks to the temporary unification of Spain and the Holy Roman Empire in the person of Charles V, thus sparked a half-century battle for supremacy over North Africa. Corsairs played a critical role on both sides, not just as auxiliaries but as admirals, leading huge fleets both in battle and on massive slave-raiding expeditions.[7]

In 1532, Sultan Süleyman summoned Hayreddin Barbarossa from Algiers and appointed him *kapudan pasha*, imperial admiral, tasking him with reversing the conquests in the Morea (as the Peloponnese was then known) that Charles V's own corsair-admiral, the Genoese Andrea Doria, had made earlier that year. With Barbarossa at the helm, the Ottoman navy took back in 1534 all that had been lost to Doria two years earlier; besieged Venetian Corfu in 1537 and, after being repulsed, captured many of the smaller Venetian-held Aegean islands in 1537–1538; shattered an allied Catholic fleet commanded by Doria at Preveza in 1538; conducted joint operations with the French against Nice in 1543; and raided the islands of the central and western Mediterranean in 1544 and 1545, carrying off thousands of Christians into captivity. When Hayreddin Barbarossa finally retired to the Bosphorus in 1545 to relax and dictate his memoirs, other North Africa–based corsairs who had risen under his command were ready to take his place.[8]

Charles V and his son and successor in Spain, Philip II, enjoyed the support of their own, Catholic corsairs. Among these, the Knights of Saint John, or Knights Hospitaller, a Crusader-era military order turned anti-Muslim corsairing enterprise, were of lasting importance. Evicted from their base on Rhodes by Sultan Süleyman in 1522, they became a far more serious threat to the security of the Ottoman Mediterranean after Charles V permitted them to settle on Malta in 1530, for which they were expected to provide one falcon annually and defend Spanish-occupied Tripoli. Although the Knights lost Tripoli to an Ottoman fleet commanded by Barbarossa's protégé Turgud Reis in 1558, Malta itself successfully withstood an Ottoman siege in 1565, marking the logistical limits of the Ottomans' naval power. From that point on, Maltese corsairs—both the Knights themselves and the many Catholic entrepreneurs who sailed under the Order's flag—would plague Ottoman waters, carrying out regular cruises into the Levant until the early eighteenth century, when French pressure forced them to restrict their activities to the central Mediterranean.[9]

Both Catholic and Muslim corsairs thus played pivotal roles in the Habsburg-Ottoman struggle for Mediterranean supremacy. Ultimately, through Istanbul's mutually beneficial military alliance with Muslim corsairs, Ottoman sovereignty was extended to all of North Africa east of Morocco. But piracy and amphibious slave raiding proved to be an enduring aspect of Mediterranean life in peacetime as well, and they frequently exposed the limits of Ottoman power. Never was this truer than in the period following the Ottoman defeat at Lepanto on October 6, 1571. Two months after the Ottomans completed their conquest of Venetian Cyprus—precipitated in part by the Venetians' inability to prevent the predations of the Maltese corsairs in the area—the allied naval forces of the Holy League (chiefly comprised of Venice, Spain, the Knights of Saint John, and the papacy) met the Ottoman fleet at the entrance to the Gulf of Patras and smashed it. Ottoman losses of ships and, more importantly, men, were staggering. Although no territory changed hands and the Ottoman fleet was rapidly reconstituted afterward—indeed larger than it had been before—that battle, "the greatest naval engagement between Actium and Trafalgar," proved to be the last major maritime confrontation in a century that had witnessed numerous decisive engagements between corsair-augmented fleets.[10] In 1574, the Ottomans cemented their conquest of the North African littoral when they retook La Goletta, the fortress at the entrance of Tunis, from its Spanish garrison, and with that, the age of large-scale galley conflict in the Mediterranean was over.[11]

The Ottoman defeat at Lepanto was not, as some popular histories would have it, the turning point in an "epic" battle between Islam and Christendom.[12] In fact, Ottoman military capacity remained high and expansion continued, albeit irregularly, for another century. But neither the Ottomans nor the Habsburgs were especially interested in continuing the conflict at sea. The multidecade naval arms race between Spain and the Ottoman Empire had led to the annual construction of enormous armadas of ever larger galleys bearing more and heavier cannon that required seemingly endless numbers of men (paid, purchased, or imprisoned) to row them and vast quantities of hardtack to feed their swelling crews. The exponentially inflating cost of the escalating conflict had contributed to the first of several Spanish bankruptcies in 1575 and stretched the limits of the Ottomans' financial, natural, and human resources. Large-scale naval warfare had simply become too expensive.[13]

The Ottomans accomplished all of their strategic objectives in the war despite the tactical reversal at Lepanto. Once the Venetians pursued a separate peace in 1573 and the Spanish were finally expelled from Tunis in 1574, there was little reason to continue with the outrageous and unsustainable expense of maintaining the imperial fleet on war footing each year. Although both the Ottoman Empire and Spain continued to mount desultory annual patrols of their maritime domains, other political and military priorities, not to mention fiscal necessity, dictated a new policy.

Both sides thus turned to more pressing affairs on the frontiers of their empires—Spain to the resurgent Dutch revolt and the Ottomans to renewed war with Safavid Iran—eventually agreeing to a truce in 1580.[14] This coincided with what Fernand Braudel termed the "Northern Invasion": the penetration of the Mediterranean by heavily armed English and Dutch merchant ships, fitted for piracy as much as for trade.[15] It also permitted the growing independence of the corsairs of North Africa. Thus, at this point of naval disengagement, of reestablished relations with Venice and détente with Spain, the sea did not become a safer place. On the contrary, incidents of piracy increased dramatically, as both Mediterranean corsair proxies and Atlantic entrepreneurs filled the power vacuum at sea, undisturbed by the once dominant Mediterranean superpowers. By 1580, the age of the *corso*—the simmering, low-intensity pirate warfare that persisted into the early eighteenth century—had begun.

Previously, Ottoman naval strength had safeguarded merchant traffic in the Eastern Mediterranean while the imperial rivalry with Spain had provided the impetus for dispatching successive fleets into the western Mediterranean to pillage Spanish dependencies. After 1580, however, the corsairs of North Africa and Malta were left to pursue their two-sided holy war at sea, while well-armed English and Dutch broadside sailing ships drove their Venetian competition from the waves, rapidly taking over much of the intra-Mediterranean carrying trade.[16] Corsairs from the North African city-states of Algiers, Tunis, and Tripoli—equipped with the latest sailing technology thanks to an influx of English and Dutch renegades left unemployed by the end of England's war with Spain (1604) and the Spanish-Dutch "Twelve Years' Truce" (1609) and buoyed by the arrival of thousands of Morisco refugees from Iberia after their expulsion in 1609—ranged the Mediterranean and beyond, staging dramatic raids as far as Ireland and Iceland in the 1620s and 1630s.[17] Meanwhile, Catholic corsairs—including the Knights of Saint John of Malta and their compatriots, the Tuscan Knights of Saint Stephen—wreaked havoc on the vital sea lanes connecting Istanbul and the Aegean ports to Egypt and ravaged the Levantine coastline. Both sides took a significant cut of the wealth from passing shipping and carried thousands into captivity, leading to the establishment of a thriving, trans-Mediterranean ransoming industry that supported a plethora of lenders, brokers, and investors in captive bodies, not to mention the many more who worked to clothe, feed, and house slaves held for ransom in Algiers, Malta, Tunis, and Livorno.[18]

However opportunistic piracy sometimes was, it was not random; it flourished along well-trafficked routes in areas with favorable geography, seascapes embroidered with small islands and cove-filled coastlines that offered myriad hiding places, choke points that funneled merchant vessels through narrow corridors where pirates could lie in wait. Nowhere was more inviting than the Ottoman Mediterranean, which attracted the big players from the corsairing capitals and sustained local small-fry as well. Weak defenses and permissive politics made piracy possible, but robust trade was what made it profitable; all three abounded in this bustling, diverse maritime ecosystem.[19]

The Ottoman Empire was a source of and a market for a wide variety of raw and finished goods in the late sixteenth and seventeenth centuries. Even as the spice trade declined toward the end of the sixteenth century (thanks to Portuguese and later Dutch efforts in the Indian Ocean) Ottoman markets continued to provide Europe with sundry luxury goods; raw wool, linen, cotton, and silk; coffee, olive oil, wine, and especially grain. Imperial authorities tried in vain to control the grain trade to preserve the supply for domestic markets, but smuggling was constant in war and in peace. For their part, European merchants brought finished cloths, lead, tin, tobacco, paper, and specie.[20]

But long-distance "international" trade was only part of the picture. The Ottoman Mediterranean supported a vast internal trade which, if not disconnected from the vicissitudes of the global economy, of necessity persisted through its ups and downs. The enormous, insatiable capital itself sustained a vigorous shipping industry, which worked constantly to provision it. After the conquest of Mamluk Egypt in 1517, the north and south of the Eastern Mediterranean became politically linked and economically integrated to a great extent. Wheat, corn, rice, lentils, sugar, linen, coffee, oil, honey, slaves, and gold flowed north to Salonica and Istanbul, while southbound traffic carried not only goods and raw materials like wood but wealthy pilgrims to the Hajj and Ottoman officials to their posts.

All this meant that, although the Mediterranean as a whole no longer commanded the central role in Europe's increasingly global economy, the Ottoman Mediterranean remained an arena of tremendous, constant internal and external shipping activity. And even as the cast of characters expanded in the second half of the sixteenth century to include the French, English, and Dutch alongside the formerly dominant Italians, much intra-Ottoman shipping and trade remained in Ottoman—Greek, Armenian, Muslim, and Jewish—hands.[21] For the piratically inclined, then, there was never a lack of potential targets in the Ottoman Mediterranean, from small fishing vessels and coastal traders on up to long-haul merchantmen, all of which might be profitably supplemented with the human bounty to be found on shore.

The Ottoman sultans' failure to effectively defend their vast maritime frontier in the century and a half following the Battle of Lepanto has been variously interpreted as evidence of their turning away from the sea, their indifference to or outright complicity in the "Muslim" piracy that preyed on European shipping, or sheer administrative incompetence and military decline.[22] Each of these interpretations contains a grain or more of truth, but they vastly oversimplify the situation, precluding discussion of regional variation or change over time. The Ottoman Empire was not a monolithic entity possessed of unlimited coercive capacity, but rather a massive, complex polity comprised of multiple layers of authority knit together over long distances.

The options available to Ottoman policy makers in Istanbul who might otherwise be inclined to suppress homegrown piracy were limited by the need to maintain frontier defense and access to experienced auxiliary forces, which naval irregulars along the Adriatic-Ionian and North African coasts provided in times of conflict. They were further constrained by the severe financial difficulties that gripped the Mediterranean throughout the late sixteenth and early seventeenth centuries, successive land wars, multiple serious rebellions, famine and pestilence, and severe dynastic turmoil through the first decades of the seventeenth century. It was not a coincidence that the period of the *guerre de course*'s greatest ferocity and the North African corsairs' most audacious activities—the 1620s and 1630s—occurred during an era of profound domestic challenges for the Ottoman central government, and indeed for much of Europe as well.

The Sublime Porte's lack of a robust military response to the growing pirate threat must be considered in its historical context. In 1578, the Ottoman Empire initiated a war with Safavid Iran—during which the truce with Habsburg Spain was secured—that dragged on until 1590. Prosecuting the war in the distant and difficult terrain of the Caucasus demanded tremendous military and financial resources that left little room for Mediterranean adventures, and so the neglected imperial fleet was allowed to molder on the shores of the Golden Horn. With the end of the war, some Ottoman officials, egged on by their English allies who hoped to see the conflict with Spain rekindled, began to seriously explore what it would take to bring the navy back onto war footing. These embryonic efforts had to be abandoned, however, when the Ottoman governor of Bosnia's bellicose posturing and independent raiding into Habsburg territory in 1591 set off a tit-for-tat pattern of reprisals that escalated into full-scale war in 1593.[23] With barely a break from the twelve years of war with Iran, the Ottoman Empire now faced a much more potent foe in the Austrian Habsburgs. Thanks to advances in fortress design that led to long sieges replacing the massive pitched battles of earlier conflicts, the "Long War," as it came to be called, rapidly settled into a stalemate that continued until 1606.

This all took place in an era of extreme economic distress. The empire had been gripped by severe inflation since the 1580s, driven by the influx of New World silver and exacerbated by the Ottomans' repeated debasement of the silver coinage to meet salary payments. The treasury further suffered from the decline in customs receipts from the spice trade, which no longer flowed through the Red Sea and Persian Gulf. More ominously, the slowing of conquest, dating to the latter decades of Süleyman's reign, rendered unsustainable the system of revenue assignment in lieu of direct payment on which the empire had relied for centuries to supply the bulk of its fighting forces and administer its lands. Changes in war fighting also meant that the cavalry that system had supported were no longer useful. The need for greater numbers of infantry in the new siege-based warfare meant more janissaries and contract irregulars, who would all have to be paid in cash. Transitioning from a military that provided administrative service and was compensated in kind to one paid in specie led to seemingly endless cash-flow problems. It also destabilized provincial society; tax-farming and confiscations from disgraced officials provided short-term solutions to the pressing need for coin, but inevitably led to abuses of the peasantry and declining productivity, as revenue raisers squeezed as much as they could from their assignments.[24]

The consequences of war, compounded by rampant inflation and the cumulative effects of the "Little Ice Age"—the centuries-long period of longer, harsher winters that hit Anatolia especially hard in the late sixteenth and early seventeenth centuries—reverberated far from the battlefield. Istanbul's efforts to provision and pay its army in the field led to demands for grain and meat that the Anatolian peasantry were unable to bear, culminating in open revolt in 1596.[25] Known as the *celali* revolts, the uprising kicked off a vicious cycle of banditry that caused massive peasant flight and forced many of the dispossessed to join the brigands to survive. For many of the same reasons—famine, war, the growth of the armed unemployed class, population dislocation—the banditry that gripped Anatolia was mirrored in Rumeli as well. In coastal areas, this activity often spilled onto the sea, manifesting as piracy.[26] As European diplomats began to complain with greater frequency about North African corsairs at the Sublime Porte, many Ottoman district governors were facing a plague of local piracy which some, unprepared to beat, joined.

In 1603, the Safavids under Shah Abbas decided to take advantage of the disarray among the Ottomans and invaded the territories lost in the last war. Fighting on two fronts and with most of Anatolia convulsed in rebellion, the Ottoman center's ability to communicate with its provincial leadership and enforce its will was severely weakened. Frontier auxiliaries, including the naval paramilitaries the Ottomans relied on for coastal defense, and the local officials responsible for their oversight had often tested the limits of legality in the past, but they now discovered that contumaciousness might go unpunished to an extent unthinkable decades earlier. Paid in debased, nearly worthless coin at rates unchanged despite decades of inflation—if paid at all—many of the rank and file turned to piracy out of financial necessity. At the same time, European pirates and Catholic corsairs established themselves on the smaller, underpopulated but strategically located Aegean islands, which had always had a light Ottoman administrative footprint. The resulting situation was not dissimilar from that facing the Spanish in the Caribbean around the same time: a permanent pirate gauntlet astride the empire's most critical sea corridor.

And the wars raged on. Only after peace was concluded with the Habsburgs in 1606 were Ottoman forces able to turn their attention to stamping out the rebellion in Anatolia, which was finally accomplished with tremendous bloodshed in 1609. Peace with the Safavids was more difficult. Concluded in 1612, war resumed again in 1615, ended in 1618, and then resumed yet again in 1623. At the same time, Cossack pirate attacks on the Anatolian Black Sea coast and even the environs of Istanbul forced Ottoman authorities to redirect the entire fleet to the Black Sea through much of the 1620s and 1630s, leaving the Ottoman Mediterranean almost completely undefended.[27] Even the North African corsairs could not pass up the opportunity presented by the navy's absence, repeatedly sacking the defenseless Mediterranean port of Iskenderun and making prizes of European merchantmen which would otherwise have paid much-needed customs dues.

In those years, the future of the dynasty itself was brought into question. Sultan Ahmed I died unexpectedly in 1617, leaving behind a "soft in the head" brother, Mustafa, and minor children.[28] Mustafa reigned for only three months before palace officials replaced him with Ahmed's son Osman II. His efforts to live up to the legacy of his namesake, the eponymous founder of the dynasty, collided with the reality of an entrenched, privileged military elite no longer suited to the nature of contemporary warfare. His brief reign (1618–1622) ended in tragedy when those elites, fearful of rumored plans to move the imperial capital to Cairo and replace them, rose up and murdered their young sovereign.[29]

In the turbulent aftermath, Sultan Mustafa I was re-enthroned, then deposed again sixteen months later, and replaced by the eleven-year-old Sultan Murad IV in 1623, with the queen mother (*valide sultan*) Kösem serving as regent. Meanwhile, the governor of Erzurum in eastern Anatolia declared his intention to march on the capital to seek justice for Osman II, building an army of the disaffected, mercenaries, and brigands as he marched westward. Abaza Mehmed Pasha's revolt, which continued until 1628, marked the start of a pattern of so-called *celali* governors—statesmen who acquired private armies and led them against the center to advance their interests—that persisted into the 1650s.[30]

Taking advantage of the ongoing disorder in Istanbul and Anatolia, Shah Abbas again invaded Ottoman territory in 1623, this time taking Baghdad. The entirety of Sultan Murad IV's reign would be devoted to reversing the Safavid advance, a task that was finally accomplished in 1639. Sultan Murad IV's majority had been a period of recovery that augured well for the future, but he died childless the following year, having previously executed, in the old Ottoman tradition, all but one of his brothers: the mentally unstable Ibrahim (r. 1640–1648), who had been spared owing to the pleas of their mother and his apparent lack of fitness to rule. Thus, in 1640, the survival of the dynasty lay solely with a man known to posterity as Deli "Crazy" Ibrahim. He was, fortunately, capable of reproducing. Finally, in 1648, as his behavior became more erratic and dangerous to the circle around him, he was deposed in favor of his eight-year-old son, Mehmed IV (r. 1648–1687), and subsequently executed—but not before he had ordered the invasion of Crete, inaugurating a generation-long war (1645–1669) with Venice.

In short, whereas maintaining maritime security and policing Ottoman corsairs in the 1570s and 1580s was difficult due to the military and financial strains of over a decade of continuous combat in the Caucasus, by the first decade of the seventeenth century, it would not have ranked highly on any administrator's priority list. That would begin to change in the mid-1650s, with the program of reforms enacted by the grand vizier Köprülü Mehmed Pasha (r. 1656–1661) and his son and successor, Fazıl Ahmed Pasha (r. 1661–1676), but by then North Africa was operating largely independently of Istanbul, engaging in foreign relations on its own account; European pirates had colonized the nominally Ottoman Aegean archipelago; and the Ottoman government was forced to hire European carriers to safely transport men and material between its coastal and insular possessions.

Characterizing the Ottomans' inability to prevent piracy as a matter of complicity or weakness would be missing the point. Just as King James I of England could not put a stop to English piracy after peace was reestablished with Spain in 1604, despite threats, offers of amnesty, and dozens of executions, so too Ottoman authorities had to contend with a problem which could hardly be realistically contained militarily in light of the economic constraints and competing local interests facing them.[31] Certainly King James's Ottoman contemporary, Sultan Ahmed I, shared his fellow monarch's contempt for pirates. In 1605, he personally ordered that a group of pirates captured by an Ottoman patrol "be dashed head foremost on the ground and then flung into the sea" in full view of the palace and the city. The immediate result—"everyone is terror-stricken" wrote Ottavio Bon, the Venetian ambassador (*bailo*)—was as intended, but it had no more a deterrent effect in the long run than James I's efforts.[32]

Whereas French and English diplomats advocated military action against North Africa at the Sublime Porte in the first decades of the seventeenth century before adopting a policy of direct negotiation and direct bombardment, the Venetians understood that confronting the pirates head-on was not a viable solution for the eastern half of the Mediterranean. For the maritime neighborhood the Venetians and the Ottomans together shared, the root problem was not the unrestrained predations of the North African corsairs. Rather, what needed to be done was to deprive pirates of markets to sell their stolen merchandise and to crack down on the local officials who looked the other way or supplied them with provisions, safe harbors, and information.[33] The Venetians advocated this approach throughout the seventeenth century's periods of peace.

Easier said than done. Many people, including Muslims, Christians, Jews, Ottoman subjects, English, French, and Dutch, profited immensely from the black market trade in pirate booty, which sustained whole economies in increasingly marginalized ports like Avlonya (Valona, present-day Vlorë in Albania) in the Adriatic and islands like Milos in the Aegean, not to mention Malta, Livorno, Algiers, Tunis, and Tripoli. Shifts in the world economy made maritime predation the only growth industry for those Mediterranean ports that enjoyed strategic locations but were increasingly excluded from participation in other avenues of legitimate commerce.[34]

Without significant military involvement, the occasional Ottoman attempts to crack down on this activity on the frontier could end in tragedy for the unfortunate officials sent to carry out such unpopular orders. Besides, as the Venetian *bailo* Sebastiano Venier noted in 1627, in spite of the pirate threat, the European merchant ships that provided the Ottomans with much needed customs revenue continued to call in Ottoman ports.[35] So long as they reliably did so, the Ottoman government had little reason to commit precious and scarce resources to what would likely be a futile, costly effort with what must have seemed to be little upside, considering the fact that their European treaty partners—with the notable exception of Venice—were doing no better in restraining their own subjects' predations in Ottoman waters.

Ottoman trade and Ottoman subjects suffered greatly from the pervasive piracy in the Ottoman Mediterranean, which Ottoman officials ascribed principally to Europeans, friend and foe alike. Particularly galling was the fact that Catholic corsairs were annually exporting hundreds of Ottoman Muslims to Malta and Livorno to be held for ransom or sold as slaves, often as oarsmen for French or papal galleys. At any given moment there were dozens of Ottoman functionaries, picked off en route to their coastal postings, awaiting redemption in Maltese dungeons. Their plaintive letters arrived regularly at the Sublime Porte. This fact, alongside the English and Dutch introduction of Atlantic sailing technology into the Mediterranean, colored Ottoman views of and reactions to Mediterranean piracy. In 1612, during one of the Venetian *bailo*'s regular discussions with the grand vizier about the pirate scourge, Nasuh Pasha recalled wistfully that "in the old days a caramursale [*karamürsel*, a common medium-size Ottoman cargo vessel] without artillery went and returned alone from Alexandria; now the galleons must sail fully armed and in company, nor is that enough, they must have an escort of galleys too." As far as the Ottoman center was concerned, the Mediterranean piracy problem—from the European renegade captains who commanded most of the vessels of Algiers and Tunis to the English merchant-pirates and the Maltese-flagged French corsairs—was one of the European trading nations' creation and one which they, together, ought to resolve.[36]

From the naval perspective, the galleys and other oared vessels on which the Ottomans relied until the late seventeenth century had several distinct advantages in Mediterranean warfare—maneuverability, speed, and the ability to operate close to shore and without wind—but were costly to man and provision and limited to operating during the "sea season" (roughly late March to October). Pirates could simply disperse upon learning that the *kapudan pasha*'s fleet was approaching on its annual cruise through the Aegean and return after it had passed, enjoying extensive freedom for the rest of the year. "Control of the sea," in the sense originated by the naval captain and historian Alfred Mahan (d. 1914), was not an option for a fair-weather, oar-craft-based navy.[37]

The Ottomans maintained several permanent galley squadrons that provided coastal defense, but a permanent, year-round system of patrols in their maritime empire would have required a colossal investment in new types of ships and a significant expansion of the Ottoman administrative presence on the Aegean islands, the smaller of which were essentially self-governing.[38] Ottoman observers like the polymath and naval historian Katib Çelebi (d. 1657) were well aware that an Ottoman galley could not hope to win in a head-to-head fight with a well-armed galleon.[39] However, it has been estimated that the cost for the Ottomans of building, equipping, and operating a galleon fleet in the mid-seventeenth century would have been as much as five times that of an equivalent galley fleet.[40] The price of making the switch completely from oar to sail was thus too much for the cash-strapped state to bear so long as some of the Ottomans' naval needs could be semi-reliably outsourced to irregulars based on the North African and Adriatic-Ionian coasts. Notably, the other Mediterranean powers had not abandoned the galley either: Venice and Spain both relied heavily on galleys throughout the seventeenth century and the French continued to maintain a fleet of galleys at Marseilles well into the eighteenth century, for aesthetic as much as military purposes.[41] That the Ottomans' failure to develop an all-season fleet before the late seventeenth century would prove so costly in the long run—so much so that they could not operate safely in their own maritime backyard—could hardly be predicted in the early years of the century when far more pressing concerns loomed.

The inherent ambiguity of much seventeenth-century piracy was a more serious problem than the qualitative deficiencies of the Ottoman navy. Unless caught in the act or identified through reliable intelligence, a galleon flying the flag of a friendly state might appear to an Ottoman patrol to be nothing more than a well-armed merchant, like the Venetian merchant-pirate Nicolo. Though the corsairs of Malta and North Africa deployed distinctive, highly recognizable ensigns bearing cross and crescent, respectively—the better to terrorize their quarry—many more pirates large and small relied on disguise and surprise to corner their victims and would never allow themselves to end up in a battle with the Ottoman fleet.

The Ottomans' failure to effectively combat piracy does not mean they were entirely passive in response. On the contrary, rising maritime violence after the war for Cyprus resulted in dynamic diplomatic, legal, and administrative action. Shifting the spotlight from the pirates to the Ottoman administrators, jurists, and victims illuminates the considerable effects of piracy on foreign and domestic policy and on Ottoman legal theory and practice. A significant proportion of the Ottomans' diplomatic correspondence and internal decrees centered on combating piracy and effecting the release of the illegally enslaved, both foreign and Ottoman. Clauses concerning piracy turned up in every bilateral treaty (*ahdname*) the Ottomans concluded with maritime powers from the late fifteenth century onward. Ottoman treaty law, shared in the seventeenth century with Venice, Dubrovnik, France, England, and the Netherlands, embraced the Ciceronian concept of the pirate as the "common enemy of all" and obligated all parties to find and destroy those that threatened them; prescribed what would happen when ships met at sea; regulated the activities of corsairs and required the return of wrongfully taken captives and cargo; and laid out the mechanisms for their repatriation or the provision of restitution.

The treaty law of the *ahdname*s fell within the sphere of secular, imperial law, or *kanun*. But piracy left an indelible mark on seventeenth-century Ottoman interpretations of Islamic law as well. Ottoman Islamic law (*şeriat*) reigned in the courts that heard disputes over ships and cargo resulting from piratical incidents, decided cases of contested enslavement, and registered ransom transactions—including on Malta, where imprisoned Ottoman judges were frequently called upon to exercise their training to draw up surety and loan agreements between Muslim captives, their Catholic captors, and a diverse mix of Christian and Jewish intermediaries and brokers. The coexistence of these two systems of law, *şeriat* and *kanun*, within Ottoman domains led to a unique set of challenges.[42]

Hanafi Islamic law conceived of a world divided into *darülislam* ("the Abode of Islam," the lands ruled by Muslims) and *darülharb* ("the Abode of War," the lands not yet under Muslim rule); residents of the Abode of War were *harbi küffar*, "enemy infidels," who might be enslaved and whose property might be seized unless they were recipients of the sultan's *aman*, or safe-conduct, as were the subjects of powers with which the sultans had treaty relations. Whereas in the realm of *kanun* the differentiation between corsair and pirate and the juridical identity of attacker and victim were of the utmost importance for any dispute, in the writings of the jurists and in the courts of the *kadi*s distinctions beyond that of Ottoman subject versus "enemy infidel" were often irrelevant. Managing the differences between *şeriat* and *kanun* and locating the dividing line between the realms of war and peace thus assumed great importance for both Ottoman subjects and the foreigners who traded in the Ottoman Mediterranean, as well as for their respective governments. The complexity of the maritime legal issues emerging from an increasingly chaotic sea led the compilers of the Ottoman chief jurists' legal opinions to devote ever more space in their collections to these problems.

For centuries, Western legal scholars have ignored or been ignorant of the multisourced body of Ottoman maritime law. In his treatise on European maritime law, first published in Italian in 1795, Domenico Azuni wrote, "We do not know of any maritime laws peculiar to the Ottoman empire, and to the regencies established on the Barbary coast, subject to the grand Seignior. It appears, that they are acquainted with no other than those of the nations with whom they traffic." He went on to argue that the French consuls were "the only judges of all differences relative to maritime commerce, either between Frenchmen and Turks," or among themselves.[43] Azuni's pronouncement that the Ottomans lacked an indigenous body of maritime law or venues where maritime cases were heard is unsurprising in light of the common misconception that, by the end of the sixteenth century, the Ottomans had turned away from the sea, but it is also incorrect. Though diffuse, spread between treaties and compilations of legal opinions, early modern Ottoman maritime law was very real and applied in Islamic courts throughout the Ottoman Mediterranean. Knowledge of it among seafaring Ottoman Muslims, Christians, and Jews, and among foreign merchants and the ambassadors and consuls who represented them, was both widespread and essential.

Although, as Azuni writes, foreign merchants did make use of consular courts to resolve disputes within their communities, they also made use of Ottoman courts. In cases involving Ottomans and foreigners, the treaties stipulated that the matter could be brought before the Imperial Council (*divan-ı hümayun*) instead of to the local Ottoman court—an option open to all Ottoman subjects as well—but the Ottoman legal system could not simply be circumvented unless both parties agreed to it. Ottoman non-Muslims had the right to bring intra-communal disputes to their own communal and ecclesiastical courts, but they too frequently made use of Ottoman *kadi*s to register all manner of transactions and to resolve lawsuits, not only with Muslims (which was required) but among themselves (which was not).[44] The Ottoman Mediterranean was a plural legal space to be sure, but one over which Ottoman religious-legal authorities presided, dispensing justice to all comers and validating and authenticating the decisions and transactions of others.

In the early modern Mediterranean, there were no hard and fast lines separating Christian and Muslim spheres, but rather a culture of legal pluralism in which merchants, travelers, and seamen took advantage of multiple overlapping jurisdictions.[45] This was certainly true of the Greek victims of Catholic corsairs, who made use of Catholic institutions in the Eastern Mediterranean to build support for their cases before heading to Malta or Rome to demand restitution, but were equally adept at obtaining Islamic legal opinions from Ottoman jurists and pressing their subsequent claims against one another in Ottoman Islamic courts.[46] It was likewise true of the Christian ransom brokers, Ottoman and foreign, who worked to free Ottoman Muslims held captive on Malta and made use of the Ottoman courts that were maintained in the slaves' prison on Malta in order to procure the documentation they would need to enforce the contracts once returned to the empire proper. Like a parasite to its host, Malta was fully attached to the Ottoman legal world. Ironically, perhaps,

Ottoman North Africa was not. Piratical violence engendered new and unexpected connections and shattered others.

This book is organized in three parts. The first two chapters approach the epidemic of piracy in the Ottoman Mediterranean from the Ottoman perspective, framing it as a domestic problem. Chapter 1 explores the connections between local and long-distance manifestations of piracy; it chronicles the rise of Ottoman-on-Ottoman maritime violence in the post-1570 period, accounting for its endurance and examining its significance for the Ottoman state and its implications for our understanding of Ottoman power and center-periphery relations. Chapter 2 explores the impact of Catholic corsairing in the Ottoman Mediterranean by focusing on the *kadi*s who, as judge-notaries, as captives, and as official mouthpieces of the Ottoman state, were involved in every stage of the ransom slavery industry. The phenomenon of the captive *kadi*s of Malta reflects the essential paradox of the seventeenth-century Ottoman Mediterranean: the inverse relationship between Ottoman maritime security and the importance of Ottoman law.

Chapters 3 and 4 examine the political and diplomatic framework through which the Ottomans and their treaty partners handled incidents of piracy and illegal slave raiding, and the consequences of such raids and the subsequent negotiations for both the powers involved and their subjects. Focusing primarily on Ottoman-Venetian relations, Chapter 3 parses the form and content of their treaties, examines how their anti-piracy provisions were understood, and traces their development from the late fifteenth century to the early seventeenth century, by which point *ahdname*s with similar anti-piracy clauses had been extended to France, England, and the Netherlands. The chapter considers the dramatic impact of both Northern Europeans and North Africans on the treaty regime around the turn of the seventeenth century and addresses the critical question of enforcement, drawing on numerous cases of the treaties being contravened and the efforts taken to obtain or provide redress.

Chapter 4 discusses the political and legal challenge that the increasingly independent and disobedient corsairs of North Africa posed to the Ottoman treaty regime in a post–"Northern Invasion" Mediterranean. It explores the diplomatic divergence of the 1620s, when England, France, and the Netherlands began to conclude treaties directly with the North African port cities while Venice continued to remonstrate at the Sublime Porte. The chapter argues that the legal and diplomatic fallout from a series of joint Algerian-Tunisian raids in the 1620s and 1630s led to a permanent restructuring of the imperial center's relationship with North

Africa and created the conditions that led to dozens of European punitive expeditions against the North African port cities, continuing from the 1660s until the French invasion of Algiers in 1830.

The final chapters delve into the role of Ottoman Islamic law in theory and practice, asking how disputes stemming from incidents of piracy were resolved within the Ottoman Mediterranean. Chapter 5 examines the responsa (*fetvas*) issued by the chief Islamic legal authorities of the empire concerning maritime violence and explores the implications of these legal opinions for law students, litigants, and judges throughout the empire, who turned to them for guidance. The chapter establishes the kinds of legal questions that piracy and captivity posed for Ottomans and how they were answered as the intensity, frequency, and focus of piracy in the Mediterranean mutated in alarming ways.

Chapter 6 looks at how individuals and communities affected by piracy interacted with Ottoman legal structures. Relying on Ottoman court records from Istanbul to Crete, it shows how merchants, monks, and mariners, Muslims, Christians, and Jews, Ottomans and foreigners used the courts and how victims of piracy sought restitution and justice. In so doing, the chapter ties together the threads from the preceding examination of Islamic law, the Ottomans' diplomatic dealings, and Ottoman administrative responses to piracy. Narrating the experiences of Ottoman victims of piracy in the Ottoman courts of the late sixteenth- and seventeenth-century Ottoman Mediterranean, we see the forces of law, religion, state power, and conflict at work on the local and individual level, and how they developed over the course of the so-called golden age of Mediterranean piracy.

PART ONE

Chaos and Captives

CHAPTER ONE

Ottoman Pirates, Ottoman Victims

Where do Ottoman pirates come from? The Ottoman bureaucrat, poet, and historian Mustafa Ali had a theory. In his didactic etiquette manual/book of rants, *Tables of Delicacies Concerning the Rules of Social Gatherings*, completed shortly before his death in 1599, he argued that they were predominantly Muslim Turks from northwest Anatolia who started off as small gangs of amphibious bandits preying on nearby Ottoman Christians. With time and success, they graduated to larger-scale piracy and ultimately abandoned illegal attacks on Ottoman subjects in favor of joining the ranks of the corsairs of North Africa, where they devoted themselves full time to marine jihad. He ascribed these obscure origins to the most famous corsairs of the sixteenth century, like Hayreddin Barbarossa, though he noted with somewhat less romanticism that the destructive process of local Ottoman-on-Ottoman piracy continued in his day.[1]

Mustafa Ali's conception of the multistage pirate life cycle, from local predatory raider to long-distance corsair, is borne out by the Ottoman documentary record of the late sixteenth and seventeenth centuries.[2] It thus provides us with a ready-made, if incomplete, framework for understanding some of the differences and connections between local and long-distance piracy in the early modern Ottoman Mediterranean. While the line between the two was more porous and multidirectional than he suggested—and Ottoman-subject pirates had been joined by a host of others by the time he was writing—Mustafa Ali's observations give some indication of the complex relationship between the practitioners of piracy and amphibious slave raiding, on the one hand, and government and victims, on the other. In the petri dish of the Mediterranean, Ottoman subjects—Muslims, Christians, and Jews—constituted the agar substrate that sustained pirates and enabled them to grow and reproduce.

Informed by Mustafa Ali's insights, this chapter charts the connections between licit and illicit forms of maritime violence and their practitioners and chronicles the explosion of Ottoman-on-Ottoman piracy and amphibious slave raiding after 1570. Geographic, demographic, economic, political, and military factors account for why this activity flourished when and where it did and for the uneven Ottoman efforts to combat it. By comparing the manifestations of and responses to Ottoman-on-Ottoman piracy in the two regions where it was most pronounced—the Aegean until the 1590s and the southern Adriatic, Ionian, and Morean coasts—the impact of human and physical geography on piracy and the reasons for the discrepancies in Ottoman countermeasures become clear. Mustafa Ali's remarks also invite us to reconsider the complex role—rhetorical, legal, organizational, tactical—that religion played in Ottoman piratical enterprise at all its various stages. And they underscore the fact that subjecthood as much as religious identity mediated the boundary between licit raiding and illegal piracy.

In Mustafa Ali's view, the metamorphosis from local pirate to long-distance corsair comprised four distinct stages. It began on land with just five or ten men:

> They attack a little boat owned by tax-paying infidels [i.e., Ottoman-subject Christians], board it, and take it to the islands. With that one boat, they launch their important career in plundering and severing family lineages, capturing men, and filling out their stores of articles of war. They bind the Ottoman-subject *zimmi* sailors and put them to the oar. At first they think they have but acquired galley slaves, then as they attack whatever vessel transporting day-laborers that strikes their fancy, they set off in pursuit of wealth. Still, they do not abandon Islam all at once; they do not put merchants and sailors to the sword out of spite. As things develop, they in no way hesitate to seize bows and arrows useful to them or limitless numbers of weapons, or beardless lads or youths who comfort the hearts of the afflicted.[3]

Small criminal bands of amphibious raiders, employing repurposed fishing boats to raid seaside villages and coastal traffic, appeared before the sixteenth century, but they flourished in its final decades. Their proliferation was paralleled by the rise of banditry throughout Anatolia and the European provinces in the late sixteenth and early seventeenth centuries. Both were symptoms of growing numbers of armed, demobilized irregular infantry, unemployed provincial law school graduates, and desperate peasants, the products of constant war, famine, and financial collapse. The main difference was that enterprising gangs in coastal areas enjoyed the opportunity provided by geography to take their activities onto the water. Starting in the 1570s, such bands popped up with alarming frequency not only along the Anatolian coastline but especially along the remote and perpetually unruly Adriatic-Ionian-Morean littoral.

Their targets at this stage were, essentially, their neighbors. Predators and prey were often already known to one another. The victims were "tax-paying Ottoman subjects," a phrase that appeared constantly in Ottoman administrative records describing the raids. These were unambiguously criminal attacks. Both in terms of Islamic and Ottoman sultanic law, the enslavement of non-Muslim Ottoman subjects was patently illegal, in contrast to the enslavement of "enemy infidels" (*harbi kafirler/kefere/küffar*) from the Abode of War, which was permissible under Islamic law but restricted in practice. Ottoman Christians and Jews, by virtue of paying a tax (*cizye*; Arabic: *jizya*) signifying their acceptance of Ottoman overlordship, were *ahl al-dhimma*, or *zimmi*s in Ottoman usage, people of the pact. This pact could be repudiated (*nakz-i ahd*) by flight to the enemy, which resulted in the loss of protected status and implicitly of Ottoman subjecthood. But so long as *zimmi*s paid their taxes and obeyed their sovereign, they were permitted to keep their faith and their property and were entitled to the state's protection.

Their enslavement was thus a grave violation of ancient Islamic legal strictures and the dynasty's solemn obligation to protect its subjects—one sufficiently serious that Mustafa Ali considered such pirates to be on the verge of abjuring Islam. Nevertheless, human booty was, besides grain in this age of frequent famine, that which pirates in the Mediterranean most prized, and nearby *zimmi*s provided an irresistible target. Word of small-scale activity of this sort rarely reached the Ottoman center, which would typically not be informed of the fledgling pirate band's actions before they advanced to Mustafa Ali's second stage:

> But over time that boat can carry them no more, which is to say it becomes apparent that the cargo of sin they have loaded has become too ponderous a burden. When this happens they attempt to obtain a small frigate. By taking these steps they gradually expand ranks and become a gang.[4]

Success meant expansion. With more men joining the gang, by this point possibly numbering up to a few dozen, and the regular haul of captives and loot threatening to capsize the boat, the pirate band would have the motive and the means to trade up to a larger vessel. This of course meant the ability to range farther out to sea and thus to engage larger prizes. At this stage, the enterprise could move beyond attacking small fishing boats and focus on larger coastal traders, as well as engage in amphibious raids on larger and more distant villages. Already engaging in the lucrative on-the-spot ransom and extortion business, the upgrade to a frigate enabled full entry into the illegal slave trade.

Whereas before the pirates' abductions of Ottoman subjects primarily served their needs for a captive workforce or—as Mustafa Ali repeatedly mentioned elsewhere—to satisfy their lust, the ability to carry off more people longer distances facilitated selling Ottoman Christian subjects just far enough away from their homes to pass them off as legally enslaved "enemy infidels." In the Ottoman world, slavery was widespread, but so too was manumission, generating constant demand. The transition from keeping slaves to selling them was a critical aspect of this stage in the pirate life cycle, for it exposed both pirates and slave buyers to the Ottoman legal system. Slaves, women and children in particular, were most often employed in domestic (including sexual) service and were frequently resold, with buyers and sellers often registering the transaction with the local courts. Brought before the judge, enslaved persons could and often did file freedom suits with the courts; if they could produce two male Muslim witnesses who could attest to their free (Ottoman) origins, they would be released with their erstwhile owner left holding the bill. Deprived of his slave, he could sue the seller to recover his losses, kicking off a chain of lawsuits that could lead back to the perpetrator of the illegal raid. Consequently, pirates trafficked their captives across the sea to complicate efforts to find them and to protect themselves from the repercussions if the slaves' free origins were discovered. Engaging in larger slaving raids, it was often at this point that the local frontier pirate might, through the complaints of villagers and provincial officials, attract the attention of the central government.

Upon learning of such incidents, Istanbul typically ordered administrators in the affected district to investigate, find and free the enslaved Ottomans, and punish the offenders. Yet by this point, pirate bands were often entrenched in their areas of operation. In many such cases, local forces were simply not strong enough to take them on directly (and lacked the capacity to do anything at sea) or had already been co-opted by them for a share of the profits; in those instances, the center was casting its orders into the wind. In the meantime, continued success permitted further upgrades and opened up a far richer buffet of potential targets farther offshore:

> In the third stage they come to rely as they must, upon those infamous perpetrators of malice and those evildoers of the human race known as "shipmaster's sailors." They comb their hair and get some new clothes—which is to say they obtain some arms and provisions. Following upon this, they accumulate arms and provisions and weapons and tools, and enough money to build a galliot, which is a vessel somewhat smaller than a galley but slightly larger than a frigate, and they become rich. Sometimes, on the coast of the Morea and Lefkada (Aya Mavra), with the collusion of one of the sea captains there, they build the kind of boat

they want. Or they find one already built and buy it. But sometimes they don't trust those captains, and when the captains give safe quarter they do not believe the agreement is truthful, so they weigh anchor and head for Samos. Or they conceal themselves on some similarly wooded island. Incorporating within it a thousand fears and precautions, they construct a ship. As soon as it is ready they board it, cast off, and meet up with one of the corsair (*levend*) admirals wintering in Algiers. They offer gifts and present themselves for service and are honored with being recruited into their ranks.[5]

Upon acquiring a large enough ship, the pirates no longer needed to limit themselves to attacks on Ottoman shores and subjects. On the Adriatic and Ionian coasts, they could now profitably expand their target list to include Venetian and Ragusan regional trading vessels carrying salt, timber, or grain.[6] Although the enslavement of the subjects of both powers was similarly illegal thanks to the sultan's treaties, these captives might be sold off rapidly or ransomed on the spot, and the same was true for their cargoes.

Mustafa Ali did not single out Lefkada, the Morea, or Samos on a whim. The only Ionian island held by the Ottomans (the others belonged to Venice), Lefkada hosted a fortress manned by naval irregulars that was a perennial source of anti-Venetian and anti-Ottoman piracy and abetted the predations of those coming from farther afield. The rugged, inaccessible coast of the Morea, parts of which could be reached only by sea, was also a hotbed of piratical activity, while Aegean islands like Samos provided the isolation and timber necessary for more independent-minded, upwardly mobile pirates to engage in clandestine shipbuilding and hide their loot and captives far from prying eyes. With at most a light Ottoman administrative presence, these advantages would soon attract foreign Christian pirates in search of safe harbor as well.

Finally, with a seaworthy vessel and a large enough crew of pirates and galley slaves, the band could embark upon the final stage of Mustafa Ali's pirate metamorphosis, emerging from the chrysalis of local marine banditry as mature, high-seas raiders bound for the big time in Algiers. "Having reached this stage," Mustafa Ali declared, "they no longer attack Muslims and merchants and tax-paying [i.e., Ottoman] infidels." Drawing a firm line between their past activities and their new careers, he argued:

They never venture one step from Algiers except in jihad and *gaza*. They even abundantly repent their earlier sins. Not postponing any of their prayers, they make righteousness and piety their example. Certainly Barbarossa, whose name was Hayreddin Pasha, Salih Pasha, Yahya Pasha, and Turgutça [i.e., Turgud Reis] all emerged along this path. They all came from one of the villages or towns on the Anatolian straits and rose up the ladder first through banditry, secondly through piracy, and thirdly through ownership outright of a galliot and supremacy over others in what is known as captaincy (*riyaset*, the act of being a *reis*).[7]

Although Mustafa Ali was mostly correct about the small-scale piratical origins of men like Barbarossa in the late fifteenth-century and early sixteenth-century Aegean and Eastern Mediterranean (though Hayreddin Barbarossa was actually originally from Mytilene and Turgud was a Greek Christian by birth from near Bodrum), the situation he was describing was actually a late sixteenth-century reality, projected backward to serve his critique of the contemporary Ottoman admiralty. Mustafa Ali's claim that "these evils did not exist in the time of Sultan Süleyman"—a common refrain from a man who idealized that period and always drew a negative contrast with the state of affairs in his own day—was in this instance demonstrably false, but there was no mistaking the fact that maritime security had deteriorated significantly in the generation since the defeat at Lepanto in 1571.[8] The blame for this, in his mind, was tied to the sultans' failure to consistently appoint qualified corsairs to the post of imperial admiral (*kapudan pasha*). Since 1495, corsair-origin admirals had provided the Ottoman sultans with the most experienced and skilled naval leaders available in the Mediterranean. From Kemal Reis (d. 1511), Sultan Bayazid II's formidable admiral and uncle of the famed geographer Piri Reis, through Hayreddin Barbarossa (d. 1546), Turgud Reis (d. 1565), and Uluc (later Kılıç) Ali (d. 1587), such men had overseen the dramatic expansion of the Ottoman seaborne empire and the extension of the blanket of Ottoman sovereignty over North Africa.[9]

In contrast, palace-trained bureaucrat admirals had presided over the Ottoman navy's two greatest failures to date, the unsuccessful siege of Malta in 1565 and the defeat at Lepanto in 1571.[10] To fight the Christian and Muslim pirates and corsairs that infested the eastern seas and to deter potential enemy attacks, the Ottomans required a cadre of talented and loyal Muslim corsairs of their own to command their fleets, supply auxiliaries, and defend the coasts. Thus, by Mustafa Ali's day and long thereafter, Ottoman commentators and historians argued that the only people worth installing in the post of imperial admiral were those with experience as corsairs, and if a non-corsair were given the position, he had best surround himself with some. In the 1650s, as the Ottoman fleet found itself repeatedly blockaded within the Dardanelles by the better-trained and better-equipped Venetian navy, defeated in battles, and struggling to provision the ground forces besieging Candia on Crete, the geographer and historian Katib Çelebi echoed Mustafa Ali's conclusions in his history of Ottoman naval campaigns, *Tuhfetü'l-kibar fi esfari'l-bihar*. He wrote in the concluding advisory section—the collective lessons learned from the preceding chronicling of Ottoman naval history—that if the *kapudan pasha* was not a corsair (*korsan*) himself, he should seek the advice of and listen to corsairs in matters of the sea and naval warfare. Failure to do so was a sure path to disaster.[11]

Unlike the landlubbers who had occupied the post since the death of Kılıç Ali Pasha in 1587 (elevated to the position after Lepanto), the ideal corsair admiral in Mustafa Ali's view would have perfect knowledge of the coasts and the conditions of his fleet. "When a sailor attached to one of the fleet captains turns to piracy," he argued, "that esteemed gentleman knows of it."[12] Yet fleet captains turning to piracy, which had been a recurring problem since the late fifteenth century, was not at all the situation he was describing in his pirate life cycle, nor was it the principal source of the piracy epidemic in the decades of peace separating the end of the 1570–1573 war for Cyprus and the invasion of Crete in 1645.[13] Indeed, Mustafa Ali concluded his discussion of piracy with a prayer and a bitter observation of the present situation:

May an honored admiral be blessed with success and good fortune in the form of a ministry or a governorship. And beneath his command may many Admirals of the Sea and captains and officers become prominent on land and sea. While in this position of strength, five or ten contemptible, worthless *levend*s (i.e., pirates/bandits) will commit bloodshed among the islands, and leaving their reflection upon the ocean of murder and plunder and mayhem at sea, spread their visage. They descend upon the tax-payers (i.e., Ottoman subjects) of that land and clime by boarding the small, insignificant ships of the petty unbelievers, who are the Christians of Rum, seizing them and putting them to the oars. Once their strength is exhausted, they fix a price on them and sell them.

In particular, the merchants of Salonica and the Muslims and the non-believers among the toiling people of Rumeli and Anatolia, the bad and the good, are always vexed by them. They single out beardless boys and use them as did the people of Lot. Once this has occurred, certainly there is no need to listen to the admiral's apologies and excuses.[14]

Returning to the image of the five to ten men gathering to raid with which he opened his discussion, Mustafa Ali recapitulated the origin story in darker tones. His outrage at the Ottoman pirates' despoiling of other Ottomans—his description indeed emphasizes that these pirates were a plague on all Ottomans, irrespective of faith or moral character—was shared by the central government, which by the mid-1570s dispatched dozens of decrees annually to coastal districts ordering them to suppress the plague of local piracy. However, the impediment to more effective action was that the pirate life cycle now encompassed—in addition to common bandits—irregular military forces, rogue officials, and others who were intimately tied to local government. In many cases, the ones being ordered to fight piracy were themselves the culprits. From Mustafa Ali's standpoint, holy warrior heroes like Barbarossa and Turgud might be forgiven their ignoble origins, but the present situation demanded that someone like them step up to put an end to a cycle of violence that was spinning out of control. As for what Mustafa Ali wanted to see happen to the pirates of his day, a macabre verse in his discussion leaves no doubt—"May he [the admiral] drown the sea in blood from executions, so that to every anchor / Coral branches offer a severed hand fouled with blood."[15]

Mustafa Ali appears to have doubted that the next generation of Ottoman corsair admirals was coming of age among the pirates of the Mediterranean, whose predations affected Muslims and Christians alike. Eventually the new crop of Ottoman pirates, like their more illustrious predecessors, might sail off to join the large-scale operations in Algiers, Tunis, or Tripoli. But for many there was no need. Already by 1599 the situation on the Adriatic-Ionian frontier had deteriorated to the extent that it had become relatively hospitable for larger and potentially more disruptive pirating operations. So much so, in fact, that those pirates operating out of Algiers, Tunis, and Tripoli might come to them, make use of their bases, and engage in joint operations. Pirate coalitions became increasingly common after central authority in North Africa slackened as a result of the administrative reorganization of 1587. This established triennial pashas in the three port cities who, with no local power base (unlike their predecessors, who had risen through the ranks of the corsairs before entering imperial service) and little time on the ground, rapidly became sidelined figureheads.[16] Collaboration increased further in the first decade of the seventeenth century, with the advent of sail in North Africa and the reinvigoration of its slaving industry by Morisco refugees. If it had ever existed, the idealized final stage of Mustafa Ali's pirate life cycle—that of the true holy warrior corsair—had become twisted beyond recognition.

Mustafa Ali's views to the contrary, the qualitative decline of the imperial admirals was not the only or even the most important cause of the broader rise of Mediterranean piracy, the start of which coincided with the long tenure of the former corsair and victor at Tunis, Kılıç Ali Pasha. Successive land wars, financial collapse, and many other deeply imbricated factors contributed to the Ottoman piracy problem and the simultaneous explosion of banditry across the core lands of the Ottoman Empire, both of which developed apart from but concurrently with the rise of foreign Christian piracy in the Ottoman Mediterranean. Indeed, the influx of Catholic corsairs and northern European merchant-pirates exacerbated the problem and, perversely, increased the center's reliance on the perpetually disobedient corsairs of the southern Adriatic coast, Lefkada, and North Africa to counter it. This outsourcing of maritime security to naval irregulars, most unpaid volunteers, had a venerable history, but without the checks imposed by an active navy, it virtually guaranteed disaster. No admiral, no matter how talented, could substitute for the state's continued investment in a large, state-of-the-art fleet and the many thousands of men needed to crew and row it, which was no longer possible or even desirable in the economic and military environment of the post-1580 Mediterranean.

The primary source of our knowledge of the Ottoman center's response to piracy is the record books of the Ottoman administration's outgoing correspondence, known as the "registers of important affairs" (*mühimme defterleri*). The pages of these registers, extant from the mid-sixteenth century, are filled with letters to foreign rulers and orders to judges, governors, military leaders, and other provincial officials throughout the empire. The decrees, each written in the first person as if by the sultan himself and often publicly promulgated, were typically responses to petitions and letters from ordinary subjects and provincial officials. Each was carried by messenger to its intended recipients, often over tremendous distances and difficult, dangerous terrain. The registers make manifest the government's enduring interest in punishing pirates and their collaborators and providing victims with redress, but they also reveal the many competing concerns facing the Imperial Council and the limits of its ability to independently gather information and compel or verify compliance with its orders.

Poring over the documents produced by the central administration in the decades separating the wars for Cyprus and Crete, we see what it saw, and we miss what it missed, or chose to ignore. Such documents do not represent the full range of experiences of Ottoman piracy, very much including that perpetrated by Ottoman subjects. But these central administrative sources, however incomplete, open a crucial window into the dynamic structures of power linking center to periphery and the unique set of challenges that Ottoman-on-Ottoman piracy posed for the government, beginning with finding the right words to describe it. By examining the phenomenon of endemic domestic piracy from the perspective of Istanbul, we locate the context necessary to make sense of the persistence of piratical violence of all sorts perpetrated in Ottoman waters and the Ottoman legal and administrative responses.

A PIRATE BY ANY OTHER NAME: THE OTTOMAN VOCABULARY OF MARITIME VIOLENCE

Mustafa Ali introduced the connection between the two opposing legal poles of Mediterranean maritime raiding—piracy and corsairing—and the two Ottoman Turkish words most frequently associated with the practitioners of both—*levend* and *korsan*. These are the terms used most frequently in Ottoman administrative documents to denote pirates, naval irregulars, and corsairs. The question of what separated pirates from privateers, legally and semantically, is not easily resolved. The line between legal and illegal raiding was thin, and the temptation to cross it omnipresent. In that vein, Mustafa Ali admonished his readers in a verse to "think of jihad as an island: on its right is a sea of wealth, on the left is corruption."[17] The religious justification Muslim corsairs claimed to raid and enslave the "enemy infidels" with whom they considered themselves at war—only Catholic corsairs claimed the blanket right to enslave any and all adherents of the enemy faith—collided with political and legal realities that identified people by their subjecthood as well as their religion and extended special protections to some. When corsairs transgressed the limits imposed on them by their sovereigns, they crossed into piratical territory.

Corsairs who served the interests of their sovereign and fought the designated enemies of the faith at the designated times—like the idealized corsairs of Algiers Mustafa Ali described—were lauded as *mücahid*s and *gazi*s, holy warriors of the sea. Indeed, all those who fought in the sultan's wars enjoyed these honors, as every war, including those waged against fellow Muslims, was construed by the Ottomans as a holy war. When corsairs turned on the sultan's subjects or the subjects of the powers to which the sultan had extended his protection or safe-conduct, however, they became rebel pirates—a point the central government was not shy about making. From the perspective of Istanbul, sultanic authorization was what made a raid *halal* and kept the corsair on the right side of jihad island—a point to which we will return in subsequent chapters.[18]

The meaning of *levend*, a word of Persian origins sometimes translated as "adventurer" or simply "young man," is ambiguous and varied according to context. It could denote officially recognized Ottoman corsairs, independent freebooters with no ties to the state, or naval auxiliaries more generally. It could be used to describe the ship, its captain, or the fighting men on board (each of whom was a *levend*). It carried no specific geographic connotation. It was usually, but not exclusively, used for Muslims.[19] The word was used for auxiliary forces on land as well, though by the second half of the sixteenth century it had also acquired the pejorative meaning of "bandit."[20] The Turkish words *korsan* and *korsanlık*, derived from the Arabic *qurṣān*, which in turn was derived from the Italian *corsaro*, carry the meaning of "pirate" and "piracy," respectively, in modern Turkish. In the early modern period, however, as many scholars have pointed out, they would usually be more accurately rendered as "corsair/privateer" and "corsairing/privateering."[21] Both Ottoman and foreign (Christian) maritime raiders, including those from North Africa and Malta, could be called *korsan*, but non-Ottoman corsairs/pirates were almost never called *levend*.

The inconsistency and ambiguity of Ottoman usage was somewhat mitigated in administrative documents by the use of various modifiers and word collocations that help clarify the Ottoman center's views of such actors or their methods, such as *harami firkate levendleri* (*levend* robber frigates), *levend eşkiyaları* (*levend* rebels or bandits), *kayık levendleri* (*levends* operating small skiffs—i.e., coastal raiders), *gönüllü levend korsanları* (volunteer *levend* corsairs—corsairs in imperial employ and stationed in an Ottoman port), *harbi kafir korsanları* (enemy infidel corsairs), or sometimes just descriptions of the types of ship, such as *harbi kafir kalyonları* (enemy infidel galleons), or the sailors of them, *firkateci* (frigateer) being an especially common byword for pirate.[22] Some of these, like *harami levend* (robber *levend*) and *levend eşkiyası* (outlaw or rebel *levend*) can be quite clearly interpreted to mean "pirate," though in many instances they indicate auxiliaries gone rogue. In the Ottomans' treaties with the Venetians, early references to pirates were to "robber ships" (*harami gemisi*) and only later in the sixteenth century did the texts' authors begin replacing the sea-robber appellation with *levend* and *korsan*.[23]

However, the usage of *korsanlık* to mean exclusively corsairing or privateering as we might understand these terms, with all their religious and statist connotations, was in fact not consistent over time and space. In the seventeenth century, the small-scale attacks of Greek Christian pirates against their coreligionists in the Aegean, committed without any state's authorization or the cover of religious justification—that is to say, unambiguous acts of piracy—were sometimes characterized as *korsanlık* by Ottoman scribes.[24] In short, the semantic distinction between simple piracy and corsairing was not quite as firm in the seventeenth century as it has sometimes been portrayed.

How the practitioners of maritime raiding conceived of their activities, what justifications they employed, and how they selected their victims are questions that are worth asking. However, the Ottoman central government seemingly had little interest in the answers. The documents it generated shed little light on the motives of pirates, whether economic or religious, personal or political, nor do they tell us much about their background or origins. In decrees issued in the aftermath of an illegal attack, it is often unclear whether the implicated *levend*s were formally licensed corsairs—who were required to post a cash bond or name a guarantor in their home port to ensure their good behavior—or just some men stealing things with a ship. The Ottoman administrative and legal response to maritime raiding hinged entirely on the subjecthood and religion of the raiders and their victims, and the wrong combination at the wrong time resulted in official condemnation. No further distinction between the various species of Ottoman *levend* and *korsan* was necessary when the targets they chose ran counter to the Ottoman central government's wishes.

It is also critical to keep in mind that a significant number of those we might call pirates were not engaged in predatory raiding full time but did so whenever it was convenient and profitable. This was certainly the case for the English and Dutch vessels that appeared in the Mediterranean in ever greater numbers after 1580 and often raided indiscriminately, even when laded with cargo for legitimate trade. In 1599, the same year that Mustafa Ali completed his musings on the origins of pirates, the ship carrying England's new ambassador to the Sublime Porte and the accession gift for Sultan Mehmed III tarried repeatedly on its journey across the Mediterranean to take prizes, including some belonging to Ottoman subjects.[25] But it was not just the Atlantic intruders who dabbled in piracy; many others large and small, local and foreign, alternated between raid and trade with alacrity. Again, the question for us is not who is a pirate, or what is a pirate, but *when* is a pirate? That is, at what point did maritime raiding become illegal, and what was to be done about it?

Modern linguistic conventions do not map well onto Ottoman usage, but we must take care not to confuse popular notions of holy war with Ottoman conceptions of legitimate and illegitimate sea robbery, which could be and often were practiced by the same individuals and groups, not just at different stages of their career, but on the very same cruise. Furthermore, the cessation of conflict would transform privateers into pirates for continuing to do what they had been doing all along. This was certainly true for the Ottomans vis-à-vis Venice after 1573, just as it was for the English vis-à-vis Spain after 1604. What remained *guerre de course* or *korsanlık* to its practitioners was transformed overnight into a criminal act from the perspective of the Ottoman imperial center. It became, in essence, piracy, even if we might hesitate to anachronistically apply the label *pirate* to those Ottoman administrators called "rebels" and "thieves" when they attacked Ottoman subjects or the subjects of Ottoman allies. The tendency of outsiders like the English to call all Mediterranean sea robbers "pirates" when their Venetian victims called them "*corsari*" and the Ottomans "*korsanlar*" or "*levendler*" should not obscure the more important differentiation the Ottoman central government made between legal and illegal acts of maritime violence.

The Sublime Porte relied heavily on *levend*s for maritime security and intelligence gathering before, but especially during and after, the 1570–1573 war against Venice and its Holy League allies. For example, in 1571, Istanbul's orders to a recently promoted volunteer *levend* commander named Kara Hoca, based out of the southern Adriatic port of Avlonya, were to "protect the places in those parts that need protection and guarding and endeavor so that no damage may come to a single place from the Venetians; never stop spying and following to [learn] whatever there is, whether the circumstances of their fleets or other plans and preparations and continuously inform of correct news."[26] For this he drew a daily salary of one hundred *akçe*. Because mobilization of the imperial fleet, based in Istanbul and Gallipoli, was a costly and time-consuming affair and it could not be everywhere at once, nor indeed could it operate outside the sea season from March to October, *levend*s like Kara Hoca and the men he commanded were employed to augment the galley squadrons permanently based at Kavala on the Aegean mainland, the islands of Rhodes and Mytilene, and at Alexandria, which together were responsible for providing coastal defense in their respective districts and protecting the annual grain convoys between Egypt and Istanbul.[27] In times of war, the government gave blanket authorization for entrepreneurial volunteers to build and man their own warships, and provincial officials were ordered to give these men all necessary aid and support to do so.[28]

Of course, it was understood that state-sanctioned *levend*s would raid enemy shipping and shores and share the spoils with their partners on land. After peace was reestablished with Venice in 1573, the volunteer *levend*s were encouraged to continue to raid the ships of Spain and the pope. To that end, they had an acceptable corsairing target right across the water in the lands and peoples subject to the Spanish viceroys in Naples and Sicily. Essentially the entire Italian coast outside the Veneto was fair game.[29] However, distance from the center complicated efforts by the government to bring its servants into line when they exceeded their charge. Although it appears that Kara Hoca was relatively diligent in carrying out his orders,[30] six months after his promotion he was implicated in the capture of seven or eight Ragusans. He was ordered to return the Ragusan captives and admonished not to interfere with the rights of the ships of Dubrovnik (Ragusa).[31] Kara Hoca would have been fully aware that the independent Adriatic trading city of Dubrovnik was an Ottoman tributary and that Istanbul considered its subjects to be full-fledged Ottoman *harac veren reaya*,[32] that is, tax-paying subjects, but this was evidently no impediment to his seizing the merchants in the hopes of an easy payoff. While the Ottoman order in response to his transgression was unequivocal in its expectations, there was clearly no question in this instance of serious disciplinary action. Indeed, just days earlier, Kara Hoca had been tasked with an important reconnaissance mission.[33] And he delivered, subsequently entering the harbor of Messina by night to count the galleys stationed there.[34] Faced with the prospect of upsetting its immediate security needs in wartime, the Ottoman administration could do little more than admonish *levend*s like Kara Hoca to behave themselves. An analysis of the war years and their aftermath in the Aegean serves to clarify the trade-offs associated with the employment of *levend*s, at once privateers and pirates, and their consequences for the Ottoman inhabitants of the region.

PIRACY, SLAVERY, AND THE FOG OF WAR IN THE AEGEAN

In the fog of war, the *levend*s knew they could just as easily raid the places they were tasked to protect and expect to get away with it. Thus, in September 1570, not long after Ottoman land forces stormed Nicosia, Istanbul received reports that *levend* galleys traveling between the eastern Morea and Anatolia had landed on Andros and taken grain and three hundred captives. At the same time, a detachment of *levend* galliots abandoned the imperial fleet, raided Lemnos, and sold their captives in Anatolia. When some of the galliots were beached there as a result of contrary winds, local officials asked them to produce their import papers (*temessük*), which they lacked. As a result, the commander of the naval squadron based at Kavala was ordered to apprehend any *levend*s who oppressed Ottoman subjects (*reaya*, lit. "flock") and to inform the Porte of their crimes, but not to interfere with any *levend* ships that appeared to be performing their duties properly, such was the need for their services.[35]

As the slaves began to flow into Anatolia from Cyprus in the fall of 1570—nearly all the inhabitants of Nicosia were put to the sword or sold off—the opportunities for black market slave dealing increased dramatically. Legally imported slaves were subject to the *pencik* tax, derived from the traditional fifth of the booty owed to the sultan, and this could be a tremendous source of income for the state in times of conquest.[36] Needless to say, pirates illegally seizing Ottoman subjects did not pay this tax, but with Greek Cypriot slaves pouring into the Ottoman heartland, even a centralized bureaucracy as accomplished as that of the early modern Ottomans was hard pressed to keep track of the flood. By late October the central government was already aware that criminal entrepreneurs were selling off Ottoman Greeks in the Anatolian ports nearest to Cyprus and passing them off as legitimate Cypriot captives, but in wartime it was difficult to muster the manpower necessary to suppress the problem. Although the government ordered its field commanders to deploy men to the southwest Anatolian ports to ensure that *reaya* were not being sold as slaves and, implicitly, that the appropriate taxes were paid on legally imported captives, the multitude of safe harbors in Anatolia where *levends* could offload captives meant that the center's efforts could be easily circumvented.[37]

The enslavement of Ottoman subjects did not decrease after the conquest of Cyprus concluded with the surrender of Famagusta on August 1, 1571. The near-total destruction of the Ottoman navy at Lepanto on October 7, 1571, left the Ottoman state deprived of tens of thousands of skilled and experienced sailors, soldiers, oarsmen, master gunners, and captains. Although the Ottomans managed to rebuild their fleet on an even larger scale over the course of the winter off-season—an incredible logistical accomplishment that astounded contemporary observers and modern historians alike—no amount of money could make up for the loss of experienced men.[38] The North African contingents that participated in Lepanto came out of the engagement with the fewest losses, and the *levends* who had been active elsewhere in the Mediterranean at the time were also unaffected by the defeat. Now the Ottoman government turned to these men to look to the empire's maritime security while the Imperial Arsenal worked furiously to rebuild.

Two months after the destruction of the Ottoman navy, as Venetian ships raided up and down the Ottoman Adriatic littoral, the Ottoman government actively encouraged the construction of privateering vessels on the coasts near Lepanto and granted authorizations (*icazet*) to all who desired to go raiding.[39] Amnesties were offered to fugitive Ottoman pirates if they would turn their attentions to the fight against Venice.[40]

No one knew that the Battle of Lepanto would never have a sequel. As the sea season of 1572 drew near, Istanbul was especially concerned that the *levends* be prepared to engage with the enemy and constantly report back on the movements of the Christian fleets.[41] There were very real fears that the forces of the Holy League would return to wreak havoc on Ottoman coasts, and the administration was prepared to provide as much logistical and material support as it could to its naval leaders and irregulars to ensure their readiness.[42] The *levends* were crucial to Ottoman plans at this juncture, and here the story becomes somewhat more complicated than unscrupulous pirates simply seizing opportunities for profit.

During the war, many Aegean islands were briefly retaken by the Venetians—a pattern that would be repeated during the wars of the second half of the seventeenth century—and the enthusiasm with which some of the islanders aided the occupiers did not go unnoticed in Istanbul or among the fleet commanders whose ships patrolled and ultimately retook the islands. In these circumstances the legal distinction between traitorous *zimmis* and enslaveable "enemy infidels" appeared somewhat blurred.

In 1537–8, Hayreddin Barbarossa reduced much of the insular Aegean that was not already Ottoman to tributary status, but most islands continued to be ruled by the Latin dynasties that had been established there in the wake of the Fourth Crusade in 1204. That dynamic changed in 1566 when the new sultan, Selim II, oversaw the conquest of Chios from its Genoese rulers. He then deposed the last Latin ruler of the Duchy of Naxos, which included much of the Cyclades, and handed the ducal title to his ambitious confidant, the Jewish Iberian refugee and banker Joseph Nasi. But if this moment marked the formal absorption of these islands into the Ottoman Empire, it did not result in Muslim settlement or the introduction of identifiable Ottoman governing institutions as it would on post-conquest Cyprus. Even as the vestiges of Latin rule were gradually pruned away—the Duchy of Naxos, for instance, was dissolved after the death of Nasi in 1579—the Ottoman administrative footprint, especially on the smaller islands, was virtually nonexistent. On many, the only direct representative of Ottoman authority (and one of the only Muslims) was the *kadi*, and most islands did not have one in residence. Their governor was the *kapudan pasha*, and his relationship with the islands was largely limited to his annual tax-collecting visits, the burden of which was distributed internally by local elites and often by Orthodox monasteries, whose power was greatly enhanced by the Ottomans.[43]

Periodic raids of the islands by errant naval irregulars had taken place since before Barbarossa's naval campaigns and continued intermittently through the 1550s and 1560s.[44] In light of the ambiguous status of the islands and their long history with the Venetians, the fact that Ottoman *levends* returned to them again and again in the 1570s to raid should not come as a surprise. Whether in retaliation for perceived past wrongs, because the islands were not really "Ottoman," or just because the islanders made easy targets, *levend* attacks in the Aegean became especially common during the war years and persisted into the 1590s.[45] Predictably, some of the islands seen as most complicit with the enemy and most hostile to Ottoman ship captains were the same ones that had previously been victims of *levend* attacks and would be again, including Lemnos, Andros, and Naxos.

On Andros, antipathy to Ottoman *levend* captains had taken a particularly ugly turn in 1572, when the ships of the brothers Veli and Memi Reis were blown off course and ran aground on the island. The islanders took the opportunity to enact revenge for earlier wrongs, emptying the ships of their weapons and stores and imprisoning the crew. They then sent word to a nearby island where a "Frankish" ship was loitering and turned over some of the Muslim captives, killing eighteen who tried to escape. The unfortunate captains' third brother, himself likely a seaman, informed the center of what had happened and Andros was added to the list of islands that the imperial admiral would be visiting on his upcoming Aegean tour; he had orders to see to it that the remaining Ottoman captives be freed and the responsible islanders punished.[46] Similar dramas played out on Lemnos and Naxos.[47] Although the *kapudan pasha* was the recipient of these orders, the tasking for individual islands might fall to small flotillas of irregulars.

The orders to punish the islands went out in May 1572.[48] By June it had become clear that the pacification of the islands and the punishment of the traitors had spiraled out of control. The central government quickly found it necessary to remind the *kapudan pasha*—who was to pass on the content of the decree to the captains, sailors, and soldiers under his command—that the "rebellious" islands were still Ottoman and their inhabitants were still Ottoman subjects and not enemy soldiers. They were to round up the traitors and treat them as criminals (*mücrimler gibi*), throw them in chains, and put them to the oar, but it was absolutely not permissible to capture or sell the islanders "like captives who have been exported from the Abode of War."

The admiral and those below him could put the criminals to work on their ships, but they could not sell them.[49] The legal distinction was an important one; aiding the enemy was certainly reprehensible and traitorous, a serious criminal act worthy of death or a very short life as an oarsman, but it did not change one's subjecthood.[50] Nevertheless, this was a subtle distinction conveniently and frequently ignored. *Levend* captains were doing exactly what they were being warned not to do. In June 1572, a *levend* named Receb Reis raided Euboea, doing a great deal of damage and taking men, women, and children captive. Again the state sent orders to the admiral stating that the troublemakers on the island should be put to the oar but that their wives and children must be left in peace. It further clarified that on the islands in the area where the revolt persisted, the ringleaders should be killed and their possessions destroyed, but unless they tried to go over to the enemy their women and children should not be touched.[51]

Even as the islands of the Aegean were brought back under Ottoman control, *levend* attacks continued. In March 1573, it was reported that a number of *levend* frigates raided Samos and took captives whom they sold in Anatolia; the admiral was ordered to apprehend the culprits and free the slaves.[52] In April, the Imperial Council issued a decree concerning nine girls and boys who were snatched from the shores of the *kaza* (jurisdiction) of Monemvasia in the southern Morea by a *levend* captain known as Küçük Hoca and spirited clear across the Aegean to be sold in the coastal Anatolian district of Urla. In this case, a number of *zimmi*s from the jurisdiction traveled all the way to Istanbul to petition the sultan for justice. Informed that the children had been held in Urla by someone named Haci Ali, presumably Küçük Hoca's local contact and distributor, the Imperial Council ordered the *kadi* of Urla to find and release the slaves and to arrest and imprison Haci Ali and the pirates who had supplied the slaves.[53] Given the delay involved in communicating with the center over long distances—especially in the case of the petitioners coming from the Morea to Istanbul—it is likely that both of these cases took place in the late winter, when the *kapudan pasha* would still be with his fleet in Istanbul and unable to provide much protection.

The *levend*s were active year-round. Each year, as winter approached, the imperial fleet returned to Istanbul to wait out the storms. As the fleet withdrew in 1573, the government sent orders to the squadron commanders at Kavala, Euboea, Chios, and Siğacık (near Izmir) to ensure that the *levend*s that remained in those parts not oppress the people in its absence but with little success; similar incidents were reported in the following year.[54] While some of the *levend*s implicated in amphibious raids and attacks on shipping held simultaneous commissions and drew salaries from the government, others had served formerly but were entirely freelance at the time, and still others called *levend* in the records may have never had any formal or informal affiliation with the Ottoman navy at all. Between the revolving door of Ottoman irregular naval service and the ambiguity of Ottoman administrative terminology, the Ottoman administration often appears to have been in the dark about who some of these people were.

To avoid detection long enough to sell their ill-gotten captives, the *levend*s took them far from their homes. And because *zimmi*s from comparatively isolated islands and coasts would be unlikely to speak Turkish, it would have been difficult for them to communicate their free origin to potential buyers.[55] More importantly, with no ties to the community to which they had been forcibly brought, it would have been extremely difficult for them to legally prove their Ottoman subjecthood in the courts. Once such a crime had been perpetrated, someone with sufficient interest and access had to notify the Porte of what had happened. Only then could the center begin the process of resolving the problem.

Although the government struggled in vain to prevent Ottoman *levend* attacks on Ottoman subjects, it often responded dynamically after the fact. The reaction to a raid on Naxos in 1574 is illustrative of the lengths the administration was willing to go to when distance and security were less of a concern. That summer, *levend* galliots landed on Naxos, seizing hundreds of women and children whom they sold at various points on the Anatolian coast, claiming that they were legally enslaved "enemy infidel" captives. The incident spurred a nine-month manhunt, in which the Ottoman central government dispatched a messenger (*çavuş*), Tahir, to coordinate the efforts of local officials across Anatolia's Aegean coast to locate the slaves and take them from their owners.[56]

Ottoman policy in these cases was that all illegally enslaved persons should be found and freed, but only those who had not converted to Islam would be actively returned to their homes. The same policy applied in the event that Venetian, French, or other treaty-protected foreign subjects were enslaved in contravention of their treaties; the Ottoman government was unwilling to countenance apostasy, which would be the predictable consequence of returning new Muslims to Christian lands—including the Ottoman-ruled Cyclades islands.[57] But there the similarities ended. Whereas illegally enslaved foreigners were freed via executive action according to procedures laid out in the treaties concluded with their sovereigns, those claiming to be Ottoman subjects "of free origin" (*hürü'l-asıl*) were required to formally sue for their release through the Ottoman court system if they had already been sold.

In the Naxos case, as in many others like it in the Ottoman Mediterranean, this was a nonstarter. To overcome the objections of a Muslim master, Islamic law required the testimony of trustworthy male, Muslim witnesses who could vouch for the contested captives' Ottoman juridical identities, and there were none to be found in the almost exclusively Christian archipelago. The fact that the western Anatolian region had recently been flooded with legally imported Cypriot Greek slaves complicated the situation. Indeed, the Naxos raiders may have hoped that their Greek captives, once sold, would be indistinguishable from the rest of the Greek slave population. The Naxos raid had garnered the attention of the center—all the more so because of the protests of Naxos' absentee governor, the sultan's favorite, Nasi—but it certainly was not the first of its kind, and as news spread of the Ottoman administration's efforts to free the Naxiotes, the courts were inundated with freedom suits from other

Greek islanders claiming to have been illegally enslaved during the late war with Venice. The courts were overwhelmed.[58] Without the necessary witnesses, how was justice to be done?

The central government's response was pragmatic, effective, and served as a model for how it might deal with similar cases. First, the government dispatched a *zimmi* from Naxos named Marko to the districts where Naxiote slaves were suspected of being held to help Tahir Çavuş, its man on the ground, separate the right Greeks from the wrong Greeks. Marko could identify Naxiotes, but as a non-Muslim, his testimony could not be used in a lawsuit against a Muslim to legally prove the free origin of the Naxiote slaves. Instead, in the freedom suits pending before the courts in which Marko had indicated that the slave was a Naxiote or another illegally enslaved Ottoman Greek subject, the government ordered Tahir and the Anatolian *kadi*s to require the owners of the contested slaves to present documentation showing that the *pencik* tax on imported slaves had been paid.[59]

It is far from clear that all owners of legally imported slaves would possess such papers, but the owners of the illegally enslaved certainly would not. Here, an owner's failure of the *pencik* papers test would be interpreted as invalidating his ownership of the slave, providing the grounds for the government's agents to confiscate any slaves of questionable provenance while sidestepping the effectively impossible task of proving that the slave was an Ottoman subject "of free origin." Once the government had done this it could simply emancipate them and send home those who had not converted. It appears that many Ottoman Greeks were freed in this fashion between 1574 and 1576. Ultimately the same mechanism of release—confiscation followed by formal manumission—would be deployed in most cases of unambiguous illegal enslavement of both Ottoman subjects and foreigners in which the center successfully intervened.

However, the center's capacity to do so varied dramatically across time and space. For example, Avcı Oğlu, Kara Mustafa, Karaca Bali, and Aksak Hoca, pirates operating out of small skiffs (*kayık levendleri*) in the district of Albanian Iskenderiyye (present-day Shkodër), were brazen enough to forgo selling their Ottoman Christian captives, the product of numerous coastal raids in the early 1570s. Instead, they kept them as their personal slaves and settled on land with them openly in their service. Such a state of affairs could only occur with a degree of willful ignorance on the part of local officials, though it is impossible to know whether this was due to collusion with or intimidation by the pirates. Thus, when the Porte ordered the *bey*s of all the districts from the Albanian coast to Salonica to find and imprison the offending *levend*s and the slaves they had made in the summer of 1574, they were also instructed not to supply them with grain, to warn the soldiery of the provinces not to give aid to such people, and to imprison those who did.[60] But the pirates were not apprehended and, in contrast with those snatched from Naxos that same year, there was no happy ending for their captives.

In fact, with time and continued success, this quartet of local pirates graduated to long-distance status and established slave-trading networks with Egypt and North Africa that enabled large-scale human trafficking. They reappear in our sources five years later, in the summer of 1579, having disposed of cargoes of captives taken from villages in their old Albanian stomping grounds in the markets of Alexandria, and they were suspected of doing the same in Tripoli, Tunis, and perhaps even Algiers.[61] Just as with Tahir Çavuş and Marko's mission to Anatolia in search of Naxiotes, the Imperial Council dispatched a *zimmi* named "Irenc" to Egypt to work with the *kadi*s in Alexandria to locate the illegally captured Ottoman Albanians, arrange their release through the courts, and escort them back to their homes.[62] But the story invites the question: why was the Sublime Porte willing to send someone all the way to Egypt to hunt for illegally enslaved Ottoman Albanians when it did not do so in the captives' own backyard? Evidently there was some hope that the envoy Irenc might succeed in his mission in Alexandria, Egypt, but next to none that he would in Alexandria (Iskenderiyye), Albania.

By the 1580s *levend* attacks of this sort became less common in the Aegean, and by 1600 the Cyclades had much less to fear from the weakened Ottoman navy or its irregulars. This was partially due to the fact that far fewer *levend*s were deployed there. As the war with Venice faded into the past, the total number of *levend*s formally serving the empire decreased dramatically, from a high of 350 in the 1570s to around 70 in 1591, although there were of course many more ships and seamen in the wider Ottoman Mediterranean not on the state's payroll who would have been referred to as *levends*.[63] There was another important reason for the decline: the resource- and cash-poor Aegean islands had only one real prize to offer the Ottoman *levend*s and that was their inhabitants. With the conquest of Cyprus an increasingly distant memory, it would have become more difficult for slave dealers to sell large numbers of newly enslaved Greeks in Anatolian markets and hope to get away with it (other regions were another story). By this point, most of the Greek-speaking world was part of the Ottoman Empire and those parts that were not belonged to Venice, with which the Ottomans were at peace between 1573 and 1645; there was no place in the interwar years whence they could be legally enslaved.

What the Aegean did offer was a maze of islands through which much local and long-distance merchant traffic had to pass, but it was Catholic corsairs and local pirates, not Muslim *levends*, who turned the largely self-governing islands into bases and markets for booty rather than sources of prey alone. These corsairs also occasionally entered into partnerships with the Greek islanders, though sometimes their collaboration was violently coerced. Reports, like a 1591 communiqué that some residents of Naxos had been providing information on the movements of Muslim shipping and serving as guides for the Maltese,[64] would become increasingly common in the seventeenth century, as Christian piracy of all sorts turned parts of the Aegean into a nautical no man's land. The situation was different along the lower Adriatic and Ionian coasts, however, as proximity to the porous land and sea frontiers with Venice and the Habsburgs, distance from the imperial center, a rich buffet of targets, and the presence of significant numbers of poorly supervised, locally based *levends* continued to invite abuse.

The conclusion of the war with Venice in 1573 had not gone over well there. The *levends* on the western frontier who had fought through the conflict were skeptical of peace and nursed a grudge against their neighbor and erstwhile enemy. When the central government ordered the Avlonya *levend* commander, still Kara Hoca, to release his Venetian captives, he objected that they would give vital intelligence to the enemy in Messina and Venice that would put them at risk. He was subsequently ordered to stay alert and be cautious but to strictly and faithfully uphold the stipulations of the treaty.[65] Many *levends* like Kara Hoca, whose brother had been a Venetian captive, resented the peace imposed on them from afar and the lost livelihood it represented and so determined to continue their war.[66] Others looked for targets closer to home to make up the shortfall, preying on Ottoman subjects who did not have an ambassador in Istanbul to make a fuss on their behalf. They were joined by an array of economically marginalized actors, from gangs of amphibious bandits to disgruntled local officials, who helped make the waters above and below the entrance of the Adriatic among the most dangerous in the Mediterranean.

THE "LITTLE ALGIERS" ON LEFKADA

One of the main sources of unauthorized raiding in this region was the Ottoman fortress of Aya Mavra (Santa Maura). Located on an isthmus on the northern tip of the Ionian island of Lefkada, it was first conquered in 1479 and served as one of the most important corsairing bases in the

Ottoman Mediterranean until its loss to Venice in 1684.[67] It enjoyed a prime strategic location. Mustafa Ali listed Lefkada among the chief destinations for an up-and-coming Anatolian pirate, and indeed Aya Mavra's *levend*s were not locals. The volunteers who populated the fortress town were "strangers and foreigners," drawn from the coastal regions of the empire, who were rapidly acculturated to the hard-living, hard-partying, frontier pirate lifestyle. Reflecting their diverse origins, they were a polyglot bunch who spoke Greek-accented Turkish, fluent Greek, and lingua franca, the Romance pidgin tongue understood throughout the Mediterranean.[68] Although the fortress and its *levend*s fulfilled legitimate security needs and played an important role in wartime, this offshore pirate haunt was a source of either frustration or profit for the governors of the nearby mainland districts and a source of perpetual misery for their populations, whose ships and villages the *levend*s plundered mercilessly and whom they enslaved in order to build and row their frigates. At any given moment, Aya Mavra might host dozens of men occupying every stage of Mustafa Ali's pirate life cycle.

The incomparable Ottoman traveler Evliya Çelebi, who visited the island in 1670, called it "Little Algiers." The connections, actual and aspirational, between the North African capital of Muslim corsairing and the Ionian island fortress community were unmistakable to the visitor. "All of them, large and small," Evliya wrote of its frigateer (*firkateci*) *levend*s, "in their manner and in their dress are like those of Algiers." Donning red fezzes, the *levend*s of Aya Mavra wore matching red vests open against their bare chests and printed silk sashes about their waists with their forks and knives tucked in them; in their hands they carried spears or hammer-axes and a white handkerchief. Walking with a distinctive swagger, they appeared to Evliya otherwise destitute.[69] Many likely hoped to one day join the Algerian corsairs whose fashions and carriage they self-consciously imitated.

Aya Mavra was large enough to contain a small town within its walls, with two hundred stone homes separated by narrow cobbled streets. These housed the fortress' garrison, which in the 1580s numbered between 261 and 299 men, roughly half of which were captains and *azab*s who would crew the galleys. Similar numbers of men appear to have been employed in the seventeenth century, supplemented by varying numbers of *levend* volunteers not on the payroll. Just outside the fortress walls was a town (*varoş*) surrounded on both sides by the sea and inhabited almost exclusively by Greek Christians. There, the homes were built of wood, lest a besieging enemy fortify them against the defenders. There was a single, wooden mosque at Aya Mavra, but there were many Christian-run taverns. These, besides piracy, provided the *levend*s with their principal occupation: "day and night the *levend*s of the fortress drink and make merry in the taverns with drum and *zurna* (a reed instrument), and it's a tumult of song and *saz* (a stringed instrument) and vice as if it were the *vilayet* of Algiers."[70] Evliya's visit to the island took place shortly after the conclusion of twenty-four years of war with Venice, during which the *levend*s of Aya Mavra had played an important role in harassing the Venetian-held Ionian Islands and interdicting Venetian merchant traffic. In recognition of their recent service, Evliya called them holy warriors and heroes, but with the 1645–1669 war freshly over, Aya Mavra's *levend*s had lost their primary legitimate target—Venetian ships and shores. The *levends*' profligate ways would soon force them to seek out some source of booty, licit or not.

There was no question that they would continue to be aided in their endeavors by the salaried garrison of the fortress, especially the low-ranking *azab*s who might serve as oarsmen and marines. In the early years of Sultan Süleyman's reign (1520–1566), the *azab*s of Aya Mavra were paid just over four *akçe* per day. Almost a century later, a salary register from 1610–1623 shows the *azab*s of the fortress earning roughly the same amount.[71] But four *akçe* in 1623 was worth far less than four *akçe* in 1523. In the 1580s, inflation caused by the influx of New World silver and exacerbated by the ongoing war with the Safavids (1578–1590) led the Ottoman treasury to repeatedly debase the silver *akçe*—its name, "little white thing," once synonymous with purity—in order to pay the troops. Inflation spiraled out of control as a result, leading to social unrest and inflicting lasting damage on the Ottoman economy. Foreign currencies with higher silver content—especially Spanish *real*s (*riyal guruş*) and Dutch *leeuwendaalder*s ("lion dollars," *esedi guruş*)—rapidly replaced Ottoman coins in Ottoman markets and became the currencies of account for nearly all commercial transactions in the seventeenth-century Ottoman Mediterranean. Nevertheless, government salaries and procurement contracts continued to be denominated in the debased *akçe*, meaning that salaried troops like the *azab*s had their pay fixed in nearly worthless coin at rates that had not been adjusted for inflation in more than a century and were barely at subsistence levels. For them and for many poorly paid frontier officials, participation in piracy and supplementing their meager salaries with plunder was a matter of financial necessity. It should not come as a surprise, then, that Evliya could not help noticing that the local authorities seemed to be studiously turning a blind eye to the often-illegal behavior of Aya Mavra's *gazi*s.[72]

For many of the *levend*s of Lefkada, however, the freebooting lifestyle was the real draw, not just the money. In much the same way that the early seventeenth-century Spanish adventurer Alonso de Contreras blew all the money he earned from anti-Muslim corsairing with the Knights of Malta and the Spanish viceroys of Naples and Sicily on prostitutes and alcohol, Evliya wrote that "every time its *gazi*s take their frigates to sea and strike deep into *Frengistan* (the land of the Franks) and return to Aya Mavra victorious with their booty, they give away the raiding monies generously and they drink and make merry until they're broke good-for-nothings and then they again go to sea."[73] Although Evliya insisted, somewhat credulously, that some of Aya Mavra's pirates were "very devout," illegal attacks on Ottoman and Venetian subjects would be the erstwhile holy warrior corsairs' first move once they reached the bottoms of their cups. By 1673, they were back to raiding the neighboring Venetian Ionian Islands and enslaving their inhabitants.[74] Although the governor of the Morea sent a force there in 1675 to burn the pirates' ships, the attacks persisted until the resumption of hostilities in 1684, at which point the conquest of Aya Mavra was the Venetian navy's first major objective.[75]

That pattern emerged a century earlier. In the spring of 1573, just as the war with Venice formally ended, *levend*s based at Aya Mavra were reported to have built frigates with which they were raiding nearby Ottoman subjects. In response, the *kadi* of Aya Mavra was ordered to record the names of the *levend*s responsible and forward the list to the *divan*.[76] But it was not long before the *sancakbeyi* of the Morea reported that apparently undeterred pirates sailing from Aya Mavra and Inebahtı (Lepanto) had been plundering his district and taking Ottoman captives. The *sancakbeyi* of Inebahtı was ordered to use the forces at his disposal to apprehend the pirates and put them to the oar on his galleys.[77]

Surrounded by islands subject to Venice and a constant flow of coastal and long-distance merchant vessels, the temptation to raid these or the Ottoman-subject Christians settled on the mainland was omnipresent and, apparently, irresistible; piratical incidents were reported with striking regularity up until the resumption of legal raiding with the start of the war for Crete in 1645. Aliens with no connections to or affinity for the region and its inhabitants, the *levend*s maintained a parasitic relationship with the neighboring populations. Clearly this was a problem, but Evliya identified the tradeoff facing the central administration: the *levend*s of Aya Mavra may "not have good relations with the people of other places, but they are brave and courageous and talented soldiers and they are a thorn in the eyes of Frengistan." With the hostile shores of the kingdoms of Naples and Sicily nearby and renewed war with Venice always a possibility, the *levend*s of Aya Mavra were a necessary and cost-effective evil. Clearing the *levend*s from Aya Mavra would thus be neither easy nor desirable, but the Ottoman government sent frequent orders in the late sixteenth century to try to curtail the attacks launched from Aya Mavra and smaller bases in the Morea against nearby Venetians and Ottomans.

Similar attacks did take place in the decade before the war for Cyprus, but they appear to have been comparatively rare. And, in contrast with the situation between 1573 and 1645, the central government typically knew exactly who was responsible and could demand their apprehension by name and order that they be sent to Istanbul for exemplary punishment.[78] After the unrestrained buildup of naval irregular forces in the early 1570s, however, it became far more difficult to keep track of the various paramilitaries operating on the frontier. Venetian intelligence often filled the gap when there were attacks on Venetian subjects, with the *bailo* in Istanbul informing the Imperial Council of incidents and identifying those responsible whenever possible, but when the culprits were unidentified *ehl-i fesad*, "people of corruption," it was hardly straightforward for the Imperial Council to follow up on its orders to provincial officials to apprehend and punish pirates.

The center recognized that these *levend*s did not operate in a vacuum. The government repeatedly ordered provincial military forces not to supply the pirates with water, grain, guides or information, and to burn any ships built without authorization or belonging to those suspected of engaging in piracy.[79] But if the Porte occasionally succeeded in winning the release of Ottoman or Venetian subjects put to the oar on the frigates of Aya Mavra's pirates, it completely failed to halt the local Ottoman leadership's growing investment in piratical activity.

In these trying times, provincial (*beylerbeyi*) and district (*sancakbeyi*) governors on the empire's western frontier enjoyed a great deal of discretionary power and minimal supervision. Those who were sufficiently enterprising could, if so inclined, make quite a profit during their tenures. This was certainly true for the *sancakbeyi*s of the district of Karlieli (in present-day western Greece), who had formal authority over Lefkada from their seat at the coastal fortress of Angilikasrı, itself a source of frequent *levend* raiding. Any incoming governor faced the choice of combatting piracy and trying to maintain order in his district or profiting from the authority and connections the post brought with it. Recognizing that the former would be difficult under the best circumstances and that their relatively short terms in office—never more than three years and often much less—could make unorthodox revenue gathering a necessity to secure the next posting in this age of secular simony, a number chose the latter. For instance, in 1591 the district's former governor, Mustafa Bey, was found to have been "disobeying the noble *şeriat* [i.e., Islamic law]" by "always committing corruption" and working in concert with the "rebel *levend*s" based at Aya Mavra.

Using the resources at his disposal, Mustafa Bey had been equipping the frigates of Aya Mavra's *levend*s for raids, enslaving Ottoman subjects from his district and from nearby islands and coasts, and using them to build galliots with which his pirates harassed passing merchant ships. As a sitting governor, Mustafa Bey rapidly cycled through Mustafa Ali's first three stages of piratical development without even setting foot on a ship. The Ottoman government learned about his criminal activities only after he had been routinely rotated out of his position and his successor, Murad Bey, informed the Porte of what had been happening. The Sublime Porte instructed Murad and the castellan (*dizdar*) of Aya Mavra to see to it that any captives held there be immediately freed, to put a stop to the *levends*' attacks on Ottoman shores and merchants, and to write if the problem persisted.[80] But of course the activities of the *levend*s stationed at Aya Mavra could not be news to its castellan, and since no attempt was made to replace him and no military force was sent to restrain the men who sheltered their ships under his cannon, the decree may have had only a limited impact, if any.

Not all Ottoman governors were engaged in piracy, and even those who were presumably did not appreciate having their districts impoverished by the piratical predations of their neighbors, but complaints to the center seem to have accomplished little.[81] The recipients of these orders certainly knew about the *levends*' raiding beforehand; it is inconceivable that they did not. But they were either partially responsible for it or incapable of stopping it. In 1564, for example, during the supposedly golden years of Sultan Süleyman, a *sipahi* (cavalryman) resident of Aya Mavra's extramural town who had attacked the ship of some local *zimmi* merchants declared to the representative of the pasha who was investigating the attack, "Long live the *padişah*, but what power does Ahmed Pasha have? We are fief-holders. Who are you to talk to us?" The local magistrate, reporting to the Porte on the activities of this and another *sipahi* run amok, complained that "it is not possible to restrain them and all the *reaya* complain about them."[82] The task of policing the *levend*s and their official supporters only became more difficult in subsequent decades. The fact that the *levend*s still fulfilled a vital security function and, more importantly, that some control over them was better than none, meant that the center would respond to the most egregious excesses but otherwise left its district governors in peace.

History repeated itself in 1617 when the Porte responded to a letter from a new *sancakbeyi* of Karlieli, Hasan, regarding the depredations of his predecessor, Mahmud. Mahmud Bey had come up with a new twist to the pattern of abusing the locals, however. Likely using muscle from Aya Mavra and Angilikasrı, he had seized numerous Ottoman subjects from every village in his district and put them to the oar on his own ship. Sailing to North Africa, he traded his Ottoman captives in the markets for legally enslaved "enemy infidels" the North African corsairs had captured. It was effectively money laundering but with slaves.[83]

By trafficking his captives across the sea, he quite literally disposed of the evidence of his crimes, returning from North Africa with a hold full of slaves who could be openly sold for cash in local markets, kept, or traded without subterfuge. Mahmud's trans-Mediterranean slave-laundering operation provides evidence for the kinds of complex, long-distance connections and illicit commercial relationships that Ottoman provincial leaders and pirates in the Adriatic-Ionian corridor and North Africa were able to establish with each other, independent of the center and contrary to its wishes.

The *levend*s of Aya Mavra—Evliya's "Little Algiers"—and those of other Adriatic-Ionian ports engaged in the piracy business played a critical role in facilitating operations like Mahmud Bey's. They maintained strong working relationships with the North African corsairing enterprises to which some of their number had graduated and which many probably aspired to join. After 1590, Aya Mavra and the ports of the Morea and the Ottoman Adriatic regularly hosted North African corsair fleets and collaborated with them in expeditions against nearby, often Venetian, targets.[84] The illegal captives they took, like those trafficked by Mahmud Bey, would often be sent to North Africa, where the sultan's peace with Venice counted for little and where his agents would not be able to confiscate them as they might in much of Rumeli or Anatolia. Indeed, there is no evidence that any attempt was made to retrieve the villagers from Mahmud's district. Ports like Tunis were already sufficiently outside the purview of the Ottoman center that such efforts would likely be fruitless. As for the slaves imported from North Africa by Mahmud, there was nothing objectionable about their capture, enslavement, or sale that would require government action.

The situation at Aya Mavra, an island fortress hosting a diverse population devoted entirely to the pursuit of the *corso*, was arguably unique in the Mediterranean outside of Malta and, in the seventeenth century, Christian corsair–dominated Aegean islands like Milos and Ios. However, the symbiosis between provincial administrators—from the local judge, castellan, or customs official on up to the district governor—and pirates that Lefkada supported was not. In particular, the southern Adriatic ports of the Ottoman Albanian coast, which had steadily lost commercial importance in the second half of the sixteenth century, were revitalized and sustained by the trade in stolen goods and captives offloaded by pirates. Economic necessity and a co-opted local government facilitated the rise of sophisticated local piratical enterprises, collaboration with long-distance pirates and corsairs, and, inadvertently, the emergence of parasitic piratical strongmen on the outskirts of towns.

THE PIRATE PORTS OF THE OTTOMAN ADRIATIC

The case of the Ottoman Albanian port of Avlonya is instructive. Located at a narrow point at the southern end of the Adriatic, Avlonya's gradual transformation from a relatively prosperous commercial port to a forward base and entrepôt for corsairs toward the end of the sixteenth century reflects many of the causes of the great increase in piracy during the period and the difficulties faced by the distant Ottoman center in imposing its will on its recalcitrant servants.

Its story is in many respects quite similar to that of other formerly marginalized Ottoman Adriatic ports, like Draç (Durazzo, present-day Durrës in Albania). Owing to shifting trade patterns, Avlonya began to lose its share of trans-Adriatic commerce in the second half of the sixteenth century and, with the establishment of Split as a viable transit port after 1590, survived primarily as a base for naval irregulars, like the aforementioned Kara Hoca, who played an important role in the late war with Venice. However, increasing piracy in the Adriatic after the 1570s, much of it perpetrated by the same naval irregulars, only reinforced this decline. It drove more and more merchants to abandon the sea for trade routes on land and employ the more secure short-haul transit ports in the north to traverse the Adriatic, thereby further accelerating the southern Ottoman ports' descent into commercial irrelevance.[85]

Local administrators in a declining port, deprived of adequate customs revenue (and presumably the bribes that would accompany it), would logically see facilitating, or at the least turning a blind eye to, piracy and smuggling as the best ways to supplement their shrinking incomes. With the drying up of licit commerce, the port's survival and that of its denizens, sailors and permanent residents alike—the entire local economy—would depend on making up the shortfall through piracy and contraband trade, including the illegal export of grain. Senj, the northern Adriatic base of the infamous Uskok corsairs, underwent a similar transformation, with similar causes, after the Ottoman conquest of the port's hinterland in the late fifteenth century.[86] Ultimately, the embrace of piracy for economic survival in the Adriatic—though its practitioners might not have articulated their motives or justified their actions in this manner—and the Mediterranean *corso* in general must be understood as, to quote Pal Fodor, "the attempt of impoverished societies excluded from the mainstream of development to compensate themselves—at least in part—for the losses caused by the commercial ascendancy" of others.[87]

Thus, pirates based in or stopping at Avlonya captured the ships of Venetians and others, brought them back to Avlonya, and sold their contents and crews there. Its prime strategic position turned the entrance to the sea into a dangerous gauntlet. Avlonya did far more than facilitate the legitimate privateering and occasional piracy of locally stationed squadrons of *levends*. By opening itself to the English (who made their Mediterranean debut in the 1580s), the North Africans, and other *levends*, it made long-distance piracy in and around the Adriatic possible and profitable. No longer limited by how much they could haul back to their home ports or the number of days' worth of provisions they could store, pirates of diverse origins could loiter in the area indefinitely, repeatedly off-loading their prizes at port, taking on fresh supplies, and heading back out for more booty. In this way, Avlonya became a major hub on Mediterranean piracy networks of the late sixteenth and seventeenth centuries.[88]

This situation was not acceptable to Istanbul, but its ability to control the *levends* on this distant frontier was severely constrained by political, military, and logistical realities. The Porte had long recognized Venice's rights in the Adriatic Sea, even adopting their styling of it as the "Venetian Gulf," and in peacetime the Ottoman navy did not enter it, going no further than Avlonya.[89] Responsibility for maritime security in the Adriatic thus devolved to Venice, for which reason the Ottomans held Venice responsible for the depredations of the Uskoks of Senj, which was in Habsburg territory. However, since there was no large, centrally controlled naval force nearby besides that of Venice, the Ottoman center both required the *levends*' services to look to their interests in the region and lacked the means to bring them into line when they misbehaved. In contrast with Aya Mavra, most of the *levends* operating out of ports like Avlonya and Draç in the late sixteenth and seventeenth centuries were of local, Albanian origins. However, here too, the fashions of Algiers had taken hold among its *levends* by the mid-seventeenth century.[90] This should come as little surprise, as both ports frequently hosted corsairs from North Africa who cruised in the Adriatic in violation of Istanbul's agreements with Venice. Most famously, in 1638, Avlonya opened its harbor to a fleet of marauding North African corsairs that was being pursued by the Venetians, leading the latter to fire on the town and enter the port by force; we will return to that incident, which brought the two powers to the brink of war, later in this book.

Just as on Aya Mavra, the *levends* of Avlonya and Draç often targeted Ottoman subjects—in most instances other Albanians—sometimes but not always as a stepping-stone on the path to taking Venetian or Ragusan prizes. However, these port cities were larger and had a more significant Ottoman administrative presence than did Lefkada, which led to periodic clashes between officials obeying their sultan's orders and the pirates and their allies who were determined to resist. Such confrontations could end in bloodshed. The flagrant lack of respect shown by some *levend*s to the representatives of Ottoman authority was manifested in the 1584 murder of Sinan, *kadi* of Belgrade and treasury inspector (*müfettiş-i emval*), in Avlonya. In the course of the subsequent investigation, suspicion fell on the *levend* captain Yaya Aşık, who witnesses attested had openly declared his intention to kill the *kadi* and who was already implicated in other murders. Yaya Aşık was a powerful character, operating two frigates with fifty to sixty *levend*s under his command. Members of the local landed cavalry (*sipahi*s) were suspected of colluding with him.

It was no small thing to kill a *kadi*, who was both judge and administrator and who, more than any other local figure, represented the law and the dynasty's commitment to the provision of justice. In a tacit acknowledgment of the considerable strength of their target, the Ottoman central administration instructed the *kadi* of Avlonya, the judge-inspector of Belgrade, and Piyale, former commander of the naval squadron at Avlonya, to take the accused and other suspected persons into custody by any means necessary and, failing that, to do whatever could be done in its place.[91]

It is not clear why Yaya Aşık and his accomplices decided to kill Sinan, but it seems likely that the *kadi*, in his capacity as treasury inspector, had somehow interfered with their plans or profits. Perhaps the outsider Sinan had tried to bring a reformist agenda to Avlonya that threatened the status quo and a preexisting, cozy relationship between the *levend*s and local officials. Evidently, the power and prestige of Sinan's office did not give the conspirators much pause, nor did the prospect of the inevitable imperial reaction to their crime; this was not the first time that the *levend*s of Avlonya had murdered Ottoman officials who stood in their way.[92] Istanbul's failure to maintain a credible threat of coercive force on the frontier, to effectively prosecute this affront or supply sufficient, loyal manpower to destroy the offending party speaks volumes about the limits of Ottoman central control on the margins of the empire and the enormous challenges facing local leaders tasked with independently taking on members of the highly mobile paramilitary groups formerly expected to defend them.

The reinvention of Avlonya as a port catering to pirates depended as much on the involvement of the local administration as it did on the activities of the pirates themselves. Indeed, without their complicity, Avlonya would not have been able to take on the role it did. Even if local administrators could not prevent piracy or restrain determined *levends* without help from the center, they might have denied pirates a market for their goods and dungeons for their captives or moved to confiscate booty brought to shore. Sometimes they did these things. More often, however, officials in Ottoman ports actively participated in pirating ventures, bankrolling operations or buying up captives and stolen property. In some instances, they planned the expeditions themselves, using the intelligence and connections at their disposal to assemble intercontinental partnerships to capture specific prizes or raid the territories of regional or personal rivals.[93]

The tone of cease-and-desist orders sent from Istanbul to provincial officials suggests that, at least from the perspective of the central government, there was no wink-and-nod situation with respect to their piratical activities. Orders sent were often concerned with preventing support being given to errant corsairs in the form of provisions or providing markets for goods or captives, and Ottoman officials from top to bottom were warned not to support or participate in unauthorized raiding on land or sea.[94] The fact that these orders were repeatedly sent out—indeed, the frustration with disobedient officials is palpable in some imperial decrees—reveals the clear problems that the administration had with enforcement. A 1617 order to the governor of the northwest Anatolian district of Biga to combat local piracy and a rash of banditry, for example, included the arch warning not to take fifteen years to do what was necessary.[95] That said, many of the petitioners to the central government regarding cases of piracy and illegal enslavement were local judges and district and provincial governors who struggled mightily to protect the inhabitants of their domains from pirates and border raiders and, sometimes, neighboring governors. Nevertheless, pirates and their partners on land had little to fear from the center so long as all the state's resources were tied up fighting wars on two fronts and combatting the worst rebellion in the Ottoman Empire's history in Anatolia.

THE RISE OF THE AMPHIBIOUS STRONGMAN ON THE WESTERN FRONTIER

As we have seen, piracy and amphibious slave raiding in the Adriatic-Ionian region, just as in the broader Ottoman Mediterranean, broadly took one of two forms: local piracy and long-distance piracy. Although the boundaries between the two were fluid and there was a continuum of professionalization within the local rubric, the differences were significant. However, both coexisted uniquely in this region. The long-distance piracy umbrella includes the corsairs from North Africa and the pirates from England. These raiders made great use of ports like Avlonya for resupply and sale of stolen merchandise. They undoubtedly had business relationships with and were familiar to officials in the region, but they were not permanently based there and were not typically invested in the functioning of local government. Long-distance pirates certainly did indulge in shore raids, but in the southern Adriatic-Ionian-Morean region, they were the least of the worries of Ottoman subjects settled along the coasts and the near interior. Rather, the local pirate was their scourge.

Local pirates were not just those based in ports like Avlonya, Aya Mavra, and Draç who might have some loose affiliation with the government and may have continued to serve its needs in legitimate security and intelligence capacities while moonlighting as sea-raiders attacking both licit and illicit targets. Beginning in the later sixteenth century and increasing rapidly in the first quarter of the seventeenth century, local strongmen featured prominently in coastal power structures. These strongmen were often decommissioned naval irregulars or lower-level members of the Ottoman military-administrative establishment—janissaries, *sipahi*s, *çavuşes*—who took advantage of local power vacuums or the opportunities provided by their offices in the absence of close supervision, but sometimes they were men from outside these backgrounds who succeeded in accumulating power and attracting others to their banner by means of daring, reputation, or some other combination of factors. Most were Muslim, but some were Christian. They shared much in common with the bandit leaders of the Balkans and Anatolia and with the rebellious *celali*s, and they were able to proliferate for much the same reasons.[96] But these were not ordinary bandits.

The coastal strongmen who established themselves on the outskirts of the main towns, supported by gangs numbering in the teens to dozens, were truly amphibious criminals who operated in more or less fixed zones. By the time Istanbul learned of their activities, the culprits were already too well entrenched and too powerful to confront directly without committing to an open conflict, and in most cases the government, beset by crisis on all sides, had to be content with scolding and negotiation. By following the career trajectory of one of these *levend* strongmen, a "rebel" by the name of Ahmed active in the early seventeenth century around the port of Draç in the district of Elbasan (in present-day Albania), we see why this was so.

Ahmed began his criminal career—which bears an eerie resemblance to the early stages of Mustafa Ali's pirate life cycle—in the hinterland of Draç. A man with no identifiable prior connection to the Ottoman military, Ahmed started out as a small-scale brigand. He and his gang terrorized the villages in the area, carrying off women and children, raping, murdering, and stealing livestock and movable goods. With the labor from his captives and the money earned from their sale, Ahmed was able to set his sights on the big time: piracy. He had a frigate constructed from scratch, with which "he plundered passing Venetian merchant ships and murdered Muslim and infidel merchants and others on board and stole [their] property." The extent of Ahmed's depredations was such that, by the end of the summer of 1604, it had had a serious impact on trade and, "due to fear of the aforementioned rebel, merchant ships did not venture out onto the surface of the sea." All the while, Ahmed gathered more *levend*s under his command and continued his raiding and slaving on land, "roaming day and night in the fashion of the *celali*s, committing acts of corruption and depravity."[97]

Ultimately, the *sancakbeyi* of Elbasan sent a letter to the Porte informing it of the dire situation in his district, and it responded with a decree addressed to him and the *kadi* of Draç in late September 1604. But how long had this been going on before he did so? Many months at the least, possibly years. Certainly the *kadi* in Draç had to have known about Ahmed from the beginning; disorder on this scale could not have escaped his attention. The center ordered the *sancakbeyi* and the *kadi* to investigate the claims, to find and free the abducted Ottomans "in accordance with Islamic law (*şer'*)," and to capture the murderers and apply the punishments required by law should they be found guilty.[98] However, the center did not offer any suggestions as to how, precisely, governor and judge were supposed to accomplish all of this.

The decree was thus divorced from reality. Ordering recipients to "investigate" was a standard cliché in Ottoman imperial commands, but it rang particularly hollow in instances like this. The *sancakbeyi* and *kadi* were expected to investigate when the *sancakbeyi* himself was the one who had reported the problem. If there had been a point when they could have done something about Ahmed on their own, it had long since passed. What they needed now was a small army, not an investigation. When had Ahmed's activities become intolerable and why?

Certainly Ahmed was no poster child for those, then or now, who argued that the frontier raiders were simply carrying on the old Ottoman *gazi* tradition of attacking the infidel enemy as required by custom and Islam. His victims were not only Venetian merchants and Ottoman Christian villagers, but Muslims too. Some historians have ascribed religious motives to the Ottoman sea raiders of the Adriatic and North Africa and some contemporaries did indeed defend their actions in this way, but the sources do not give Ahmed and those like him the chance to explain themselves.[99] Nevertheless, there is no question that had Mustafa

Ali lived long enough to become acquainted with Ahmed, he would not have hailed him as a heroic *gazi*; on the contrary, Mustafa Ali would have declared him an infidel (*takfir*) and an apostate for his crimes.

Ahmed was a harbinger of things to come, as local Ottoman piracy intensified along the Adriatic-Ionian coasts and spread across the Morea in the first quarter of the seventeenth century. It was compounded by the growing presence of Catholic and North African corsairs and English pirates in the area. By 1618, officials in the Morea acknowledged that piracy, perpetrated both by "damned infidel" corsairs and Ottoman "rebel" pirates, had risen markedly in recent years. To protect the shipping and shores of this strategically important zone, which nearly all traffic from the Adriatic to points east and from the Aegean to points west had to traverse, the Porte ordered the *kapudan pasha* to have six large galleys built in the Morea, to be operated year-round in defensive patrols with a complement of sixty fighting men apiece drawn from the local *sipahi*s and their retainers. Authorization was given to divert the tax revenues from specific estates and the *cizye* receipts of certain villages to cover the costs of constructing, manning, and provisioning this coastal defense force.[100]

Despite these efforts, the cataclysmic events of the 1620s, with the future of the dynasty in the balance and the imperial fleet withdrawn to the Black Sea to hunt the Cossacks through much of the decade, invited further disorder and six Morean galleys could hardly stem the tide. The regional situation had so deteriorated by 1631 that a *çavuş* by the name of Yahya, the beneficiary of a *zeamet* (revenue-bearing land grant) in the Morea worth 27,000 *akçe* annually, had established a criminal empire that would have impressed even Ahmed. "He is," the *kapudan* Mustafa Pasha declared to the Porte, "a rebel and a criminal (*ehl-i fesad*) and a murderer and a frigateer oppressor (*firkateci zalim*)."[101]

Operating three frigates, he and his men had been kidnapping and raping their way up and down the Morean coast for some time when they came to the seaside village of Anatolikoz to raid. There they took property and cash and carried off twelve Ottoman Christians in chains. It just so happened, however, that this village was among those whose tax revenues supported the grand vizier, Hüsrev Pasha. The targeting of Anatolikoz got the attention of the area's *kadi* and ultimately of the *kapudan pasha*, at which point the *kadi*s of Londra and Kalamata spoke up. They reported to the *kapudan pasha* that Yahya Çavuş had been, in true amphibious fashion, going through their jurisdictions village by village with forty to fifty men in tow, abducting women and young girls, and had killed a janissary who stood in their way. The *kapudan pasha* then assembled these accounts and submitted a petition to the Porte detailing these offenses and requesting that Yahya be formally stripped of his *zeamet* and punished. This the Porte duly ordered, and to give Yahya neither succor nor respite once he had been captured and his guilt proven in court.[102]

Thus, in this case which directly affected the financial interests of members of the ruling elite, the Porte was informed of events after Yahya touched a nerve with his raid on lands paying out to the grand vizier, but once again, nothing happened until after Yahya had become a formidable power in his own right. Unlike in the case of Ahmed, however, Yahya's zone of activity was not so far away as to escape the *kapudan pasha*'s attention or wrath. The admiral's petition to the Porte was not asking for guidance or support. It was a request to rubberstamp a decision already made to crush the rebellious messenger's personal pirate flotilla. Proximity, the fact that Yahya was a *çavuş* (a highly esteemed position in the imperial service), and the impact of Yahya's raids on the grand vizier's purse made it both possible and necessary to respond with force to the affront, but this was no longer the norm in this piratical theater.

CONCLUSION

Throughout the late sixteenth and seventeenth centuries, the Sublime Porte had to engage in a precarious balancing act in its coastal possessions. The illegal activities of Ottoman *levend*s, especially the enslavement of Ottoman subjects, demanded a response, but the complex security situation and differing political and military interests involved made it difficult to proactively combat piracy. Instead, the central administration largely confined itself to ordering the release of the illegally enslaved and the apprehension of the responsible, while doing little to deconstruct the dynamic that made their seizure and sale possible and profitable.

The situation was especially complicated for the linguistically and religiously diverse inhabitants of the Adriatic and Ionian coasts. Distance from Istanbul and a complicated relationship with local officials and (para)military leaders meant that efforts to prevent piracy or free captives there were compromised from the start. And with the populations of various ethnic groups traversing religious and political borders, the opportunities for raiders to conflate "enemy infidels" with protected subjects increased exponentially. Although the Ottoman government employed a similar legal vocabulary in its decrees, ordering always that contested slaves be identified and released "in accordance with Islamic law," it is unclear whether or how it expected its commands to be carried out, especially when their recipients doubled as perpetrators. The semantic challenges associated with defining terms like *levend* in any given context reflect the complex and fluid situation on the Ottoman Empire's maritime frontier which, viewed from Istanbul, could appear hopelessly tangled.

Examining Ottoman-on-Ottoman maritime violence uncovers the connections between local and long-distance piratical actors and between legal and illegal raiding. The *levend*s of Aya Mavra, who styled themselves after their colleagues and sometime partners from Algiers and who raided friend as often as foe, are a case in point. The boundaries between pirate and corsair were fluid and shifting. Erstwhile full-time pirates might obtain formal commissions and privateers might indiscriminately raid the subjects of their own sovereign, to say nothing of persisting in attacks against former enemies after the restoration of peace. Pirates and corsairs were the same people, not just at different points in their career, as Mustafa Ali suggested in his description of the pirate life cycle, but often on the very same cruise. Those in the service of the state might look for ways to position their activities within socially and legally acceptable norms, or to conceal evidence of their crimes, but such concerns were far from universal. Nevertheless, unambiguous pirates are difficult to identify in the sources. Piracy, on the other hand, is everywhere.

The Ottoman central government responded with principled outrage when the situation dictated, but it was forced to tolerate a certain amount of frontier violence as a sort of pressure-release valve for the otherwise unremunerated security forces it maintained in the region. Thinking about Ottoman-on-Ottoman piracy in the post-1571 Mediterranean as a symptom of decline oversimplifies the problem. The Ottomans faced innumerable, concurrent military threats, dynastic turmoil, and a staggering financial crisis during the decades separating the wars for Cyprus and Crete. The differing responses to piracy and amphibious slave raiding perpetrated by and against Ottoman subjects were not a function of decline. This was triage.

However serious the damage done by the *levend*s to Ottoman domestic interests and foreign relations, the threat from Catholic corsairs and Atlantic merchant-pirates was greater and growing. The government's register books reveal how the center grappled with the need to defend against their attacks with limited resources in an era of seemingly endless land wars. Inevitably, locally based irregular forces and the corsairs of North Africa were asked to pick up the slack, thereby guaranteeing that their crimes could never be fully prosecuted. Their predations were the least of Istanbul's problems, as Christian corsairs operating in the Ottoman Mediterranean continued to pick off the servants of the state traveling to and from their posts and to capture many hundreds more Muslim merchants, pilgrims, seamen, and coastal residents each year. It is to their plight that we now turn.

CHAPTER TWO

The Kadi of Malta

On March 19, 1597, Macuncuzade Mustafa Efendi, an Ottoman judge living in Istanbul in between appointments, learned that he had been assigned to a new post, the judgeship of Baf (Paphos) on the southwest coast of Cyprus. It was another step up the career ladder for the Istanbul-born *kadi*. In his mid-forties and with multiple successful rotations already under his belt, Mustafa Efendi could expect that after a couple of years in Baf he would be elevated to a more prominent post with a higher salary elsewhere within the European half of the empire.[1] He promptly secured permission to depart, packed his belongings, and said goodbye to his friends, but the sudden onset of severe eye inflammation stopped him in his tracks. A month elapsed before his doctors cautiously gave him permission to travel, but they ordered him not to take the more common land route, which entailed traversing the difficult, corrugated terrain of Anatolia and making the short hop to Cyprus from one of the ports on its southern shores. Passage by sea, faster and dust-free, offered the best prospects for his continued recovery. Acceding to his physicians' prescription, Mustafa Efendi boarded a *karamürsel* in Galata on April 22—the fifth day of the holy month of Ramadan—and embarked on a voyage that would take him not to Cyprus, but to Malta.

After three weeks of smooth sailing, the Ottoman vessel was only seventy miles from Baf when it was intercepted by four heavily armed galleys of the Order of Saint John of Jerusalem, the Hospitaller Knights of Malta. Commanded by the French knight Saint-Aubin, the galleys' red banners emblazoned with flared white crosses announced their hostile intentions long before the first shot was fired. Too far from shore to abandon ship, too slow to escape, hopelessly outnumbered and outgunned, the ship's captain, Alaiyeli Mehmed Reis, determined not to surrender without a fight. Thirty Muslims perished in the ensuing melee but, Mustafa would later claim in his account of his captivity, they took eighty of the damned

Maltese infidels with them and wounded one hundred more. In the end, however, ship and passengers were overwhelmed and subdued.[2] The Maltese clapped the survivors in irons and threw them below decks. The Knights had departed Malta on April 24, two days after Mustafa had left Istanbul.[3] They spent another twenty-six days at sea—too horrible to describe, Mustafa declared—before arriving in Valletta in mid-June. The six-week cruise netted the Maltese twelve sail and 283 Muslim prisoners.

Mustafa Efendi was not the only Ottoman judge among them; three others had been traveling with him on Alaiyeli Mehmed Reis' ship. The new *kadi* of Pendaye on Cyprus, Sivaslı Bekir Efendi, was killed in the Knights' assault, but Antakyalı Abdurrahman Efendi, the *kadi* of Erbid and Aclun (in present-day northern Jordan), and Sinan Efendi, *kadi* of Güvercinlik, joined Mustafa in the ship's hold. When they arrived on Malta, they and the other captives were assembled before the Grand Master of the Order and the leading knights in front of the palace, counted, and then marched into the slaves' prison. There, Mustafa Efendi encountered a familiar face, that of Haşim el-Haşimi, the titular *kadi* of Hacısofu on Cyprus. Haşim Efendi had never taken up his post. Fearful of enemy capture, he had taken the land route that Mustafa had eschewed for health reasons, but in those years even the shortest sea journey was fraught with danger. The Maltese picked off his ship just outside Silifke, whence he had embarked. That was exactly six years earlier, in June 1591.[4] Now Mustafa Efendi would join him in waiting for an uncertain redemption.

There was a constant flow of *kadi*s moving in and out of the capital region. *Kadi*s for the entirety of the empire save North Africa—where they were appointed locally—were dispatched to their posts from Istanbul for terms of one to two years. They returned to the capital upon the completion of their rotation, where they waited at least a year before receiving their next assignment and departing once more.[5] The frequent moves were the most dangerous part of a *kadi*'s job. Every time a *kadi* set foot on a ship, both his life and his freedom were at risk.

Hundreds of Ottoman judges were among the many thousands of Ottoman Muslims captured by Catholic corsairs in the early modern Ottoman Mediterranean. Some were snatched on their way to or from seaside posts as Mustafa had been. Others were abducted from their homes in brazen amphibious raids on the islands where they held court, the only Muslims in a sea of Greeks. Well into the eighteenth century, a number of Ottoman judges could always be found imprisoned in Maltese dungeons. Yet the *kadi*s of Malta were not simply valuable captives, symbols of Ottoman authority who would fetch a high ransom. Their captors and fellow captives alike needed them for their knowledge and legal training.

Carried off along with their writing stands, seals, and reed pens, the *kadi*s of Malta were put to work in their capacity as judge-notaries, drawing up surety agreements, assignations of legal agency, and ransom contracts that bound together Ottoman Muslim captives, Catholic captors, and a diverse assortment of Christian and Jewish middlemen who facilitated the transfer of men, women, and money across the liquid borders of the Abode of War. They represented one end of a triangular legal web that connected the Ottoman captives of Malta, Messina, Livorno, and Rome to the ports of Egypt and the Ottoman heartland, including Salonica, Istanbul, and Izmir.

Focusing our gaze on the *kadi*—as captive, as notary, as local representative of the Ottoman central government and official conduit for communication with it—grants us a unique, multivalent perspective on the shape and impact of Catholic corsairing and ransom slavery in the Ottoman Mediterranean. Following the *kadi*s and the documents they produced carries us from the Aegean and the Levant to Malta and Italy and back again. The plague of pirates that descended on the Eastern Mediterranean beginning in the late sixteenth century betrayed the weakness of the Ottoman navy and the Ottoman state's utter inability to protect not only its most vulnerable subjects but its most important servants as well. Despite this fact, Ottoman Islamic law and Mediterranean custom, sanctioned by Ottoman *kadi*s from Malta to Istanbul to Alexandria, underpinned the entire ransom slavery industry. Ottoman norms were the legal lingua franca of the Ottoman Mediterranean, even on Malta, that most reviled insular patch of the Abode of War. The phenomenon of the *kadi*s of Malta is a testament to the simultaneous, seemingly contradictory processes of the precipitous decline in maritime security in the early modern Mediterranean and the expansion in the power and reach of Ottoman law.

INVASION OF THE BODY SNATCHERS: CHRISTIAN CORSAIRING AND ITS IMPACT

It was in part due to Maltese attacks like those that netted Macuncuzade and Haşim Efendi that Sultan Selim II had ordered the invasion of Cyprus in 1570. Cyprus, Mustafa Ali wrote in his *Künhü'l-Ahbar* (The Essence of History), "is close to Syrian Tripoli and Silifke, both of which are on the coast of the Well-Protected Domains. Every year large and small ships of necessity pass through those straits. Now [the Venetian owners of Cyprus] present a face of obedience and offer the pretense of vassalage, but whenever there is an opportunity they board their ships and capture and raid the ships of Muslims en route toward Egypt. When asked 'Why do you commit such acts of rebellion?' they give such evasive answers as 'It is the ships of Messina and Malta, not we,' although their treachery has been demonstrated many times."[6] Mustafa Ali was not being entirely fair, conflating the Venetians with the corsairs of Malta and the Spanish viceroyalties of Naples and Sicily, but Venice's inability to prevent their regular landing and resupply on Cyprus suggested that the Ottoman seizure of the island was both just and necessary to secure the vital sea roads joining the northern and southern halves of the Ottoman Mediterranean. It also promised far greater rewards than a renewed attempt on Malta itself, the failed siege of which in 1565 still smarted.

However, the Ottomans failed to fully capitalize on this strategic acquisition, which would have required establishing a major naval base on the island and instituting a system of regular patrols.[7] And so the Ottomans proved no more capable of preventing the incursions of foreign corsairs and pirates than the Venetians had been, and in the succeeding decades the reallocation of resources previously earmarked for the navy and maritime defense opened the floodgates to swarms of them. The Istanbul-based imperial fleet's once-a-year circuits of the Ottoman Mediterranean routinely resulted in the capture of numerous pirates—more than fifty ships large and small between 1609 and 1611, for example[8]—but these were not enough to deter foreign activity nor to prevent corsairs from openly settling on the Aegean islands for the rest of the year, especially since there was next to no Ottoman administrative footprint or Muslim settlement on most. By 1600, pirates and Catholic corsairs infested every corner of the Ottoman Mediterranean, scurrying away whenever the Ottoman fleet appeared and returning as soon as the danger had passed to interdict local and long-distance shipping and stage amphibious raids on the islands and coasts.

Mr. Roberts, an Englishman pressed into service on a Corsican-captained, Livorno-flagged corsair in the 1690s, described the modus operandi, by then well-established, of these corsairs, who remained in the Ottoman Mediterranean year-round with impunity. From mid-December to March, they careened—laying their ships up on their sides, scraping the hulls clean, and tarring them to keep out water and improve speed—on Paros, Antiparos, Milos, or Ios. They then proceeded to the small isles in the channels beside Samos and Ikaria, where they lay in wait for prizes until midsummer, at which point they headed to the coast of Cyprus. If they received intelligence that the Ottoman fleet or Algerian corsairs were at Rhodes, they headed south to ply the waters off Alexandria and

Damietta, knowing well that the shoals there were too dangerous for the fleet to operate in strength. In late summer, they would set sail for the Syrian coast and send out their felucca on shore raids. Dispatching the boat by night, the men hid themselves along the coast, "where they way-lay the Turks, and take sometimes a dozen of them at a time."[9]

In early autumn they returned to the Cyclades, selling pilfered cargo on Milos or Paros before laying up once more for the winter. The French traveler Chardin estimated in 1671 that there were at least forty such private corsairs operating in the Aegean.[10] They could stay out at sea almost indefinitely, cannibalizing prizes to repair their ships and returning from the archipelago in better condition than when they had left Malta or Livorno. Purchasing gunpowder from French merchants at Milos and extorting bread from the Greek islanders, they had no need to return home to resupply and nothing to fear from the Ottoman fleet in winter. Roberts' ship, the *St. Helena*, had been out for nine years before returning to Livorno on its previous voyage. When Roberts was brought aboard in 1692, after being marooned on Ios, it had already been out for four years. Roberts was acquainted with seven other private Catholic corsairs operating in like fashion at the same time, most Livorno or Malta-flagged with Corsican captains. One, the *Caravel*, a Corsican-captained vessel of twelve guns flying Portuguese colors, had been continuously at sea for nineteen years, a sort of nautical "Hotel California," whose quasi-captive crew could check-out, but never leave.[11]

After engaging in amphibious raids or capturing smaller coastal trading vessels, corsairs would typically sail to the towns where their captives lived, anchoring just beyond range of shore batteries and raising the white flag of truce to announce their intention to open ransom negotiations. A white flag raised in response from land would signify agreement to parley, after which the ship or ships would approach the shore and bargaining would commence.[12] Evliya Çelebi witnessed the practice at Abukir, east of Alexandria, in 1672, after two corsair galleons seized a ship full of Muslim passengers just outside the port. In that instance, Evliya prevailed upon the fortress commander to fire on the ships after they had begun ransoming their captives, destroying one and damaging the other, resulting in the release of 145 captives for the cost of some powder and shot.[13] In a seascape ruled by custom and reciprocity, however, such violent breaches of a mutually agreed truce were unusual, even when the parties failed to make a deal.[14] Captives who were unable to redeem themselves would be packed off to Malta or Livorno, but captain and officers would be able to pocket all the money obtained from those ransomed on the spot without giving notice to the ship's owners, providing an enormous incentive to engage in the activity, "for the money will stow in little room." Roberts estimated the number of captives caught and released in this manner by his ship alone at fifty to sixty a year.[15]

Untold numbers of Ottoman subjects—predominantly Muslims, but also Jews and Greek and Armenian Christians—were caught, redeemed, and released in short succession in the early modern Ottoman Mediterranean. But many thousands, like Macuncuzade Mustafa Efendi and his fellow *kadi*s, were spirited away to Malta or Livorno, where those of status or means would be held for ransom and the rest would be sold as slaves, often to row the galleys that the Catholic rulers of the Mediterranean continued to operate well into the eighteenth century.[16] In 1599 there were roughly eighteen hundred slaves on Malta, comprising 5.5 percent of the total population of thirty-three thousand. As the island's population gradually grew to nearly sixty thousand souls, so too did the number of slaves in proportion, constituting 4–5 percent of the population throughout the seventeenth century.[17] Over the course of the seventeenth and eighteenth centuries, at least thirty-five thousand to forty thousand slaves passed through Malta.[18]

The Knights of Saint Stephen, founded in Pisa by the Tuscan Grand Duke Cosimo de Medici in 1562 in imitation of the Knights of Saint John, were likewise responsible for the importation of significant numbers of captives, bringing more than fourteen thousand back to Livorno between 1563 and 1642.[19] This was a fraction of the total imported into Livorno, where as much as 10 percent of the burgeoning population between 1600 and 1750 were enslaved persons, the majority Ottoman subjects.[20] The annual raiding activities of the two Catholic military orders, neither of which operated more than a handful of galleys at a time, were dwarfed by the many private corsairs—like the *St. Helena* on which Roberts served—that Malta, Tuscany, and other Christian states licensed each year, not to mention the pirates operating without commission. These private operators were responsible for bringing back the lion's share of the captives taken in the Ottoman Mediterranean. For instance, of the 4,538 slaves registered with the Maltese quarantine between 1655 and 1674 (a figure that does not include the many captives diverted to fill open spots on the galleys' benches), only about a quarter (1,141) were brought in by the Knights. The rest were taken by corsairs licensed by the Order, the Grand Master, or other Catholic powers.[21] These sailed under their respective banners and made use of the infrastructure that both Malta and Livorno maintained, in particular the slave prisons, or *bagnos*, modeled after those in Algiers and Tunis, that securely housed thousands of captives.[22]

The detailed archival records preserved in these capitals of Christian corsairing have allowed scholars to offer tentative estimates of the size and scope of their human-trafficking operations, but the mechanics of the Ottoman end of the ransoming business and the overall social, legal, and economic impact of this persistent piracy remain understudied and poorly understood.[23] To some contemporary observers, the Catholic corsairs were as mosquitoes to the Ottoman behemoth, incapable of doing any real harm besides arousing its anger. Such was the view espoused by the Venetian *bailo* Antonio Valier in 1616, who argued that the predations of the Catholic corsairs would serve only to justify Ottoman rage which, Malta and Tuscany being out of reach, would inevitably be directed against Venice instead.[24] Such had been the case with Cyprus of course, and Valier's remarks proved prescient when in 1644 a Maltese flotilla seized an Alexandria-bound Ottoman galleon carrying numerous important Ottoman personages—*kadi*s among them—and stopped on Crete's southern coast to share out the booty, thereby supplying the *casus belli* for the Ottoman invasion of the Venetian-held island the following year.[25]

But the corsairs' raids were hardly mosquito bites, annoying but harmless. They were rather more like the malaria mosquitoes carried: a serious, recurring, incurable menace that was extremely disruptive to Ottoman state and society and affected lives and livelihoods throughout the empire. Ships from Egypt brought north staples and luxury goods like rice, lentils, sugar, linen, cotton, henna, and coffee. The loss of these goods to corsair attacks could drive up prices and cause "a sort of famine" in the capital, especially among the elites denied sugar for their sherbets and rice for their meals.[26] News of the disruption of the Alexandria route could cause riots in Istanbul. Carefully orchestrated convoys, preferably with an escort of galleys, provided some security, but like impalas on the edge of the traveling herd, some ships might still be picked off by the circling predators familiar with the seasonal rhythms of their migrations.[27] There was nowhere to hide in the open sea north of the ports of Egypt. Every seventeenth-century Ottoman seafarer knew one thing to be true: "In these waters no galleon sails alone, unless it be a corsair."[28]

Although Ottoman customs receipts from English, French, and Dutch merchants were largely unaffected by Christian corsairing—indeed they increased at the expense of Venice during this period of "Northern" expansion—intra-Ottoman trade suffered greatly. It was not just the vessels carrying valuable commodities, government officials, and wealthy pilgrims that were targeted. Whereas the heavily armed galleys of the Knights of Saint John, which usually carried upward of three hundred highly trained fighting men apiece, sought the biggest prizes in the Ottoman Mediterranean and were prepared to sustain serious losses to obtain them, many of the piratical entrepreneurs who sailed under Maltese or Tuscan colors aimed for easier scores. Small and medium-size vessels owned, crewed, and laded by Ottoman subjects, often Christians, were especially vulnerable and took the brunt of the damage from the pirates. As Roberts put it, "We acted our part, not in taking Turkish vessels, but Greek Saicks, or any small Ships that came in our way."[29] The religious ideals and formal licensing of the Catholic *corso* provided legal cover for activity that was, in practice, often little more than indiscriminate piracy.

In the Ottoman Mediterranean, the economic damage from piracy rippled outward across the bonds of credit and blood that underlay most mercantile activity, and it was often a source of grief for years after an attack. El-Hac Ahmed, who entered into a *mudaraba* (that is, commenda) contract with Ramazan Reis (wherein he provided the capital and the captain the labor), lost everything when the latter's ship and all its cargo were seized by pirates in 1626; ten years after the attack, he was still trying to recover his investment from the unfortunate captain, who had neither the ability nor the legal obligation to compensate his former partner.[30] Yorgi, a Cretan *zimmi*, borrowed money from a butcher in Candia named Abdi Beşe to purchase sheep he intended to import to Crete and was ruined when, in 1672, pirates captured both ship and sheep; although he escaped with his life, he couldn't escape his debts, which he was unable to pay.[31] Ahmed Ağa of Cairo died intestate as a captive in the Abode of War in 1617, leaving it to the court and his heirs to dispose of his possessions and slaves to settle his accounts.[32] The *zimmi* Corci veled Frani fronted the money to ransom his friend, the *kadi* Mehmed Ali Efendi of Gallipoli, from Malta in 1644 only to discover that the *kadi* had misrepresented his finances and could scarcely afford to pay back half of the 1,293 *guruş*—a veritable fortune—that he had handed over on the *kadi*'s behalf; as Corci had not required his friend to supply collateral or a guarantor for the loan, he eventually had to agree to write off a huge portion of the *kadi*'s debt.[33]

Outside the major port cities, on the islands and along the coasts, the danger from pirates took a more immediate form, affecting not only those who sailed the sea, but all those who resided within a day's march of it. The plague of piracy dramatically altered the human geography of the Ottoman Mediterranean. In the Cyclades, pirates became a permanent fixture. Milos became a thriving entrepôt for stolen goods, especially during and after the war for Crete, with Latin pirates trading booty for food or equipment and keeping homes, wives, and mistresses there.[34] A Latin ecclesiastical register dated 1667–1669 for nearby Kimolos, effectively a piratical suburb of Milos, gives some indication of the diversity of the adventurers attracted to the Aegean free-for-all: Swiss, Dutch,

Italians, Veneto-Dalmatians, Ragusans, Maronite Lebanese, Maltese, and French, who married local Greek women through "temporary" unions that, in many instances, created permanent offspring who followed in their fathers' footsteps.[35] Islands like Mykonos and Ios were said in the 1670s and 1680s to be populated almost entirely by pirates, many second generation, who served with the Maltese and Livornese.[36] "The Turks call it Little Malta," the French traveler and botanist Tournefort wrote of Ios in 1700: "'tis a harbouring place for most of the corsairs of the Mediterranean."[37]

Muslim raiding in the fifteenth and sixteenth centuries had already driven much of the Greek population away from the shores and lowlands of the Aegean islands to higher altitude settlements that were safer from amphibious attack, but the process continued through the seventeenth century and spread to the Anatolian and Syrian coasts as well. In southwest Anatolia the predations of foreign pirates—"enemy infidel galleons in winter and galleys in summer"—grew so severe that, in 1629, the predominantly Christian residents of Meğri (present-day Fethiye) were given extraordinary permission to stockpile muskets and other arms to defend themselves against the landing parties that plundered their homes and carted off their women and livestock year-round.[38] Meanwhile, Haifa, little more than a village in the seventeenth century, also became known locally as "little Malta" and was employed by the corsairs as an advance base. Undeveloped and in ruins since the Mamluk conquests of the thirteenth century, the former Crusader ports of the Palestinian coast frequently played host to seafaring Latins who were the ideological descendants of those expelled centuries earlier.[39]

A single, well-executed amphibious raid could wipe out an entire settlement. The French traveler Jean Thévenot recounted the experience of the residents of Castel Pelegrino, a small fortified village between Acre and Jaffa ten miles south of Mount Carmel, whose former residents he met on a Livornese corsair that had captured his ship on the road to Damietta in May 1657. As corsairs often did, these had obtained intelligence from a Muslim captive who was promised his freedom in exchange for leading them to a promising spot for a slaving expedition. There they went, sacking the unsuspecting settlement and carrying off men, women, and children and killing any "without regard to age or sex, that would not willingly go along with them." The corsairs took fifty captives in the raid, and left behind considerably more dead; there were no survivors in Castel Pelegrino.[40] Nor did the corsairs' commander choose to honor his promise to the captive who had led them there—a dishonorable decision that alarmed the crew—taking him back with them to Livorno as well.[41]

The permanent loss of so many men, women, and children to pirate raids, and the continuous export of specie to retrieve others, did incalculable damage to families, businesses, and communities. Women whose husbands had disappeared into the Abode of War would be unable to remarry unless they received news of their husband's death and might struggle to support themselves and their children.[42] For those fortunate enough to receive word from their loved ones that a ransom had been set, the process of redemption could drag on for excruciating months or years, during which success and safe return were hardly guaranteed. All too often, illness or natural disaster struck at the moment of redemption, with the cumulative stresses of captivity and temptations of fate conspiring to rob families of long-awaited reunions and the forked-over ransom money in the process. Even with receipts, there were no refunds in this trade.

Of the half dozen courts operating in greater Istanbul in the seventeenth century, it is unlikely one could find a single *kadi* or deputy judge who had not drawn up documents certifying loans and surety agreements for ransoms, formalizing ransom arrangements with specialized brokers, and notarizing the repayment of the debts incurred bringing friends, relatives, business partners, and loved ones back home. This was quotidian business in Salonica, Izmir, and Alexandria as well, with each court serving as a hub for ransoming captives who hailed from those cities and often from further afield.[43] After 1669 Crete too became a way station for both brokers and returning captives, and entries in the Candia court records suggest that its proximity to Malta made it a node on trans-Mediterranean ransoming networks.[44]

Men and women who spent long years in captivity before obtaining their release often returned home to find changed circumstances. Ottoman court records are filled with stories of challenging reentries into Ottoman society, a powerful reminder that the tribulations and trials of captives did not end with their homecoming. Many struggled to repay those who had arranged their release or had loaned the money to pay the broker. Ketuna, a woman of the Portuguese Jewish community of Ortaköy in greater Istanbul, found herself indirectly indebted to the Ottoman dynasty after she was captured by pirates while on a pilgrimage to Jerusalem. Süleyman Pelini, her community's agent, traveled to Edirne—home to the royal family at the time—to borrow 700 *guruş* from the princess Ayşe Sultan in order to pay Ketuna's ransom. Pelini, understandably anxious about his outstanding debt to the princess, sued Ketuna before the Rumeli *kazasker* (the military judge of the European half of the empire and its highest-ranked judge) in January 1668 when she was slow to secure the funds after her return.[45]

Others attempted to collect on old debts or recover inheritance shares and lost property, often with limited success. In 1638, after twenty years as a captive in the Abode of War, Mehmed bin Ali sued his sister Kerime in the court of the Eyüp neighborhood of Istanbul for the inheritance from his uncle that she had claimed in his absence. Kerime admitted she had inherited from her uncle, but she denied that the Mehmed standing beside her was her brother. She insisted she had no idea who he was. Rejected by the only living relative who might have known him, Mehmed could bring no evidence to prove that he was who he said he was. He left the court defeated, alone, and likely destitute.[46] For all those former captives warmly welcomed home by elated family and friends, there were many Mehmeds who returned to find themselves deprived not only of their youth but their property, their birthright, and even their family name.

Beyond the deleterious micro- and macroeconomic effects, perhaps the greatest damage done by the corsairs was symbolic. The fact that the sultans, as Protectors of the Holy Places, could not safely facilitate their subjects' performance of the Hajj, the annual pilgrimage to Mecca, was damning. The corsairs specifically targeted these pilgrims. Gathering intelligence as to when they would depart each year, they loitered along the routes they traveled. In 1642, for example, the *kadi* of Kalamata reported that seventeen or eighteen Maltese frigates had been plying the waters between the nearby islands, plundering, killing, and capturing the Muslim pilgrims from the Balkans who had mustered for the Hajj at the ports of the Morea.[47] The security situation was even worse off the southwestern coast of Anatolia, where all traffic bound for Cyprus and Egypt passed and where Macuncuzade Mustafa Efendi was captured; a seventeenth-century Ottoman account remarked that "the damned infidels are capturing pilgrims (*huccac*) and holy warriors (*guzzat*) and merchants in that place all the time."[48] Owing in part to the increasingly predictable perils of sea travel, the Ottomans encouraged pilgrims to take the land route through Syria. This was not without its dangers, including Bedouin raids on the passing caravans, but these paled in comparison.[49] The capture of numerous wealthy and prominent pilgrims by Catholic corsairs was an enormous embarrassment that deprived the Ottoman state of important and experienced servants and siphoned away resources from the Ottoman economy to procure their release. The lost pilgrims were only one manifestation of a much larger problem.

What did it say about Ottoman power in the Mediterranean when the Istanbul government could not ensure the safe arrival of its administrators at distant posts? Or when some of those who did successfully occupy their positions, like the *kadi*s on seventeenth-century Samos or Syros, were literally forced to run for the hills every time a strange sail appeared in harbor, lest they be carried off?[50] How did it reflect on the dynasty when the local embodiments of Ottoman authority, the official mouthpieces of the Lords of the White and Black Seas, if required to traverse the former, might very well end up rotting in a Maltese dungeon alongside dozens of pilgrims, descendants of the Prophet, and men of the pen and the sword? Macuncuzade Mustafa Efendi summed up his incredulity and anger at what he perceived to be the injustice of this situation, of the cream of Ottoman Muslim society being locked up among the infidels, and contrasted it with the lofty ideals of the dynasty in a verse:

> Yatur bend-i belâda nice esnaf
> Kimi hacı kimi kadi kimi eşraf
> Değildir padişah-ı dehre insaf
> Tegallüb göstere eşrafa eclaf[51]
>
> (There are people of every class in the snare of evil
> Some are pilgrims, some *kadi*s, some nobles.
> It is contrary to the justice of the *padişah* of the age
> For the ruffians to lord over the noble ones)

As for what Mustafa Efendi wanted, the refrain of his poem, which he dispatched to Sultan Mehmed III in lieu of a ransom note, left no doubt: "the faithless infidels enslaved us, O helper of the ones who wish for help, help us!"[52] He wanted the sultan to bring him home. He wanted the sultan to bring them all home.

KADIS, CAPTIVITY, AND REDEMPTION

Claiming that his experiences were "one in a thousand," Macuncuzade Mustafa Efendi titled his account, completed in 1599, *The Singular Voyage of the Poor One of Malta, the Adventure of the Maltese Captive.*[53] "One in a thousand" was hyperbole meant to underscore the exceptional nature of his misfortunes, not an attempt to estimate the rate at which Ottoman Muslims became Maltese captives. Yet while Mustafa's account is indeed exceptional as one of the few extant Ottoman captivity narratives, his experience on Malta was entirely typical for an elite, male Ottoman Muslim. Even the bumper crop of captured *kadi*s of which Mustafa Efendi was a part in 1597 was unexceptional for the time. In 1586, for example, French pirates captured an Ottoman Greek-captained vessel traveling from Alexandria to Istanbul that carried at least three *kadi*s among its many elite passengers, which also included the future Sultan Mehmed III's chief treasurer. All were taken to Malta.[54]

But it is precisely because experiences like Mustafa Efendi's were becoming increasingly common lines on the curricula vitae of Ottoman notables that his account is of such great value. Men of letters bearing the sobriquet *esiri* (from *esir*, captive or prisoner) as a mark of their time in captivity crop up with some regularity in the historical record starting in the sixteenth century. Most prominently, Esiri Mehmed Efendi of Bursa (d. 1681) spent five years on Malta after being taken from the galleon whose capture in 1644 triggered the invasion of Crete; he had been sailing to take up the judgeship of Mecca. He returned from Malta to occupy successively more important judgeships before being appointed *şeyhülislam* in 1659, while the war for Crete still raged.[55] Esiri Mehmed Efendi, like many prominent Ottoman jurists, wrote a number of Islamic legal works, but had no words for his time on Malta. Few besides Mustafa Efendi did.[56]

Modern readers conditioned by the conventions of the genre of early modern European captivity narratives are likely to be disappointed by Macuncuzade Mustafa Efendi's *Singular Voyage*. Mustafa eschews the personal catalogue of torment the reader of European narratives might expect in favor of a more collective representation of the group's suffering. Indulgence in salacious descriptions of misfortune, of specific longings, hopes, and fears, let alone discussion of any family waiting back home, was beneath the stoic dignity of the Ottoman gentleman.[57] Glossing over the particularly difficult periods, the author and his views are most visible in the narrative whenever he recalls or is asked by his companions to produce a verse, which he does frequently and at great length in a variety of metrical forms and in the three languages—Arabic, Persian, and Ottoman Turkish (which draws heavily on the former two)—that any well-educated Ottoman Muslim man was expected to command.

Mustafa Efendi was not writing for a mass audience like those European Christian captives returning from Algiers, Tunis, or Salé, nor were his words reshaped like theirs by an editor with a print shop and a strong commercial sensibility. Only one copy of the twenty-seven folio work survives, prepared by a scribe named Ömer in 1602 as a section of a *mecmua*—a curated collection of miscellaneous writings bound together into a single volume.[58] We have no way of knowing how widely read it was, but Mustafa probably wrote with a small circle of well-educated and well-connected friends, colleagues, and potential patrons in mind.[59] These would have circulated the manuscript among themselves, had it copied into their *mecmua*s, or heard it read aloud in their salons. Considering his illustrious intended audience, Mustafa was determined to showcase his erudition and his multilingual poetic chops, including his ability to extemporize fully formed odes and chronograms upon request, but his primary aim was to expose the plight of the many Ottoman Muslims, of all ranks, being held against their will on Malta. As a midlevel member of the Ottoman learned hierarchy captured in the line of duty, Mustafa Efendi may have humbly believed that there was no one better qualified than he to bring the true state of affairs to the attention of Istanbul's ruling elites.

In European captivity narratives, the crux of the story was the moment of redemption, whether by escape or ransom, which provided the payoff for the Christian captive's Christ-like endurance of physical torture and spiritual temptation.[60] In contrast, Mustafa concludes abruptly upon learning that he would be ransomed after twenty months of captivity. The time frame, route, and experience of his reentry are left undescribed, an unimportant distraction from the Muslims' trials on Malta. For Ottoman Muslim captives like Mustafa, capture and release had already been decreed from on high. The language of fate pervades the narrative; whenever one of Mustafa's companions was redeemed, he wrote that it was "their portion" from God to go.

Mustafa Efendi would have been instantly recognizable to his captors as someone who would fetch a ransom far greater than his value as a slave on the open market, justifying a substantial investment in food, shelter, and security. For this reason, he was immediately consigned to the *bagno* and spared the most dangerous labor. The same could not be said for Mustafa's slave Ridvan, who was captured alongside him.[61] Mustafa left Ridvan's subsequent fate to the reader's imagination, but like others of lesser status or means, Ridvan could expect to be put to the oar on the galleys of the Order during the sea season and employed in backbreaking work on land the rest of the year or, even worse, to be sold to the agents of the pope or the king of France, who kept their galley slaves chained to the benches year-round.[62] Reconciliation with the church, a possibility for formerly Christian captives, might lessen the harsh decree but offered no promise of freedom from bondage. Mustafa Efendi was thus comparatively fortunate, but life in the *bagno* was bleak.

It was an entirely male world. On Malta, nearly all male slaves, even those in private hands, were required to return to the *bagno* every evening to spend the night, though exemptions were occasionally granted and masters often ignored the orders.[63] In contrast, women captured by the galleys of the Order, like those taken by the private corsairs, were as a rule sold to private parties to be employed as domestics, held for ransom, or both; they were in any event kept apart from the *bagno*. Though greatly outnumbered, the female captive population was not negligible on Malta. For example, auction records from 1659 to 1664 show that of 769 captives brought in and sold by private corsairs, 69 were women or girls, or about 9 percent.[64] Nevertheless, Ottoman court entries concerning the ransom of individual women, as opposed to those included in family groups, are relatively rare, indicating perhaps the relative poverty of many, especially those captured in amphibious raids; the higher rates of conversion among those employed as domestics; and the disadvantages of isolation from the well-connected if generally miserable Muslim community of the *bagno*.[65]

Mustafa Efendi spent his days excavating rocks and dirt from a ditch, "shedding tears of blood."[66] Although they were generally free to move about the *bagno* and to pursue work outside it during the day, prisoners were locked in leg irons in the dungeon for weeks on end for the slightest infraction. The guards liberally employed "the pit" both as a disciplinary measure and as a negotiating tactic when setting ransoms.[67] In the spirit of reciprocity that governed the Mediterranean ransom industry, Muslim and Jewish captives on Malta were permitted to practice their religion, as they were in Livorno, but the guards allowed the Maltese youth to taunt the enslaved Muslim worshippers during Ramadan, telling them that God had abandoned those of their faith and pelting them with stones.[68] The captives in the *bagno* subsisted on a daily allowance of three loaves of black bread and a gruel that would be at home in a "dog's bowl." The wells and cisterns supplying the *bagno* with water, which flowed into two troughs, were polluted with effluent from the streets and "resembled hell."[69] No effort was made to remediate the squalor, and Mustafa became violently ill within a fortnight. However, valuable captives were treated in the Order's famous hospitals—there were no ransoms for the dead—and Mustafa spent two bedridden months recuperating in the nearby Hospital of Saint John before being returned to the *bagno*.[70]

Upon his arrival in the *bagno* in early June 1597, Mustafa Efendi found a group of others like him, members of the military-administrative (*askeri*) class, *ulema*, and the scribal service distinguishable by their carriage and their titles. It was with these men that he spoke, ate, and prayed during the day; with whom he was counted by the guards during their evening rounds; and alongside whom he slept at night.[71] Among these the *kadi*s stood out, thanks to their religious-legal knowledge and the authority it conferred, which was of use to both captors and fellow captives.

One of their number would be nominated by their fellow prisoners and confirmed by the Grand Master as "the slaves' Cadi," who would serve both as their liaison with the Maltese authorities and their magistrate. The position had a long history, one which predated the Knights' tenure on Malta. When Evliya Çelebi visited Rhodes, the former home of the Order of Saint John, in 1671, he toured the dungeons in which the Knights had incarcerated their Muslim prisoners in the century before the Ottoman conquest and took note of the graffiti etched into the walls. Alongside heartbreaking examples, such as "I fell captive three times" and "I suffered and prayed here for forty years," he recorded intriguing autobiographical evidence for the ancient pedigree of the Maltese *bagno*'s *kadi*: "I was the Hanafi *kaziasker* for Sultan Inal [r. 1453–1461], the [Mamluk] ruler of Egypt, and I served as *kadi* to all the prisoners in this pit of woe."[72]

When the Muslim prisoners communicated collectively with their Maltese captors, as when they petitioned the Grand Master regarding their preferred candidate for the *bagno*'s interpreter in 1640, they did so through their *kadi*. The Maltese similarly used the *kadi* to convey orders to the prisoners. They also obliged the *kadi*s to write to North African authorities periodically to debunk complaints from returned Muslim captives about their ill treatment and prevent retaliation against the Christian captives held in North Africa. It was not just local authorities who tried to co-opt the slaves' *kadi*. In 1685, Pope Innocent XI conveyed his wish to the Order's ambassador in Rome that the "cadi of the slaves in Malta" write to the pasha of Tripoli to request that he moderate his treatment of the Missionary Fathers there.[73] It was the same in the *bagno* of Livorno, where men with religious-legal backgrounds, referred to as "coggia" (Turkish: *hoca*), were spared hard labor, maintained the *bagno*'s mosques, and helped facilitate communication between masters and the captives' homelands.[74]

In essence, the *kadi*s of Malta fulfilled the same role as they did within Ottoman domains, serving as judge-notaries but also as local administrators and as the principal conduit for communication between central authorities and the sultan's subjects in his jurisdiction. Of course, the slaves' *kadi* was still a slave, awaiting his ransom just like the others. One holder of the office is mentioned in a Maltese decree of 1638, when he was released to fetch his own ransom, with his son remaining behind as security.[75] When he left, another *kadi* took his place, just as the *kadi*s in the Ottoman Empire were routinely rotated. Through at least the first quarter of the eighteenth century, when Maltese corsairing in the Levant was sharply curtailed at French insistence, there was a surfeit. As we shall see, in addition to their importance in representing the interests of the prisoners and the Maltese authorities, the *kadi*s of Malta played a crucial role in propping up the legal order of the ransom industry throughout the Ottoman Mediterranean.

The ransoming process was difficult and slow under the best of circumstances. Although prisoners were often paroled, given permission to travel home and collect their own ransoms and those of their fellows within a set period of time and with other captives standing surety for their ransom price if they failed to return, this was more likely to occur when family members or close associates were captured together.[76] Communication between Malta and Ottoman domains otherwise mostly took the form of letters carried by passing merchants and ransom brokers, who shuttled back and forth. Dedicated brokers could make the roundtrip in under four months in ideal conditions, but it often took considerably longer to make arrangements.[77]

More than eight miserable months passed before Mustafa Efendi had his first opportunity to make contact with home. In late February 1598, Haci Hasan, one of his companions in the *bagno*, was ransomed, and Mustafa gave him letters to bring back to Istanbul. It is clear from comments later in the narrative that Mustafa asked Haci Hasan to deliver notes to friends and family, but he discusses only the poems he dispatched to the "Throne of Justice" and to Mehmed III's mother, the powerful *valide sultan* Safiye. The former, quoted above, was specifically intended to inform the sultan and those around him of his plight and of the condition of the captives generally, many of whom had been captured in the line of duty.[78] A second poem, directed explicitly at Sultan Mehmed III, underscored the latter point. Praising the sultan for his recent victory at Eger (Eğri), it contrasted the dynasty's glory with the ongoing shame of those representing its banner being packed tightly together in the *bagno*, wailing and moaning night and day. There were three other *kadi*s imprisoned on Malta besides himself, Mustafa wrote, and it was God's wish that the sultan free them immediately from infidel captivity. Naming his colleagues, their ranks and positions along with his own, he described their collective trials and, invoking the promises of the sultan's loftiest titles in the poem's refrain, demanded that the sultan help them.[79]

"Help" meant money, or the provision of prisoners for an exchange. Whereas some European governments became more proactive in retrieving their subjects from North Africa over the course of the seventeenth century, paying group ransoms, negotiating treaties, and threatening bombardment for the release of all their subjects, such actions were impossible or unpalatable for the Ottomans. Malta and Istanbul had no formal diplomatic relations and their rhetoric left little room for their negotiation; at the same time, lump-sum payments for the release of Ottoman subjects or large-scale fixed-rate exchanges were too costly for the Ottomans in both prestige and coin and such offers were categorically rejected.[80] Tuscany, in contrast, made occasional efforts in the late sixteenth century, the last in 1598, to revive commercial relations with the Ottoman Empire and obtain an *ahdname*, but negotiations always foundered over the Ottomans' entirely reasonable demand that the Grand

Duke put an end to Tuscan corsairing and the enslavement of Ottoman subjects.[81] As a result, though the Ottoman government could and did intervene directly on behalf of its subjects when its treaty partners, like Venice or France, were implicated in their capture, ransom payments and small-scale prisoner exchanges arranged through intermediaries were the only options for obtaining the release of Ottomans held in places like Malta, Livorno, Messina, and Rome.

Members of the *askeri*, or military, class—the men of religion, the pen, and the sword—could look to the treasury for their ransoms, but it is clear that this was more custom than official policy. Many *askeri* captives, including *kadi*s, ultimately arranged their own ransoms. For all other non-*askeri* (*reaya*) captives, the Ottoman government would facilitate safe passage from Malta, as it did in 1585 for a fleet of eleven galleys and one galleon carrying freed Muslim captives to Alexandria, but the work and cost of their redemption remained in private hands.[82] Ottoman Jewish communities often took up collections to free their captured coreligionists, but there is no evidence for the same sort of collective action on the part of Muslim communities in the core Ottoman lands.[83] Some individuals of means undertook to ransom Muslim prisoners whenever they encountered them as an act of piety. Evliya Çelebi claimed to have ransomed 170 Muslims from captivity in the course of his travels, but he noted "that many thousands have been sent off to the lands of the infidels . . . it is impossible to help them—may God in His omnipotence rescue them from captivity!"[84] For those who lacked the wealth to redeem themselves or the good fortune to encounter someone like Evliya, family and friends shouldered the burden.

Negotiated prisoner exchanges for prominent *askeri* Ottomans took place on a handful of occasions, with the Adriatic city-state of Dubrovnik, a Catholic Ottoman tributary, reluctantly serving as the go-between.[85] Such swaps were more often a feature of the Ottomans' post-hostility relations with their Habsburg and Venetian neighbors, however. The Ottoman central government usually stayed out of the orchestration, if not necessarily the financing, of redemption from Malta, leaving the arrangements to the professionals. Unlike in the central and western Mediterranean, where Muslim brokers (*fakkak*) also played a prominent role, these were almost exclusively Christians from France and Malta or islands like Chios and Mytilene, as well as some Jews who mostly worked on behalf of their coreligionists.[86]

Requests for help from *askeri* captives were handled ad hoc on a case-by-case basis, and there were no guarantees. Appeals like Mustafa's—from a midlevel official posted to the boondocks, not someone with close connections to the most powerful and wealthy—were thus sent to any person thought receptive. The families of *askeri* captives could also petition the Imperial Council for help on their behalf, which might come in the form of a cash grant or, more often, the bequest of a state-owned Catholic captive for exchange. The latter might have significant value as slaves and, if they were themselves prominent personages, would be worth very much more in ransom money, but their donation did not deprive the state of hard currency, which was perpetually in short supply and was desperately needed to pay the troops.

Those who were fortunate enough to receive such aid would still have to make their own arrangements and contract with brokers in the courts. In 1614, Ayşe Hatun bint Yunus secured a Frankish slave from the sultan in order to free her son, Hüseyin bin Mahmud, from Malta. Ayşe was a resident of Kilidü'l-Bahr, the fortress guarding the European side of the Dardanelles, and it is fair to assume that Hüseyin had been serving in some naval capacity when he was captured. To free her son, Ayşe traveled to Galata to make arrangements. In April, she contracted with two Frankish Christian merchants, Tumaz veled Frençus and Natun veled Narsed, to trade the Frankish slave she had received, Gaspar veled Françesko, for her son in Malta. The merchants would take Gaspar with them to Malta and free Hüseyin within four months. Gaspar's ransom value was pegged at 36,000 *akçe*.[87] This was ten times his value as a slave on the domestic market, according to the documents; such a large difference between his "exchange value" and his "use value" suggests that Gaspar was a man of considerable importance and wealth in his home country and reminds us how immensely profitable ransom slavery could be.[88] Each merchant posted half this amount as bond, with the total of 36,000 *akçe* held in escrow by a local Jew. If they failed to return with Hüseyin after four months, they would forfeit their bond to Ayşe.[89]

Of course, Maltese captors were not necessarily more interested in freeing their coreligionists than in receiving stacks of gold and silver. Five months later, Ayşe, Tumaz, and Natun were back in the court of Galata. The merchants had failed in their mission to redeem Hüseyin, and they were there to confirm that they had handed over 300 *filori*, the equivalent in gold of 36,000 *akçe*, to compensate Ayşe for her loss. She in turn swore that she had no outstanding claims on them, thereby concluding their business with one another.[90] Despite this setback, 300 *filori* would go a long way toward future efforts to free her son. Other exchanges met with greater success, as when Ahmed Odabaşı bin Ali from Iznikmid contracted with the Maltese merchant Tarako veled Ulo in the court of Galata in 1663 to free his brother Arslan from his Maltese captor, Ser Cuvan, in exchange for a Frankish slave named Karlo veled Malinor.[91]

Succor for Ottoman *askeri* captives on Malta could come from the state's coffers or the Imperial Arsenal's prison cells, but individuals within the imperial administration also sometimes paid ransoms in their capacity as quasi-private individuals, using the substantial resources at their disposal to do some good and build their patronage networks at the same time. It was for these reasons that Mustafa wrote a lengthy poem to the *valide sultan* Safiye, in which he recounted his story and reminded her that freeing a slave was a greater deed in God's eyes than the Hajj or even building a mosque or a soup kitchen (*imaret*), the acts of pious charity for which both sultans and royal women, Safiye included, were best known and which they endowed with their personal fortunes. Although Mustafa Efendi suggested that it would be right for his ransom to be paid out of the "treasury of the Muslims," he was equally amenable to having his freedom come via a private act of charity. Money has no value, he argued, compared to having knowledgeable men by your side.[92]

But first, the ransom price had to be set. Captors often waited some time to do this, using the harshness of life in the *bagno* to soften the captive in advance of the bargaining. Mustafa could guess what the price of his freedom would be based on precedent—he had told Safiye it would be five hundred gold coins—but another six months would pass before the matter was formally settled. Before the negotiations were to begin, important captives would be isolated from their groups and forced to sleep in an outer courtyard of the *bagno* for a few days. Sleep-deprived and discomfited, Mustafa was brought before his captors and asked: "What will you pay for your ransom?"

> Pleading destitution, we said "we'll pay 300 gold," and they said they wanted 1,000 coins. Saying "I can't," they said, "it's enough." Then they called for Kadi Abdurrahman. He said "I'll pay 400 *filori*." The response they gave to us they also gave to him: "The pit," they said.[93]

Ultimately Mustafa Efendi and his captors agreed to a ransom of 500 *filori* on September 6, 1598.[94] That seems to have been the going rate for the *kadi*s of Malta.[95] As the months passed without word from Haci Hasan, however, Mustafa became desperate. When another of his companions, Ibrahim Çelebi, received a letter from his father, a *çavuş* (an imperial messenger), telling him that the incumbent governor of the Morea, Mehmed Bey, had contracted to free him, Mustafa decided to write another of his poetical ransom notes to this new potential savior. That month, a *zimmi* ship captain named Yakomo arrived on Malta with a cargo of olive oil and the ransom for an Ottoman frigate captain. Mustafa gave this Yakomo his letter for Mehmed Bey, who was still in Istanbul, in which he told the governor his story in meter and asked him to send Yakomo back with his ransom without delay.[96] Similarly, when Hızır Pasha of Tunis ransomed Seyyid Mehmed Çelebi along with Mehmed Çelebi's mother and his female slave for 1,800 *filori*—which Mustafa commemorated with verse chronograms in Persian and Arabic—he acceded to their advice to "tell him about your story and your ransom and write a poem by way of request" for them to give to him in Tunis. True to form, Mustafa included each of these poems in his narrative, cycling through multiple permutations of poetic supplication in the process.[97]

In the end, Mustafa Efendi's exhaustive efforts bore fruit. On December 29, 1598, a non-Ottoman "infidel merchant" named Marko arrived on Malta from Istanbul carrying the ransom payment for Ibrahim Çelebi and letters for many of the captives. Mustafa learned that Haci Hasan had written to him in May 1598; his letter had thus taken nearly eight months to arrive. Haci Hasan relayed that many of Mustafa's friends had thought he was dead and had read prayers for his soul. They had since written him to express their joy and explained that the *nişancı*, the imperial chancellor, Musa Çelebi, "had arranged for an order to be produced from the *padişah* regarding your being freed for the release of an infidel." Such an arrangement would have won him release eventually, either through a head-for-head exchange or by using the proceeds from the Christian captive's ransom to pay for Mustafa's freedom, but Mustafa learned in a letter from another friend that Mehmed Bey had contracted to free him upon his arrival in the Morea and had suggested that he resign his judgeship, still awaiting him on Cyprus, and become his *hoca*, or spiritual adviser.[98] A copy of Mustafa Efendi's safe-conduct survives in the Maltese archives. Dated December 29, 1599, it was made out to "Mustafa Cady Mahamed ogli turco di Costantinopoli," a man of upright stature about forty-six years old.[99] It would take a little longer, but Mustafa was going home.[100]

Mustafa Efendi's narrative was completed on Malta in 1599, and on Malta it ended.[101] Afterward, he disappears from the historical record. We can only guess as to the long-term physical, psychological, and professional repercussions of his years as a captive. For one who believed, as he did, that both his captivity and his redemption were preordained by God, the voyage home and its aftermath did not warrant, and were not appropriate for, description. Mustafa's fatalistic attitude aside, the story of the *kadi*s of Malta and of ransom slavery in the Ottoman Mediterranean did not begin or end when money changed hands on Malta nor upon embarkation in Valletta. To fill in the blanks, we need to turn to the documents produced by the *kadi*s themselves on both sides of the Ottoman Mediterranean.

THE *KADIS* OF MALTA AND THE MECHANICS OF RANSOM

On December 18, 1693, the *kadi* Ahmed Efendi ibn Mehmed made his way from his house in Galata, where he normally held court, to the nearby home of a French merchant. He and his scribe squeezed into a parlor already crowded with prominent local Muslims and Frenchmen who were waiting for them to arrive. On that winter day, the court of Galata would be convened in Monsieur Jean's living room to solemnize the arrangements for the redemption of an Ottoman admiral, Mehmed ibn Abdallah, for which purpose *kadi* and scribe would draw up a *hüccet*, or legal document. War was raging in the Ottoman Mediterranean, where the nearly ten-year-old conflict with the Holy League (1683–1699) had merged with the Europe-wide conflagration known by many names but most succinctly as the Nine Years' War (1688–1697), pitting privateers and corsairs of all nations against one another. Mehmed Kapudan had been a casualty of this conflict and was now languishing on Malta, the captive of a knight named "Ser Cuvan" (Jean, Juan, Giovanni—the Ottoman orthography rarely helps with such distinctions). To free him, the French merchant and his Ottoman interlocutors would embark upon a series of legal transactions on both extremes of the Ottoman Mediterranean, predicated on trust and verification, following a pattern that had emerged over a century earlier.

The plan was to bring Mehmed Kapudan back to Istanbul in exchange for a slave of Maltese origin, Francesco veled Matteo. The French merchant would serve as both broker and guarantor, receiving 150 *guruş*' worth of gold from a certain Mehmed Çelebi ibn Ömer, possibly of the scribal service, as a nonrefundable security deposit for the Maltese slave, who had probably been donated by the palace. After Mehmed Kapudan's arrival in Istanbul, escorted by Monsieur Jean, the Maltese slave would be turned over to him and sent back to Malta. The deal came with the following conditions: if Ser Cuvan were to demand the gold as security for the safe arrival of Francesco, Jean would be reimbursed the 150 *guruş* as compensation for his efforts. And, "if the *kadi* of Malta produces a *hüccet*" certifying Mehmed Kapudan's release and Mehmed Kapudan died after weighing anchor, Francesco would still be freed. Otherwise, Francesco would not be sent home until Mehmed's safe arrival.[102]

In this manner, the *kadi* Ahmed Efendi of Galata invoked his unnamed colleague on Malta in his *hüccet* formalizing the agreement between Mehmed Çelebi ibn Ömer and the French merchant Jean. Made out to Mehmed and witnessed by half a dozen prominent Muslims, both men would have received a signed and sealed copy of the document. Yet as the *hüccet* drawn up in the Frenchman's living room made clear, everything depended on the "*kadi* of Malta" certifying that its conditions had been fulfilled. It was as if the *kadi* of Malta were appointed to his post like any other in the Ottoman Empire, rather than a victim of maritime misfortune who had had his beard forcibly shaved and held court in a filthy corner of the *bagno*. Only a signed, sealed, and witnessed *hüccet* produced by one of these captive judges could protect the French merchant-cum-ransom broker, assuring him of repayment for services rendered if Ser Cuvan claimed the cash and, in the event of Mehmed Kapudan's untimely death, ensuring the eventual release of the Maltese slave Francesco.

Macuncuzade Mustafa Efendi makes only one vague allusion in his *Singular Voyage* to his employing his legal expertise on Malta, referring to his involvement in making appropriate arrangements for other captives with Ibrahim Çelebi's broker Marko "because he [Marko] was a Frank,"[103] but it is abundantly clear from this aside that he too did his duty as a *kadi* of Malta—if not necessarily as the *bagno*'s designated "slaves' *kadi*"—drawing up surety contracts, loan agreements, and notarized receipts to which his fellow Muslim prisoners bore witness. Experienced ransom agents, whatever their origins, knew that it was absolutely necessary to document their arrangements in front of an Ottoman judge and Muslim witnesses, since documents produced outside the Ottoman Islamic legal tradition would not be admissible in an Ottoman court in the event of a legal challenge.[104] Thus, it made little difference if the contract was first agreed on Malta or Istanbul—*kadi*s would be involved and the deal would be concluded according to the norms and expectations of Ottoman Islamic law.

The *hüccet*s produced by the *kadi*s of Malta were virtually identical in appearance to those produced elsewhere within the Ottoman Mediterranean. Between marbled-paper boards with a red leather spine, the French consul in Izmir Jean Depuy had bound a selection of the *hüccet*s generated from his side-business as a ransom broker in the second half of the 1620s. Serving as the Ottoman-end interlocutor and money man, he worked with two Malta-based partners to free dozens of Ottoman Muslims and Jews, most hailing from western Anatolia, in a span of just three and a half years. Of the thirty-six *hüccet*s preserved in his volume, held today in Paris at the Bibliothèque nationale de France, twenty-seven were drawn up on Malta by four different *kadi*s. From the characteristic shape and layout of the page down to the *kadi*s' seals and signatures, the Maltese *hüccet*s followed the same conventions as those produced in Izmir or Istanbul.[105]

Aside from the fact that the paper used in the Maltese *hüccet*s was not glazed and polished as it would have been in Ottoman lands, a post-manufacture procedure that gave Ottoman documents and manuscripts their distinctive sheen, smoothness, and ivory color, the only differences are in the text itself. The *kadi*'s signature at the top, traditionally composed in Arabic and giving the author's name and position followed by an apologetic, disclosed the unfortunate *kadi*'s current status. For example, Ahmed bin Ali wrote that he was "previously the incumbent *kadi* of protected Üsküb (Skopje), currently captive on Malta, may God Almighty free him."[106] Ahmed bin Ahmed likewise informed the reader that he had been the incumbent *kadi* of Ayasoluk, the Aegean town beside the Roman ruins of Ephesus.[107] Halil bin Zülfikar, following the same pattern, described himself as the former *kadi* of the town of Nimçe, suggesting that, unlike the others, he had been captured on the way home from his posting.[108]

The body of a *hüccet* typically began by noting the place of composition, such as in "protected Izmir" or "protected Galata." These *hüccet*s documented proceedings on "the island of Malta, may God Almighty destroy it." One wonders whether the *kadi*s and the Ottoman captives they worked with appreciated the irony of Maltese and other Christian ransom brokers relying on documents that explicitly called for their destruction. The *kadi*s acknowledged the abnormal circumstances of their notarial function on Malta by noting that the parties made their attestations "in the presence of this poor one and captive, servant of the straight path [i.e. Islamic law]."[109] The existence of these stylistic conventions, peculiar to the captive context but shared across the Maltese *hüccet*s, makes it clear that these were not exceptional or unusual documents. There was, as Jean Depuy's volume attests, more than enough work to go around for the *kadi*s imprisoned there.[110] Unlike other jurisdictions, there could be more than one *kadi* of Malta at a time. These *kadi*s almost certainly received compensation, in coin or food, for their services, though it is unclear whether there was a quasi-formal fee structure paralleling that in place within the empire proper.

The documents they produced provided the legal foundation for further arrangements on the other side of the Ottoman Mediterranean. In 1672, el-Hac Şaban bin Abdallah contracted with the French merchant "Garasko veled Cako" on Malta for his own release, much as Marko would have done with Macuncuzade Mustafa Efendi's fellow inmates. Together, Şaban and Garasko obtained a *hüccet* "from a *kadi* who is one of the judges in the slaves' prison on the aforementioned island" for Garasko to bring back with him to Istanbul to secure the funds for Şaban's ransom. These documents not only gave someone like Garasko the legal authority to act on a captive's behalf, they would help him to convince the captive's family and friends to trust him—a man they had never met before, a man who may have hailed from the same place as their loved one's captors and shared their language and faith—with enormous, life-altering sums of money.

Garasko brought the *hüccet* to a certain Mustafa Ağa, who handed over 543 *esedi guruş* and, before a judge and witnesses, appointed Garasko his legal agent (*vekil*), thereby giving him the power to act on his behalf on Malta. Garasko then returned to Malta, doubtless bearing letters for other captives and transporting trade goods, and paid Şaban's ransom. Another *hüccet* was obtained from one of the *kadi*s of Malta to certify that Şaban had been freed before they set sail for Istanbul. Upon their return, Garasko arranged for Mustafa Ağa to appear in the court of Galata by proxy to certify that Garasko had faithfully discharged the terms of their agreement, leaving the court with yet another *hüccet*.[111] Such faithful documentation was standard operating procedure, and ransom brokers like Garasko—French, Maltese, or Ottoman Christians—were a common sight in the court of Galata.[112]

For example, the Maltese merchant captain Andrea veled Gabriele, who was permitted to sojourn in Istanbul with a safe-conduct, appeared in the courts of Galata and Istanbul no less than seven times over the course of just two months in the spring of 1663, registering ransom debts from the recently redeemed, suing the guarantors of former captives for overdue payments, and arranging new ransom contracts (see Table 1). On April 5, 1663, Captain Andrea registered the debts of four Muslim captives hailing from Bulgaria, the Marmara region, and south-central Anatolia who had arrived in Istanbul together just days earlier. After making arrangements in the court of Istanbul concerning another freed captive who had remained on Malta as security for the debts of one of his companions, Andrea returned to the Galata court on two separate occasions to sue guarantors for payment after former captives who had been freed months earlier on his previous voyage skipped out on their debts. In the case of an extremely wealthy *seyyid* (a descendant of the Prophet Muhammad) redeemed captive, Andrea's Muslim agent in Galata received mixed security of cash and goods worth a total of 2,000 *guruş*, combined with a cash payment of the other half of the ransom, to secure the release of his companion. In June, as Captain Andrea prepared to return to Malta, he began arranging new business, contracting to free a certain el-Hac Mustafa for the comparatively modest sum of 200 *guruş* after accepting his standard nonrefundable down payment of 50 *guruş*. The largest ransom in his previous voyage had topped out at 4,500 *riyal guruş*.

Table 1. *The Ransoming Activity of the Maltese Merchant Captain Andrea, Son of Gabriele: Spring 1663*

Captive's Name	Date of Entry	Origin	Length of Captivity	Total Ransom	Captor	Guarantor	Description
Ahmed b. Abdallah[1]	April 5, 1663	Vize	8 years	352.5 *riyal guruş*	Seranyoz Anton	Self	Owes 302.5
Ahmed b. Mehmed[2]	April 5, 1663	Zagra-ı Atik	2.5 years	202.5 *riyal guruş*	Karlo	Self	Owes all
Ahmed b. Abdallah[3]	April 5, 1663	Vize	2.5 years	352.5 *riyal guruş*	Seranyoz Anton	Self	Owes 302.5
Burak Bey b. Mehmed[4]	April 5, 1663	Sis	10 years	990 *riyal guruş*	Fransiz Mosiler	Self	Owes all
Mehmed b. Mansur[5]	April 18, 1663	Istanbul	?	3,620 *riyal guruş*	Cemarya, Aptriko, and Anton	es-Seyyid Ali Efendi b. Hasan and es-Seyyid Şaban Çelebi b. Mahmud	Ransomed but remained on Malta as security for Zeynelabidin, below
Şaban[6]	April 20, 1663	?	?	852.5 *riyal guruş*	?	Mehmed b. Mehmed	Freed three months earlier; Andrea sues Şaban's guarantor for payment
Uzun Mehmed b. Veli[7]	April 28, 1663	Galata	?	500 *riyal guruş*	?	Şaban b. Veli and Mustafa b. Veli (captive's brothers)	Andrea sues the guarantors who had hired him for payment
es-Seyyid Zeynelabidin Efendi b. Ahmed[8]	May 20, 1663	Istanbul	?	4,500 *riyal guruş*	Cemarya, Aptriko, and Anton	es-Seyyid Şaban b. Halil	Pays 2,000; guarantor puts up 2,500 in goods and cash as security for the rest
el-Hac Mustafa[9]	June 1, 1663	Istanbul	?	200 *riyal guruş*	Anton	Ahmed Efendi b. eş-Şeyh İbrahim Efendi	Initial contract to ransom Mustafa; 50 *guruş* nonrefundable down payment

[1]Galata 90, 11r (26/Ş/1073); *İstanbul kadı sicilleri*, 40:94.
[2]Ibid.
[3]Ibid., 40:95.
[4]Ibid. The captor's "name" here actually means "French gentlemen."
[5]İstanbul 12, 2r (10/N/1073); *İstanbul kadı sicilleri*, 16:109.
[6]Galata 90, 17v (12/N/1073); *İstanbul kadı sicilleri*, 40:135.
[7]Ibid., 18v (20/N/1073); *İstanbul kadı sicilleri*, 40:140.
[8]Ibid., 27v (12/L/1073); *İstanbul kadı sicilleri*, 40:186.
[9]Ibid., 36r (24/L/1073); *İstanbul kadı sicilleri*, 40:230.

This was not the only business the Maltese merchant captain was conducting in greater Istanbul. On June 9, 1663, he appeared in the court of Galata to settle his debts with an Ottoman Muslim merchant named Osman Çelebi bin Habib. For various goods, unfortunately undescribed, purchased in connection with his voyages and mercantile activities, Captain Andrea owed Osman 723,000 *akçe*. At this point, taking the profits from his ransoming activity, he paid Osman 596,000 *akçe*, leaving 127,000 outstanding. This amount Osman forgave, considering the debt settled.[113] The debt cancellation might indicate the existence of a hidden loan and interest contained therein, or it might have been in consideration of longstanding and profitable business ties. Certainly, despite the cash value attached to ransoms on Malta, many were paid in trade goods. Wheat especially, but also raw cotton and wool and finished cloth, legumes, hides, and other goods could be profitably traded or given in lieu of gold and silver.[114] Captain Andrea was not engaged in a one-off moneymaking venture. Despite being a Maltese infidel, he freely shuttled back and forth between Malta and Istanbul, a participant in an established and long-term business arrangement, perhaps an informal partnership, that transcended the constantly shifting cast of captors, captives and their families who enabled it. The trade in Muslim bodies both permitted and disguised a robust trade with Malta in all that the Ottoman Mediterranean had to offer.[115]

Captain Andrea was not working alone, though most of the Galata court documents he obtained could easily create that impression. As an unusual transaction in the Galata court that same day in June makes clear, Captain Andrea was part of a much larger consortium of interests, which had multiple nodes in the Ottoman Mediterranean and close connections with the French diplomatic and merchant communities. On June 9, the agent in Galata of an Izmir-based French merchant named Gaspar veled Folt appeared in court to register the safe arrival in Istanbul of three Anatolian Muslim captives who had been freed from Malta by Gaspar's French partner there. The plan had been for them to sail to Izmir, but when they could not find a departing ship, they contracted with a French captain to take the Anatolian Muslims to Istanbul instead. Local Muslim witnesses were brought to court to verify the former captives' safe arrival so that a legal document would be issued accordingly, thereby guaranteeing the French merchants' full payment if one of the captives should suddenly die. Notably, the Muslim witnesses were joined by Captain Andrea veled Gabriele and the French dragoman (interpreter) Batista veled Tomazo.[116] From the Islamic legal perspective, the attestation of these foreign Christians, *müstemins* (foreigners with safe-conduct) all, was entirely unnecessary; in the event of a court challenge from a

Muslim, their testimony would be inadmissible. But their inclusion by name in the proceedings and the resulting document surely mattered to their various Christian partners, who also needed to know with certainty that the French merchants' voyage had been successfully concluded. We thus get some indication of the French connection between the Izmir and Istanbul ransoming operations, and the division of turf between merchants operating in more or less exclusive spheres.

There is rarely any indication of the ultimate source of the capital behind these operations, but the involvement of European diplomatic figures is frequently detectable. Just as Jean Depuy, the French consul in Izmir, was active in the ransom business in the 1620s, the presence of the French dragoman in the Galata court on that June day in 1663 suggests a continuing, if in that instance peripheral, involvement. The French ambassador himself sometimes directly engaged in the ransoming business, trading on his overseas connections with the Knights, most of them French, and French merchants to make some extra money with little or no risk. On June 18, 1614—the same year that he negotiated a new *ahdname*—the French ambassador Achille de Harlay, Baron de Sancy (served 1611–1618) undertook through his agent and dragoman Lior veled Domeniko to free Mehmed bin Ömer from Malta for 36,000 *akçe*. Mehmed's brother Ali paid 30,000 *akçe* upfront with the understanding that if Mehmed died before being freed, he would be reimbursed, but if Mehmed were freed and then died en route to Istanbul, Ali would still pay the remaining 6,000 *akçe*.[117] Although it was not explicitly stated, the actual cost of redemption was most likely 30,000 *akçe*; the 6,000 due upon delivery represented the ambassador's commission—20 percent of the ransom—meaning that the ambassador had no personal financial exposure in this transaction at all.

Nor were the French alone. Harlay-Sancy's English contemporary, Paul Pindar (served 1611–1620), also played a role in facilitating the ransom of Ottoman subjects. Unlike the French, however, who were visibly involved in every stage of the process from capture to release and profited from every angle, the English could play the role of impartial third party, through which cash or captives might be held in escrow, and gain Ottoman goodwill in the process. When in July 1614 the son and wife of Hasan bin Musa hired the "Frankish" merchant Çavluvizu veled Anton, resident of Chios, to free him from captivity in Messina, ambassador Pindar served as the mutually acceptable escrow agent for the agreed up-front half payment of Hasan's 72,000 *akçe* ransom, with all the usual provisions for full payment if Hasan died subsequent to his release.[118] English consular officials in Izmir provided similar services in the seventeenth century, aiding in the redemption of both Ottoman subjects from Livorno and English subjects snatched by the Greek Maniotes in the Morea.[119] The Venetian consuls in Salonica likewise offered escrow services for the redemption of Ottoman subjects from Malta.[120]

When disputes arose, as they often did with such enormous sums of money at stake, the combination of legal documentation adhering to Ottoman Islamic norms and Muslim witnesses, usually former fellow prisoners, provided powerful protection for Christian brokers operating in the Ottoman Empire. Such was the case when Pavlu veled Anton, a *zimmi* from Chios, sued Salih Reis ibn Mehmed in the court of Galata in January 1617 for failing to repay the agreed upon amount for ransoming him from Malta. Pavlu claimed that, while on Malta, Salih Reis had pledged to pay him 52,000 *akçe*, and Pavlu had advanced the ransom to Salih's captor and freed him. Salih Reis had paid Pavlu only 30,000 *akçe* upon their return, and when the rest was not forthcoming, Pavlu sued Salih for the remaining 22,000 *akçe*. In court, Salih Reis confirmed that he was a captive on Malta and that he pledged himself (*haviyye kefalet*), but he claimed that the agreed-upon amount was 30,000 *akçe*; that was the figure he had pledged to pay his Maltese captor, so that was what he paid Pavlu. He denied that he owed a single *akçe* more. Pavlu then called two Muslim witnesses who had been captives on Malta with Salih Reis and had witnessed the surety *hüccet* drawn up on Malta between Salih and Pavlu by a captive *kadi* there. They confirmed that Salih had pledged himself to pay Pavlu 52,000 *akçe*. With this unimpeachable evidence, the court ordered Salih to pay Pavlu the remaining 22,000 *akçe* without delay.[121] In-person witness testimony like this was required to back up documents in the Islamic courts—they could not stand up alone to a defendant's denial—but surety agreements and loans were neither valid nor defensible without them. Both documents and the Muslim witnesses to their composition were required to prevail in these kinds of suits. The *hüccet*s were not just socially or symbolically significant; they were legally necessary.

The large discrepancy between the figures in the case above comes from the associated costs of ransom, which were often concealed in Ottoman legal documents and were undoubtedly resented by both captives and the friends and family who struggled to pay them. Besides the ransom itself, these included the fee for the safe-conduct, an exit tax levied by the Maltese (the *diretto della porta*), currency exchange fees, ship hireage costs for the passage home, and—most irritating—the broker's percentage, which could be 20–30 percent of the ransom.[122] Because usury was not formally permitted and loans were often involved, the latter in particular was routinely folded into the ransom itself, creating the false impression that the brokers offered their services for free. Salih Reis very likely did agree to pay his captor the equivalent of 30,000 *akçe* in gold, but the deal he made with Pavlu, who provided the money for his release with no surety besides Salih's word—that is, no one back home arranged for Pavlu's mission, fronted the money, or posted some portion of it as a security deposit—was for a total of 52,000 *akçe*. The disputed 22,000 probably represented the fees owed to the Maltese and the price of the homeward voyage plus Pavlu's payment for services rendered, including reimbursement for his expenses, interest on the loan, and a healthy profit for his time and risk. At roughly 73 percent of the ransom itself, Salih Reis may have considered the amount over and beyond his ransom extortionate—it was, in fact, precisely that—but that was the price of freedom. Because Pavlu had both the contract concluded on Malta before a *kadi* there and the witnesses to back it up, his case was ironclad, and Salih's attempt to escape his obligations doomed.

For all the importance and power of the *kadi*s of Malta, it is evident that the *hüccet*s they prepared, though binding for the Muslim prisoners and legally admissible and enforceable in any Ottoman court, carried limited probative value when disputes occurred between captives and their would-be brokers on Malta itself. In 1635, an Ottoman Greek from Lefkada, Filippo Precante, was arrested on Malta on charges of having defrauded an Ottoman Muslim slave whom he had previously agreed to ransom. The slaves' *kadi* was called to testify before the Tribunal Aerarium, where he declared that Precante and the slave in question had appeared before him the previous year to solemnize their agreement, in which Precante undertook to free the slave upon his return from his voyage to Lefkada. A document to that effect was duly drawn up in Ottoman Turkish and witnessed by eight Muslims. The *kadi* swore that there had been no mention of payment in the agreement. Three other Muslim captives testified that they had seen the slave give multiple small payments and gifts of food to Precante—slaves could earn money through a variety of small trades—which had added up to his ransom price of 250 *scudi*; they further stated that they had heard Precante himself admit to having received 100 *scudi* and promise to free the slave upon his return. Precante admitted that he had shared dinner at the slave's expense a number of times, but he declared that he had promised only to try to obtain the slave's ransom from his family on the Ionian mainland. During his recent sojourn on Lefkada, he had traveled inland at his own expense to meet the captive's family, and they were unable to pay anything. Any misunderstanding about the nature of the agreement, he claimed, lay with the *kadi* and was not his fault. The court, he argued, ought to trust the testimony of a Christian over that of a Muslim. The court agreed, and a few days later Precante was released.[123]

Precante's example is a powerful reminder that while a parallel quasi-Ottoman legal system operated in the *bagno* with the full knowledge and encouragement of the Maltese authorities, outside the prison walls it offered far greater protection to Christian captors and brokers than it did to the Muslims who wrote, witnessed, and were legally bound by its terms. It was in the interest of Malta's Tribunal Aerarium to seriously investigate claims like those lodged against Precante, for accusations of dishonesty were bad for business and trust across political and confessional lines was essential for its smooth operation, but even when testimony from multiple individuals and documentary evidence were available, the odds were clearly stacked against the Muslims. Despite the fact that Precante's victim—if we choose to believe the slaves' *kadi* and the other Muslim witnesses—did not obtain justice through the Maltese court, it is safe to assume that news of Precante's behavior would ensure he would never do business in the *bagno* again.

Of course, foreign Christian brokers were also vulnerable in Ottoman courts, where the testimony of Muslim witnesses trumped that of Christians and where uncorroborated documentary evidence had limited value. It was not enough for a ransom agent to simply obtain a *hüccet* from the *kadi* of Malta. Lining up trustworthy witnesses in the event of a dispute was critical, and care had to be taken to follow the norms of Islamic legal procedure to the letter, lest he be swindled once on the former captive's home turf. No one would know how to manipulate the rules better than the *kadi*s themselves.

A certain Mustafa Efendi (no relation to Macuncuzade) from Istanbul, a *kadi* captured en route to Egypt by the Maltese, escaped repaying his ransom broker in 1671 because he and a captive companion had mutually pledged to free one another with money borrowed from their broker, who subsequently made the mistake of ransoming him outright instead. When the broker, Garskar, asked to be repaid upon their arrival in Galata, Mustafa was able to claim that he had never asked Garskar to free him, only to loan him the money to free his companion. Ignoring what appeared to be an unnecessarily convoluted, seemingly pointless exercise—the financial outlay for their identical ransoms would be the same—cost Garskar 400 *guruş*.[124] One was not obligated to repay a ransom one had not requested, for which reason Ottoman ransom agreements always included an explicit affirmation from the captive that the money had been handed over to their captor with their knowledge and at their request.[125] Using his knowledge of the law, the *kadi* Mustafa was able to outmaneuver the enemy infidel merchant attempting to profit from his plight. More often, however, assiduously documented and attested ransom agreements drawn up in the prescribed fashion ensured that, in the event of a dispute, the lender-broker would always prevail in an Ottoman court.

It is abundantly clear that the *kadi*s of Malta, in concert with their colleagues on the Ottoman mainland, were essential for the smooth operation of the ransom industry. Their knowledge and expertise protected the interests of the men who moved vast quantities of capital and goods across a dangerous sea and, simultaneously, across an inhospitable juridical divide. They solemnized agreements made between enemies. But of course, the diversion of Ottoman *kadi*s to Malta meant that there were posts left unfilled in the Ottoman Mediterranean proper. What impact, actual or symbolic, did these developments have? As noted above, Macuncuzade was grudging in his provision of personal detail and ended his narrative too soon for us to know what captivity meant for his personal and professional life, but, just as important, what did the loss of a *kadi* mean for the people of Baf? Or for the populations of those places, like the smaller islands of the Aegean archipelago, where the *kadi*s were literally the only representatives of Ottoman political authority and Ottoman justice? To answer these kinds of questions we must leave behind the Ottoman courts of Galata and Malta and head instead to the seas and the isolated Ottoman island outposts where the *kadi*s were most often captured to consider the role that *kadi*s played there and what happened when they were lost.

LOCAL CONSEQUENCES

In 1707, Mevlana es-Seyyid Yusuf Efendi was the *kadi* of Santorini. But he did not live there. The danger of being a prominent Ottoman functionary on a small, entirely Christian Aegean island frequented by pirates made the otherwise picturesque volcanic rock an unappealing place to live. He chose, instead, to reside in Candia on Crete during his tenure.

Non-resident *kadi*s were common in the early modern Aegean. *Kadi*s were a permanent presence only on the larger islands (for example, Chios, Mytilene, Naxos, Andros). Smaller islands often shared a *kadi*, who traveled a circuit, "causing notice to be given wherever they pass, that all such as have any lawsuits on their hands, bring their papers or witnesses, and they shall be immediately and with a moderate charge dispatched."[126] There was also a "sea judge" (*deniz kadisi*) who traveled on the *kapudan pasha*'s flagship and, along with the admiral himself, dispensed justice wherever the fleet might roam.[127]

As *kadi*s were a visible, and often the only, Ottoman Muslim presence on many islands, they were extremely vulnerable, especially during the second half of the seventeenth century when Ottoman control of the Aegean was effectively lost to the Venetians, their corsair allies, and apolitical pirates. Between 1645 and 1699, the Eastern Mediterranean experienced only fifteen years of formal peace (1669–1684), during which the Ottoman navy struggled to reassert itself. The primary goal of the 1645 invasion of Crete had been to deny Catholic corsairs access to the Aegean, but the island's conquest twenty-four years later notwithstanding, the war only exacerbated the problem. It transformed the Venetians from maritime policemen, effectively Ottoman auxiliaries in the fight against piracy, into enthusiastic supporters and practitioners of corsairing in their own right. Smarting from the loss of Crete, after 1669 Venice was a far more reluctant ally in the war on Catholic corsairing, and the return of peace did nothing to remove the corsairs from the archipelago. The Ottomans' initial efforts to evict them failed miserably. A fleet sent to Milos in 1670 to clear out the pirates was repulsed. Better results were obtained toward the end of the decade, but the resumption of conflict on land and sea in 1683–1684 rapidly undid the progress the Ottomans had made.[128]

The situation improved somewhat around 1700, thanks to the return of peace—the Nine Years' War and the War of the Holy League had ended in 1697 and 1699, respectively—and, more importantly, the withdrawal of French privateers and of tacit French support for Maltese corsairing in the Levant, which increasingly threatened the profits of the resurgent French trade in the region more than it did "Turkish" shipping.[129] More and more, Ottoman merchants were freighting European ships and Ottoman officials were traveling on French and English bottoms to protect themselves from the corsairs, making the Maltese *corso* increasingly untenable in the Levant. But the situation was still precarious. That year, Tournefort observed that when the itinerant *kadi* arrived on Kimolos, he "dares not talk big, for fear the inhabitants should send him packing on board some corsair of Malta."[130]

Nevertheless, *kadi*s played an essential role in the legal structures of even those places that were entirely devoid of Muslim settlement, and periodic Venetian occupation of the islands did little to change that. Ottoman Greeks and other non-Muslim communities were permitted to operate their own ecclesiastical and communal courts, but *kadi*s confirmed those courts' rulings, provided courts of appeal, and issued legal documents that were acceptable throughout the Ottoman Mediterranean world, including in those same ecclesiastical and communal courts.[131] In this plural legal world, the Catholic corsair captains themselves, as outsiders capable of wielding force, heard disputes and decided cases on the smaller islands they frequented, especially those with Latin Christian communities, throughout the seventeenth century.[132] But neither communal legal institutions nor the corsairs could fully supplant the need for *kadis* among those Greeks whose interests extended beyond the confines of their island communities, nor those who required permanent, properly documented legal solutions that would still hold on the day when, eventually, inevitably, the "Turks" returned. During the years of war and instability, when *kadis* were sometimes evacuated for their safety or were abducted and not replaced, Greek islanders often made the trek to Istanbul to submit entirely quotidian disputes and transactions to the *kadi* of Galata or the Rumeli *kazasker* via the Imperial Council, where both legal certificates and binding decisions might be obtained.[133] Ottoman subjects had broad discretion to choose the venue for their cases; the *kadi*'s court did not have to be the court of first instance for *zimmis* (nor was one obliged to go to the nearest *kadi*), but it was usually the last.

So it was that in 1707, Yusuf Efendi, *kadi* of Santorini and resident of Crete, was called upon to perform his judicial duties. A group of ten notables from the exclusively Christian island came by caïque to Candia and told Yusuf Efendi that they had a suit waiting and asked him to come back with them to hear the case. Before departing, "in order that no harm might come from enemy infidels," the notables were required to pledge themselves as guarantors for Yusuf's safety in the Ottoman court of Candia. Such precautions were no longer unusual for the judge asked simply to do his job in the archipelago, and similar expectations obtained elsewhere. On Skyros, for example, it was understood that if the *kadi* were kidnapped by corsairs, the local Greek administrators would pay his ransom.[134] After the notables had pledged themselves, Yusuf, his small entourage, and the Santorine *zimmis* boarded the caïque and set sail.

Santorini is roughly 130 kilometers from Candia. Today, the trip takes about three hours by ferry. In 1707, however, the journey could be the distance between freedom and slavery. Although the caïque traversed the Sea of Crete without incident, an enemy infidel saettia was lying in the harbor of Santorini when they arrived. Yusuf, his son, and four other Muslims who had accompanied him from Crete were immediately taken captive. The other four were probably, in addition to the *kadi*'s scribe and assistant, the court's Muslim witnesses, brought along expressly to enable the production of legally valid documentation, which would have otherwise been impossible on the Christian island. The six captives were then sold to another set of "enemy infidels" and brought to Malta.

Two years later, the Maltese released Yusuf Efendi so that he could collect the ransoms for himself and his compatriots. As Yusuf "left for the Abode of Islam," his son and the four others remained behind on Malta. Once back in Candia, Yusuf informed the local government of the perfidy and injustices he had experienced. "In the legal manner," he summoned his Santorine notable guarantors to the court in Candia to hold them accountable for his captivity. To resolve his case and determine what should be done next, he wrote to the central government.[135] Yusuf evidently believed that the men who had brought him to Santorini had given him to the infidels or at least should have done more to protect him. Some degree of complicity was not out of the question. He would not have been the first *kadi* in the Cyclades sold out to the corsairs who, as Tournefort put it, "would often go and take them by the beard, and away with them on board ship, where they made slaves of them."[136]

What had happened to Yusuf Efendi—abduction in the line of duty, years of captivity on Malta, parole—was hardly unusual at this historical and geographical conjuncture, but the local consequences of those events are indeed remarkable. The sultanic decree that Yusuf requested after his release in 1709, copied into the registers of the court of Candia as was standard procedure, was not dispatched until June 1714. More than six years after his capture and four years after his release from Malta, Yusuf Efendi had not been replaced as *kadi* of Santorini, and the suit that he had been traveling there to hear was still awaiting his decision.

Although the residents of Santorini theoretically had recourse to other Ottoman courts, Yusuf Efendi's abduction brought the orderly dispensation of Ottoman justice on Santorini to an abrupt halt. The island's communal and ecclesiastical legal structures, though autonomous, still depended on the *kadi* for confirmation, authentication, notarization, and appeal. And the center had been unable or unwilling to move forward with a replacement until Yusuf's case had been resolved and his term served.

His disappearance also meant Santorini's traditional lines of communication with the imperial center were cut. Elsewhere in the Ottoman Mediterranean, the *kadi*s' role as conduit for information, documenter and legitimizer of local activities was of critical importance. This was especially true for the Orthodox monasteries that controlled much of the land and collected taxes throughout the Aegean.[137] For the monasteries on Andros and Patmos, for example, the courts of the *kadi*s of Andros and, for Patmos, Kos, provided the primary venue for them to perform their loyalty to the sultan, inform him and local government of important news, and confirm and strengthen their own positions.

During the disorder of the seventeenth century, the monks of Andros and Patmos, islands located at strategic points on major shipping lanes, were routinely called upon to shelter and ransom Muslim travelers and seamen from corsairs and warn the Ottoman authorities of the corsairs' movements. At the same time, they had to combat the persistent, sometimes justified, Ottoman suspicions of their complicity with the corsairs.

This they did, always appearing before their local *kadi* to document their successes and failures in the constant battle with the corsairs, retaining copies for their records and forwarding duplicates to the administration to remind it of their good behavior.[138] When the *kadi* of Andros was withdrawn in the 1650s during the worst years of the war for Crete, the monks sailed to neighboring Euboea to maintain the practice, informing the judge of their efforts to protect Muslims from capture and enslavement.[139] The removal of the local *kadi*, as on Andros or Santorini, did not remove the islanders from the Ottoman Mediterranean legal space they inhabited, but it could complicate their ability to operate efficiently within it.

This was clearly the case with the abduction of Yusuf Efendi in 1707. We do not have the whole story of what occurred in the intervening years, but in 1714 the Sublime Porte decided that the Santorines should come to Candia once more and Yusuf should finally hear their case—this time safely behind the Cretan city's massive walls—and any others that had accumulated over the previous years. Yet there was still the sticky issue of responsibility for Yusuf's captivity and the payment of his and the other Muslim captives' ransoms. Obviously, Yusuf Efendi could not decide his own case, especially when the residents of his jurisdiction were the defendants. Instead, the Porte decreed that Yusuf and the governor of Candia should inform the Rumeli *kazasker*, Mevlana Ahmed Efendi, of the details of the case. The *kazasker* would then send them his judicial decree (*'ilam*), in accordance with which justice would be done in Candia. Both men were ordered to take pains that excessive demands for money not be made and that the islanders not be oppressed.[140]

Given Yusuf's unpleasant experience on Malta and the fact that he himself was both the judge for and a plaintiff against the inhabitants of Santorini, the Porte had a delicate and complicated situation to manage. Here, in an uncommon view into the inner workings of the Ottoman judicial hierarchy, the disruption caused by corsairs forced the triangulation of justice across the sea between the Imperial Council, the local judge, and the *kazasker*. The Porte's decree suggests that there were procedures in place that enabled the empire's senior justice to be apprised of the details of complex interjurisdictional cases from a distance, allowing him to offer advisory rulings that could then be formally implemented, in accordance with the evidentiary standards of Ottoman Islamic law, by the local, subordinate *kadi*.

Nevertheless, the saga of Yusuf Efendi and the Santorines is an indication of the extensive damage and disruption to the orderly dispensation of Ottoman justice that the corsairs wrought, especially in those corners of the Ottoman Mediterranean that typically received less attention from the center. Less obvious is the symbolic damage to the prestige of the sultan and the wider Ottoman establishment in the communities thus affected, but the extreme vulnerability of the *kadi*s and the difficulties in replacing them must have suggested an unintentional irony in the Ottomans' continued usage of the "well-protected domains" to describe the empire. In order to prevent these predictable mishaps, Ottoman officials in Istanbul increasingly turned in the second half of the seventeenth century to the European ambassadors to provide safe transport within the empire. When the *kapudan pasha* asked the English ambassador in 1689 to arrange transport for a *kadi* to Alexandria, he was engaging in a practice dating back at least to the 1650s.[141] Nevertheless, *kadi*s still fell captive to Catholic corsairs. What is clear is that every *kadi* brought to the bench on Malta represented an Ottoman jurisdiction deprived of its magistrate, possibly for many years. Such were the less obvious, but no less significant, consequences of Catholic corsairing in the Ottoman Mediterranean.

CONCLUSION

Malta's wealth was extracted from the Ottoman Mediterranean and as such, it could not fully escape inclusion within it. Never subdued by Ottoman arms, Malta and its ransom industry nevertheless depended on the unity and universal acceptability of Ottoman legal practice and Ottoman legal practitioners within the Ottoman Mediterranean to function. The captive *kadi*s of Malta thus had an essential role to play, in which they operated as full-fledged representatives of Ottoman authority and Ottoman law as if they were still within the centrally controlled and appointed network of Ottoman judges. It is worth noting that the independent sultanate of Morocco and the semi-independent Ottoman regencies of Algiers, Tunis, and Tripoli were not part of this network; the former in particular followed legal norms and styles of documentation that were quite different, but Ottoman North Africa also appointed its own judges—in contrast with neighboring Egypt, which did not. If *kadi*s from these places were among the North African captives held on Malta—and few would be, since they had less need to travel—they were certainly not among those *kadi*s of Malta invoked in the courts of Galata or Izmir when arrangements were made for the redemption of Ottoman Muslims.

These *kadi*s drew up contracts, facilitated the procedures that made friends, family, or ransom agents full legal representatives of captives or of those paying their ransoms, and confirmed the safe dispatch or arrival of prisoners and payments. The documents the *kadi*s of Malta drew up were presented, considered, and accepted in Ottoman courts no differently than those produced elsewhere. That was, of course, the point. No one doing business in the Ottoman Mediterranean, not even the Catholic corsairs of Malta, could ignore or circumvent the law and customs of the Ottomans. Followed to the letter and supported by Muslim witnesses, these practices protected captors, brokers, lenders, and even borrowers in lawsuits that could cost them dearly. They provided predictability and security in an industry borne of instability and violence. What further meaning might be extracted from this seeming paradox, wherein the reach of Ottoman law and the need for Ottoman legal professionals grew in inverse proportion to the Ottomans' ability to defend Ottoman territories and ensure that Ottoman subjects would have recourse to Ottoman judges within them? Literary sources suggest answers where the documents are silent.

Seventeenth- and eighteenth-century Ottomans were cognizant of this paradox and of the *kadi*'s position at its core. Within decades of Macuncuzade Mustafa Efendi's Maltese ordeal, the *kadi*-as-captive emerged as a trope in Ottoman storytelling, since the *kadi*—educated and trained in Ottoman-endowed institutions, representative of the dynasty both in his jurisdiction and within the Abode of War—personified Ottoman Islam. In one anonymous seventeenth-century Ottoman Turkish story, a triumphal tale of Islam's ability to take root even in the most barren and inhospitable places, a *kadi* named Mehmed captured en route to Egypt becomes the slave of a Catholic monk on Malta—the embodiment of infidelity in the very heart of the Abode of War.

After three years, the monk reveals himself to be a crypto-Muslim who had long ago received in a dream the call to "be a member of the community of Muhammad" and be among those who "guard and look after the dignity of the Sultan of Believers." Here, then, Islam and the Ottoman sultanate are tightly bound together and the *kadi*'s captivity, preordained by God, serves a greater purpose, for Mehmed serves as catechist for this monk who had already been illuminated by the light of Islam, instructing him in theology and law. The dynasty is thus absolved for its failure to provide adequate security for the seas, and after a time the *kadi* is supernaturally transported back to Istanbul, where he is reunited with his family and friends. The monk, we learn, received occasional visits from the Prophet Hızır, who taught him how to pray but also encouraged him to remain on Malta, where he might ransom Muslims and form the central node in a network of new crypto-Muslims spread throughout the lands of the infidels.[142]

The meeting of a *kadi* and a monk is repeated, though with a different twist, in an anecdote preserved in a mid-eighteenth-century Moroccan work. Here again, Ottoman weakness at sea has permitted the capture of an Ottoman *kadi* by the Maltese, in this case an Ibrahim Efendi traveling from Egypt to Crete. Although he was robbed of his money, the corsairs permitted him to keep his books and, upon his arrival on Malta, he was identified as a *kadi* and immediately released into the custody of a monk whom he was astonished to learn read and spoke fluent Arabic and possessed a collection of classic books on Qur'anic exegesis. When Ibrahim asked the unnamed monk how he came upon such works, the monk responded that he had copied them himself when he had been the *kadi* of Jerusalem, leading to the following exchange:

> I asked him, "How could you have been a judge while you are a monk?"
>
> He answered, "Blessed be God. Not long ago, I was a [slave] boy serving the judge of the soldiers [the *kazasker* in Istanbul], so-and-so. And although I continued to be a Christian, I served him and learned to read and write and copy. I was then advanced to the rank of a jurist and excelled. And when he [the judge] saw my dignity and competence, he advanced me to higher positions. I became a judge, in so-and-so year, and once more, in so-and-so year, and after seven positions, I became the judge of Bayt al-Maqdis [i.e., Jerusalem]. And when my teacher died, and I had spent so many years there, I returned to my country, my luggage full, and I reassumed the religion of my fathers and ancestors. By God, I only work with Muslim books, which are my companions, although I keep my Christianity, which I do not wish to change."[143]

Ibrahim Efendi spent a further month with this former crypto-Christian *kadi*, who became his "friend and host," until a ship arrived that took him, free and clear, to Crete.

Both stories, however implausible, are suggestive of the permeability of the religious, political, and intellectual boundaries separating Abode of War and Abode of Islam in the Mediterranean. They are indicative of an Ottoman world-view in which, despite the insecurity of the Ottoman sea, the learning, culture, and dignity of the Ottoman *kadi* are immediately recognized and respected on Malta and even the apostate *kadi*-monk acknowledges the superiority of Muslim, implicitly Ottoman, learning. Both stories encourage us to think of an Ottoman Mediterranean in which the boundaries of law and faith defy those of strict sovereignty or military power. In this world, monks can be Muslims, and *kadi*s ambassadors for the faith. Macuncuzade Mustafa Efendi was not prepared to elevate his captivity into a personal religious trial like the European Christian authors of captivity narratives; in contrast, these quasi-fictional stories employed the *kadi*'s captivity on Malta to create unique encounters between Ottoman Muslim and Catholic Christian that defied the simple binaries familiar to both sides, and then saw their protagonists safely home.

This chapter has argued that the persistent salience of Ottoman law on Malta is illustrative of the fact that the Ottoman Mediterranean of the seventeenth century is best thought of not in terms of the territory within which the Ottomans had the capacity to project force by land or sea, nor even the space encompassed by the penumbra of Ottoman sovereignty, but rather as the space within which Ottoman law had force and meaning. The following chapters continue to explore this point, and elucidate how, in treaties with European powers and in their abrogation, the borders of the Ottoman Mediterranean legal space were gradually brought into relief.

PART TWO

Piracy, Diplomacy, and International Law

CHAPTER THREE

Piracy and Treaty Law

In the early months of 1627, a party of Venetian merchants hired a Dutch ship in Venice and laded it with goods bound for the markets of Alexandria. The outbound voyage proceeded without incident, and the merchants took on a new cargo in the Egyptian port and set sail for Crete. Shortly before making land, however, the merchant vessel was seized by pirates. The pirates left a number of their men aboard the subdued ship to pilot it, along with its captive crew and cargo, back to their base on Samos, but a severe storm blew both pirates and prize off course. They made for the safety of the small port of Kuşadası on the Aegean Anatolian coast and entered the harbor, taking shelter beneath the fortress walls.

The pirates and their captives were still anchored in Kuşadası when the *bailo*, the Venetian ambassador to the Sublime Porte, learned of the incident. He immediately reported it to the Ottoman government, submitting a petition to the sultan requesting an investigation and the return of the goods and captives. In response the Porte dispatched a decree in early March to the *kadi* of Izmir, in whose jurisdiction Kuşadası lay, and to the chief Ottoman administrator in Kuşadası, ordering them to liberate the prize ship and prevent the further sale of its stolen merchandise. The decree declared that piratical acts and the enslavement of Venetian subjects were violations of the peace and of the imperial treaty (*ahdname-i humayün*), and so the *kadi* was required to apprehend and punish the pirates, locate and gather the Venetian captives and their goods, and turn them over to the protection of the Venetian consul in Izmir.[1] A personal letter from the imperial admiral, Hasan Pasha, was sent at the *bailo*'s behest to the same recipients and echoed the sultan's demands that the *ahdname* be upheld.[2] The matter of who these pirates actually were, their subjecthood or religion, was never mentioned.

What precisely did this treaty promise the Venetians? How did Ottomans and Venetians understand its provisions and how had that understanding evolved across time and space? On what legal bases were the Ottomans and their treaty partners entitled to demand action against pirates and restitution for their losses? What practical legal and diplomatic structures facilitated that process? On what sources of law did they draw?

This chapter examines Mediterranean piracy in the context of interstate relations. Setting aside the aspects of Ottoman maritime raiding that would have been encouraged, or at least not actively discouraged or prohibited—such as attacks against Spanish subjects, or the conduct of corsairs in times of armed conflict—this chapter focuses on the origins and development of the diplomatic and legal framework through which piratical incidents were dealt with by the Ottomans and the ways in which changes in the political, economic, and military environment of the Ottoman Mediterranean impacted policy. The bilateral treaties and commercial agreements concluded between the Ottoman Empire and European powers regulated their relations and dictated the mutual expectations for dealing with pirates and amphibious slave raiders. By 1612, the club of seafaring treaty partners had expanded to include France, England, and the Netherlands, but the form and content of their treaties had their origins in the relationship between the Ottoman Empire and Venice, the Ottomans' neighbor and longtime trading partner.

These treaties and their provisions cannot be understood in isolation from the historical context which birthed them. Their anti-piracy articles, the first of which appeared in 1482, developed not out of theoretical concerns but as a practical response to real issues, and they evolved to meet the challenges of the day. Ultimately, the *ahdname*s began to promise more than they could deliver, and the rash of piracy around the turn of the seventeenth century stretched them to the breaking point. When the gap became too big to paper over, the *ahdname* snapped back to size.

The anti-piracy articles of the Ottoman-Venetian *ahdname*s outgrew their medieval historical precedents in the early sixteenth century, as successive Ottoman conquests in the Aegean, along the Morea, and in the Adriatic brought Ottoman naval forces in ever closer contact with those of Venice, and growing imperial ambitions and sympathy with the plight of Iberian Muslims propelled Ottoman-aligned corsairs across the Mediterranean Sea.[3] The first expanded anti-piracy clauses emerged during a period of maritime violence that was predominantly state sponsored, even as the line between regular navy forces and irregulars and corsairs remained blurred. After 1570, however, the centers of gravity and practitioners of piratical raiding shifted largely beyond the control of the central states most affected by it. As a result, Ottoman and Venetian negotiators expanded the treaty language concerning piracy, language that would be carried over to the treaties the sultans concluded with the emerging European maritime commercial powers.

Piracy was a major source of friction between the Ottomans and those who came to trade in their domains, and as a result of increasingly ineffective policing of the seas, the articles that dictated what would happen after pirate attacks became considerably more important than those that forbade them. Piracy was the primary engine driving the development of interstate law throughout the sixteenth and seventeenth centuries, and dealing with its consequences became a central pillar of early modern Mediterranean diplomacy. Frequent negotiations in the respective capitals and the dispatch of case-specific orders and elaborative decrees added to and clarified anti-piracy law between treaty issues and reflected shifting understandings of their provisions, even when the original articles retained their form. They thus created a new body of maritime law that guided domestic and interstate policy and could be referred to as necessary to resolve disputes.

Scholars have taken note of the connection between piracy and the theorization of international law by European jurists in the early modern period.[4] It was the London-based Italian jurist Alberico Gentili (d. 1608) who, taking an obscure saying by the Roman orator Cicero, advanced the idea that pirates were "the common enemy of all mankind." His younger contemporary, the Dutchman Hugo Grotius, employed to defend Dutch interests against the Portuguese in the Indian Ocean, wrote extensively about freedom of navigation and what constituted piracy, formulating the definition cited at the beginning of this book.[5]

That Gentili in particular had much to say about the Ottomans is well known. As both a theoretical jurist and an advocate for Spanish interests in London in the first decade of the seventeenth century, Gentili found himself considering the complex question of whether Ottoman North Africa, by then a serious threat to European shipping, was imbued with sovereign authority or just a constituent part of the empire. The answer to this question determined whether its corsairs were in fact pirates and consequently whether their booty had legally changed owners and could be licitly purchased. If they were pirates, the booty would have to be returned to its original owners; if, however, they were privateers waging war against their enemies, their takings were fair prizes and the new owners would prevail in court. Gentili found himself arguing both sides during his career in London.[6]

But if the importance of these issues in Gentili's writings and those of his contemporaries has been recognized, the Ottomans' own views on them have gone unexplored. Gentili's dismissal of the Ottomans as unreliable and untrustworthy was informed not only by religious prejudice—he rejected any possibility of an alliance with infidels—but by the North African paradox, which by the 1620s would become no less vexing to the Ottomans themselves.[7] The persistent question of the legal status of North Africa and whether its activities constituted legitimate privateering or illegal piracy, which arose first in the 1580s, and the inability of European jurists like Gentili to decouple Istanbul from Algiers in their appraisal of Ottoman law and diplomacy, obscured the fact that the Ottomans and their treaty partners were contending with precisely the same legal quandaries. Their responses developed in parallel, if not always in concert, and had much in common. The relative congruence should come as little surprise. Through the seventeenth century, the Ottoman Mediterranean was a Venetian space as well, and the interimperial law that reigned over it emerged from a shared history and drew on shared sources—ancient custom, treaties, and municipal (that is, Ottoman Islamic and sultanic, as well as Venetian) law—for meaning and legitimacy.[8]

The commercial treaties first granted to France in 1567, England in 1580, and the Netherlands in 1612 were based directly on and essentially mirrored the language of the Ottoman-Venetian agreements.[9] In contrast with these entirely commercial relationships, however, the Ottomans and Venetians shared a long, dynamic frontier on land and sea that resulted in constant contact—mostly peaceful but punctuated by both isolated violent episodes and periods of sustained conflict. The intimacy and history of this relationship meant that piracy was first and for far longer an issue for the Ottomans and the Venetians, and they were forced to develop lasting legal and procedural solutions to the problem very early. As the Ottomans' ability to maintain security in the Mediterranean declined in the late sixteenth century, the Venetians were forced to pick up the slack, effectively propping up the Ottoman legal order in the decades leading up to the war for Crete. Much of Venetian diplomacy was, of necessity, geared toward goading Ottoman officials in both the capital and the provinces to act in accordance with the law they shared, while the Venetian navy worked tirelessly to uphold its end of the bargain.

The other members of the increasingly crowded diplomatic quarter in Pera had initially shared some of Venice's goals, but their decision in the first decades of the seventeenth century to answer the questions surrounding the nature and extent of North African sovereignty by entering into direct diplomatic negotiations rapidly undermined both the shared legal regime and the Ottomans' relations with their overseas provinces. The Venetians, as neighbors and symbiotic partners with an Ottoman host that was gradually consuming them, had no choice but to continue to rely directly on their relations with the Sublime Porte to safeguard their rights. The precipitating causes for this diplomatic divergence and its consequences are the subject of Chapter 4. Here we explore how the Ottoman-Venetian diplomatic framework took shape, how it worked in practice, and how it came to encompass the French and the Northerners.

Through their pragmatic, negotiated agreements—and in the regular violations of them—Ottomans and Venetians laid the groundwork for principles that would become enshrined in modern international law. Combining maritime custom, negotiation, and the legal traditions of both sides, Istanbul and Venice constructed a platform of codes of conduct at sea, expectations for how to deal with pirates, and a formal system for providing restitution for damages and the return of illegally enslaved, treaty-protected subjects.

THE *AHDNAMES*: BACKGROUND

The diplomatic instruments through which relations between the Ottomans and foreign powers were defined were called *ahdname*s. The term combines the Arabic word *ahd*, for promise or pact, with the Persian *name*, for letter. Europeans referred to them as "capitulations," for the sections, *capitulo*, into which they were divided. As international legal instruments, the *ahdname*s have most often been studied in the eighteenth- and nineteenth-century context, by which point their contents were effectively fixed and their duration perpetual. As the Ottoman Empire was territorially contracting and its economy was increasingly captive to European interests, changes in the *ahdname*s' interpretation were almost exclusively to the Ottomans' detriment. But in the sixteenth and seventeenth centuries, these were dynamic instruments, frequently renewed and revised, and their content and interpretation were constantly in flux.[10] The story of piracy in the Mediterranean is incomplete without considering these instruments, the context of their creation, and the history of their implementation and violation.

The first *ahdname* granted to Venice was issued in 1403 and was likely based on a combination of Mamluk and Byzantine models.[11] It, like all the *ahdname*s that followed, extended legal protection (*aman*) to the subjects of a power which was, in Islamic legal terms, within the Abode of War, and who were, as a result, "enemy infidels" whose lives and possessions would otherwise be forfeit. The *ahdname*s permitted them to travel to and remain within the Abode of Islam in security as *müstemin*s, or recipients of safe-conduct, and exempted them from the taxes owed by *zimmi*s; over time, the *ahdname*s set aside the traditional one-year time limit on *müstemin* status, preventing long-term foreign residents from becoming "naturalized" *zimmi*s (with the concomitant tax burden) unless they wished it. As charters of commercial privileges, the *ahdnames* dictated the legal and commercial rights of foreigners in the Ottoman Empire, opened markets to trade, determined the commodities that might be exported, and fixed customs rates.[12] The *ahdnames* with Venice also delineated borders, set tributes, determined procedures for dealing with fugitive slaves, and established codes of conduct for naval and merchant vessels meeting at sea.[13]

Although early *ahdnames* had a bilateral character, by the sixteenth century they had assumed an increasingly unilateral tone.[14] They were "given" at the request of Venice as an expression of friendship and as a reward for peaceful behavior. Nevertheless, this was a rhetorical fiction; the *ahdnames* were extensively pre-negotiated. And even as the *ahdnames* granted to Venice and other powers in the sixteenth and seventeenth centuries came to resemble sultanic decrees to circumvent the Islamic prohibitions against negotiating perpetual peace with the Abode of War, they operated on the principle of reciprocity.[15] In some key areas, especially those having to do with maritime issues, the *ahdnames* maintained explicitly reciprocal articles throughout their history.

Venice confirmed, renewed, or acquired a fresh *ahdname* at the accession of every new sultan or following the end of hostilities. Although the Ottomans employed very similar terminology in their peace treaties and in their commercial agreements—and those with Venice essentially conflated the two—the *ahdnames* discussed in this chapter were not strictly speaking peace treaties like those that ended conflicts with the Habsburgs in southeastern Europe. Unlike the *ahdnames*, those instruments did not contain any unilateral grants of privileges, though there were certain common expectations, including the return of captives taken in violation of the peace.[16] Tributary states and polities that might be (or definitely were) considered to be part of Ottoman domains also received *ahdnames*. For example, Galata, the former Genoese colony across the Golden Horn from Constantinople that was home to most of the European merchant communities and their diplomatic representatives, received an *ahdname* upon its submission to Sultan Mehmed II in 1453. This pact was renewed a number of times over the centuries that followed, and it established the community's special status within the Ottoman sphere.[17]

Somewhat different were the *ahdnames* given to the Adriatic city-state of Dubrovnik (Ragusa), which retained nominal independence from the Ottoman Empire in exchange for an annual tribute and obedience to the sultan. Like Venice, Dubrovnik's *ahdnames* promised peace and prosperity and granted favorable trading rights and extensive freedom of movement within Ottoman domains. However, Dubrovnik was sometimes considered to be a part of the empire itself. Whereas the Ragusans were not technically Ottoman subjects, at times the city's leaders and Ottoman administrators conspired to paper over this fact. The Ottomans often dispatched decrees to Dubrovnik as if its leaders were provincial officials, and Dubrovnik often made appeals for Ottoman aid in finding and freeing abducted Ragusans on the basis of its protected status within Ottoman domains.[18]

Part of the problem, and the solution to the quandary of the religious-legal basis of the *ahdname*, was the matter of subjecthood and tribute. Non-Muslim Ottoman subjects, *zimmi*s, were liable to pay the poll-tax, the *cizye*. Yet the *cizye* was typically referred to in Ottoman usage as the *harac* (Arabic: *kharaj*), the canonical land tax. The same term was used for the tribute paid by submissive states. The conflation of these taxes proved legally useful. This way, by extension, when the Ottomans referred to Ragusans as "tax-paying subjects," *haracgüzar reaya*—the same formulation the Ottomans used to describe their own subjects—they could avoid the complicated question of whose subjects, precisely, they were.[19] By virtue of the fact that Venice, too, paid a tribute—likewise referred to as *harac*—the Ottomans could dispel some of the Islamic legal proscriptions against making perpetual peace with them and construe the tribute as submission, an interpretation the Venetians no doubt would have rejected.[20] This proved not to be a factor for the French, English, or Dutch when they negotiated *ahdname*s, largely because they did not share a border with the Ottomans; their *ahdname*s were almost exclusively concerned with regulating commerce. In short, the *ahdname*s with Venice and other foreign powers were framed as unilateral charters of privileges to satisfy Islamic legal strictures but were in reality bilateral treaties that were mostly, but not exclusively, concerned with commercial matters.

THE EARLY EVOLUTION OF OTTOMAN-VENETIAN ANTI-PIRACY LAW

Piracy in the Mediterranean increased dramatically in the century after 1570, but piratical violence accompanied every naval conflict of the preceding century and persisted to varying degrees in peacetime as well. As war and trade brought Venice and the Ottoman Empire closer in the late fifteenth century, the two powers together evolved their first diplomatic and legal responses to piracy. They did not start from scratch, however. The roots of the form and content of the first Ottoman-Venetian accord to deal with piracy, concluded in 1482, lay in the Venetians' long history with the Mamluk Sultanate.

Between 1250 and 1517, manumitted military slaves, *mamluks*, reigned over a state composed of Egypt, greater Syria, and the Hijaz. Much of the Mamluk Sultanate's wealth was derived from its control of the lucrative trade in spices, which crossed the Indian Ocean and were transported from the Red Sea to Alexandria, where they were warehoused and sold in fixed quantities at fixed prices to merchants from the Italian maritime republics.[21] The Mamluks never developed a strong navy, and they razed the towns, ports, and fortifications of nearly the entire coastline of greater Syria to prevent the return of the Crusaders. This left coastal dwellers vulnerable to amphibious assaults from the Franks, who came to raid and plunder with regularity. Turkish pirates from the Anatolian coast also took advantage of the Mamluks' naval weakness to prey upon the Italians' shipping. By the fifteenth century, the Venetians effectively became the Mamluks' navy by treaty.[22]

Those treaties dealt extensively with piracy. The Mamluk-Venetian treaty of 1442, for example, dealt with both Frankish and Turkish piracy. One article noted that Turkish galleys were "lying in wait to commit robbery" and plunder the Venetian merchants and obligated the Mamluk sultan to "promulgate his command prohibiting the aforesaid from interfering" with the Venetians and to seize any pirates they might find and punish them accordingly.[23] Another established the principle that signatories would be responsible for paying the ransoms of Muslims captured by pirates of their own nation and brought to Mamluk ports, but that they would not be liable for those taken by others.[24] The spirit of both articles would outlive the Mamluks themselves. The 1497 Mamluk-Florentine treaty, modeled after the former, also included an article stating that "one merchant be not held for another except when he is a guarantor by contract," adding that "when the corsair on the open sea seizes a ship belonging to the Muslims they (Florentines) shall not be held for it." The treaty authors explained their rationale: "for a merchant is a merchant and a corsair a corsair."[25] No one would be able to make that claim with such certainty a century later.

But when the Ottomans and Venetians reestablished trading relations in the late fifteenth century after sixteen years of war, the groundwork for an international legal order concerning piracy had already been laid. Much of the language and content characteristic to subsequent *ahdname*s first took shape in the Venetian *ahdname* of 1482, which drew on those Mamluk precedents while incorporating many of the articles of the peace treaty that ended the first Ottoman-Venetian war in 1479.[26] Unlike the Mamluks, however, the Ottomans had aspirations to naval supremacy, and these influenced the content of their treaties and the conduct of their relations immensely. The 1463–1479 conflict marked the emergence of the Ottomans as a formidable maritime power, and as a result the *ahdname* of 1482 had to address issues like how Ottoman and Venetian naval forces would interact in peacetime. This instrument, which established broad trading rights and freed all Venetian slaves taken during the previous hostilities, also mentioned piracy.[27]

It stipulated that when Ottoman and Venetian ships met at sea, they should be friendly and not do any damage to one another, and that if either "captured the ships of pirates (*haramiler*, lit. "thieves" or "robbers") in any place, they should punish them and execute them." In a later clause, the 1482 *ahdname* established another principle that would carry over into every subsequent issue—that of procuring bonds from non-fleet vessels to ensure their good behavior. In addition to a unilateral promise that Ottoman naval vessels would not engage in *haramilik*, by which the drafters meant predatory raiding, the treaty stipulated that both Ottomans and Venetians would take a "strong surety" from the captains of ships going out to sea in order to discourage acts of piracy against the other. Those captains who did not provide surety would be viewed as "criminals and sinners" and would be strongly punished, and those who did give surety and then engaged in piracy would have the restitution for the damages they caused paid out from their bond.[28] As we shall see, the issue of actually getting ship captains based in ports sustained by the profits from piracy to post bond continued to vex Ottoman and Venetian central administrators for the next two hundred years, but versions of this clause became a fixture in every subsequent Venetian *ahdname*.

The next Venetian *ahdname* was issued in 1503 after the conclusion of the second Ottoman-Venetian war (1499–1503). Like that of 1482, it was granted by Sultan Bayazid II, and it was substantially similar to the earlier treaty. Nevertheless, further Ottoman territorial gains in the Aegean brought Ottomans and Venetians into ever closer contact in the politically divided archipelago. The concomitant danger of piracy and the increasing importance of maritime affairs necessitated the first in what would be an extensive series of elaborations and expansions of the *ahdname*'s anti-piracy clauses over the course of the sixteenth and seventeenth centuries.

In the years leading up to the second war, Ottoman power was first projected beyond the Eastern Mediterranean. The raids of the notorious Turkish corsair Kemal Reis stretched across the sea and even into the Atlantic. He caused serious economic and psychological damage throughout the Christian Mediterranean in the 1490s and into the early years of the sixteenth century, and Venice was not spared his wrath.[29] At the same time, the Hospitaller Knights of Saint John, based on the island of

Rhodes, were a continuing threat to Muslim pilgrims and merchants and a tremendous irritant to the Ottomans. The failed Ottoman siege of the island in 1480 had not dampened their enthusiasm for raiding, and with Cyprus and numerous Aegean islands still in Venetian hands, it was up to Venice as much as the Ottomans to defend against Hospitaller predation until the Ottomans finally expelled the knights in 1522.[30]

For all these reasons, the matter of piracy had to be dealt with in greater depth in 1503. As before, the treaty stipulated that when Ottoman and Venetian ships met at sea, they should be friendly and do no harm to one another, but gone now was the vague commitment to punish captured pirates. A strongly worded reciprocal anti-piracy clause took its place that, like the surety clause of 1482, became a fixture in all future agreements in one form or another. It stated:

> Venice shall not equip, give refuge or provisions to other countries' pirate (*harami*) barques and galleys when they come to its islands and ports and if their capture is possible, they shall capture and punish them and they shall absolutely prohibit and repudiate [them]; and I also shall not equip, give refuge or provisions to the pirate galleys, barques, and caïques that come to my islands and ports and, if their capture is possible, I shall capture and punish them and I absolutely prohibit and repudiate [them].[31]

Thus, both sides undertook to deny shelter and aid to pirates of any nation, essentially adopting the view of pirates as the "common enemy of all." While this clause was new to the 1503 *ahdname*, its inspiration can easily be traced back to the Mamluk-Venetian treaties, which included similar articles. These had precedents in the maritime legal tradition of the Mediterranean dating to antiquity. The "Roman Piracy Law" of 100 BCE, for example, similarly required the Mediterranean powers who were friends of Rome to deny pirates access to their harbors, prevent them from operating from their territory, and capture them whenever possible.[32] Both Roman and Ottoman-Venetian law framed combatting piracy as the mutual obligation of friends and allies, to be achieved principally by depriving pirates of bases of operation and markets for stolen goods. In both instances, pirates were unequivocally excluded from any legal protections afforded by subjecthood and declared to be thieves punishable by any and all.

Many of the "thieves" at issue were not full-time pirates but rather errant naval vessels, and Ottoman and Venetian negotiators were most anxious to prevent this sort of activity by their subjects. This is clear from the wording of the 1503 treaty's reciprocal surety clause:

> When the galleys and caïques and other ships go out to sea from those places in my well-protected domains and my admiral is not together with them, the cap-

tains of the aforementioned ships shall give strong sureties (*kefil*) that they will not go and do damage to the dominion of Venice; if they go without giving surety, they are criminals and sinners (*mücrim ve günahkar*) and shall be punished; if, after giving surety, they go and do damage, however much damage they do shall be given from their surety. In the same way also, if the captains of the ships that go out to sea from the side of Venice without the Venetian admiral, after giving strong surety, do damage to my well-protected domains, they shall give their sureties for those damages; if they go without surety they are sinners and shall be strongly punished.[33]

The clause singles out galleys and caïques, swift oared ships better suited to combat than commerce, among the vessels whose captains had to provide surety when they went out to sea unaccompanied by their fleet admiral. Captains participating in fleet actions were not required to post bonds, the implication being that they would be controlled by their respective leaders. At this stage in the development of the treaty language, the surety clause does not appear to have applied to private merchant vessels or fishing boats (though this would be reinterpreted a century and a half later) but only to ships associated with the Ottoman and Venetian navies, including irregulars that set out to sea independently to raid enemy shipping. Neither the Ottomans nor the Venetians equated this practice with piracy. The purpose of taking surety was not to prevent Ottoman corsairs from setting upon legitimate targets but simply to discourage attacks of convenience on Venetian ships and shores. Only failure to give surety, and thus obtain official authorization, made corsair captains into "criminals and sinners" and, by extension, into pirates.

The renewals of the *ahdname* in 1513 and 1517 (following the accession of Sultan Selim I and his conquest of the Mamluk Sultanate, respectively) reproduced the two anti-piracy clauses of 1503 almost verbatim.[34] However, in light of the increased activity of the Ottoman fleet, these *ahdnames* included a new provision that when the Ottoman imperial navy went on campaign, it would not stop in Venetian ports. In return, Venice's fleet was expected "to remain silent in its place in friendship and not set sail."[35] This warning to stay out of the way meant, essentially, that the Venetian peacetime navy was expected to remain sequestered in the Adriatic whenever the Ottoman navy entered the Mediterranean. It also meant that Venice had to cease naval patrols in the furthest parts of the *stato da mar* during Ottoman campaigns, leaving large parts of its maritime empire defenseless when it was most vulnerable.

The Ottomans' absorption of the Mamluk Sultanate in 1516–7 completely reshaped the maritime power dynamic in the Mediterranean. Reuniting the north and south of the Mediterranean for the first time since the Islamic conquests of the seventh century ripped the Eastern Roman

Empire in half, the Ottomans now controlled an uninterrupted stretch of Mediterranean coastline from the borders of Venice in the Adriatic to the ports of Egypt and, with it, access to the rich trades, especially in spices, that had long sustained Venice's economy. Even though the Portuguese in the Indian Ocean had begun to threaten the flow of pepper in the decade before the fall of the Mamluks, there were still tremendous profits to be had in the trade with Egypt and other Ottoman ports. Venice's fortunes now rested entirely on maintaining peace with the Ottoman Empire and security in the eastern half of the Mediterranean, which they together shared.[36]

EXPANSION: THE *AHDNAMES* OF 1521 AND 1540

During the last five years of his eight-year reign, Sultan Selim I routed Safavid Iran, doubled the size of the empire and assumed the protectorship of the Holy Cities of Mecca and Medina with the Mamluk conquests, and oversaw the symbolic extension of Ottoman sovereignty to Algiers. The latter set the stage for a contest with Spain over North Africa that, thanks to European aristocratic inbreeding, became a theater in a much larger conflict with the far-flung Habsburg Empire of Charles V. It was a rivalry that would occupy Selim I's son and successor, Süleyman (r. 1520–1566), for the entirety of his long reign.

The Süleymanic *ahdname*s of 1521 and 1540, the first granted following his accession to the throne and the second after the conclusion of a three-year war, mark the growing maturity of the format and the crystallization of many of its core elements and their language, which served as the basis for later treaties with Venice and for those concluded with other powers. The *ahdname* expectations regarding piracy had remained similar, if vague, since 1503, but the brewing imperial contest for dominance in North Africa and the growing role of corsairs on both sides of the conflict left Venice uncomfortably in the middle, geographically and politically, and necessitated further expansion and clarification of the treaty language.

The 1521 *ahdname* marked a significant change in the tone and content of the *ahdname*s, reflecting the Ottomans' enhanced confidence as a naval force and their growing imperial pretensions. As before, Ottoman and Venetian naval and merchant vessels were urged to be friendly when they met on the high seas, "but they [the Venetians] must also lower their sails and make known their friendship and obedience when they meet my personal fleet, my galleys, and my other ships sailing at sea, as before in accordance with my imperial decree." This humiliating demonstration of Venetian obeisance and respect before Ottoman naval might, beyond the traditional salute, had previously been decreed by Sultan Süleyman and was now permanently enshrined in the *ahdname* text, but it also had the practical implication of forcing Venetian ships to make themselves vulnerable whenever they encountered Ottoman ships. "And if, after lowering sail and making their friendship known," the text continued, "they are damaged, if a man or possession or goods are harmed, whatever it may be shall be replaced."[37] This latter part was then expressed in reverse, committing Venice to provide restitution should any harm come to Ottoman naval vessels or merchant ships, Ottoman subjects, or their possessions at Venetian hands.

Although the new addition emphasized Ottoman dominance through the required sail lowering, it also formalized the procedures for Ottoman and Venetian maritime encounters, prescribing a submissive display of friendship that, properly and promptly performed, would defuse what was always a potentially dangerous situation. The reciprocal agreement to provide restitution for damages and losses of ships, men, and material was an even more important development. While the 1521 *ahdname*, like those before and after it, maintained the surety clause essentially intact, this new promise of restitution independent of the captains' sureties placed the financial responsibility for any damages caused by Ottoman or Venetian subjects squarely on their respective governments. This guarantee marked a practical and logical step forward in the development of Ottoman-Venetian relations that would serve as the legal basis for dozens, if not hundreds, of claims for losses presented by both Venice and the Ottoman Empire over the course of the sixteenth and seventeenth centuries.[38] We return to the question of how such claims were handled in practice later in this chapter.

The reciprocal assurance of financial restitution for losses was followed by several new provisions that expanded and elaborated upon the preexisting anti-piracy clauses and did away with much of their earlier ambiguity. Immediately after the restitution clause, the 1521 *ahdname* included a strongly worded new provision that marked the first time the Ottoman word *levend* appeared in the *ahdname*s (though *korsan* was still absent) and introduced specific new procedures for Venice to take when combating piracy perpetrated by Ottoman subjects:

> If they [the Venetians] should happen across and meet a pirate or *levend* ship (*harami ve levend gemisine*), it is incumbent upon them to attack that pirate ship (*harami gemisi*) and by the grace of God almighty they shall be victorious over that pirate ship; let them kill however many men they kill at the time of battle,

> but if they capture and take implicated men alive, they shall never kill them themselves; without fail they shall send them healthy (*sağ ve selim*) to my threshold of felicity (i.e. Istanbul) where I will strongly punish them and have them executed in such a way that they shall be a necessary warning and admonition to others.[39]

This clause unambiguously gave Venetians the right to defend themselves against Ottoman pirate attacks. Indeed, it actually required them to engage and defeat Ottoman pirates whenever they encountered them, though this was a rhetorical twist meant to obscure the fact that Venetian ships were more likely to be accosted by Ottoman-subject pirates than the other way around. It did implicitly recognize Venice's right to mount galley patrols of her maritime possessions for the express purpose of protecting against and hunting down marauding Ottoman pirates, and this included corsairs breaching the *ahdname*, but the Venetians were denied the right to punish Ottoman-subject pirates themselves. This responsibility the sultan reserved for himself, promising to make a gruesome example of convicted pirates in the imperial capital.

This strong assurance aside, however, the clause demonstrated a new Ottoman unwillingness to have the sultan's subjects, no matter what the crime, tried and punished by a foreign power. In practice, the Ottoman government did at times make serious attempts to find notorious Ottoman pirates and executed no small number.[40] As for those the Venetian navy encountered, however, it proved easier and perhaps more satisfying to kill them all on the spot, though a number of cases of mistaken identity, in which overzealous Venetian galley commanders assaulted nonpiratical Ottoman ships, revealed the dangers of such unofficial policies.

The novel requirement to send Ottoman pirate prisoners safe and sound to Istanbul for punishment established a double standard in the *ahdnames*' anti-piracy clauses that would remain on the books for a century and a half. The article of the 1521 *ahdname* stipulating that neither side would give refuge or support to foreign pirates, which had been a hallmark of these agreements since 1503, still contained the requirement that Ottomans and Venetians capture and punish such pirates whenever possible. This meant that while both sides continued to recognize the principle that pirates could be theoretically tried and punished by anyone, a special exemption had been made for Ottoman-subject pirates—one that was not explicitly mirrored for the Venetians.

Both the assurance of the Venetians' right to self-defense against Ottoman pirates and the expectation that those they captured be sent to Istanbul were composed before the Ottomans became the dominant power in North Africa. Though the Ottoman standard now fluttered above the citadel of Algiers, the authors of the clause did not envision a world in which the Ottoman sultan presided over multiple ports that derived the bulk of their revenues from attacks on the sultan's friends, Venice included. Venice's right to vigorously defend itself, though repeatedly upheld by Istanbul, would prove to be a serious sticking point in North Africa, especially since the Venetians were disinclined to take prisoners. The result was a vicious cycle of raids and reprisals that the Ottoman government was hard-pressed to stop.

Although constructed in almost exactly the same form as before, the 1521 anti-piracy clause contained important additions to the wording that were indicative of some of the growing sources of tension for Venetian and Ottoman subjects at sea. Chief among these was the complicity of fortress commanders on the frontier, which worsened with time and ultimately caused numerous diplomatic scandals and severely damaged Ottoman-Venetian relations at several points in the late sixteenth and seventeenth centuries. The 1521 additions to the treaty language are given in bold:

> Venice shall not equip, give refuge or provisions to other countries' pirate (*harami*) barques and galleys **and other ships** when they come **across** its islands, ports, **and fortresses** and if their capture is possible, they shall capture them and **however many men they capture they shall not give them any opportunity and never treat them with respect or affection** but they shall **strongly** punish **all of** them **immediately** and **if they are unable to capture them** they shall absolutely prohibit and repudiate [them]; and I also shall not equip, give refuge or provisions to the pirate galleys, barques, and caïques that come to my islands and ports and, if their capture is possible, **I shall not give them any opportunity** [to escape] and they shall be **strongly** punished **immediately and if capture is not possible,** I will prohibit and repudiate [them].[41]

The addition of fortresses (*hisarlar*) was of paramount importance, as their castellans played a key role in facilitating piracy. Their appearance here anticipated what would become a common complaint among the Venetians, that Ottoman fortress commanders were doing precisely what the provision forbade. At the same time, the addition of the word "across" expanded the sphere of responsibility for preventing piracy, which no longer applied only to pirates who came to their islands and ports, but also to those passing through their coastal waters. Now in its mature form, this clause laid the legal grounds for later Ottoman complaints about Venice's failure to stop Maltese and Uskok piracy when it transited or stopped in Venetian territory, culminating in the Ottoman invasions of both Cyprus and Crete.

The language also tried to take into account the problem of local sympathies with corsairs and pirates, demanding not only that neither side abet piracy but that captured raiders be immediately and severely punished and given no opportunity to rally support or chance of escape. There was to be no quarter in the war on piracy.

Of all the additions and modifications to the anti-piracy clauses in the 1521 *ahdname*, perhaps the most important was that concerning illegal slave raiding. Whereas earlier *ahdname*s implicitly prohibited the enslavement of the subjects of the other side, there had been no specific mention of slave raiding by land or sea, nor any indication of what should be done if and when it occurred. Venice would have demanded the return of its subjects, but determining who, in fact, was Venetian was hardly straightforward, and religious conversion complicated matters further.

In a Mediterranean world in which slavery was legal and integral to the social and political order, in which the constant import of slaves was necessary for the system to function and the question of who could be enslaved was a matter of subjecthood as much as religious identity, no aspect of the issue could be taken for granted. The *ahdname* of 1503 had ordered the release of all Venetian captives taken during the 1499–1503 war,[42] but Venetian subjects were periodically captured in illegal slaving raids along the land and sea frontiers. As a result, the 1521 *ahdname* not only explicitly forbade the enslavement of Venetian subjects, it also fixed detailed procedures for finding, identifying, and returning them:

> Should the pirate ships (*harami kayıkları*) go by sea and others by land and raid the islands belonging to Venice and enslave their people and take them to and sell them in Anatolia and Rumelia (i.e. the European part of the Ottoman Empire), as before, when a slave is found, it will be investigated with attention and care as required; in whoever's possession he is found, he shall be taken from him. Furthermore, if the person who took him turns out to be a *levend* and if that *levend* is captured and if the slave is actually a Venetian, then that *levend* shall be severely punished; and if that slave became a Muslim, he shall be emancipated and freed, and if he is still an infidel, he shall be turned over to the Venetians. If [his Venetian identity] is not known from whom he was taken, then that slave himself shall be brought to my exalted court and it shall be investigated with complete care at my threshold of felicity, and if it is revealed that he is Venetian and if he has become a Muslim, he shall be emancipated and if he is still an infidel, he shall be turned over to the *bailo*.[43]

This clause was included unchanged in every subsequent *ahdname* until 1595, when it was expanded and subtly altered. It served as the model for similar clauses that appeared in every other *ahdname* given to foreign powers for the duration of the regime, including those of Dubrovnik, France, England, and the Netherlands, and it established a lasting Ottoman policy for dealing with illegal enslavement.[44] Venetians who were captured in contravention of the treaty were to be found and freed no matter the circumstances, but they would only be returned to Venetian custody if they had not converted to Islam, since doing so would facilitate apostasy. As we have already seen, this was intra-Ottoman policy as well.[45]

However, the methods for determining Venetian subjecthood on the ground were left deliberately vague. In intra-Ottoman cases, local courts were the primary venues in which Ottoman subjecthood had to be proven in order to earn release, and these typically required Muslim testimony. This was not the case for Venetian slaves. While local magistrates might bear some responsibility for identifying Venetian slaves, the process of freeing them and turning them over to Venetian authorities was otherwise an executive matter that circumvented the Ottoman Islamic legal system. Indeed, in cases where Venetian subjecthood was suspected but uncertain, only the sultan's court—the Imperial Council—was competent to adjudicate the issue. This was congruent with policy elsewhere in the *ahdname*s, which held that legal disputes involving treaty-protected foreigners could always be heard by the Imperial Council.

Later in the sixteenth century, as the number of peacetime raids against Venetian targets spiked, the stipulation that "Venetian-ness" be determined on the spot or investigated in Istanbul was quietly dropped in favor of allowing the Venetians to take a more active role in helping to identify and retrieve their subjects, but the procedures described in the 1521 *ahdname* for freeing the illegally enslaved were otherwise fixed. While this clause was not expressed reciprocally, it was understood to apply in reverse. Ottoman captives taken in peacetime were similarly expected to be found, freed, and returned to Ottoman custody.

This unilateral article included the first mention of amphibious slave raiding by Ottoman pirates in the *ahdname*s. Although it was hardly a new practice, it was certainly on the rise by this time, as the Ottoman navy and Ottoman-aligned corsairs prowled the Mediterranean and carried off thousands into captivity, mostly from southern Italy, the Balearic Islands, and the Iberian coast. This activity was condoned by the Ottoman government, except when it was directed against protected powers, like Venice or Dubrovnik. For this reason, attacks on Venetian territorial possessions were, just as in the preceding clauses, framed as criminal acts.

The culprits were still assumed to be primarily Ottoman naval units and corsairs gone astray, accounting for the language about establishing whether the attacker was indeed a *levend* and the victim indeed a Venetian before prescribing exemplary punishment. The term *levend* had not fully acquired the more pejorative overtones that it would possess later in the century and did not on its own suggest disobedience.[46] The treaty authors could not have anticipated how political, military, and economic developments would reshape the maritime landscape later in the century, when the frequency of amphibious raids in the eastern half of the Mediterranean increased even as their scale shrank, and the number of actors responsible for such attacks and the bases from which they operated multiplied.

Another Ottoman-Venetian war resulted in the second and final *ahdname* of Sultan Süleyman's reign. The anti-piracy clauses were reproduced largely intact from the 1521 instrument. However, the decisive Ottoman victory at the Battle of Preveza in 1538 and in the 1537–1540 conflict as a whole consolidated the empire's control over the Morea and the Aegean, leaving only Tinos in Venetian hands, and the new *ahdname* hardened the boundaries between the two states. Every earlier *ahdname* had explicitly given the Venetians the right to visit and trade unimpeded in Ottoman domains and come and go as they pleased.[47] This changed in 1540.

Venetian merchants traveling by land and Venetian ships were now admonished not to enter "heedlessly" into the straits of Lepanto and Preveza, the port of Modon in the Morea, the Dardanelles, Istanbul, Galata, or Alexandria without first notifying the local fortress commanders and obtaining their leave to enter or pass. Exceptions were made in the event of contrary winds or storms, or if "pirate (*harami*) or *levend* galliots were pursuing them" and there was no other safe harbor to put into, in which cases they were permitted to seek shelter unannounced. Even in such instances, however, the *ahdname* text suggested that Venetians should attempt to provide some warning of their imminent arrival if possible. Venetian ships that entered Ottoman ports in emergencies were not to be harmed, but they were required to obtain the permission of the fortress commander before departing after the danger had passed.[48]

The Ottomans were not trying to discourage Venetian trade, but with Ottoman hegemony in the Aegean and the Morea complete, they were inclined to and capable of regulating contact far more closely. The language also suggests an Ottoman desire to avoid creating situations where violations of the treaty were more likely to occur. A cursory look at later Ottoman and Venetian records uncovers numerous instances of Venetian merchant vessels that were blown into Ottoman Adriatic ports by storms or entered to escape pirates only to have the goods confiscated, the ship impounded, and the passengers and crew sold into slavery. For example, in the early days of 1630, five Venice-bound ships were caught in a fierce gale and foundered on the rocks near Draç. The men of the fortress charged the Venetian admiral 2,700 *guruş* to salvage the ships, then promptly enslaved the 130 crewmembers and stole all the cargo and cannons, some but not all of which ended up in the fortress.[49] Such violations were not necessarily the norm—after all, the records mostly preserve cases of things going wrong, not the many instances where Ottoman port authorities assisted endangered Venetians and upheld their treaty obligations—but they were a legitimate concern.

Merchant traffic in and out of Venice had to pass through a long Ottoman gauntlet above and below the narrow entrance to the Adriatic, with no friendly port until Venetian-held Corfu (the conquest of which had been the initial objective of the late conflict). The 1540 *ahdname* included a clause promising that "the ships that sail in the straits above Corfu, whether they be Venetian or others coming to Venice for trade, shall not be hindered or harmed," but this was a hollow assurance.[50] In succeeding decades, local and long-distance pirates attacked the shipping of Venetians and others passing through the straits with regularity.

WHAT DIFFERENCE DOES A WAR MAKE? PIRACY AND LAW BEFORE AND AFTER CYPRUS

The 1540 *ahdname* remained in force for twenty-seven years, and it defined Ottoman-Venetian relations for far longer. It was confirmed and renewed without amendment in 1567 upon the accession of Sultan Selim II, suspended during the 1570–1573 war, and then renewed again.[51] The 1575 *ahdname*, given by Sultan Murad III, again quoted the entirety of the 1540 text, tacking on only one new article at the end. There would be no substantial changes made to the structure or content of the treaties until 1595. In the intervening fifty-five years, however, the maritime situation did change. There was no lack of piratical activity during the 1550s and 1560s, as the Ottoman fleets embarked on far-flung slave-raiding tours of enemy Christian coasts, conquered Tripoli in 1551, and unsuccessfully besieged Malta in 1565. However, in this period, attacks on Venetian ships and possessions were largely collateral damage, an unfortunate but predictable consequence of the chaos that accompanied large fleet movements and the irregulars who joined them. Ottoman naval commanders were thus ordered to keep their men in line, and whenever Venetian ships and men were taken, as they were in one incident near Alexandria in 1558, to promptly return them and punish those responsible.[52]

As a result, the Ottoman government began the regular practice, at the *bailo*'s request, of dispatching orders at the start of each sea season to the imperial admiral and to the commanders of the provincial naval squadrons and North African units that joined the main body of the fleet on campaign. On April 2, 1560, for example, the Porte sent orders to the *kapudan pasha* and the governors of Rhodes and Mytilene, urging them to ensure that the ships under their command not interfere with Venetian vessels or harm the merchants they carried, and not do any damage to Venetian coasts, islands, or subjects "in contravention of the imperial *ahdname*."[53]

It was not the imperial fleet but rather the local galley squadrons and naval irregulars based on strategic islands and coasts in the Aegean and along the Adriatic and Ionian Seas that were increasingly the source of friction with the Venetians. So long as they were occupied with missions from the imperial center or sailing with the combined navy, major incidents were comparatively infrequent, and when they did occur—in contrast with later years—the Ottoman government often knew the names and identities of the culprits, precisely because they were ship captains who drew state salaries. The former corsair admirals lauded by Mustafa Ali did indeed know when their captains turned to piracy.

Thus, on May 20, 1560, less than two months after dispatching orders to leave the Venetians in peace, the sultan sent a decree concerning the predations of two salaried *levend* captains based out of Aya Mavra fortress, Divane Nasuh Ali and Memi, who had seized a small Venetian ship, killed its captain, and sailed off with the cargo and crew. The goods were ordered returned, the captives found and freed, and the *levend* captains punished.[54] As the same sea season drew to a close that fall, the Porte issued orders concerning an attack on Venetian Crete, in which the *levend* captains Karaca Ali and Divane Yusuf raided a village with their three galliots and made off with two hundred captives. Afterward they sailed to Mytilene, where they were likely stationed, and tried to sell their catch to the governor, who was now ordered to turn over those captives who were verifiably Venetian to the *bailo*.[55]

These two incidents reflect several common features of anti-Venetian Ottoman piracy in the period and the Ottoman center's response to it. Encompassing ship-on-ship and amphibious slave raids, in both instances the central government was aware of the names of the accused captains before it dispatched its orders and, in the latter case, seemed to have already corralled the captives in anticipation of their return. Both decrees were instigated by Venetian petitions to the Porte, a pattern that would be repeated in nearly every such case, and in the latter instance, the Porte was explicitly abiding by the language of the 1540 *ahdname* that called for an investigation to determine Venetian subjecthood before turning over the captives to the *bailo*. In short, anti-Venetian Ottoman piracy was largely a problem of ship captains on the state payrolls freelancing before or after fleet maneuvers, and the Ottoman central government was capable of identifying the culprits and meting out punishment. All this changed in the aftermath of the 1570–1573 war with Venice over Cyprus.

Piracy was not a one-sided problem before the war for Cyprus, however. Although the Venetian government strove mightily to avoid provoking the Ottomans, Venetian subjects were occasionally implicated in pirate attacks and Venetian provincial officials, like their Ottoman counterparts, were frequently accused of turning a blind eye to, if not actively facilitating, piracy. This had been the case on Cyprus. Although Sultan Selim II coveted Cyprus even before he renewed the Venetian *ahdname* in 1567 and sought religious justification for breaking the pact from his chief jurist, the *şeyhülislam* Ebu Su'ud, Catholic corsairing provided an official, secular *casus belli*. The Venetians' failure to deny the Maltese and other corsairs access to Cypriot ports and provisions, indeed their failure to capture passing pirate (*harami*) ships whenever possible, was a clear breach of the *ahdname*, similar violations by Ottoman fortress commanders notwithstanding.[56]

When the Venetians finally decided to cut their losses and sue for peace in 1573, the *ahdname* of 1567 was reaffirmed, but tensions remained high along the shared Ottoman-Venetian maritime frontier.[57] Some *levends* found it difficult—whether for financial or ideological reasons, or both—to adjust to the return of peace and resisted the calls to discontinue raiding their erstwhile enemy.[58] Venetian forces thus remained on high alert and patrolled the Adriatic constantly for the decommissioned privateers whose war had not ended. In the spring of 1574, for example, a *levend* galliot intent on raiding islands subject to Venice encountered a Venetian galley patrol. Facing this superior force, the galliot made for land, coming ashore near Draç. The *levends* ran away, but the Venetians succeeded in capturing two of them and promptly turned them over to local Ottoman officials, scrupulously following the protocol prescribed in the *ahdname*. In response, the Ottoman administration ordered the castellan, the head of the guard, and the *kadi* in Draç to interrogate the men and find out who their comrades were, and then round them all up and send them to Istanbul for punishment. It reminded the recipients that "the pact (*ahd*) was renewed and peace restored," that *levends* no longer had permission to raid the Venetians, and that earlier orders to that effect should be respected. The decree concluded with warnings, doubtless unheeded, not to provision *levends* and to prevent them from equipping their ships.[59]

But too spirited a defense could lead to local conflict and a pattern of raids and reprisals that the distant governments of both sides were powerless to prevent. In a decree dated May 25, 1574, issued thirteen days after the aforementioned one, it was revealed that the doge had sent a letter to the Porte informing it that a Venetian galley captain had, in violation of the *ahdname*, taken a number of captives from the shore below Draç Castle. Perhaps this was the same Venetian galley that had successfully chased down the *levend* galliot before, venting its frustration on the *levend*s' home base, or, given the lag times in communication, the incident may very well have preceded the failed attack described above. The doge reported that the galley captain had been punished for his violation and the Ottoman captives had been freed. As the Ottoman central administration had clearly been unaware of this incident before, it now ordered the Elbasan *sancakbeyi* to investigate when the captives had initially been taken, confirm that they had in fact been released, and find out where they had gone.[60]

The doge's letter is indicative of the care with which Venice was trying to adhere to the *ahdname*'s requirements, as both sides gradually readjusted to peace. Both sultan and doge were anxious to defuse potential flare-ups of violence on the frontier. Cognizant of the likelihood of reprisals, the Ottoman decree closed with a reminder that the *levend*s were forbidden to attack the Venetians.[61]

However, Ottoman prescience had not been accompanied by a credible threat of force. Later that summer, *levend*s from Draç captured a Venetian galley in violation of the recent Ottoman orders. Once again, the government turned to the Elbasan *sancakbeyi* and ordered him to recover the galley and, in accordance with the doge's request, see to it that the ship was returned to Venice. The blame was laid firmly at the feet of the leaders on the border, that is, the local officials in Draç who had received the initial decree several months previously, along with others who had a stake in the *levend*s' projects. Evidently these men had taken it upon themselves to avenge the earlier Venetian galley's intrusion, and the situation had escalated. This time it was left to the Elbasan *sancakbeyi* to make clear to the officials in his district that violations of the peace with the Venetians would not be tolerated. It was decreed that captains who equipped galliots for raids against the Venetians would be arrested and sent chained together to Istanbul for execution while their *levend* crews would be condemned to the oar.[62] Sentencing pirates to life on the galleys had a certain poetic justice and, regardless of whether it was an effective deterrent, promised to help relieve the chronic shortage of oarsmen that the Ottoman navy had suffered since the defeat at Lepanto.

The piracy epidemic of 1574 was not limited to the Adriatic, and as we have seen Ottoman subjects also suffered greatly from *levend* attacks. The Ottoman government did not need to be petitioned by the Venetian *bailo* to recognize that the maritime security situation remained unacceptably unstable. On July 7, 1574, the Porte dispatched a decree to Alaüddin

Bey, *sancakbeyi* of Üsküp (present-day Skopje in Macedonia) and commander of the Ottoman forces responsible for the defense of the Lepanto-side of the Morea, that neatly summed up the problem:

> When the *kadi*s and *bey*s on the Mediterranean coasts were ordered not to give provisions to the pirate *levend* frigates (*harami firkate levendlerine*) and to capture them when they came ashore, the aforementioned persisted in corruption, continually raiding [our] tax-paying subjects (*haracgüzar*) and the subjects of the islands belonging to Venice and sacking merchant ships. Since it has been learned that they captured a Venetian oil ship and brought it to Preveza and the *bey*s and *kadi*s and castellans and irregular commanders took shares in the despoliation and that many provincial soldiers have been guiding [them] and receiving stolen goods, they are to be captured when they come ashore for water and grain; the captains are to be punished and their men clapped in chains.[63]

Alaüddin Bey was to ensure that the fortress commanders and their men no longer provision the pirates or purchase stolen cargoes, and he was ordered to record the names of all those who did not obey. The decree, more concerned with the insubordination of the Ottoman frontier government and its soldiery than the actual piracy, nevertheless mirrored the form and tone of orders sent out at the request of the Venetian *bailo* in response to similar incidents, and it anticipated the problems the center would have with the periphery regarding piracy for the next century. As the capacity of the Ottoman navy declined and attentions turned to successive land wars after 1578, enforcement of such decrees—especially along the Adriatic-Ionian frontier and in North Africa—became increasingly difficult, but the Ottomans and Venetians continued to cooperate to effect the return of cargo and captives when possible and to provide restitution when it was not.

In the mid-1570s, however, piracy and border raiding were an additional complication to a still lingering issue from the war. During the conquest of Cyprus, the Ottomans had taken a large number of high-value Venetian prisoners of war and enslaved an enormous part of the island's population. Unlike in 1503, the Ottomans had no intention of unilaterally freeing any of these captives. The Cypriots taken during the war would remain slaves, but what of the "Venetian" Venetians? Shortly after the end of hostilities, the Sublime Porte and the Signoria began arranging prisoner swaps, a process which continued for several years. However, many Venetian nobles were in private hands, and their owners expected ransoms, as did those Venetians holding Ottoman prisoners. Given that mutual enslavement was prohibited in the *ahdname*s, and that captives taken by pirates after the war ended were being returned as a matter of course, it was determined that clarification of the rules was necessary.

The result was the only new article in the *ahdname* of 1575. Issued upon the accession of Sultan Murad III, it stated, "On the matter of captives taken in contravention of the treaty before and after the hostilities, it shall be carried out in accordance with the conditions expressed in the treaties, but on the matter of captives taken from the two sides during the hostilities, that article is not in force; slave owners are free to choose if they wish to release them in exchange for ransom or if they want they can use them and no one may prevent or prohibit this."[64] The great numbers of captives taken during the war and the rash of illegal enslavement of Venetians that had begun before 1570 and persisted after 1573 made the article necessary. Nevertheless, it was no simple matter to differentiate between legally and illegally enslaved Venetians so soon after the war.

The investigations prescribed in the *ahdname*s since 1540 took on added meaning after 1573, since Ottoman officials would have to determine not only whether contested captives were Venetian, but when they had been taken. Only in 1595, when twenty-two years had passed since the end of the war, was the clause and the investigation requirement officially dropped, though it fell into desuetude earlier. In the meantime, the Ottoman and Venetian governments stuck to the pattern when pirates struck: the Venetian *bailo* would submit a petition describing the incident and requesting the return of plundered goods and captives and the punishment of the culprits. The Porte would duly order that the *ahdname* be respected, the goods returned, the captives found, the culprits punished, and that such acts be prevented in the future.

In 1578, for example, the *bailo* submitted a petition to the *divan* reporting that two *levend* galliots based at Aya Mavra and equipped at Angilikasrı—suggesting the complicity of the often piracy-inclined *sancakbeyi* of Karlieli—had captured some of the small boats plying the waters around the Venetian Ionian islands of Cephalonia and Zante and taken prisoners; now six of the Venetian captives were being employed as galley slaves in Lepanto. The Venetian petition resulted in two decrees: one to the *sancakbeyi* of Karlieli prohibiting *levend* attacks on Venetian subjects, and the other to the *sancakbeyi* of Inebahtı (Lepanto) ordering him to investigate and free the six unfortunate oarsmen if they were truly Venetian subjects.[65]

Even as the Ottomans were increasingly ineffective at restraining their frontier naval forces as required in the *ahdname*s, Venetian attacks on Ottoman subjects and ships that were perceived to be unprovoked drew a sharp reaction from Istanbul and unsubtle threats of harsh reprisals. After Venetian ships landed on the coastline of the *sancak* of Herzegovina in

1583 and disembarked soldiers who pillaged and made off with captives, the Porte sent along a list of the names of the abducted and demanded that Venice return them and their possessions and punish those responsible. Such incidents, the letter noted, would lead to a breach in the *ahdname* and retaliation.[66]

In another well-known case, Gabriele Emo, a Venetian galley commander patrolling for pirates, captured an Ottoman ship near Cephalonia in 1584 that was carrying Ramazanpaşazade Mehmed Bey of Jerba, son of the recently deceased governor of Tripoli, and his mother back to Istanbul. Thinking them pirates, the Venetians cut down nearly all those they encountered, the young man and his mother included, and took the ship as a prize. Emo would pay dearly for his zeal. Returning the ship and its cargo was not enough to staunch Istanbul's growing anger over the incident, and Emo was put on trial and executed for his crimes the following year, a sacrifice on the altar of maintaining good relations with the Ottomans. This, and substantial cash payments, satisfied the Sublime Porte. In North Africa, however, the memory of what had happened to Mehmed Bey and his mother lived on—decades later, corsairs in Tunis were still citing the incident as an example of Venetian perfidy and brutality and a justification for their own bellicose attitude toward the Venetians they encountered.[67]

The predations of Uskok corsairs also frequently excited Ottoman passions. Because the Uskoks had to cross Venetian territory to raid the Ottomans, and because the Venetians claimed sovereignty in their "gulf," the Ottomans held them responsible for coastal security and accused them of complicity if they failed to prevent attacks.[68] Indeed, in the 1590s the Ottomans interpreted the *ahdname* provisions regarding restitution to mean that the Venetians were financially responsible for damages caused by the Uskoks and supported Ottoman merchants' claims against the *bailo*.[69] This changed by 1605, however, when the Ottoman government decided that only the Habsburg government, with which it had been at war since 1593, should be held responsible for Uskok attacks, not Venice.[70]

In sum, although the core content of the treaties remained fairly stable after the 1520s, there was significant flexibility in interpretation as both sides reacted to changing circumstances. The declining stability of the Adriatic-Ionian region and the extension of Ottoman sovereignty to North Africa were only part of the story of the second half of the sixteenth century. The rise of Catholic corsairing, the growth of trade with western Europe, and with it the expansion of the *ahdname* regime to France and England had a dramatic impact on the shape of Mediterranean piracy and the conduct of relations.

THE *AHDNAMES* COME OF AGE

Although France did not receive its first *ahdname* until 1569, it was by then hardly a newcomer in the Levant trade. With the Ottoman conquest of Egypt in 1517, the trading privileges the French had enjoyed there under the Mamluks were confirmed, and France continued to operate on this basis. King François I's ambitions in Italy brought him into conflict with the Habsburgs under Charles V, and he was defeated and captured at the Battle of Pavia in 1525. He would find a ready ally in Sultan Süleyman, whose victories in Hungary the following year put the Ottomans and Habsburgs on a collision course on land as well as at sea. Early in 1535, Francois dispatched an ambassador, Jean de la Foret, to Istanbul. The commercial treaty he concluded in 1536 with the grand vizier Ibrahim Pasha was never ratified, but the resulting Franco-Ottoman alliance proved to be an enduring cornerstone in the foreign policy of both powers; henceforth there was almost always a French ambassador in the Ottoman capital. In the short term, the alliance led to military cooperation: in 1543, Ottoman and French naval forces conducted joint maneuvers in the western Mediterranean and besieged Nice (then part of the Duchy of Savoy), after which the Ottoman fleet overwintered in Toulon.[71] Over the longer term, the relationship led to increased trade, and France sought to obtain from Süleyman's son and successor an *ahdname* that would formalize the rights of French merchants and permit them to trade under their own flag throughout the sultan's domains.

The resulting *ahdname* of 1569 borrowed heavily from that of the Venetians while leaving out the portions that did not apply to a friendly power that was not also a neighbor. It granted them the same customs rates, 5 percent, and promised protection from piracy and enslavement in words nearly identical to those in the relevant clause of the 1540 Venetian *ahdname*. This document, in turn, would serve as the model for the next expansion of the *ahdname* regime. When England obtained its first *ahdname* in 1580, it was an almost verbatim copy of the French *ahdname*.[72]

France and Venice had fought hard to prevent the English from gaining admittance to their exclusive club. Up until the mid-sixteenth century, Venice had supplied the north with nearly all the dried fruits, spices, silks, and wines that it had required, and state-sponsored merchant galleys had made regular voyages to England and the Netherlands. The Ottoman threat forced the redirection of Venetian maritime resources, however, and the English began making occasional forays into the Mediterranean to meet their needs. But it was the disruption caused by the war for Cyprus which flung open the doors to the Levant and the Mediterranean carrying trade. Both the French and the English took advantage of the gap left by the Venetians during the war, but the English were forced to trade under the French flag, for France had won a concession in its *ahdname* requiring any other enemy infidels besides Venetians wishing to trade in Ottoman domains to do so under French protection. This meant both prestige and profit, through the payment of consulage dues, for the French. Thus, when William Harbourne arrived in Istanbul in 1578 intent on securing an *ahdname* for the English, the Venetians fought to keep out a dangerous competitor and the French fought to keep them under their protection. They ultimately failed, in part because of England's potential as an ally in any renewed fight against Spain and because of the militarily useful materials like lead and tin that the English could provide the Ottomans. A similar conflict would be repeated a generation later with the Dutch, who traded variously under English or French protection and who promised further unwelcome competition in the diplomatic quarter of Pera, but who prevailed for similar reasons in their efforts to obtain an *ahdname* in 1612.[73]

The English and the Dutch rapidly came to take control of much of the Mediterranean carrying trade, elbowing out Venetian shipping along the routes they had long controlled and taking on Ottoman merchants' freight as well. This they did through cheaper rates, faster service, innovative business arrangements, and, above all, through violence. That Braudel's coinage for their penetration of the Mediterranean from the 1580s, the "Northern Invasion," has proven so popular among historians reflects the jarring reality of their arrival and rapid rise to dominance.[74] The English and the Dutch came in square-rigged sailing ships, which carried more cargo and more guns than anything operating in the Mediterranean at the time. The merchant vessels the Northerners encountered en route to their destinations were detained, despoiled, and often destroyed.[75]

These tactics were brutally effective, and by the turn of the century, Venetian and Ottoman merchants alike increasingly chose to ship their freight on English and Dutch bottoms, which could promise a safer passage at lower insurance rates, in part because they themselves were among the greatest threats to Venetian shipping. In few places was the impact of the English invasion more keenly felt than on the Ionian island of Zante, which supplied the English market with the much-prized little raisins known erroneously as currants, and in 1603 its Venetian governor, Maffio Michiel, summed up the grave situation in a letter to the Senate:

> The English are becoming absolute masters of these waters; for apart from rapine and robbery perpetrated daily on all sorts of vessels, and more especially upon those of your Serenity's subjects, they are utterly supplanting your subjects in

the carrying trade, weakening your customs and ruining the merchant service, as your Excellencies must be well aware. The English are not satisfied with having absorbed Venetian trade in the West entirely, but are devoting themselves to a similar object in the Levant. They trade in their own ships to the ports of Alexandria, Alexandretta, and Smyrna and other Turkish cities in Asia Minor, and in the Archipelago, where our ships only used to trade, to the great benefit of the State and of private individuals. All this merchandise they carry to these ports and make bargains for return cargoes without paying any customs dues above the ordinary, which is very light.[76]

English piracy did not go unnoticed in Istanbul either. It led to frequent complaints and occasional reprisals against English merchants, but the English privileges were never revoked as a result.[77] In part this was because English piracy, at least in the eastern half of the Mediterranean, was piracy in its purest form: nonideological, opportunistic business. It damaged the reputation of the English in Istanbul, but their representatives could and did outwardly repudiate it, while anti-Catholic solidarity still bought them goodwill in some quarters. In contrast, Florentine efforts to obtain an *ahdname* in 1598 fell through over the corsairing activities of the Tuscan dukes, who sponsored the Knights of Saint Stephen. Sultan Mehmed III's demand that Tuscan corsairing cease as a precondition for further negotiations proved unacceptable, as too much of the Grand Duke's symbolic capital was invested in the legitimacy obtained from despoiling and enslaving "Turks."[78] Ironically, Tuscan corsairing was often subcontracted to English ships and English mariners, who happily targeted Ottoman Christians as well in spite of their commissions.[79]

However, it was not English or Dutch piracy that affected the content of the *ahdname*s around the turn of the seventeenth century so much as that emanating from North Africa, though English and Dutch renegades contributed greatly to its intensification in the first decade of the seventeenth century. North African piracy increased shortly after the Ottoman reconquest of Tunis in 1574, aided by sharply decreased interest from the Ottoman center in North African affairs. France was supposedly protected under its *ahdname* from such attacks, and so when several French ships were captured by corsairs based out of Tunis and Tripoli in 1576, it complained to the Porte, which decreed that French captives should be freed and the treaty with France respected.[80] Similar orders were sent again to Algiers in July of 1580,[81] April of 1582,[82] March of 1586,[83] and June of 1591.[84]

Nevertheless, the Porte's intervention was mostly limited to cases involving the capture of important personages, whose release from North Africa it could demand by name. The Ottoman government did on occasion send out proactive decrees, such as one dispatched to Algiers, Tunis, and Tripoli in February 1588 that forbade attacks on the ships of Venice, England, France, and Dubrovnik and the enslavement of their subjects. In fact, the recipients were ordered to *protect* the merchants of these powers, in accordance with their *ahdname*s.[85] It is unclear, however, whether such orders—meant to shore up the authority of the *ahdname*s between re-issues—had any effect.

Local representation, however, could help with both raid and trade. The English sought and obtained the right to open consulates in the North African ports in their 1580 *ahdname*, and the French, not to be left out, acquired the same right the following year.[86] The English, French, and Dutch sailing to the eastern half of the Mediterranean had no choice but to transit Algiers and Tunis. Besides protection from corsairs, they required safe harbors for watering and victualing and they saw valuable opportunities for trade in North Africa. Venice, unlike its rivals, never sent consuls to Algiers or Tunis; its eastern trade routes did not pass those cities and their markets offered little to entice Venetian merchants.

The rise of North African piracy impacted the content of the Venetian *ahdname* and those of the other treaty-protected powers when they were renewed by the new Sultan Mehmed III beginning in 1595. The 1595 Venetian *ahdname* marked a new step in the development of the form, abandoning the practice of quoting the 1540 *ahdname* in favor of a fresh text, though one that still preserved much of the wording and content of the earlier treaties. The essence of the anti-piracy clauses that had matured in the 1540 version was carried over, but the sections regarding illegal enslavement underwent several critical changes. The new clause simplified and consolidated the earlier, separate provisions that touched on slavery and expanded their coverage:

> If the *levend* galliots of the Maghreb (i.e., North Africa) and the *korsan* caïques of other places go by sea, or if other thieves go by land, and raid the islands and other places subject to Venice and capture their people and take them and sell them in Rumelia or Anatolia or in the Maghreb or in other places, or if they use them themselves; that sort of slave, in whoever's possession he is found, shall be taken from them without delay and be turned over to the Venetian Senate's *bailo*s or their deputies or their agents and those pirate *levend*s shall be captured and strongly punished and if that slave became Muslim he shall be emancipated and freed.[87]

Besides integrating the earlier provisions, the new version now specifically recognized the North African port cities as one of the chief sources of illegal raiding. It also marked the first time that the word *korsan* appeared in the *ahdname*s, reflecting the complicated relationship the Ottoman center had with its nominal North African provinces and Adriatic-Ionian periphery, as well as the proliferation of third-party piracy, especially that of the English. The treaty now recognized that the *levend/korsan* of North Africa and elsewhere could be corsairs, insofar as they were openly supported by their local governments, and still be pirates by the standards of the respective imperial centers.

Whereas the language of the original anti-slave-raiding clause of 1521 had reflected Venice's previous status as the holder of far more of the Aegean's real estate and identified the primary raiders as errant irregulars from the fleet, the new version mentioned "other places" beyond just islands. This meaning had long been assumed but was now made explicit. Likewise, the list of places where Venetian captives might be sold was expanded to include North Africa along with Anatolia and Rumelia and, again, "other places," making it clear that there were absolutely no exceptions to the rule that enslaved Venetians must be found and freed. It also added the possibility that pirates might keep captives for themselves, whether for use as oarsmen, personal slaves, or for ransoming. The new language thus closed every potential loophole.

More importantly, the procedures for returning Venetian captives were simplified. Gone was the tortured language about investigations to verify Venetian subjecthood. Rather, slaves would be located wherever they were held, released, and turned over to the relevant Venetian authorities or those deputized to receive them as soon as possible, unless they had converted. The word order regarding conversion was reversed, so it no longer implied that this was the most likely outcome of illegal capture. All this was followed by a further provision stating that the escape of Venetians enslaved in contravention of the treaty would not be viewed as a breach of the peace.

Decades of amphibious raids, disorder on the frontiers, and the rising threat from North Africa demanded revision of the language and expansion of the content, but as with every previous iteration of the *ahdname*, the adjustments were the result of actual experience and negotiation. The Venetians themselves were the party most competent to identify Venetian slaves, not the Porte, and it made no sense to send captives liberated from, for example, the ports of the Morea to Istanbul for careful examination before turning them over to the *bailo* when they could simply be sent home. The experience of resolving dozens of such cases determined the next step in the evolution of the treaty language, while the sultanic decrees sent out over the years in response to them comprised the legal basis for the changes. The precedent-based origins of the new form of the law were spelled out in the treaty itself. The 1595 *ahdname* declared that, as imperial decrees had previously been issued concerning the punishment of those who violated the peace by enslaving Venetians, "it shall be dealt with as it was by the understanding of those imperial decrees."[88] Sultanic law, *kanun*, was both the foundation and the legal glue of the *ahdname*s.

The French *ahdname* of 1597 adopted the same language regarding enslavement and North Africa. However, there were key differences. It forbade the taking of "enemy" goods from French ships. This was a direct reference to one of the major issues concerning privateering and merchant shipping. Going back to the *Consolato del Mare*, the great medieval compendium of Mediterranean maritime customary law, it was permissible for corsairs to remove the goods belonging to enemies from friendly or neutral ships so long as they paid the freight. North African corsairs did this. So too did the Maltese, who claimed the right to seize the goods of "Turks and Jews" from Christian ships. The *ahdname* attempted to exempt the French from this practice, much as the Venetians attempted to do vis-à-vis Malta. Likewise, the *ahdname* held that French traveling on enemy ships could not be enslaved, but that protection did not apply to those caught in the act of piracy/corsairing, meaning that the many French sailing under Maltese colors could be legally enslaved.[89]

The corsairs of North Africa continued to follow the customary practice, however, removing "enemy" goods from French ships even when they declined to seize the ship itself, and like the Maltese, they often compelled French crews to admit that their cargoes belonged to enemies, giving them the necessary pretext to seize the goods.[90] Consequently, contending with North Africa occupied a growing portion of the French ambassador's time. Of the 179 Ottoman documents issued at the request of François Savary de Brèves between 1592 and 1604, 158 were addressed to particular Ottoman governors or *kadi*s, and nearly half of those were dispatched to North Africa: 39 to Algiers, 24 to Tunis, and 10 to Tripoli.[91]

Thus, the French, who already automatically enjoyed all privileges granted to the Venetians, requested and received a new addition to their *ahdname* when it was renewed in 1604. Now they too had enshrined in their *ahdname* an explicit right to defend themselves against North African corsairs.[92] As for the Venetians, their treaty text concerning piracy and slavery was, by 1595, as comprehensive as could be hoped for, and further additions within the treaty would only muddy the waters.[93] Renewals of the Venetian *ahdname* in 1604, 1619, 1625, and 1641 had little more than the names and dates changed from the 1595 version.[94] After 1595, modifications to and new interpretations of Ottoman-Venetian anti-piracy policy, beyond case-specific orders, were elaborated through dedicated sultanic edicts (*nişan*). These were typically issued at the request of the *bailo* in Istanbul and were usually the product of some prior negotiation. Before the 1595 *ahdname*, they recalibrated procedures between treaty issues; after 1595 they obviated the need to amend the treaty text itself. In August 1595, for example, several months before the new *ahdname* was granted, a spate of attacks in the Morea spurred the *bailo* to request action and so, in addition to a series of case-specific orders sent to the Morea, the Porte disseminated a *nişan* across the empire that firmly established the new policy that Venetian slaves must be freed wherever they were and those who had not converted should be turned over to the nearest appropriate representatives of Venice.[95] This *nişan* was then specifically referenced as a binding source of law within the 1595 *ahdname*.

In March 1605, four months after the *ahdname* was next renewed, Sultan Ahmed I dispatched a wide-ranging anti-piracy *nişan* that responded to some of the present issues with specificity in areas where the treaty itself did so only generally. Produced in response to a petition from the *bailo*, the decree opened by noting that both Muslim *levend*s and enemy infidel pirates had been staging attacks at sea and within ports on Venetian merchant ships sailing for the Ottoman Empire. The sultan confirmed that the Ottoman Empire was responsible for Venetian losses in the areas under Ottoman jurisdiction, whether they were caused by (Ottoman) Muslim or foreign Christian pirates. Ottoman authorities were expected to locate and return stolen goods, and if Ottoman subjects bought anything from the "corsair rebels" (*korsan eşkiyasından*), the goods or slaves would be confiscated regardless of whether they claimed to have paid for them "with our own money."[96]

This meant that even if the goods had changed hands multiple times, they would still be taken from whoever held them without compensation. In contrast with the *ahdname*, the *nişan* singled out several maritime problem areas, ordering the fortress commander of Aya Mavra, among others, not to admit pirate ships nor purchase stolen merchandise and to prevent others from doing so. The *nişan* would be unlikely to have much deterrent effect, considering Aya Mavra was perhaps the most consistent violator of the *ahdname* outside North Africa, but it did lay the legal groundwork for Ottoman administrators' efforts to locate stolen goods after successful attacks.[97] By this point, the sultan's pronouncements about what would happen after attacks had taken on much greater importance than the empty promises that the Venetians would be protected from them. The prohibition of piracy was more aspirational than enforceable, but the procedures for responding to attacks, though subject to local contestation, were often followed, making them the area of greatest change in these texts.

Decrees from the sultan and less compromised administrators on the ground could still get results, but total success was often elusive, especially as the "Long War" and the Celali revolts dragged on through the first decade of the seventeenth century. For example, after a Venetian galley was captured at Draç in 1594, the *bailo* Marco Venier petitioned the Porte as usual and a messenger was dispatched with orders to Draç to resolve the situation. The person tasked with executing the orders was Hamza Bey, the former *sancakbeyi* of Elbasan (the central Albanian district that included Draç) and still its military administrator. Hamza Bey successfully rescued the galley's captain, a Venetian nobleman, and the nobleman's two sons and sent the four to the fortress of Modon in the Morea, which was evidently a more secure location than hostile Draç for the former captives to await transport home. Likewise, Hamza Bey recovered fourteen cannons from the galley and these too were sent to Modon, where they awaited the Venetians below the fortress walls.

However, despite the standing orders to free Venetian captives without ransom, most of the Venetians taken from the galley had been purchased by men of the town, some of whom held military positions—their names were known to both the Ottomans and Venetians—and Venice quickly ransomed twelve of these directly from their captors. It is unclear whether Hamza had been unable or unwilling to secure their release without payment, but where they were being held was certainly not a secret. As a result, Istanbul ordered Hamza Bey to reimburse the Venetians' representatives for the total ransom they had paid. As for the men responsible for the piratical attack, they had been positively identified as irregulars employed in the fortress at Draç. The ringleaders, the irregular commander Mustafa and soldiers named Hüseyin, Uzun Mustafa, and Hano, had already been implicated in the murder of a visiting Ragusan priest and various previous piracies, but they had escaped capture and months later had still not been apprehended. It is unclear how hard local officials were trying to find them.[98]

A little more than a decade later, the situation in the Adriatic was far less stable and outcomes like that achieved by Hamza far more difficult. In 1605, a coalition of pirates working in concert with administrators in Draç captured a Venetian barque laden with cotton. The names of the pirate captains implicated in the attack give some indication of the geographic medley that had lately been drawn to the chum-filled waters of the Adriatic: Cezayirli ("Algerian") Cafer Reis, Arabacı Hüseyin, Tunuslu ("Tunisian") Hasan, Mehmed Reis, Novalı ("from Nova") Umuroğulları Hasan, and a Mustafa for good measure. Killing some of the Venetian crew and enslaving the rest, they towed the ship back to Draç, where officers from the fortress helped them plunder cargo worth more than 200,000 pieces of gold. Many of the Venetian captives were quickly ransomed, just as had happened in the incident described above. Likewise, an official, Ali Kethüda, was sent from the seat of the provincial government to confiscate the stolen cargo and arrest and punish the pirates and the administrators who supported them.

The similarities ended there, however. Ali Kethüda did not come with sufficient backup for his task, and the group he had come to Draç to arrest joined together and murdered the unfortunate man, then rapidly sold off the remaining slaves and goods they held from the Venetian barque while they still could. The *sancakbeyi* of Avlonya was ordered to do what Ali Kethüda could not and bring the perpetrators to justice, and an official was dispatched from the center to ensure adequate force was brought to bear this time.[99] Nevertheless, the incident was emblematic of how decrees and good intentions no longer sufficed to right piratical wrongs and how collaboration with North Africa and a decade of war had emboldened local pirates and administrators.

Venetian shipping in and around the Morea and the Adriatic was a favored target of English and North African piracy, and pirates developed close relationships with local Ottoman administrators, to whom they fenced their booty. Although the Ottoman central government ordered that these pirates be captured whenever possible, it was more concerned with closing the markets for stolen goods. In the summer of 1605, it sent a list of names, produced through Venetian intelligence, of Ottoman officials who were collaborating with English pirates in the Morea to the *sancakbeyi* and *kadi* and ordered them to apprehend the accused and punish them in such a way that they would serve as an example for other Ottoman subjects.[100] Similar orders were dispatched regarding North Africa–based pirates, who found the Morea to be an equally convenient place to dispose of stolen goods.[101]

Yet the extent of the pirate cooperation extended beyond the Morea and crossed religious and political boundaries in sometimes surprising ways, further complicating Ottoman efforts to prevent it. English pirates increasingly worked together with North African administrators to avoid the long arm of the Ottoman central bureaucracy, which was largely neutered there. In 1607, English pirates captured a Venetian ship and took it to Tunis, where they sold the Venetian passengers and crew into slavery. This was an unambiguous violation of the *ahdname*s on the part of both the English and the Tunisians, but it was rather more difficult to retrieve Venetian captives from Tunis than from the Morea. The Porte nevertheless ordered the Tunisian authorities to find the Venetian slaves, return their goods, and send them home.[102]

Although failure typically generated the more robust paper trail, it is important to note that there were success stories in both North Africa and the Morea. In February 1601, for example, two English pirate vessels captured a Venetian ship in Spanish waters, dumped its captain and crew with the ship's boat on Mallorca and brought it to Algiers, claiming it was a Spanish ship. As the English began unloading their prize, however, the Venetian master and crew arrived in the port. The Algerian officials realized they had been deceived and "seeing the trick, resolved to restore the ship." But the English pirates chose to burn it instead. Some of the pirates were imprisoned, and the officials decided to give one of the English pirate ships to the Venetian master as restitution. The matter ultimately got transferred to Istanbul, where the English and Venetian ambassadors fought over the issue, but in the end, decrees were sent in May upholding the Algerians' initial decision to restore the goods and turn over one of the pirates' ships to the Venetian captain.[103] In another instance, English pirates brought a Venetian ship with a cargo of wood into the Morean port of Modon in April 1603, looking for buyers. Seeing the Venetian markings on the cargo, local officials refused, saying they would have purchased it if it had been Spanish. Instead, the Ottoman authorities arrested the English pirates and turned them over to the Venetian governor of Zante, Maffio Michiel. Some of the pirates who had escaped Modon were captured separately by the Venetians and were condemned to death in late May. Those who were turned over by the Ottomans, including the English captain, were held for some time in Zante, after the *sancakbeyi* of the Morea began demanding that the pirates be returned to him for further examination; the Venetians suspected that this was a ploy to free the English pirates in exchange for a fat bribe. Ultimately, Venetian diplomacy in the capital convinced him to relent and he dropped his demands, writing to Michiel to do as he saw fit. The remaining pirates were hanged on September 11, 1604, as their compatriots had been, their bodies left to swing from the castle in sight of town and port to be consumed, by the birds and the elements, to serve as a warning to others.[104] Stories such as these tend to be obscured in a documentary record that preserves more evidence of clashes than cooperation, but the system worked more often than not.

CONCLUSION

The changing nature of maritime violence between the fifteenth and seventeenth centuries was reflected in the *ahdname*s granted to Venice. Repositories of interstate law grounded in Mediterranean custom as well as the legal practice of both sides, the *ahdname*s not only governed the relationship between the Ottomans and their treaty partners, they defined the form and the language of the Ottoman center's relationship with its own provinces. When violations occurred, as they often did toward the end of the sixteenth century, Istanbul responded with principled outrage and blasts of decrees. These were, it is true, issued at the behest of the powers affected by piracy in Ottoman waters, but when the orders of the sultan were ignored or flagrantly disobeyed, the fates of captives and cargoes became intertwined with the internal struggles of empire and thus of far greater concern to the capital. Because the *ahdname*s were part of the sultanic *kanun*, the imperial law governing the Ottoman Empire, they were Ottoman law as much as they were interstate law and the failure to observe their provisions was no less serious a challenge to the sultan's authority than any other.

The expansion of the *ahdname* regime in the second half of the sixteenth century was soon followed by developments that undermined the core promises of safety, security, and freedom of movement on which they were founded. The rise of North African corsairing and "Northern" piracy, the latter often in the guise of the former, stretched the *ahdname*s to the breaking point. If Algiers, Tunis, and Tripoli were Ottoman, and the *ahdname*s' anti-piracy provisions were not observed there, what did this mean for the regime as a whole? The treaties provided some recourse, permitting their recipients to defend themselves and punish pirates as necessary, but this was a half solution. The corsairs threatened to drive an irreparable wedge between North Africa and Istanbul, if not between the sultan and his friends.

For Venice, the situation was especially vexing. Unlike their recently arrived Atlantic rivals, Venetian merchants did not need to frequent North African ports to pursue their trade in the Ottoman Mediterranean, nor could they bond over or profit from a shared enmity with Spain, as the English and Dutch might. It was demobilized English and Dutch privateers who introduced the latest sailing technology to Algiers and Tunis when they transferred their bases of operations against Spain there in the first decade of the seventeenth century, increasing the range and enhancing the prowess of the ports' corsairs immeasurably.[105]

The diplomatic and commercial infrastructure the French, English, and Dutch built in North Africa permitted first informal negotiations over navigation rights and the fate of their nation's captives and, ultimately, the conclusion of formal peace treaties with Algiers, Tunis, and Tripoli. In contrast, the Serenissima could not and would not negotiate directly with North Africa. Deeply invested in preserving peaceful relations with its larger, more powerful neighbor, Venice sought instead to work within the legal and diplomatic framework that Venetian and Ottoman administrators had painstakingly built over the previous centuries and see the implications of Ottoman sovereignty fully realized in North Africa. In this, the Venetians would be consistently frustrated. The causes and consequences of these developments, for Istanbul, North Africa, and the shape of the Ottoman Mediterranean, are the subject of Chapter 4.

CHAPTER FOUR

Diplomatic Divergence

Giovanni Battista Salvago probably knew his mission was doomed long before the members of the Tunisian ruling council threatened to burn him alive, but if there had been any lingering doubts, the bellicose posturing of the men with whom he had been sent to negotiate rapidly dispelled them. Salvago, an Istanbul-based Venetian dragoman, had been dispatched to Algiers and Tunis in 1625 to coordinate the release of hundreds of Venetian subjects taken captive the previous year. Accompanied by a janissary and another Ottoman envoy bearing Ottoman imperial decrees and letters ordering their recipients to cooperate with him, Salvago had arrived in North Africa to a welcome quite different from the one he had expected. Events leading up to Salvago's star-crossed voyage and in its aftermath mark a critical moment in the shared histories of Istanbul, Venice, North Africa, and Northwest Europe which would set them all on different courses, leaving Venice diplomatically isolated and dependent on Istanbul, and Algiers and Tunis openly declaring war and making peace of their own accord.

The story of Salvago's mission begins not in Tunis, but in the small Adriatic port-town of Nova, or Castelnuovo (present-day Herceg Novi in Montenegro). In 1624, the leading men of the town dispatched letters, hand-delivered by their emissaries, to the corsairing leadership in Tunis and Algiers with a proposal: to conduct an expedition that spring against the nearby Venetian coastal town of Perast, located only thirty kilometers away from Nova inside the Bay of Kotor. The residents of Nova and Perast had been trading raids and reprisals for years, part of a wider pattern of small-scale piratical violence and banditry common along the Adriatic frontiers.[1] After the most recent raid ascribed to the Perastini, the notables of Nova decided to enlist the corsairs of Algiers and Tunis in their feud. With the corsairs' help, they could deliver a devastating blow to their neighbors and enrich themselves in the process.[2]

As for the corsairs, this formal invitation—not to mention their perennial hatred of Venice, nourished by the Venetians' merciless execution of their captured comrades—was more than adequate justification for embarking on an Adriatic cruise with the advent of the sea season. In late June 1624, a thirteen-ship fleet from Algiers and Tunis arrived in the Adriatic and rendezvoused with pilots and fighting men from Nova. Landing at Perast, the raiders ransacked the town and returned to their vessels with 443 captives, mostly women and children, and large quantities of goods and cash. Their primary mission accomplished, the galliots disembarked their local partners with their share of the booty and captives in Nova, and then headed south to raid the Venetian Ionian Islands.

At Corfu, the corsairs seized thirteen women and three men and captured a number of merchant ships plying the straits. At Paxos and Antipaxos, they carried off 264 captives.[3] The corsairs then sacked Cephalonia, laying waste to the island. There a Venetian relief force found the North Africans, who promptly weighed anchor and escaped unharmed. More than seven hundred Venetian subjects were captured on the cruise, most of whom were sold into slavery in Algiers and Tunis.[4] Disease and privation would claim nearly a third within a year.[5]

That peacetime raid, and the involvement of local Ottoman officials in its planning and execution, led to outrage in Venice and Istanbul. But another North African attack on the opposite end of the Ottoman Mediterranean a little over a month earlier had been even more shocking to Ottoman authorities. In May 1624, five bertons—three-masted broadside sailing ships—sailed east for Iskenderun, stopping along the way to burn two Venetian ships in the Cypriot port of Larnaca. Located in the armpit of the Mediterranean, Iskenderun, known to Europeans as Alexandretta or Scanderoon, was a miserable place—hot, humid, malarial, underdeveloped, and undefended—but it was also the outlet for the enormously important inland trading city of Aleppo. Silk, cotton, finished cloths, tobacco, spices, and numerous other goods of distant and local origin passed through Iskenderun on their way to or from European markets.[6]

The Syrian coast had long been a popular hunting ground for corsairs, who might loiter close to shore and pick off ships as they approached or departed. Over the previous thirty years, Aleppo's official outlet had repeatedly been moved from Syrian Tripoli to Iskenderun and back again, depending on which area pirates were favoring. In 1609, for example, the port of Aleppo was switched to Syrian Tripoli after the Venetians suffered severe losses at Iskenderun, but because European merchants preferred Iskenderun for the shorter, two- to three-day camel trek to Aleppo and the absence of Tripoli's extortionate powerbrokers, many continued to use it. It was formally redesignated Aleppo's port in 1613.[7] In 1624, however, the North African corsairs did not stand off close to shore and wait for the prizes to come to them. Instead, they headed straight for the landing stage and sacked the town itself. They burned the Ottoman customs house to the ground, looted the warehouses of the European merchants, and plundered the ships anchored in the harbor. Ottoman customs officials in Iskenderun, reporting the event to their superiors, employed the language of natural disaster to describe the raid, an inscrutable act of God for which there had been neither warning nor explanation.[8] The corsairs tarried at Iskenderun for the next eight days before leaving with prodigious English, French, and Dutch booty. The damages inflicted on European shipping were estimated to exceed 50,000 *esedi guruş*.

Ottoman losses were severe as well. Trade was brought to a grinding halt by the destruction of essential infrastructure and by the persistent fear, wholly justified, that the pirates would return.[9] The port was deprived of the myriad taxes and duties imposed on all those who used it, which included, in addition to the flag-specific duties, a 1 percent tax on cash brought to port, a tobacco tax, a stamp tax, and a port-use tax.[10] Eight months passed before the customs house was functioning again, eight months in which no large ships came to unload cash or goods. When the customs receipts for the 1624–1625 fiscal year were tabulated in March 1625, they amounted to only 60 percent of the port's expected annual revenue of 40,000 *guruş*. That money, after expenses, was earmarked for the upkeep of the queen mother, the *valide sultan* Kösem, who ruled as regent for her minor son Sultan Murad IV.[11] At Iskenderun, the corsairs had not only violated the promise of peaceful trade granted in the sultan's name to the European commercial powers whose ships and goods had been seized, they had effectively robbed the sultan's mother.

The attack sent shockwaves through Istanbul and its diplomatic community, leading the English ambassador Sir Thomas Roe to remark that "The piratts of Algier and Tunes have cast off all obedience to this empire, not only upon the sea, where they are masters, but presuming to doe many insolences even upon the land."[12] The two 1624 raids described above were neither the first nor the last of their kind, but they hastened conversations already underway between the ambassadors and their masters back home over what to do about the predations of the North African corsairs, who were at the peak of their powers in the 1620s, and it forced them to reevaluate their traditional responses. The raids raised critical questions about the future of the relationship between Istanbul, Algiers, and Tunis, and, for Roe, of the dynasty itself.

The brazen attacks at opposite extremes of the Ottoman Mediterranean exposed fissures in the facade of a unified Ottoman Empire that would never be repaired. As important as the raids were, their aftermath was more telling. As the Venetians pursued their time-honored strategy of carefully working their contacts in Istanbul, generating overwhelming numbers of letters, decrees, and legal opinions in support of their cause, the English, Dutch, and French redirected their efforts from the Sublime Porte to North Africa, thereby undermining both the Ottoman center and Venice in the process. Increasingly unable to have its orders respected in Algiers and Tunis and seeing its prestige damaged at home and abroad as a result, Istanbul gradually, but irreversibly, washed its hands of responsibility for the actions of North Africa's corsairs. The divergence between Istanbul and North Africa that had begun within decades of the littoral's conquest broke out into the open in the 1620s and 1630s and solidified in the 1670s, hardening the boundaries of the Ottoman Mediterranean and ultimately leaving Algiers, Tunis, and Tripoli at the mercy of the European powers on which they had preyed.

The growing audacity of the corsairs coincided with a period of extreme, persistent crisis that significantly weakened Istanbul's ability to project its authority on distant frontiers, including both the Adriatic and North Africa. Dynastic turmoil gripped the capital following the premature death of Sultan Ahmed I in 1617, with the brief reigns of the twice-deposed, mentally unstable Sultan Mustafa I (r. 1617–1618; 1622–1623) bookending that of the young Sultan Osman II, who was murdered in a janissary uprising in 1622. Despite the resolute efforts of the queen mother, Kösem, stability did not return until the 1630s, when Murad IV took up the reins of government and led a series of successful campaigns against the Safavids. The troubles of the dynasty were accompanied and compounded by a dizzying array of existential threats that persisted through the first third of the seventeenth century, including near-continuous warfare in the east, natural disasters, rampant inflation, widespread rebellion, endemic banditry, peasant flight, and the sudden appearance of the Cossacks in the Black Sea.[13]

The last of these menaces had an outsize impact on Mediterranean security. As the Cossacks' raids inched closer to the imperial capital in the early 1620s, Istanbul was forced to repeatedly divert the entire Mediterranean fleet to the Black Sea to engage in costly, mostly fruitless hunts for the Cossacks, who employed swarms of small rowboats that dispersed in all directions whenever the navy's galleys were sighted.[14] The results were predictable. With the *kapudan pasha* frequently occupied in the Black Sea, the Ottoman Mediterranean was left completely undefended. In the spring of 1625, Roe reported that, thanks to the Cossacks, for "two years they [the Ottomans] have not been able to looke in to the Levant."[15] Pirates and privateers of all stripes took full advantage of the resulting chaos.

Thus, while the raids of 1624 were shocking, they were not at all surprising. Although theoretically bound by the *ahdname*'s guarantees, without fear of serious consequences from Istanbul, the leadership in North Africa had been safely disregarding them for years. In the aftermath of the raids on Cyprus and Iskenderun in May and again after the attacks on Perast and the Ionian Islands in June, the Venetian *bailo* Zorzi Giustinian met with leading Ottoman officials—including the grand vizier, the *kaymakam* (the grand vizier's deputy), the *kapudan pasha*, and the *şeyhülislam* (the mufti of Istanbul and the Ottomans' chief religious-legal authority)—to remonstrate and coordinate responses to the incidents.

The *kaymakam* assured him in May that the Ottoman officials in Cyprus who had failed to protect the Venetian ships would be punished and that "he would give this matter his chief attention." But as far as the *kaymakam* was concerned, and this was a lament the Venetians no doubt shared, "the fault lay with those who introduced these pirate bertons at Tunis and Algiers, who were English, French, and Flemings. They taught the people of Barbary, who before that time had not known what bertons were."[16] Indeed, it was pirates and renegades from the Atlantic, many of them Britons and Dutchmen who had served their countries as privateers until peace with Spain left them unemployed, who brought broadside sailing ships to the region in the early years of the century. Although oared vessels remained in use—the North Africans' Adriatic-Ionian cruise had been carried out with galliots, which were better suited to the requirements of amphibious raiding—the sail-powered bertons brought to bear against Iskenderun were, in terms of range and firepower, equal to or better than any operating in the Mediterranean at the time. And beyond: Algiers-based corsairs were by this point regularly raiding Britain and Ireland and, in 1627, a fleet captained by a Dutch renegade and guided by a captive Dane sacked unsuspecting Iceland.[17] Ottoman officials, entirely unprepared to respond militarily to a problem from which they might still derive some benefit, were inclined to view it as an intra-European conflict rather than one they were themselves obliged to solve.

After the sack of Iskenderun, the consuls of the four major trading nations in Aleppo agreed to send a joint note to the Porte to protest their treatment by local officials and pirates alike. Giustinian, an experienced diplomat who had once served as ambassador in London, believed that a similarly coordinated response from the European ambassadors in Istanbul might spur the Ottoman leadership into action. On the basis of the consuls' note, he proposed that the four ambassadors submit a joint *arz* (petition) to the sultan on the matter. Such an *arz*, he argued, would carry considerably more weight at the Porte. There was but one hitch, he thought: "Joint action by the ambassadors is rendered difficult by the quarrel for precedence between France and England."

In late June, as he worked to corral his colleagues, he reported to the Senate that English and French egos continued to obstruct his progress, even though "as regards the pirates, we all four recognize the supreme importance of attempting a final remedy by jointly presenting an *arz*."[18] Two weeks later, Giustinian could finally claim that the four ambassadors had "drawn up a very efficacious *arz* about the pirates," but he admitted with evident frustration that its submission remained impossible so long as the problem of precedence was unresolved.[19]

Giustinian was correct that precedence was an issue. Ambassador Roe was quite determined to battle his French colleague on this point. But he was entirely unconcerned with the content of Giustinian's carefully crafted *arz*. Instead, Roe wrote at length to his superiors regarding the jockeying for position for their signatures on the document, relaying with satisfaction that he had placed his such that the French ambassador could not sign above him.[20] Roe may have been willing to humor the Venetians in the summer of 1624, but he was busily trying to deal with the pirate problem at the source.

When Roe first took up his position in the fall of 1621, he was ordered, just like his French and Venetian counterparts, to remonstrate about Algiers and Tunis at the Sublime Porte and seek redress.[21] These orders were repeated the following spring. Roe was vocal about his doubts that a solution could be found in Istanbul and repeatedly advocated a more bellicose policy toward North Africa, suggesting blockade, bombardment, or invasion to neutralize the threat. Nevertheless, he complied with his orders and sought relief from North African attack through official channels.[22] These efforts culminated in 1622, when the *kapudan pasha* mediated a peace "agreement" with Algiers and Tunis that was signed by representatives of both cities in Istanbul.[23] The agreement met with resistance back home, however, and rapidly collapsed.

After this failure, Roe moved to negotiate directly with North Africa. At his own expense and with the Porte's blessing, Roe arranged in early 1623 for Ottoman and English envoys to travel together from Istanbul to Algiers to broker a peace and secure the release of the roughly 800 English captives held there. Roe's efforts were likely inspired by the Dutch, who had acquired their first *ahdname* in 1612 and had engaged in a similar bout of three-way negotiations in Algiers in 1617 before adopting a more direct diplomatic policy in 1622.[24] The French likewise initiated talks, ultimately unsuccessful, in 1622.[25]

As far as Whitehall was concerned, these talks were not meant to result in a separate treaty but rather the enforcement of the one they already had with Istanbul.[26] Roe had previously had to reassure his superiors that in seeking a peace at Algiers and Tunis consonant with the *ahdname* he was not trying to conclude a formal treaty with those cities.[27] To do so risked a breach with the Porte. Indeed, the failed peace agreement of 1622 had carefully avoided any language that could be construed as conferring legitimacy on North African self-rule or acknowledging North African sovereignty. It was concluded with the "soldiery and people" of Algiers and Tunis, not with specific officeholders, and the state of conflict between the regencies and England was referred to not as war—impossible since the Ottoman Empire of which they were a part was at peace with England—but rather as "diverse discontents and quarrels" which did "mutual damage contrary to . . . the said capitulations (i.e., *ahdname*)."[28]

The murder of Sultan Osman II in that year and the chaos that followed may have opened the door for England, France, and the Dutch Republic to begin direct talks with North Africa, but it was the Iskenderun attack that changed the nature of the conversation. Although Roe was already orchestrating the negotiations with Algiers from Istanbul, the North Africans' sack of this port in the Ottoman heartland added urgency to his mission and seemingly vindicated his longstanding position that the Ottoman central government had no further role to play in safeguarding English trade interests in the Mediterranean. For Roe, the Ottoman government's inability to secure its home waters and harbors from the predations of its own subjects was deeply troubling, and he considered a permanent rupture between the North African port cities and Istanbul very likely.[29] He gave little thought to whether his direct diplomacy might hasten that outcome. Owing to the long-distance transit requirements of English shipping, coming to an understanding with the North African ports was essential. Unlike Venice, the English and French (and more recently the Dutch) also had the diplomatic infrastructure on the ground to accomplish this, thanks to the consulates they had won the right to establish there beginning in the 1580s.[30]

The English agreement with Algiers and Tunis was largely settled in the fall of 1624 and publicly proclaimed in January 1625.[31] The Porte had been involved in various phases of the process, dispatching ever more emphatic orders to Algiers and Tunis to respect the *ahdname* and acceding to the removal of a particularly obstructionist pasha from Algiers and the installation of one more favorable to the English. But if outrage within the Ottoman central government subsequent to the Iskenderun attack enabled Roe to pursue his goals with the support of leading officials, it was direct engagement and direct payments that secured the peace Roe sought. The temporary success of the pact—hundreds of captives were freed and English ships were largely spared from North African attack during the next "sea season"—was a source of significant pride for Roe and demonstrated quite clearly that direct diplomacy could accomplish what remonstration at the Porte could not. What had begun as an effort through official English-Ottoman channels to compel Algiers and Tunis to obey the *ahdname* had, in the aftermath of the Iskenderun raid of 1624, morphed into a formal set of peace articles conveyed by an Algerian envoy to London for the king's signature.[32]

But in the summer of 1624, Giustinian continued along the procedural path that he and his predecessors had followed for decades, unaware that Roe's negotiations had already torpedoed any chance of success he had to secure the release of the Venetian subjects from Algiers and Tunis on the strength of imperial authority alone. On July 20, 1624, Giustinian wrote that he had met with Halil, by then the former *kapudan pasha*, to discuss the matter. In addition to commanding the fleet and serving as governor of the Aegean archipelago, the imperial admiral was the Sublime Porte's primary liaison with North Africa, so maintaining good relations with the men who held, or might again hold, that office was critical for the Venetians. This was especially true with Halil Pasha, who had previously distinguished himself in the fight against piracy in an era of limited resources and declining nautical competence. Halil, Giustinian said, "swore he was as much disturbed as I at the pass things had come to." Ideally, Halil suggested, the best course of action would be "to take a force to Barbary and execute the captains," but this would require an impossible number of galleys. The pirates presented a threat, the former admiral admitted, that the Ottoman navy was quite incapable of confronting at the moment.[33]

Halil was not bluffing about taking a force to North Africa. As *kapudan pasha* a decade earlier, he had sailed with the imperial fleet to Tripoli after a busy spring spent chasing pirates and raiding Malta. The fleet arrived on July 9, 1614, and the ruler of Tripoli, Sefer Dey (Turkish: *dayı*, lit. "maternal uncle," a high rank in the janissary corps and the title used by many of the Maghreb's military commanders), was invited aboard the admiral's flagship. It was a trap. The unsuspecting *dey* was seized while the *kapudan pasha*'s forces stormed the fortress. Sefer Dey had presided over corsairs who had exceeded their commission, partaking in piracies and murders that were, to the *kapudan pasha* and to the Porte, unacceptable, and the admiral had come to Tripoli to deliver harsh justice. The goods and ships that Sefer Dey and his men had seized were inventoried and confiscated for the state, and then a court was convened. The suits against him for theft and murder were conducted in public with all the townsfolk and local *ulema* in attendance. After the necessary evidence was provided, the *kadi*—probably the "sea judge" who traveled on the admiral's flagship—found him guilty. Sefer Dey was hung from the fortress gates to serve as an example for the people of Tripoli and a warning for their neighbors.[34]

But no North African strongman would fall for the same trick again. Future invitations to join a *kapudan pasha* on his flagship would be politely refused.[35] And Algiers and Tunis were not nearby, puny Tripoli; it would take much more to bring them to heel. Unfortunately, the outclassed imperial fleet had not even sailed as far as Algiers in decades, and containing the Cossacks was now its chief operational priority. It would remain so through the 1630s.[36] Even if armed suppression were possible, Giustinian argued that the more serious problem was the complicity of Ottoman provincial officials, who admitted pirates and errant corsairs into their ports and shared in the spoils.

He complained that "the Sultan's mere commands did not suffice and they ought to execute the ministers who broke them." Halil, he wrote, "admitted the truth" of what he had said and promised that he would punish the officials in question if he were ever reappointed to the admiralty.[37] Giustinian was correct that, rather than attempting to suppress piracy by military means, the first step ought to have been to deny pirates safe harbor and markets for their booty, but managing frontier officials in a time of crisis was hardly straightforward and those in North Africa were another story altogether. However insufficient they were without a credible threat of force, the sultan's commands were what the Venetians had, and Giustinian and his superiors still fundamentally believed that they could be effective.

For months after the Adriatic-Ionian raids, Giustinian bombarded Algiers and Tunis with paper, inducing important Ottoman personages to write in support of the sultan's orders. In late August, Hüsrev Pasha, the newly appointed *beylerbeyi* of Algiers—nominally the provincial governor but in reality a ceremonial position—was sent to his post bearing both an imperial decree ordering the *divan* (the ruling council) of Algiers to free the captives and a *fetva*, a legal opinion, from the *şeyhülislam* declaring that it was illegal for all Muslims to attack the friends of the sultan.[38] The *fetva*, the first of several issued in relation to the attacks, represented a joint effort on the part of the Ottomans and Venetians to employ the religious gravitas of the empire's chief jurist to compel North African compliance.[39]

A little more than a month later, decrees were dispatched to the governor of Bosnia, in whose province Nova fell, and to key officials in Tunis, ordering them to locate the stolen goods, identify the culprits, and uphold the *ahdname*.[40] Decrees were coupled with personal letters from the grand vizier, the *kapudan pasha*, and the *şeyhülislam*.[41] As with Algiers, those bound for Tunis were conveyed personally by Abdi Pasha, the incumbent *beylerbeyi*.[42]

The letters highlighted the question of what was and was not a religiously acceptable raid, setting up a legal and rhetorical battle between Istanbul and North Africa over the definition of piracy and, by extension, the rights to declare war and make peace. The *şeyhülislam*, Hocazade Esad Efendi (d. 1625), reminded Bayram Pasha in Bosnia that there was peace between the Porte and Venice and to contravene the *ahdname* was to violate Islamic law.[43] The admiral, Topal Receb Pasha, was more explicit in his letter to Tunis. Writing to Yusuf Dey, the effective ruler of Tunis, the *kapudan pasha* lauded the *dey* as a *gazi*, a holy warrior, and acknowledged the corsairs' long history of service to the dynasty, but he disparaged the Adriatic-Ionian raiders as "rebel pirates." Venetians were not like other "enemy infidels," and an attack against them was not a "*halal gaza*," a religiously permissible raid.[44]

As the letters and decrees crossed the Mediterranean, Giustinian and his superiors in Venice blithely proceeded under the assumption that the orders they had procured would have the desired effect. To coordinate the release of the captives held there, they selected the dragoman Giovanni Battista Salvago to travel to Algiers and Tunis. Salvago's report on his experiences and observations, submitted to the Venetian Senate in February 1626, provided detailed information about the governance of the North African port cities and their complex relationship with each other and the Ottoman center that would force Venetian decision makers to reevaluate their expectations vis-à-vis Istanbul.[45]

The Senate instructed Salvago to seek the release of the slaves through the authority of the Porte alone, and only those mentioned in the orders concerning the raids on Perast, Paxos, and Antipaxos that were expected to arrive ahead of him. He was not to pay ransoms like his English, French, and Dutch colleagues.[46] To do so would undermine the authority of the Porte, and the intent was to create circumstances on the ground in which specific orders of the Porte would be obeyed. That would set a desirable precedent indeed, even if it had to be helped along with Venetian diplomacy and a few thousand liberally distributed Spanish *real*s: Salvago was authorized to promise and distribute substantial monetary rewards to cooperative North African officials, but only after the liberation of the captives.[47]

Salvago also carried letters from the Venetian Senate that highlighted the friendship between the Sublime Porte and Venice and stressed that attacks on Venice violated the *ahdname* and the express wishes of the sultan. Giustinian had placed great hope in the *şeyhülislam*'s ruling, and the Senate's letter to the *divan* of Algiers drew special attention to the *fetva* "issued by the most wise mufti . . . in which he condemns and detests the *corsi* against the ships and possessions of the princely friends of the

Grand Signior."[48] The Venetians believed that the *şeyhülislam*'s opinions were incontrovertible.[49] Outside North Africa, they were right.

Carrying the letters and his instructions, Salvago traveled via Livorno to Marseilles, where he embarked a leaky vessel for Algiers. Arriving on February 14, 1625, Salvago's first meeting with Hüsrev Pasha did not inspire confidence. Salvago found the Porte's symbolic viceroy feigning ignorance of the *bailo* Giustinian's efforts and the very orders he had borne with him. Hüsrev predicted that Salvago's negotiations would be difficult, both because of the large number of captives involved, in which many leading figures had a financial stake, and because the Venetians were universally hated for beheading captured corsairs. Hüsrev noted that the other trading nations obtained their slaves by treaty of peace, exchange of captives, or ransom payments as stipulated in the peace terms; the Venetians, he implied, ought to do as others did.[50]

Salvago's mission could not have been more poorly timed. Tasked with trying to retrain the corsairing leadership to obey their master in Istanbul without rewarding their previous bad behavior, Salvago had arrived in Algiers only weeks after ambassador Roe had publicly proclaimed the formal peace treaty he had bought and brokered with the Porte's blessing. The corsairs' tactics had paid off. For Salvago, all hope "rested on the efficacy of the orders."[51]

Venice had badly miscalculated, for they would have no effect in Algiers. Having been told that his mission was doomed, Salvago's efforts were unexpectedly stymied further when Hüsrev Pasha left abruptly for Istanbul, depriving him of his official interlocutor. The imprimatur of the *beylerbeyi*, who was to be treated as if he actually governed the place on the sultan's behalf, was essential for the negotiations to have the legitimacy Venice and Istanbul desired. Directly engaging local power brokers without the *beylerbeyi*'s mediation would have granted them precisely the formal recognition Venice wished to reserve for the sultan's chosen representative. Unable to proceed with negotiations, Salvago departed Algiers empty-handed in April 1625.

Meanwhile, Tunis had been ominously silent. The October 1624 decree had not been acknowledged, so a second decree had been dispatched from Istanbul that April recapitulating the first and demanding an immediate response.[52] Traveling once again via Livorno and Marseille, Salvago arrived in Tunis in late June bearing fresh letters and commands for Hüsrev Pasha's counterpart, Abdi Pasha.

Abdi Pasha claimed that he had argued for the release of the Venetian captives as ordered when he arrived earlier that year, but had been dismissed by Yusuf Dey, who asked him if he had come "to quarrel or to govern." Subsequently prevented from corresponding with the Porte,

Abdi Pasha confided to Salvago that he feared for his life.[53] Such a dynamic had become common over the previous thirty years. The *beylerbeyi*s, outsiders sent from Istanbul with no natural local constituency, had little ability to coerce compliance from the fiercely independent and cliquish factions that controlled the North African provinces, where power was unevenly divided between the local militias, corsair captains, and other elites. They had even less incentive to try. Rotated frequently, they typically became well-remunerated prisoners in their palaces, forbidden from taking an active role in governance but permitted to claim the 10 percent stake in booty their figurehead position allotted them. They provided a facade of sultanic legitimacy for what were in reality frequently unstable military dictatorships and maintained the bond with Istanbul, but in these uncertain times, powerful men like Yusuf Dey could afford to be dismissive of the sultan's servants.[54]

Salvago would come to share the pasha's fear when he finally appeared before the *divan* on August 1, 1625. When Salvago read aloud the decrees he bore with him, its members exploded in anger and the head of the militia threatened to have him burned alive to avenge the deaths of their comrades.[55] Cooler heads prevailed, however—the solidarity of the janissary and *kapıcı* attending him helped—and Salvago heard the *divan*'s reasons for refusing to hand over the slaves.[56]

Lauren Benton has described "pirates as lawyers" who, with an eye toward self-preservation, engaged in "legal posturing" in order to justify their activities and place them within a framework of legitimate practice.[57] Pirates who relished the name were a historical abnormality, and the corsairs of North Africa, just like those of Malta, always sought to situate their raids within the context of a legal and just war. If pirates were lawyers, these were among the most accomplished amphibious barristers, and they were prepared to mount a vigorous defense. Consequently, the members of the *divan* declared that they were ancient enemies of the Venetians, with whom they had neither truces nor *ahdname*s as they had with the other friends of the sultan, namely the English, French, and Dutch. In light of this historic enmity, they were not required to return the slaves.[58] This explanation got to the heart of the matter, for the Tunisian leadership was asserting its right to decide with which powers it would have war or peace. All the historical and legal justifications that followed meant little when the fundamental question was one of sovereignty and whether the sultan's *ahdname* extended to North Africa. The Tunisians argued that it did not.

Whether they would have been willing to make such a bold claim a decade earlier is unclear, but after engaging in treaty negotiations with the English, Dutch, and French over the past year, they reasonably could.

Venice's effort to prop up Ottoman sovereignty in North Africa ignored the fact that that proverbial ship had sailed. Furthermore, the North African business model meant that Tunis and Algiers could scarcely afford to be at peace with all of the sultan's friends at once. As one of the "principal corsairs" complained at an earlier meeting, having recently concluded treaties with the English and the Dutch and in the midst of talks with the French, Tunis would scarcely have a reason to fit out ships if the *corso* against Venice were suspended as well.[59]

Since Venetian ships did not call in North African ports and carried out no trade with them, there was little basis for establishing friendly relations and much to lose from doing so. Moreover, most of the leading figures in Algiers and Tunis owned Venetian slaves captured in the previous year's raids, including, Salvago later learned, the otherwise sympathetic Abdi Pasha.[60] None was enthusiastic about losing his investment without remuneration and many likely held out hope that some compensation, if not a profitable ransom, would be forthcoming if they waited long enough.[61] They were correct in this assumption. Men from Perast were shadowing Salvago and were prepared to ransom their countrymen if his mission failed.[62]

All the same, the corsairs had specific grievances. They accused Venice of complicity with their enemies, the Maltese, and complained of their treatment at the hands of Venice. Even though the Venetians were explicitly permitted to defend against, pursue, and destroy North African corsairs, the Venetians' gruesome execution of those they captured was a source of great indignation, the reason for the threats made against Salvago's person and the most common excuse for continuing to attack Venice. Indeed, when the Ottoman envoys accompanying Salvago asked Yusuf Dey why he did not obey the sultan's commands, the *dey* explained that it was not with his consent that the *levend*s enslaved Venetians, but that they did so whenever they encountered them to avenge their slain compatriots.[63] The corsairs argued that, in enslaving the Venetians instead of putting them to the sword, they were proceeding far more mildly.

The corsairs could also point to specific incidences of Venetian excesses. In 1584, a high-ranking Venetian naval commander, Gabriele Emo, captured the personal galley of the recently deceased pasha of Tripoli, Ramazan Pasha, near Cephalonia. The Venetians slaughtered nearly all the passengers, the pasha's son Mehmed and his mother among them, and towed the ship back to Venice as a prize. The incident, discussed in Chapter 3, provoked outrage in Istanbul and increasingly strident demands for retribution that came to personally involve the highest levels of the administration. It took the return of the ship, its surviving passengers and contents, and more importantly, the execution of the Venetian captain in 1585, to resolve the issue.[64] Forty years later, Salvago was confronted with the story of Ramazan Pasha's galley, as the corsairs dipped deep into their history to justify their persistent attacks on Venice. The fact that the row had been settled to the satisfaction of the Porte in 1585, that Emo had paid the ultimate price for his error, and that the corsairs had subsequently been ordered not to retaliate, did not enter the picture.[65]

As for the 1624 raid itself, they reiterated that they had been formally invited to sack Perast by all the leading men in Nova, who had been wronged by their neighbors, and they had the letters to prove it. Continuing their legal posturing, they argued, rather disingenuously, that the attack on Paxos was legitimate self-defense; they claimed that they had not intended to attack the island but a number of islanders on the shore had discharged their arquebuses and hurled insults at the passing fleet, thereby obliging them to stop and land their raiding parties. Moreover, they added, custom and their ancient sultanic privileges entitled them to fall upon any who did not obey their commands at sea.[66] For all these reasons, the 1624 raids and the seizure of the captives were legal and justified, and if the Venetians wanted their subjects back, they should ransom them as their coreligionists did.

The Tunisian leadership was determined to follow its own course—they would not budge on their position regarding the captives—but they did not want a full breach in relations any more than Istanbul did. The members of the *divan* could not simply dismiss the Ottoman envoys and the rolls of imperial decrees as they could Salvago and his letters from the Venetian Senate. They thus argued that Venice must have procured the sultanic commands under false pretenses. Surely if the sultan understood the true state of affairs, he would not be taking the Venetians' side. The corsairs told Salvago that in the time of Uluc Ali (aka Kılıç Ali Pasha, *beylerbeyi* of Algiers from 1568 to 1571, then *kapudan pasha* until his death in 1587) the Venetians had extracted similar decrees for the liberation of their subjects, and in response, the corsairs sent deputies to Istanbul to appeal the decision. After discussing the Venetians' decapitation of captured corsairs, they claimed, the Imperial Council waived its earlier decision and left things as they were. This story, Salvago wrote, was pure fantasy, the invention of self-interested men.[67] So it may have been, but the Tunisian leadership decided to pursue precisely this course of action.

Because the Ottoman envoys accompanying Salvago would not leave without some sort of response for the sultan and the Imperial Council, the Tunisian leadership resolved to send a delegation of their own to Istanbul to represent their views and assert the legitimacy of their actions. As Salvago prepared to return to Venice, his unhappy mission concluded, six Tunisian notables set sail for Istanbul, bringing with them one of two recently captured Maltese galleys. They would present their prize in triumph and then mount their defense.[68] They would also have to answer for the Iskenderun attacks. The customs house there, painstakingly rebuilt after the sack of 1624, operated for only a few months before several Algerian and Tunisian bertons returned to Iskenderun in the fall of 1625 and burned it to the ground again, doing even greater damage to the port's infrastructure and loitering in the vicinity for nearly a month while the imperial fleet chased Cossacks in the Black Sea.[69] The members of the delegation, Salvago suggested, feared reprimand from the Porte for these raids within and against Ottoman ports, which they would have a much harder time justifying.[70]

While Salvago was learning firsthand about the attenuated power of the sultan's decree in North Africa, Giustinian was gradually coming to realize that he could expect little more than sympathetic words from Ottoman officials and even less support from his fellow ambassadors in Istanbul. On April 27, 1625, Giustinian and Venice's extraordinary ambassador, Simone Contarini, reported to the Senate that, because of the "impossibility" of presenting a joint *arz*, which they still attributed to the impasse between the French and the English, they were now turning to the Dutch ambassador Cornelis Haga to see if he could "try and devise some way of bringing the true state of the business to the Sultan's knowledge in the common name of the ambassadors, urging him to see that his orders against the pirates are enforced."[71]

Months later, with Iskenderun once more in ruins and Salvago on his way home, Giustinian finally understood that his inability to advance his anti-piracy agenda stemmed neither from precedence disputes nor from the sultan's unawareness of the pirates who infested his waters. On December 28, 1625, the *bailo* wrote that he had again visited the *kaymakam*, the mufti, the *kapudan pasha*, and the former admiral Halil to complain about rampant piracy and noted bitterly that "they all made the usual promises." The ongoing Cossack threat to Istanbul itself—they had entered the Bosphorus the previous year and burned and pillaged all the way down to Rumeli Hisarı (the massive fortress that today lies beneath modern Istanbul's second trans-straits bridge)—meant that the oft-promised Ottoman naval response would continue to be indefinitely delayed.[72] He broached the issue with the other ambassadors once more and was brushed off. Although the French were supportive of joint action—no surprise given that officials in Iskenderun reported that their ships had suffered the most in the 1625 raids[73]—the English claimed that they were not being attacked by the corsairs and so "had no reason to move," while the Dutch, having sent their own embassy to North Africa, were "very cold."[74] Venice, rebuffed in Algiers and Tunis, was stuck with a hamstrung Istanbul as its only friend in the fight against piracy.

The Tunisian delegation arrived in Istanbul in early January 1626.[75] Expecting a sympathetic reception from Receb Pasha, the *kapudan pasha*, the Tunisian representatives were unpleasantly surprised to find themselves face-to-face with the *bailo* Giustinian and his dragomans, whom the angry admiral had invited to the initial meeting along with other Ottoman officials. Together, they insisted that the time had come for the Tunisians to obey the sultan's wishes: free the slaves and refrain from further attacks on Venetians. But the Tunisians were intransigent. Responding to accusations regarding the recent capture of still more Venetian ships, they argued that the corsairs had done so in reprisal and to compensate themselves for the loss of several of their galliots to Venetian patrols. The *bailo* countered that Venice seized the Tunisian galliots due to their stealing, in accordance with the requirements of the *ahdname*.[76]

After trading recriminations, the meeting ended without resolution. But the Tunisians' defiance in the presence of Ottoman officials and their responses to the complaints registered by the *kapudan pasha* and the *bailo* laid the foundation for further maneuvers. After the meeting, the admiral informed the *bailo*'s dragoman that he would procure a *fetva* from the *şeyhülislam*, now Zekeriyyazade Yahya Efendi, in order to debunk the Tunisians' excuses.[77] This time, the *fetva* would take into account the Tunisians' own arguments in defense of their actions, rather than presenting a vague declaration that the friends of the sultan were not to be harmed. The opinion of the Ottoman Empire's chief religious-legal authority would not be so easy to ignore this time, or so the *kapudan pasha* hoped.

By the time he wrote his dispatch of January 24, 1626, the *bailo* Giustinian had received a copy of Yahya Efendi's *fetva*. The opinion he obtained was favorable, notwithstanding the contrary efforts of the Tunisian delegation; they had rushed to meet with the mufti to defend themselves when they got wind of the admiral's plan. Rather than swaying the mufti to their side, their explanations provided the grist for the opinion itself, which broke down the lines of reasoning by which they had "maintained the justice of their *corsi*" against Venetian ships and shores, as well as their excuses for keeping the Venetian slaves. The *fetva* held that the Tunisians' actions were "illicit according to their laws" and, the *bailo* reported, that the Venetians' seizure of their galliots was not a valid reason for "sustaining a *corso* against us."[78] Notably, the Tunisians' justifications for their actions, both in Tunis and in Istanbul, had been secular, based on the principles of custom, reciprocity, and local sovereignty. Given the persistent assumptions in modern popular and scholarly literature about the religious motivations of North African corsairing, there is a certain irony in the fact that it was the Ottoman center, not North Africa, that deployed religious arguments, not in favor of, but against the capture and enslavement of enemy infidels. We return to this point, and to the *fetva* itself, in Chapter 5.

Within a fortnight, a new batch of letters and imperial decrees had been prepared that referenced the *fetva*s explicitly and repeatedly to explain why it was absolutely necessary to free the Venetian slaves without delay and refrain from further attacks on Venice.[79] The documents, presented to the Tunisian delegation in Istanbul, were also dispatched directly to Tunis. The messenger had orders to remain there indefinitely and coordinate the release of the Venetian slaves.[80] The contumaciousness of Tunisian authorities had made the Venetians' problem an Ottoman problem as well, but the response was simply an intensification of previous efforts: more messengers, more letters, decrees, and *fetva*s that the Tunisians might quietly ignore until Istanbul was forced to call upon them for naval aid, at which point they could demonstrate their usefulness and loyalty once more.

The diplomatic efforts on behalf of the Venetian captives between 1624 and 1626 were insufficient to arrest or reverse the changing dynamic in the Mediterranean. Once opened, the Pandora's box of direct diplomacy with North Africa could never be closed again. The efficacy of this approach was proven as soon as Roe had won his treaties from Algiers and Tunis in 1625. France was not far behind, securing a peace treaty with Algiers in 1628 through the mediation of the notorious Algiers-based French renegade corsair, Sanson Napollon.[81] After that, the Europe-wide Thirty Years' War (1618–1648), the Franco-Spanish War (1635–1659), and the English Civil War (1642–1651) led to the neglect of European–North African diplomatic relations, but when they resumed in the late 1650s, the European powers picked up where they had left off.[82]

The treaties with European powers were repeatedly broken and renegotiated. The French in particular actively sought Muslim slaves for their galley fleets in the second half of the seventeenth century, purchasing thousands of captives in Malta and Livorno in spite of the prohibitions enshrined in both the *ahdname* and the treaties with the North African powers. The repeated failure of the French to abide by treaty requirements to release all Algerians or Tunisians, as opposed to the token numbers of sick and infirm Muslims of random origin that they returned, was the most commonly cited cause for breakdowns of the peace. Abuse of the system of passes, transporting the goods of enemy powers on treaty-protected ships, was another.[83] Nevertheless, when the parties did abide by the treaties, they removed English, French, or Dutch-flagged vessels from the target lists. They also rapidly altered the diplomatic and legal relationship between North Africa and Istanbul on the one hand and North Africa and European states on the other.

The instruments themselves document the changing dynamic. In form and content, they were initially inspired by the *ahdname*s, but whereas the failed 1622 agreement had been framed as an effort to bring the signatories into compliance with the *ahdname*'s provisions in accordance with the sultan's wishes, the treaties concluded in subsequent decades increasingly stood alone. For example, in the treaties England concluded with Algiers, Tunis, and Tripoli in 1662, each was referred to in text as a "kingdom" and their principal power holders were identified by name in the preamble. However, the *ahdname*s continued to be acknowledged as a source of law and guidance in the North African treaties. Thus, the final article of the 1662 Tripoli treaty (its first with a European power) states "that in all other particulars not mentioned, the regulation shall be according to the general capitulation (i.e., the English *ahdname*) with the grand Signiori."[84]

Similar provisions appeared in the English treaties with Algiers and Tunis, the French treaty with Algiers of 1666, and many others. This meant that North African and Ottoman treaty law dovetailed, with similar rights and practices obtaining across the Mediterranean, but neither the sultan nor Ottoman overlordship was mentioned elsewhere in the texts.[85] In 1676, with the English treaty imposed on Tripoli by Admiral Narbrough, even this reference to the *ahdname* disappeared (though it likely remained implicit), delinking the Tripolitan treaty from relations with the Ottomans completely. Article 14 underscores this fact, finding that any controversy "shall be liable to no other jurisdiction, but that of Day [*sic*], or Divan," except those among the English themselves, which would be referred to the consul.[86] This followed the pattern of the *ahdname*s, of course, but the *divan* of Tripoli had usurped the rightful place of the Imperial Council in Istanbul. The treaties were not simple addenda to the *ahdname*s, but rather replicated their expectations in a completely independent bilateral relationship.

The English treaty agreed in 1625 was for all intents and purposes one concluded between sovereign powers, and thus it was only a matter of time before the texts themselves fully reflected this reality. Istanbul never accepted that the English, French, and Dutch *ahdname*s were not binding upon Algiers, Tunis, and Tripoli, but neither did it prevent the European powers from coming to terms with North Africa directly. The signatories initially reciprocated by submitting the peace treaties for the sultan's confirmation, but this diplomatic nicety did little to hide the fact that Istanbul no longer had a meaningful say in North Africa's decisions to declare war or make peace. By the 1670s, even this formality had been abandoned.[87]

Already by 1627, the quartet of ambassadors had agreed that there was little point in continuing to press the pirate issue at the Sublime Porte, the influence of which had been further weakened by the success, however ephemeral, of direct negotiations. The new *bailo*, Sebastiano Venier, reported his colleagues' views on the subject in his dispatch of May 15, 1627: "They all agree that no real remedy can be expected here by remonstrances alone, because they [the corsairs] are weakening the Christian powers and they [the Ottomans] expect great help from these Barbary people, who are their subjects, in the event of war. They do not lose heavily of their customs, as the plundered Christians continue to trade. They [the ambassadors] all agree equally that the powers concerned should apply a remedy without further delay." The remedy they had in mind was a joint fleet to destroy the North African ports. The Venetians were supportive in theory, but remained cautious for fear of upsetting the Ottoman government.[88]

The ambassadors underestimated the financial impact of the corsairs' predations. For one thing, not only European trade was targeted, though of course the European ambassadors took little notice of depredated Ottoman subjects. More importantly, the customs losses were not insignificant, cash being in particular demand in this period, and even if trade were redirected from one Ottoman port to another, customs revenues did not flow into one centralized pool on which the treasury might draw. Within the intricate Ottoman fiscal system of revenue grants and tax farms, losses in one area could not simply be compensated through gains in another.[89] The disruption of revenues from Iskenderun between 1624 and 1626, for example, led to questions from the top about what was happening there and why, driving panicked local officials to summon the English vice-consul to explain why their ships had not come from London in the summer of 1625 as usual (the answer, in that case, was plague, not pirates).[90] But the ambassadors were right about the trade-off facing Istanbul, which could tolerate some losses in the service of their security needs, especially when it could see that the culprits and the victims often shared European origins. The center was disinclined to absolve the European powers of responsibility for the increasingly mercenary tendencies of the corsairs of North Africa, given that the many European renegades among them often gave Istanbul little reason to trust in their loyalty to the Ottoman dynasty aside from their newfound religious convictions. Events at Iskenderun were only the latest manifestation of this trend.

Talk of collective punitive action notwithstanding, the reality was that the other powers did not really want to destroy the North African corsairs, not when they might make war on their competitors. England's successful conclusion of a peace with Algiers and Tunis kicked off what would become a lasting pattern: when one power won some respite, the others suffered more. This was an agreeable outcome for Roe, who had noted with some delight that a French embassy that had arrived in Algiers shortly after the peace with England was proclaimed in 1625 was rebuffed and that both French and Dutch shipping had come under greater attack since.[91] The situation was far worse for Venice, and her exposed merchants rapidly sought to take advantage of the English peace and ship their cargo under the protection of the colors of Saint George. The reason was simple: Venice had become the "common prey" of the pirates, which had driven up the insurance rates on her freight to extremely uncompetitive levels, at the time around 18 percent. English vessels, armed with more cannon and an effective peace agreement, were insuring at 4 percent in London.[92]

There was little respite for Iskenderun either. Razed in 1624 and 1625, North African corsairs raided it again in 1627.[93] That same year, a proposal to fortify Iskenderun was fiercely opposed by the English, who feared the various official and unofficial impositions that might come from expanded Ottoman infrastructure more than they feared pirates.[94] Their success inadvertently enabled the English philosopher-cum-privateer Sir Kenelm Digby to take his turn wreaking havoc on the trade of the port in 1628. Carrying a commission to attack French shipping, Digby's fleet of five ships encountered five French merchantmen lying at anchor at Iskenderun. Fearing that he would make a prize of them, the French ships put themselves under the protection of two Venetian galleasses that were anchored there as well. A firefight soon erupted between the English and the Venetians, who had endeavored to prevent Digby from sailing into the port to assault the French. The Venetians got the worst of it, and Digby subsequently captured three of the French ships. He tarried in the area for weeks until he finally heeded the pleas of Thomas Potton, the English consul in Aleppo, to leave.[95] His presence was endangering the interests of the English merchant community, for the French and Venetian representatives had complained to the Ottoman authorities in Aleppo of the violence done to their ships at Iskenderun. They "demand justice," Potton wrote, "for wee had broken the Peace" of the sultan by taking "his friends in his owne Port."[96]

The consul and the English merchants in Aleppo were soon arrested and their goods impounded due to the violation. The new English ambassador in Istanbul, Peter Wyche, managed to get the Porte to lift the embargo, but only after restitution was made.[97] There was a clear lesson to be learned here, and half a century later, the Irish jurist Charles Molloy presented the story of Digby's assault on the French and Venetians at Iskenderun to illustrate one of his principles of maritime law: "Nor may such Privateers attempt any thing against the Laws of Nations, as to assault or endamage an Enemy in the Port or Haven, under the protection of any Prince or Republick, be he Friend, Ally, or Neuter, for the peace of such places must be kept inviolably."[98]

This was an international usage that the Ottomans wholly subscribed to, and that they would jealously guard in the future, as the Europeans' wars began to invade Ottoman waters with increasing frequency in the second half of the seventeenth and eighteenth centuries.[99] Yet, as we shall see, the neutrality of Ottoman ports and the Ottomans' efforts to maintain peace within them threatened to bring the Ottomans into conflict with their European friends when those Europeans undertook to pursue and punish the corsairs of North Africa, as was their right under the *ahdname*.

Only Venice did not abandon the Porte in favor of direct diplomacy with North Africa in the 1620s, making "ye flagge of Saint Marke," in the words of Roe, "ye very temptation of a Piratt, for Venice would not scape under ye banner, if it did swimme in ye Medeteran."[100] The temptation proved irresistible indeed, and the number of North African attacks on Venetian ships skyrocketed between the 1620s and the Ottoman invasion of Crete in 1645.[101] The growing threat and the perennial absence of the Ottoman navy drove Venice into an increasingly aggressive posture. Shortly after the second sacking of Iskenderun in 1625, Venice began to assign warship escorts to convoy some of the more valuable shipping to and from the Levant.[102] Anti-piracy patrols increased. However, this more active and assertive Venetian naval presence inevitably led to friction with the Ottoman naval squadrons that were permanently stationed in and around the Aegean, especially since the identities and intentions of distant ships could rarely be ascertained before it was too late.[103]

Such was the case in late February 1626. Having received intelligence at Milos that three North African ships were in the area and fearing for the safety of a Venetian ship, the *Pellegrino Rossi*, from which no news had been received in nearly a month, the admiral of Crete, Francesco Querini, entered the archipelago with his galleys. Patrolling off the coast of Andros, Querini's galleys encountered a solitary Ottoman warship and, thinking it a pirate, proceeded to attack. In the ensuing fight, the Ottoman ship fled and ran up along the shore. The Venetian soldiers boarded the disabled vessel in force and began to plunder it, taking prisoners and goods. It was not long, however, before Querini realized that they had made a terrible mistake.

The Ottoman ship was not a pirate, but that of the *sancakbeyi* of Andros, Perviz Bey, who had been sailing between Chios and Euboea hunting pirates himself. Perviz Bey subsequently commended Querini to the doge and to the *kapudan pasha*; he understood that the battle had been an unfortunate accident, and Querini had subsequently treated him with great respect. Nevertheless, many had been killed on the Ottoman ship, a fair number of whom had been enslaved oarsmen, and dozens of Venetians lay dead. The Venetians undertook to return all the goods and captives taken and to provide compensation for the damages, with which Perviz Bey was ultimately satisfied, but the skirmish led to a strongly worded letter from Sultan Murad IV to the doge in January 1627, as well as letters from the *kaymakam* and *kapudan pasha*, demanding that the Venetians observe the provisions of the *ahdname* concerning how Ottoman and Venetian vessels should conduct themselves when they met at sea. The sultan reported that he had already dispatched orders to the border districts forbidding reprisals, and he asked the doge to do the same.[104]

Tensions remained high, however. The Venetians remained the target of North African pirates wherever they sailed—1628–1629 (H. 1038) was the worst year in memory, with more than a million *guruş* in Venetian losses to the ships of Algiers and Tunis[105]—and the raiders of the Adriatic and Ionian coasts continued to harass them whenever they passed. Although the Ottoman government scored successes in retrieving Venetian slaves and goods from North Africa in the 1630s, some of its decisions would not have inspired confidence in Venice. In 1637, for example, the Ottoman central administration rotated the former *beylerbeyi* of Tunis to a high-ranking position in the Morea. Not long after, it was reported that collaboration between North African corsairs and officials in the Morean ports of Modon, Koron, and Anavarin had spiked.[106] Who could be surprised that posting an Ottoman official with ties to Tunis in an area already prone to engagement with pirates would lead to increased cooperation across the Mediterranean and a rather more lax attitude regarding the importance of upholding the *ahdname*? A year later, tensions boiled over in the most serious diplomatic debacle since the end of the war for Cyprus.

The Avlonya incident of 1638 was a stress test of the *ahdname* that both sides failed. That summer, a fleet of sixteen Algerian and Tunisian galleys marauded up and down the Adriatic coast of southern Italy before crossing to raid Venetian Dalmatia. Venice assembled a formidable force to chase down the corsairs, sending thirty vessels from Crete under Marino Capello to engage them. At the same time, Maltese and Tuscan corsairs were pillaging in the Eastern Mediterranean. As the Ottoman fleet was tied up, as usual, pursuing Cossack pirates in the Black Sea, the *kapudan pasha* summoned the North African galleys to drive out their Catholic counterparts.[107] They had changed course to answer the call when they met the Venetian fleet near the mouth of the Adriatic, prompting the North African ships to beat a hasty retreat for nearby Avlonya. In contravention of the *ahdname*, the port permitted the North African raiders to take shelter under the cannon of its fortress, whence they disembarked. After a month-long blockade, the Venetian fleet resolved to pursue them into the harbor, forcing its entrance and firing on the fortress and the corsairs' encampment. The bombardment destroyed a mosque's minaret and a number of homes and other structures. The Venetians captured all sixteen ships, which had been abandoned by their crews, and freed the hundreds of galley slaves still chained inside. One of the corsair galleys was towed back to Venice as a prize and the others were sunk in the harbor of Corfu. Sultan Murad IV was furious.[108]

The Ottoman chronicler Ibrahim Peçevi (d. 1650), writing less than a decade later during the early years of the Cretan War, offered an account of the incident that is surprisingly sympathetic to the Venetians (though he referred to them as "enemies" due to the war) in which he suggested that the Ottoman fortress commander in Avlonya may have invited the Venetian attack: "According to what some people said, at that time the Avlonya castellan (*dizdar*) sent word to the enemy fleet (i.e., the Venetians) informing them that these were *levend* ships that neither obey the *padişah* nor protect the Ottoman ships they meet and that they are one big meeting of rebels."[109] Declaring the corsairs no better than pirates, the *dizdar*'s words in Peçevi's account square with the deep ambivalence many Ottoman officials felt toward their Maghrebi allies, who by this time bore little resemblance to the esteemed sixteenth-century corsairs who had delivered North Africa from Spain but who might still provide valuable services for the empire, as they had been preparing to do when the Venetians caught up with them.

The sultan may well have shared the *dizdar*'s disdain for the *levend*s and he recognized the Venetians' right to defend themselves, but he considered their armed assault on an Ottoman port (not least the damage to a mosque) to be an abrogation of the pact, irrespective of the events that preceded it. He immediately ordered the Adriatic transit port of Split closed in retaliation. According to the chronicler Naima, when Ottoman officials protested that this move would cost the treasury a significant amount in lost customs revenue, Sultan Murad IV declared that he wanted revenge and did not care about money, and he threatened to cut off the head of anyone who brought up the issue again.[110]

Relations were immediately suspended, and Venetian representatives in Istanbul and throughout the empire were arrested. If the sultan had not been busy attending to the reconquest of Baghdad, he might have chosen war. It took a massive indemnity of 250,000 ducats from Venice and the return of the Algerian ship taken as prize to clear the air.[111] But the episode showed how shaky the peace had become, and rampant piracy was the root cause.

In July 1639, orders were sent out across the Mediterranean announcing the restoration of relations with Venice.[112] Crucially, Sultan Murad IV conceded a point to Venice, and issued a *nişan* in 1639 concerning piracy that henceforth allowed the Venetians to defend against and destroy North African pirates without exception, and to pursue them into Ottoman ports if necessary. Such an act would no longer be considered a breach of the *ahdname*. Furthermore, Ottoman officials who sheltered pirates would be dismissed, and North African corsairs were now to have the *ahdname*'s surety clause applied to their ships when they entered Ottoman ports, an addition which underscored the fact that the North African ports were no longer considered, in theory or practice, *Ottoman* ports.[113]

Events of recent decades informed this development. Between 1613 and 1638, no fewer than twenty-eight large Venetian ships were taken by Algerian and Tunisian corsairs—most in the vicinity of Crete—along with hundreds of captives. The total damages were estimated at the staggering sum of 5,000,000 *guruş*, and this was hardly an exhaustive accounting.[114] So long as the corsairs of Algiers and Tunis were formally *Ottoman* corsairs, these were damages for which the Porte was theoretically obliged to provide restitution. Even if that compensation was not always forthcoming, the Avlonya debacle spurred the palace to take a closer look at the cumulative impact of North African piracy on Venice and to reevaluate the terms of a relationship that made it legally responsible for the actions of armed parties it simply could not control.

Meanwhile, the *ahdname* was in effect once more, and cooperation regarding cases of piracy and illegal enslavement resumed.[115] When the *ahdname* was confirmed in 1641 following the accession of Sultan Ibrahim, Murad IV's 1639 edict was explicitly renewed at the end of the document.[116] The content of Murad's 1639 *nişan* was understood to apply to France, England, and the Netherlands as well. France had a guarantee in its *ahdname* going back to its first in 1569 granting them any privileges obtained by Venice, and by the mid-seventeenth century all four were claiming the rights of the others. Regardless of intent, the allowances made in the aftermath of Avlonya would one day be interpreted by the European powers to greenlight precisely the kind of naval actions against the Maghrebian ports that their ambassadors had been advocating in the 1620s.

In 1639, however, it represented a further step in the diplomatic distancing between Istanbul and the North African port cities, with the reservations that once applied to Ottoman subjects caught in the act of maritime predation completely withdrawn from those operating out of Algiers, Tunis, and Tripoli. Over the course of the 1630s and 1640s, the territories continued to acknowledge the sultan in Istanbul as their overlord, but they were progressively less concerned with feigning obedience to his orders.

This is not to say that there were not still attempts by the center to assert some measure of authority in North Africa, but these were at best uneven. Two examples from 1644 illustrate this point. That year, the *kapudan* Piyale Pasha sailed for Tripoli and, as Halil Pasha had done thirty years earlier, invited Mehmed Dey aboard his flagship. Tripoli, close and comparatively weak, was ideally suited for the Ottoman government to make a forceful statement about its displeasure with the status quo. For his part, Mehmed Dey was justly terrified, fully aware of what had happened the last time a *dey* of Tripoli accepted an admiral's invitation. Stalling, he sent rich presents instead, writing that "the slave and his possessions belong to the master." Piyale Pasha accepted the gifts and, no longer insisting on a meeting that could easily morph into a trial, returned to Istanbul. Piyale Pasha gave some of the gifts to Sultan Ibrahim—both could be temporarily satisfied with some profitable, bloodless extortion—but kept others for himself. In a postscript to the story, the admiral was executed after a search of his home turned up an item from the *dey* engraved with the sultan's name.[117]

This lack of follow-through helps explain the rather consistent response of Tripoli's neighbors to the center's occasional attempts to appoint officials to positions of power in North Africa; men dispatched from Istanbul might be formally welcomed and accepted, but they would then be ignored, obstructed, imprisoned, or even murdered to prevent them from upsetting the local political ecosystem. That same year, Tunuslu Şeyh Mehmed, a Tunisian member of the Ottoman *ulema* who was a client of the grand vizier Kemankeş Kara Mustafa Pasha (d. 1644), obtained appointment as *kassam-ı guzat* for the Maghreb. He would, according to the decree, oversee the division of the spoils from all prizes brought to the ports by the corsairs, and he would take a share for himself in payment. This was a startling innovation, for the arithmetic of divvying up booty was already handled by members of the indigenous *ulema* in each port, who obtained their positions locally. The center's appointment of someone to this task, even though he was of North African origin, represented a significant threat to local autonomy. Aside from the fact that Şeyh Mehmed would be taking a cut of their loot, could they be certain that he would not interfere or complain to Istanbul if they brought back booty from those deemed to be the sultan's friends?

Thus, when Şeyh Mehmed arrived and produced the order, the ruling elites outwardly assented to his appointment in deference to the grand vizier, but they also did not produce anything for him to divide, making him a man with a title but no work and no income. After a time, he sailed back to Istanbul, hoping that the grand vizier would reconfirm his appointment and provide some aid in his effort to have his position recognized. Instead the grand vizier, embarrassed by Mehmed's failure but unable and unwilling to do more, banished him. Şeyh Mehmed returned to Tunis and tried again to impose himself on the corsairing system, but this time, having been officially disgraced, he was promptly imprisoned. Not long thereafter, a man was sent from the center to execute him, thereby eliminating a noisy reminder of the Porte's inability to regulate North African corsairing.[118]

His failure was predictable, considering the fact that every major administrative, military, scribal, religious, and judicial position was filled locally, though their occupants might have hailed from the core Ottoman lands, Europe, or beyond. In contrast, Şeyh Mehmed's local origins meant little when the appointment came from outside the Maghreb. The *beylerbeyi*s, the official representatives of the sultan in the North African provinces and nominally their governors, were the only locally recognized central appointees. In Algiers, their position had not improved since Salvago's journey, whereas in Tunis, the local strongman Murad Bey had prevailed upon Istanbul to grant him that title and the rank of pasha in 1631, consolidating symbolic authority and real power and laying the foundations for independent, dynastic rule. Tripoli would soon follow a similar path.[119] Meanwhile, even as Algiers was ruled without interference from Istanbul's governors, who were imprisoned in their palaces and prevented from communicating with Istanbul for the duration of their appointments, its leaders continued to recruit soldiers from Anatolia, who counterbalanced the mostly European renegades who commanded and crewed the corsairing fleet.[120]

This was not a happy arrangement from the point of view of the Sublime Porte. The services the corsairs provided could excuse a great deal, but the mistreatment of the sultan's servants and the failure to observe standards of decorum raised hackles in Istanbul. Ottoman frustration with North Africa had only increased since the accession of Sultan Ibrahim in 1640, by which point the decades-long conflict with the Safavids had been concluded and Mediterranean affairs were once more attracting the center's attention. According to Naima, early in his reign Sultan Ibrahim angrily reprimanded a group of admirals from Algiers in a speech that was alternately pleading and menacing: "Look, don't flee my kingdom; my flock is split in two—why are you being obstinate? What does it mean to come and recruit your men from the villages of the districts of Foça and Karaburun in Izmir and then arrive in the Maghreb and assemble and disobey my orders? To imprison and restrain my governors? If you act this way with the pasha I'm giving you now, I will kill you all!"[121]

Sultan Ibrahim's threat failed to conceal Ottoman impotence, however, and Algiers was not afraid. When the promised *beylerbeyi*, Ibrahim Pasha, arrived in Algiers, he was imprisoned in his palace, prevented from acting in any official capacity, and denied permission to come or go. The same was true of his successors. And then, in 1644, the letters came.

Earlier that year, a ship carrying the former chief harem eunuch Sünbül Ağa into exile and the new *kadi* of Mecca to his post, along with many wealthy pilgrims, was captured by the Knights of Malta after a bloody battle, and the spoils from the ship were divided on a deserted stretch of coastline in southern Crete. Sultan Ibrahim held Venice responsible for not preventing the corsairs from landing on Crete and began making preparations to invade the Venetian-held island. In support of that effort, and to combat the Venetian navy and the Maltese ships that would surely aid them, additional naval forces would be required beyond the galleys and supply ships of the imperial fleet. And so the grand vizier dispatched letters to Algiers, Tunis, and Tripoli declaring that there would be a campaign the next spring, that they should prepare for *gaza* with their ships and join the fleet when ordered. There was, we are told, much clamor and excitement at the call for *gaza* among the people of Algiers and Tunis, and so they prepared for war and sent a messenger to inform Istanbul of their intent to participate. But the unfortunate pasha remained imprisoned in Algiers.[122]

Thus, the sultan's murderous promise was promptly forgotten and the ongoing abuse of the pashas ignored. The North African provinces' quasi-rebellious assertions of autonomy would have to be tolerated for the sake of the coming war. Although they would prove to be of less help than in the last great naval campaigns of the 1570s, the corsairs of Tunis and Tripoli showed up when first called and those of Algiers soon followed. For the badly attenuated imperial navy, this would have to be enough. And yet more dramatic rifts between Istanbul and Algiers would form as the war dragged on. The political, if not rhetorical, distance between Istanbul and North Africa increased as the corsairs' military aid, which Istanbul had to heavily subsidize, became less forthcoming.

The Ottomans' problems in the Cretan conflict were almost entirely naval, and reinforcements from North Africa proved wholly inadequate to close the gap. Venice and its allies repeatedly defeated the Ottoman navy at sea and were able to impose a loose blockade on the Dardanelles, which bottled up the fleet and threatened the provisioning of the capital.[123] In response, the Ottomans attempted, sometimes successfully, to press English merchant ships into service against Venice throughout the war.[124] Although most of Crete had been subdued by 1647, the Ottomans were unable to cut off supplies to Candia, the stoutly fortified capital of the island, enabling it to hold out against the Ottoman besiegers seemingly indefinitely. In 1656, the reforming grand vizier Köprülü Mehmed Pasha lost patience with Algiers after a newly arrived *beylerbeyi* was turned out, declaring that "the *padişah* [sultan] has no need for your kind of service. He has a thousand countries like Algeria. There is no difference [for him] whether Algeria exists or not. From now on, you are not allowed to approach Ottoman shores."[125] The excommunication of Algiers was not lifted until after Mehmed Pasha's death in 1661.

The twenty-four-year war between Venice and the Ottoman Empire was the longest in their history and marked the end of nearly three quarters of a century of peace. Notwithstanding the fact that the Ottomans were guilty of similar breaches of the *ahdname* on a regular basis, the Maltese corsairs' landing on Crete was interpreted as a justification for war. Crete was the lynchpin of piracy in the eastern half of the Mediterranean, a frequent stopping point for both Catholic and North African corsairs, and the decision to invade emerged from the same misguided logic behind the 1570 invasion of Cyprus. Just as the European ambassadors to the Porte found it hard to believe that the Ottoman government was not winking at the activities of the North African corsairs, many in Istanbul were convinced that Venice was in league with the corsairs of Malta and Livorno who mercilessly preyed on the Ottoman traffic connecting Istanbul and the Aegean with Egypt. Although in peacetime Venice was no friend of Malta, the fact that the corsairs were embraced in wartime as valuable allies seemingly vindicated Ottoman suspicions—as no doubt did the participation of the corsairs of Algiers, Tunis, and Tripoli on behalf of the Ottomans for European observers possessed of similar views. Although Venice protested that it had had nothing to do with the 1644 attack, Ottoman perceptions of Venetian complicity in this catalytic incident were so pervasive that the Ottoman chronicler Solakzade (d. 1657), writing during the ensuing conflict, declared that it had in fact been Venetian ships that carried out the attack and violated the treaty.[126]

When Candia finally surrendered in 1669, ending one of the longest sieges in history, piracy would be one of the main topics of discussion in the negotiations for restored relations. The Signoria appointed Alvise Molin, then in Crete, extraordinary ambassador to negotiate the peace following the capitulation of the city, and to aid him in his task he was furnished with gifts, money, copies of the *ahdname*s of 1540, 1573, and 1640, and all the imperial orders pertaining to piracy. Molin was meant to see to it that the latter were restored, along with open access to Ottoman ports. In addition to a decrease in customs dues—Venice had previously been paying 5 percent while the newcomers had secured customs at 3 percent—Molin was supposed to request that orders be sent to leaders in Dalmatia and Albania, as had been done in 1639, to keep the borders quiet and suppress piracy.[127] The result of his efforts was a peace treaty formally concluding the war in 1669, organized now in the European style as a distinct list of articles, followed by a new *ahdname*. The content of Murad IV's 1639 edict was now incorporated into the text, as it would be in every subsequent version of the *ahdname*.[128] The anti-piracy and slavery aspects of the *ahdname* were also recapitulated in a dedicated *nişan* in 1670.[129] This lengthy document marked the final stage in the evolution of Ottoman-Venetian, and by extension Ottoman-European, maritime law concerning piracy.

With abundant reference to tradition and "ancient custom," the edict confirmed the validity of all preceding *ahdname* regulations and renewed them. Freedom of travel and trade was reestablished. Sureties were to be taken from all corsair ships that came to Ottoman ports, and fortress commanders were not to admit pirates who harmed Venetians to their harbors. All the earlier requirements about freeing Venetian slaves and returning Venetian ships and cargoes were repeated in full, along with the expansive permission that was first granted in 1639 for the Venetians to take whatever measures necessary to punish pirates in the event that local Ottoman officials were negligent in their duties. The requirement to send Ottoman pirates taken alive to Istanbul for punishment was dropped, though the Porte still promised to capture and strongly punish pirates and corrupt officials such that they would serve as an example for others.

What was most different about the 1670 document was the language, which now conformed completely with international maritime usages. The *nişan* did not speak of "*harami* ships" or even of "*levend*" as it once had, but used only the more inclusive "*korsan*," in light of the fact that Muslim and Christian privateers and pirates alike made use of Ottoman ports and harmed Venetian interests. The text spoke now of "when corsairs brought their prizes" to a fortress, whereas before terms like "prize" (*akdarma*) had never been used. It mentioned meetings between Venetians and corsair bertons—the sailing ships now favored by both North African and Atlantic sea raiders—"on the high seas," additions that reflected the Mediterranean's transition from oar to sail. Beyond recapitulating the anti-piracy legislation that had evolved over nearly two hundred years, the 1670 edict adjusted it for the conditions of the age.

In tacit recognition of their de facto independence, the corsairs of North Africa were placed totally outside the protections of the *ahdname*—Venice could do what it needed to do, no questions asked.[130] Otherwise, besides that single mention of the "galleys and bertons of the Maghreb," all national and religious identifiers before the word *korsan* were removed from the *nişan*'s provisions so that there was now a completely uniform piracy policy, one that would remain in place for the remainder of the empire's history. After cycling through various changes and additions over the course of the sixteenth century to accommodate Ottoman privateers generally and North African ones specifically, the Ottoman government once again adopted the blanket view of pirates as the "common enemy of all."[131]

Fifteen years of peace separated the end of the war for Crete from the Morean War, when Venice decided to join the anti-Ottoman pile-on initiated by the Ottomans' failed siege of Vienna in 1683. The conflict with Venice stretched from 1684 to 1699 and added a maritime theater to the Ottomans' land war with the Habsburgs and their allies. Between 1670 and 1684, however, the *ahdname* was in effect. Although the Venetians adhered to the letter of the law, they were noticeably less enthusiastic in pursuing their erstwhile allies during the interwar years; they would still fight and destroy any pirates they encountered, but they would fire several shots when their warships approached well-known Christian pirate haunts like Mykonos to warn any pirates present to weigh anchor before they put into port.[132] The Ottomans, however, displayed a newly proactive attitude against piracy in the areas that were still effectively under their control in the 1670s and early 1680s.[133]

Along the Adriatic and Ionian coasts, for example, the Ottomans took measures that had little precedent. In particular, the surety clause of the *ahdnames* and anti-piracy *nişans* was now interpreted extremely broadly. In its earliest manifestation in 1482, it had only applied to vessels associated with the navy. In 1639, this had been explicitly expanded to include North African corsairs making use of Ottoman ports. In 1670, it reached its logical conclusion, and sureties were henceforth demanded from all shipowners, as the Ottoman government began regulating ship-building and usage in a way it never had before. At the start of the sea season in

1673, for example, orders were sent to all levels of the provincial hierarchy in the Adriatic and Ionian districts, which included long-time problem areas like Aya Mavra and Ülgün (Dulcigno, present-day Ulcinj), to summon everyone who owned a ship or boat. Those who used their boats for trade were required to obtain a certificate (*hüccet*) from their local *kadi* showing that they had secured guarantors. The names and descriptions of all the guarantors in the districts were then to be sent to the Porte for central registration. Anyone who failed to follow the procedure or engaged in piracy was to have his boat destroyed.[134] Similar orders were dispatched right up until the start of the next war in 1684—but not to North Africa.[135]

By disavowing North Africa and making the *ahdname*'s provisions regarding piracy ecumenical, the Ottomans had washed their hands of responsibility for North Africa's predations. They maintained their obligation to deny pirates markets and shelter and to return stolen goods and slaves, but otherwise stepped back from interdiction assurances and restitution guarantees. At the same time, the vigorous new stance against pirating in the Adriatic-Ionian sphere through broader enforcement of the surety clause, however fleeting, demonstrated how Ottoman thinking on the issue had evolved. Whereas surety had once been a means of ensuring that corsairs and regular naval units stuck to the right targets, it was now intended to prevent all shipowners from engaging in illegal raids.

These developments extended to the other maritime powers as well. Over the next decade, all three obtained new *ahdname*s, their first in decades, as they were not expected to follow the traditional practice observed by Venice of getting a new one at the accession of a new sultan (or the conclusion of a war). France obtained one in 1673 and the English in 1675. The Dutch followed suit in 1680. For the English and the Dutch, these were the last *ahdname*s they would receive—France would receive one more, in 1740—and they would remain in effect until 1923, after the dissolution of the empire. All three effectively adopted the same stance toward North Africa that had first been expressed in 1639. What Murad IV's *nişan* had begun, the post–Cretan war settlements concluded, excluding North African corsairs who acted contrary to the sultan's wishes from the protections of Ottoman subjecthood vis-à-vis the Ottomans' treaty partners. That differentiation, in legal as well as social and cultural forms, had dramatic consequences. The regencies stopped asking the sultan to ratify their treaties with the Europeans, thereby breaking one of the last traditions that had, at least in theory, bound their foreign policy to his, and European powers, awarded the same rights as Venice to chase and punish the North African corsairs, took those articles to their limits. European military interventions in North Africa had begun in the

1660s, but they accelerated in the second half of the 1670s and 1680s.[136] Istanbul's reaction to the intensification of European naval actions in the Maghreb was muted, but it remained fiercely defensive of its own ports, as events in the early 1680s would demonstrate.

France and Tripoli were at war in 1681. After a period in which Louis XIV had burnished his Catholic credentials by providing thinly disguised aid to the sultan's enemies, sending units in support of the Habsburgs during their 1663–1664 war with the Ottomans and reinforcements to besieged Candia in 1668, the ancient amity with the Ottoman Empire had been restored and French shipping was ascendant in the eastern half of the Mediterranean.[137] For Tripoli, however, the commercial success of the French and Tripoli's greater fear of the English, who had burned a portion of the fleet in the harbor and imposed peace in 1676, dictated war with the former and peace with the latter.[138] When, in 1680, the French admiral Abraham Duquesne came to Tripoli to negotiate peace, he was rebuffed. War on the continent had previously prevented a decisive response to Tripoli's depredations, but in 1681 Louis XIV decided to take advantage of a respite in the fighting to teach Tripoli a lesson. France's ambassador to the Sublime Porte, Gabriel Joseph de la Vergne, Comte de Guilleragues, had been advocating such for at least a year, taking particular umbrage when Tripolitan corsairs abducted the French consul at Larnaca on Cyprus, releasing him only upon the payment of an on-the-spot ransom of 800 ducats. Meanwhile, the ships of Tripoli continued to be admitted to Ottoman ports, despite their war with the sultan's friends.

And so, in the spring of 1681, Louis XIV ordered Admiral Duquesne to the Mediterranean, to find and destroy the ships of Tripoli wherever he might find them, including within Ottoman ports. Explicit exceptions were made for Izmir and Alexandria, which were too large, too well-defended, and too important for European commerce to risk an incident. On July 5, 1681, Guilleragues wrote to Duquesne that "the occasion and the pretext are very favorable" for an attack at Chios, where eight Tripolitan ships were then careening, since the Tripolitans had "taken with them two prizes which are French ships." The *ahdname* of course specifically prohibited North African corsairs bringing prizes taken from treaty-protected powers into Ottoman ports, so this violation, Guilleragues believed, provided additional legal cover for what the French had planned. Urging Duquesne to move quickly, he declared that "nothing in the world is more important for the king's affairs in this country than that enterprise which will give an idea of his majesty's greatness that the Turks will be unable to affect to ignore."[139] Duquesne was to inform Ottoman port officials that he came as a friend, but that if he were treated as an enemy, he would respond in kind; that he had no quarrel with the Ottomans, who were the king's "ancient friend and ally," but only with, in Duquesne's words, the corsairs who, "against his [the sultan's] orders and capitulations, even against the law of nations (*droit des gens*), prey upon and make slaves of the subjects of the king on the lands belonging to the Gran Seigneur."[140]

On July 23, eight French warships appeared before Chios, entered the harbor, and dropped anchor. To the alarm of those watching from the beach, they then hoisted the battle flag and opened fire upon the Tripolitan vessels, helpless since the guns had been removed so that the hulls could be exposed and tallowed. When the fortress, temporarily commandeered by some of the Tripolitans, answered with two shots, the French fired a volley into it, after which its guns fell silent. The *kadi* of Chios immediately summoned the French consul to find out what had precipitated this unexpected assault. Two Capuchin monks were rowed out to the French fleet and they relayed Duquesne's message upon their return: "give us the Tripolitan ships or we will completely destroy this town."[141]

The one-sided cannonade lasted for four and a half hours, during which roughly eight thousand balls were discharged in the direction of the ships. Four were sunk; four others were heavily damaged. But the Tripolitan ships were the least of the casualties at Chios. The French chain-shot—pairs of iron balls or half-balls connected by a chain, deployed to devastating effect against ships' masts and rigging—ripped through the crowds gathered along the shore, local Christians and Muslims who had come down to see what was happening before the French had begun firing without warning. When the smoke cleared, 110 innocent bystanders were dead and 800 seriously wounded. In addition to the human toll, wayward shot destroyed homes, damaged the fortress, and toppled a mosque's minaret.[142]

Sir John Finch, England's ambassador to the Sublime Porte, described the French action at Chios as "the greatest affront Upon this Empire, that it wer receiv'd since the taking of Constantinople."[143] But of course it resembled nothing so much as the Avlonya incident of 1638. Venice's actions against Tunisian and Algerian corsairs within the harbor of the Ottoman Albanian port had nearly led to war—indeed, they contributed to the lingering resentment that brought about the invasion of Crete in 1645—but the negotiations that followed led to the bestowal of the right to pursue hostile North African corsairs, even into Ottoman ports if necessary, and to destroy them.[144] Was, then, the French bombardment of Chios permissible according to the *ahdname*, or a grave violation of Ottoman sovereignty and an insult to Ottoman honor?

When news of the events at Chios arrived in Tripoli, the English consul Thomas Baker wrote in his journal, "how the Violation of the Gran Sigrs. Port wilbee relished at Constantinople wee shall shortly Learne." He, along with the rest of the European commercial powers' representatives, would be watching closely: "If happen to bee well digested, It may bee noe unserviceable Precedent for His Majesties men of Warr on the like occasion against those of Algier."[145] As it happened, the violation did not go down well at all. The incremental allowances granted after 1639 presumed hot pursuit, not the premeditated destruction of unmanned, disarmed ships without warning, and they provided no license for violence against the port itself or its inhabitants. Molloy's treatise on maritime law, first published in 1676, discussed the conflicting issues arising at Avlonya with words that were no less applicable to Chios in 1681, writing that "though the Ottoman Port[e] had by Treaty permitted the Venetians to pursue the Pirates in all places, and forbad their Commanders to protect or shew them any favour, yet the Castle interdicted, and forbad the Venetian General with Cannon to attack them; for it was nevertheless intended by the Treaty that the peace of Ports must be preserved."[146]

The peace thus disturbed, the Dardanelles were ordered closed to French ships such that none might come or go, and the French merchant community braced itself for impact.[147] Guilleragues, the French ambassador, was promptly summoned to an audience with the grand vizier, Merzifonlu Kara Mustafa Pasha (d. 1683), to account for what the French fleet had done. Guilleragues' own account and the Ottoman chronicles agree that the grand vizier demanded that the French apologize and that Guilleragues produce a legal document certifying his agreement to provide compensation for the dead and the property damage. If restitution were not provided, Kara Mustafa Pasha threatened, they would toss the ambassador into the infamous Seven Towers and there he would remain until it was paid. And he warned Guilleragues that if any further damage were done to any place or ship within the sultan's domains—for Duquesne's fleet was still menacingly anchored just beyond Chios—all French consuls and merchants would be arrested. For his part, Guilleragues defended Duquesne's actions as being directed against the sultan's rebellious subjects and consonant with the *ahdname*.[148]

Finch, reporting on Guilleragues' conversation with the grand vizier, portrayed the Frenchman as even more defiant and having vowed that no compensation would be paid, just as none had been provided when the same Tripolitan vessels took two French ships at Cyprus and kidnapped the consul. For the French to attack Tripoli's ships in the sultan's ports was more lawful than it was for the French to be attacked within them.[149]

However, the words Guilleragues reported saying to his master, the king, and repeated in admiring tones by the other ambassadors, were not the only ones heard by the sultan's ministers. And those spoken in Turkish by the French dragoman on the ambassador's behalf, but not always in his presence, were far more conciliatory. According to Ottoman accounts, the ambassador initially refused to provide compensation, but on the grounds that he could do nothing without first consulting the king. The grand vizier rejected this excuse, arguing that the ambassadors of the European kingdoms were appointed precisely to conduct such business, and he ordered Guilleragues imprisoned in the nearby chambers of the *çavuşbaşı ağası*. This provided an opportunity for the dragoman to take control of the situation. Referring to the lives lost and the physical damage at Chios, he claimed that "the things that happened were not the wish of our king," but that they took place in an effort to protect his country and its people. He reiterated that Louis XIV did not know what was going to happen and suggested that the king could send an apology letter (*i'tizarname*) and, "in order to renew the pact of friendship," he would send gifts. This led to an extensive discussion of what such an apology letter might say and of the gifts, the value of which would have to reflect the seriousness of the "mistake." After all had been agreed, a legal certificate formalizing the arrangement was produced, and the ambassador was released.[150] Finch, too, noted that Guilleragues had been briefly held and released after a signing a paper "to acquaint His Most Christian Ma[jes]ty with the Gran Sig[o]rs desires," but in reality the French ambassador had formally agreed that an apology and presents of specified value would be forthcoming.[151] This was, in effect if not in name, the admission of guilt and promise of compensation the grand vizier had demanded in the first place.

But in the interpretation of the law and the practice of diplomacy, appearances were everything, and in this regard the endeavor at Chios was not without success. The French had successfully impressed upon both their rivals and the Ottomans their resolve to combat those who preyed on their shipping, all the while maintaining that they were well within their legal rights in acting forcefully against those they continually referred to as the sultan's "rebellious subjects." Their Ottoman hosts did not dispute this interpretation. The demands for compensation and apology were understood by both sides not to encompass the shattered and sunken ships of Tripoli but only the unintended damage done to Chios and its residents, and Guilleragues represented them as such to the king.[152] At the same time, Duquesne remained anchored outside Chios, bottling up the Ottoman fleet and intimidating it into inaction. Soon the *kapudan pasha* agreed to mediate a peace between France, represented by Duquesne, and Tripoli, which was grudgingly accepted by Tripoli's corsairs in late October 1681.[153]

The king's letter, which stated that the events at Chios took place without his knowledge or permission and that the admiral would be punished—precisely what the grand vizier had demanded to hear—finally arrived on May 27, 1682. As agreed, it was accompanied by nine purses of jewels and thirty purses of assorted precious objects with a total value of 60,000 *guruş*. The gifts and the letter were ceremonially handed over to the sultan with great pomp and accepted, bringing the episode to a formal close.[154] Compared to the indemnity demanded of Venice after Avlonya in 1638–1639, the price of peace after Chios was a pittance. The disparity reflected the political and economic importance of the French relationship at a time when the Ottomans were preparing for war with the Habsburgs, but the ferocity of the Ottoman response sufficed to demonstrate once again that the sultan would not countenance naval maneuvers by his friends in his own ports. Indeed, he would not tolerate violence between his friends in his ports either, as the reaction to Digby's captures of French ships at Iskenderun in 1628 had shown. But if the Porte was now satisfied, Tripoli was not, and the events at Chios accomplished little for the French in that city. Within six months of the bombardment at Chios, four of the eight ships that had been the target of Duquesne's broadsides were back at sea, and in the last days of 1682, Tripoli again declared war on France.[155]

But in the summer of 1682, France was still at peace with Tripoli and looking toward chastening more powerful Algiers, which had reopened hostilities after the French failed to release their Algerian slaves as promised. The aftermath of Chios had suggested to France that, though hunting Maghrebi corsairs in the ports of the Ottoman Mediterranean would meet with reprisals, direct action against their home ports might not. In late August, just a few months after Louis XIV's presents had restored friendship with the Porte, Duquesne arrived before Algiers with a far larger fleet than that which had been arrayed against Chios. Deploying a new naval innovation, the bomb ketch, a two-masted vessel armed with forward-facing mortars, the French fleet could fire explosive shells on a ballistic arc while remaining anchored beyond the range of Algiers' shore batteries. Over the course of two weeks, Duquesne dropped bombs on Algiers, killing five hundred and blowing up fifty homes. Duquesne returned with his fleet the following year. The bombardment of late June 1683 was far more destructive, killing more than one thousand, pulverizing the port and town into ruins, and precipitating a coup d'état in the process. Although the new government retaliated by blasting the French consul from a cannon, it ultimately acceded to the release of hundreds of captives without ransom and accepted a new peace agreement with France.[156]

In contrast with Chios in 1681, the considerably more deadly and destructive bombardments of Algiers in 1682 and 1683 led to virtually no response from the Porte. An embassy sent from Algiers to Istanbul to complain after the bombardment of 1682 was brushed off.[157] There were no demands for compensation or apology this time. On these events, the Ottoman chroniclers of the period—including the court historiographer Râşid, who wrote indignantly of the "damned French" in the aftermath of Chios—are entirely silent. Shattered Algiers did not merit the same reaction as Chios, nor a place in the official Ottoman historical record. The chroniclers do note, however, that in November 1682 the Ottoman fleet sailed to the island of Milos, the notorious Catholic pirate haven on the southwestern edge of the Cyclades where the French had recently rebuilt a large Capuchin monastery without sultanic permission. Sappers attached to the fleet were dispatched to mine the monastery, where the *pères* had ministered to pirates, and blew it to smithereens. The navy then retired to Istanbul. But if this marginally satisfying reassertion of Ottoman sovereignty in the Aegean were spurred by pique with the French over recent events, none said so.[158]

There was no question of a direct military response to the French provocations. The Ottoman fleet was not, in 1681 or 1682, even remotely the equal of the French. Duquesne's eight ships at Chios could have taken on every galley Istanbul could muster and defeated them all—and everyone knew it.[159] This embarrassing recognition, that the French might ignore the warnings of the *kapudan pasha* in his own domain, may have contributed to the increased pace of the Ottoman fleet's modernization and conversion to sail over the next generation.[160] But the Ottomans had other tools at their disposal, not least the threat to arrest French subjects, impound French ships, and confiscate French wealth within the empire. They could withdraw trading privileges. They could favor the enemies and rivals of the French king. To do so would hurt them too, and French friendship was particularly important as war with the Habsburgs loomed, but none could simply dismiss Ottoman threats, especially in these years before the fateful Ottoman defeat at Vienna in 1683. And indeed, neither France nor any of the other European powers repeated what the Venetians had done at Avlonya in 1638 and the French at Chios in 1681. Henceforth, they limited their progressively more violent reprisals to the North African ports themselves, which the Ottomans accepted without intervention or significant protest.

What happened to Algiers in 1682, 1683, and 1688, and the many similar bombardments suffered by it and its neighbors over the course of the eighteenth century, was not understood, in Istanbul or Europe, as an attack on the Ottomans themselves.[161] This would not have been the case half a century earlier. In March 1624, the *şeyhülislam* Hocazade Esad Efendi was alarmed when he learned that the French were contemplating an assault on North Africa and warned the French ambassador, the Comte de Césy, that, if the French were to declare war on Barbary, they would be "declaring war on his master," Sultan Murad IV. At the same time, however, he reminded the Frenchman that both he and his father, the *şeyhülislam* Hoca Sadeddin Efendi (d. 1599), had repeatedly issued *fetva*s saying that the French were free to fall upon the "rebels" who threatened them.[162]

Duquesne had also portrayed the Tripolitans he attacked at Chios in 1681 as the sultan's "rebellious subjects," but as the Irish jurist Molloy noted in an addition to the 1682 third edition of his treatise on maritime law, Algiers, Tunis, and Tripoli "having acquired the reputation of a Government . . . cannot properly be esteemed Pirates but Enemies." Having obtained the "right of legation" over half a century earlier, the Maghreb, though a "nest of pirates" to the Europeans in an emotional sense, was effectively sovereign and its predations legitimate acts of war.[163] The bombardments it suffered, then, were acts of war, as well. Even if these might still be framed for the Ottomans as the punishing of pirates, of "rebellious subjects," out of respect for Istanbul's de jure sovereignty, the Ottomans' turning a blind eye to the bombardments was evidence for how things had changed since the 1620s, how not just the corsairs but their ports had been placed outside the Ottoman Mediterranean in recognition of their de facto independence. The links between the core lands of the Ottoman Empire and North Africa were real, they were lasting, and they were important, but events since the turn of the century had created enough political, legal, and diplomatic distance between the two to sail a French fleet through without creating an international incident.

This process reached its logical conclusion in the eighteenth century. In its efforts to maintain the neutrality of Ottoman ports and the peace of the waters of the "well-protected domains," the Ottoman government declared that, in times of war, neither the privateers of its European friends nor the corsairs of North Africa would be welcome, and if prizes were taken within the boundaries it set, the offending power would be expected to compensate the victims or risk reprisals. Although the Ottomans still maintained a broad commitment to preserving freedom of navigation, the policy the Ottomans adopted grew out of the recognition that blocking off ports and coastal waters did not serve to protect their friends' shipping and, by extension, the goods Ottoman subjects freighted with them. For instance, in the 1740s the Ottoman government issued demarcation notices (*hududname*) to the governments of Algiers, Tunis, and Tripoli, ordering them not to enter or take prizes in the Aegean nor within thirty miles of Crete, the Dodecanese islands, Cyprus, or the mainland ports of Alexandria, Sidon, Beirut, Syrian Tripoli, Iskenderun, or Antalya—effectively encompassing all the major and minor ports of the Ottoman Mediterranean. After a Tripolitan corsair captured a Venetian ship returning from Alexandria off the coast of Crete in 1742, the principal question in the subsequent legal wrangling was not whether Tripoli had the right to make war on Venice nor whether Tripoli might make lawful prizes of Venetian ships, but rather whether the prize had been taken within the boundaries (*hudud*) previously set.[164]

Beginning with the Nine Years' War (1688–97), the British and the French were similarly ordered to restrict their privateers' movements, and as Michael Talbot has shown, with each war the Ottomans claimed a progressively larger swath of maritime space that was to be kept clear of their quarrels.[165] The orders establishing the new exclusion zone in 1744, when Britain entered the War of the Austrian Succession (1740–1748) against France, are worth quoting. Declaring that the sultan could not tolerate any warfare "in the waters of his well-protected domains, and in places under his jurisdiction," the grand vizier decreed that, "it is necessary to suppose a line, which forms the extreme end of the Islamic realms; that is, between the peninsula of the Morea, and its end the Gulf of Sidra, which is the western border of the Land of Egypt, so that in no island that is under the Ottoman dominion, nor in any waters to the east of that line, nor on the high seas, nor on the coasts of Rumelia or Asia, shall be introduced any warships of privateers."[166] Privateering and piracy forced the Ottomans to define more explicitly than they ever had the extent of their maritime legal space, and in the mid-eighteenth century the sultan's administrators drew a line on the map formalizing the borders of the Ottoman Mediterranean that had taken shape a century before.

CONCLUSION

The blanket of de jure Ottoman sovereignty continued to cover North Africa, but it would provide neither succor nor warmth going forward. At the beginning of the seventeenth century, the England-based Italian jurist Alberico Gentili had struggled with whether the North African provinces, as constituent parts of the Ottoman Empire, exercised sovereignty or not, and thus whether they were covered by the contents of the sultan's treaties. He argued both sides depending on his employer. By the 1620s, that question was putting enormous strain on the credibility of the sultan and his guarantees. That pressure was relieved, for all but Venice, by allowing the North African city-states to conduct their own foreign policy, independent from but rubber-stamped by Istanbul. Over the following half century, the combination of a local monopoly on force, independent foreign relations, and autonomous institutions reduced the political connections between Istanbul and Algiers and Tunis to the symbolic, even as military cooperation continued periodically and commercial, cultural, and personal links were maintained. By the 1680s, the question that had exercised Gentili had largely been settled in favor of the corsairs. European jurists like Molloy in 1682 and Cornelius van Bynkershoek in 1737 argued that the North African city-states had legal personality and exercised full sovereignty and theirs was not a minority opinion, but rather one given full credence by the actions of the navies and courts of European powers since the 1620s.[167] What should concern us here is the fact that, by the middle of the seventeenth century, Istanbul accepted the implications of this view of North Africa as well, even if it could not formally subscribe to the particulars; the sultans never surrendered their claim to overlordship, which continued to be symbolically acknowledged.

Ottoman sovereignty had been extended to the Maghreb in the sixteenth century, by both request and conquest, in large part to deny that space to the growing Habsburg threat. During the seventeenth century, with North Africa's usefulness in question and its loyalty in doubt, the Ottomans retrenched. Although the center would reassert itself in Tripoli in 1835, after an internal revolt toppled the Karamanlı dynasty that had ruled there since 1711[168]—a second Ottoman conquest after more than two centuries of virtual independence—the gradual separation that had begun in the 1580s and broken out into the open in the 1620s and 1630s, had otherwise become irreparable by the 1670s. With that, the seeds of more European intervention in North Africa had been sown. The Ottomans had provided a century-long reprieve from this, though they had been alien colonizers as well. In time, however, the independent negotiations with European powers in which North Africa had the upper hand gave way to bombardment and imposed treaties, and ultimately to occupation and colonization. When France occupied Algeria in 1830, there was little more than symbolic protest from Istanbul.[169]

The boundaries of the Ottoman Mediterranean gradually emerged as a result of these fundamental disagreements over the line between licit raiding and piracy. They were further defined as the Ottomans attempted to exclude the quarrels of other powers, including both the North African provinces and Istanbul's European friends, from their waters and their ports. In pirate- and privateer-infested seas, the Ottomans attempted to establish Ottoman ports and, ultimately, the Ottoman Mediterranean as a whole, as a neutral space. Within those liquid borders, the sultan's treaties and decrees still had binding force and violations might generate a response. Within the Ottoman Mediterranean, there was a whole other sea of law in which Ottoman subjects and foreigners, pirates and their victims swam.

PART THREE

Ottoman Mediterranean, Abode of Law

CHAPTER FIVE

Piracy in Ottoman Islamic Jurisprudence

Question: While Captain Zeyd is cruising towards the Mediterranean with his ship, he encounters the ships of enemy infidels. They seize Zeyd's ship. Afterwards, near the island of Cyprus, the ships of the Muslims happen upon the infidel ships and they prevail [in the ensuing conflict]. They take Zeyd's ship from their hands. If, after taking full possession of it, they sell it to Amr, and if Zeyd now finds his ship in Amr's possession, after providing proof [of his prior ownership], can he, according to the *şeriat*, take [it] from Amr's possession for free? **Answer:** Yes.[1]

Zekeriyyazade Yahya Efendi, *Fetava-yı Yahya Efendi*

This *fetva* of Zekeriyyazade Yahya Efendi, Ottoman chief mufti (*şeyhülislam*) between 1622 and 1644 with two two-year interruptions, is unusual in some respects, and typical in others. Unusual is its mention of specific place-names, the Mediterranean Sea and Cyprus; typical are the simple language and deliberate phrasing that spotlight the particular point of law at issue and anticipate the jurist's terse response. A *fetva* (Arabic: *fatwa*) is a nonbinding legal opinion delivered by a qualified Islamic jurist, a mufti, in response to a query and in accordance with the precepts of that mufti's school of Islamic jurisprudence (*mezheb*; Arabic: *madhhab*). Individually, Ottoman *fetva*s' characteristic absence of detail and dates makes them appear rather unpromising as historical sources. Only rarely can we identify who requested them, when, or why. Taken together, however, the *fetva*s of the *şeyhülislam*s provide unrivaled insights into the legal quandaries that acts of maritime raiding posed for the Ottoman administration and its subjects and detail Ottoman jurists' persistent search for solutions. They elucidate a legal worldview that was particularly Ottoman, demonstrating how the *şeyhülislam*s reconciled the sometimes conflicting precepts of Islamic law and prerogatives of the state.

In their collected form, *fetva*s like this served as a two-lane bridge between the imperatives of classical Hanafi Islamic jurisprudential theory and the pragmatics of early modern Mediterranean reality. Lived experience percolated up into legal precedents through *fetva*s that were informed as much by secular policy and political necessity as by Islamic law. These *fetva*s, in turn, were reproduced and disseminated such that they directly impacted the lived experience of others on land and sea. Together, muftis and their *fetva*s mediated the encounter between the law, the individual, and the state, guiding them together through dangerous, uncharted waters.

This chapter explores how the early modern Ottomans understood the sea in religious-legal terms and how that understanding evolved in the context of increasing lawlessness in the seventeenth-century Mediterranean. To do so it relies on collections of *şeyhülislam fetva*s compiled between the late-sixteenth and mid-eighteenth centuries.[2] It was through *fetva*s that Ottoman jurists formulated their response to the problems posed by piracy and through *fetva* collections that that response was disseminated throughout the Ottoman Mediterranean. The result was an explosion of opinions on the subject beginning around the turn of the seventeenth century where before there had been none. Ottoman jurists deployed the tools of Hanafi jurisprudence to cope with unprecedented political, legal, and military challenges that demanded novel solutions.

Though the Ottoman muftis worked within the Hanafi school, issuing opinions consistent with centuries of tradition, they were nevertheless confronting questions that their predecessors had never seen in a theater of law—the sea—that defied the rigid dichotomy of the standard Islamic binary division of the world into a zone of peace, the realm of Islam, and a zone of continuous war.[3] Their rulings touched not only on the disposition of disputed property, of ships, slaves, and cargo, but also on the fates of converts and apostates, on the rights of Ottoman corsairs to their spoils, and the rights of Ottoman subjects not to become part of them. Crucially, they tackled the complex question of holy war at sea, asserting the state's monopoly on religious violence and denying the mantle of religious justification to the pirates and slave raiders whose attacks abrogated Ottoman treaties.

Under the Ottomans, the mufti of Istanbul was known as the *şeyhülislam* (Arabic: *shaykh al-Islam*), the head of the Ottoman *ulema* (the Islamic learned class) and, by the mid-sixteenth century, a figure at the pinnacle of the Ottoman legal and religious hierarchy with authority over a broad array of judicial and educational appointments and great personal and moral influence over political and religious policy. But the primary duty of the *şeyhülislam* was, as the empire's chief mufti, to issue *fetva*s to all comers.[4] Anyone from anywhere within the empire and without, regardless of class, religion, or subject status, could submit a query to the *şeyhülislam*. As the most respected source of authoritative, Islamic legal opinions in the empire, the *şeyhülislam*'s *fetvahane*, the *fetva*-granting office, received all manner of questions, from curious Muslims looking for clarifications on correct religious observance to the sultan looking for justification for war, from Ottoman Armenian Christians engaged in contentious international litigation to the Venetian ambassador hoping to strengthen a petition for an imperial decree.

As the importance of the *şeyhülislam* increased over the course of the sixteenth century, a bureaucracy grew to facilitate *fetva*-granting on a larger scale. During the twenty-nine-year tenure of the *şeyhülislam* Ebu Su'ud (1545–1574), this bureaucracy was expanded and further institutionalized, taking on the basic form that persisted until the dissolution of the empire. This coincided with an expansion of the duties, power, and prestige of the office itself, owing in large part to Ebu Su'ud's earlier career in the upper echelons of the judicial establishment and his long friendship with Sultan Süleyman I (r. 1520–1566) and his influence over the latter's son and successor Sultan Selim II (r. 1566–1574). Though most subsequent *şeyhülislam*s did not enjoy relations as intimate or tenures as long as those of Ebu Su'ud, the prestige of the institution, its duties, its supporting bureaucracy, and the career path that led to it were firmly established. Critically, most *şeyhülislam*s of the early modern period came to their position, like Ebu Su'ud, not through previous careers as muftis, but as judges in one of the empire's most important posts (for example, Istanbul, Bursa) and/or as one of the two military judges (*kazasker* or *kadiasker*) of the empire with a seat on the Imperial Council.[5] This meant that they, unlike ordinary muftis, already had extensive experience putting the law into practice and reconciling the sometimes contradictory requirements of Islamic and sultanic law (*şeriat* and *kanun*, respectively), and were familiar with imperial policy and the inner workings of government. Ebu Su'ud was eulogized in his day for having successfully reconciled *şeriat* and *kanun*, and it was in part through his *fetva*s and those of his successors that this process was accomplished and sustained.[6]

The *fetvahane* of Ebu Su'ud and his successors was managed by a permanent staff of trained jurists headed by the *fetva emini*, the chief clerk. The questioner (*müstefti*) submitted his query (and, from the seventeenth century, his fee) to one of the clerks who would reformulate the question in consultation with the *fetva emini*. The question was distilled to its essence. Names were replaced with standardized aliases (Zeyd, Amr, Bekr, Beşr, and so on, for men; Hind, Zeyneb, Hadice, and so on, for women) and superfluous details were removed to bring the point of law at issue into relief. The new question was usually posed in such a manner that it could be answered simply yes (*olur*) or no (*olmaz*). Fair copies were prepared and presorted by the *fetva emini* into "yes" and "no" groups in anticipation of the *şeyhülislam*'s final ruling; indeed, more complicated questions were divided on the same page into an initial question with one or more follow-up questions that presupposed the mufti's response to the first. The *şeyhülislam* wrote his ruling below the answer prompt (*el-cevab*) and then added his signature. Aside from inquiries from important dignitaries or the sultan, when the *şeyhülislam* might write the question and answer himself and indulge in a more lengthy response, the *şeyhülislam* would have no contact with the questioners and no knowledge of their identities. He might not even have to read their questions. In this manner, the *fetvahane* could produce several hundred or more *fetva*s a day—Ebu Su'ud claimed to have dispensed with a staggering 1,412 *fetva*s between morning and afternoon prayers one day and 1,413 on another—and return completed *fetva*s to questioners within a few days.[7]

Written on small square pieces of paper, few original early modern *fetva*s survive. But *fetva* collections (*mecmua*) compiled after the death, dismissal, or retirement of a prominent *şeyhülislam* preserve a broad sample. These included copies of *fetva*s issued during the *şeyhülislam*'s tenure, occasionally supplemented with some number of *fetva*s fabricated later in order to showcase the legal mind of the jurist and increase the comprehensiveness and usability of the collection. In some collections, the compilers also added proof-texts in Arabic—essentially citations—showing what canonical works of Hanafi jurisprudence were (or could be) used to support the (usually) Ottoman Turkish *fetva*. Nearly all of the *şeyhülislam fetva* collections produced in the late sixteenth, seventeenth, and early eighteenth centuries were assembled by one or more of their *fetva emini*s. Spared the factional wrangling that the *şeyhülislam*s had to contend with, the *fetva emini*s often held their positions through the tenures of multiple *şeyhülislam*s.[8] They and their staff provided continuity in the sphere of *fetva* production even when political turmoil resulted in rapid changes at the top.

The fact that the *fetva emini*s, accomplished jurists responsible for overseeing the wording of the questions and anticipating the mufti's answers, were also the primary producers of *fetva* compilations meant that their selections reflected the consensus of a stable bureaucracy and not just the opinions of a particular *şeyhülislam*. Furthermore, the post of *fetva emini* was a stepping stone to high-ranking judicial positions and to the *şeyhülislam* post itself.[9] A number of seventeenth-century *fetva* collections were compiled by a sitting *şeyhülislam* from the *fetva*s of the *şeyhülislam* whom he had served as *fetva emini* some years earlier.[10] Ottoman *fetva* collections were extensively reproduced and recompiled; they were widely disseminated and often heavily annotated. They had a sizable readership in learned circles and provided ready, up-to-date guidance to judges, provincial muftis, law students, and private individuals alike.[11]

MURKY WATERS: ABODE OF ISLAM AND ABODE OF WAR AT SEA

Ottoman *fetva* collections are arranged topically, with an Arabic table of contents and chapters (*kitab*) corresponding to the traditional organization of *fiqh* (Islamic jurisprudence) manuals and allowing for easy reference.[12] The material we are interested in here generally falls into the *kitab al-siyar*, an extremely broad chapter that deals with the conduct of state and incorporates questions concerning *gaza* and jihad (holy war), the taking of captives, relations with foreign powers, travel between the *darülislam* ("the Abode of Islam") and the *darülharb* ("the Abode of War," i.e., the lands not under Muslim rule), the rights and responsibilities of non-Muslim subjects (*zimmi*) and of resident foreigners carrying a safe-conduct (*müstemin*), and so forth.[13] Though true, indiscriminate piracy should, according to classical Hanafi jurisprudence, be handled under the section dealing with highway robbery (which usually immediately precedes the *kitab al-siyar*), in no Ottoman *fetva* collection is such a case clearly identifiable there. In spite of the fact that piracy resembles highway robbery both in practice and in punishment—conceived as a crime against the state, it merits administrative execution (*siyaset*)—opinions emanating from all manner of maritime raiding are confined to the *kitab al-siyar*.[14] The reasoning behind this is clear: highway robbery is an internal affair. Conversely, piracy and corsairing occur in the murky waters separating the *darülislam* and the *darülharb*, putting it firmly within the jurisdiction of *siyar*.

Motion, either along or across the invisible line separating those two domains, is at the center of most *fetva*s in the *siyar* sections and all those concerning conflict and captivity. The Arabic *siyar*, most often rendered as "the conduct of state," is the plural of *sira*, which carries a number of meanings, including "biography" (this remains its most common usage in contemporary Arabic). But the original meaning of *siyar* was "motion," connoting travel. Abu Hanifa (d. 768), eponymous founder of the

Hanafi *madhhab*, was known to have used the term in its present juristic function, and it was the Hanafi jurists who popularized and expanded it. Muhammad al-Shaybani (d. 804), disciple of Abu Hanifa and of Abu Yusuf, authored two treatises on *siyar* that laid the foundation for much of the Hanafi thought that followed.[15] This kinetic quality is evident in the Ottoman *siyar fetva*s as well, where the outcome of a particular case often turned not on the circumstances of the originating act of seizure, but on whether or how the line between *darülislam* and *darülharb* was crossed after the fact.

A couple of examples serve to illustrate this point:

> **Question:** An enemy infidel takes Captain Zeyd's ship. After he *imports* it into the *darülharb*, the possessor of that ship in the *darülharb* gives [it] to Amr who is a Muslim [merchant] with safe-conduct. When he exports [the ship back] into the *darülislam*, can Zeyd take [the ship] from Amr's possession for free? **Answer:** No, he can take it for its value.[16]

> **Question:** After infidels capture Zeyd's ship by force, if they sell it and turn it over to Bekr without importing it into the *darülharb*, can Zeyd take his ship from Bekr for free? **Answer:** Yes.[17]

In both *fetva*s, taken from the collections of Zekeriyyazade Yahya Efendi (in office, 1622–1623, 1625–1632, 1634–1644) and Minkarizade Yahya Efendi (in office, 1662–1674) respectively, the circumstances of the initial seizure are identical. Zeyd's ship is captured by "enemy infidels," the catch-all term for non-Ottoman non-Muslims, within the *darülislam*. Nothing is said about who the enemy infidels are or whether they are part of a regular navy, semi-independent irregulars, licensed corsairs, or fully independent pirates; in religious-legal terms, the distinction was irrelevant, just as it often was in practice.

But in the first case, the enemy infidels bring the ship back with them across the divide into the *darülharb* before they transfer possession, while in the second case, they do not. It is this detail that determines the outcome of both cases, allowing Zeyd to reclaim his ship from Bekr in the latter example, even though Bekr had paid for it, while preventing him from doing so in the former, even though Amr had acquired it for free, because Amr had received it in the *darülharb* and brought it back into the *darülislam* in his possession. The forceful removal of property from the *darülislam* to the *darülharb* voids pre-existing ownership ties when it is brought back to the *darülislam* in the possession of another, since ownership ties within the *darülharb* are not recognized and persons and property in that realm can legally be taken and claimed by Muslims.[18]

The phrasing of our second example, in which the ship's continuous presence within the *darülislam* is framed as a negative—the infidels sell the ship to Bekr without first importing it (*idhal etmeden*) into the *darül-harb*—makes it immediately clear to the reader that the crossing between the two worlds, and not the originating encounter, is the act on which the mufti's decision hinges.

The wording might evoke for us the image of a tug-of-war, in which someone or something must be dragged from its natural place in the world across a thin line and, in that finite instant and in that definable place, the act of being brought over to one side and out of the other is accomplished in full. But this was a juristic fantasy. Though the Hanafi jurists' absolute binary conceptualization of the world did not allow for any physical or political middle ground—they rejected the notion, accepted by some other schools, of *dar al-sulh* or *dar al-'ahd* (Arabic for "Abode of the Truce/Treaty") for tributary, but still independent states[19]—political and administrative realities shattered this strict dichotomy in practice. Politically, the Ottomans maintained a mutually beneficial arrangement with the Adriatic city-state of Dubrovnik that treated it exactly as *dar al-sulh*, though a great deal of juristic back-bending was required to show that it, in fact, was not, leading to frequent confusion over whether Ragusan merchants were actually *zimmi*s (they were not).[20] On the ground, most Ottoman borders were not well-defined before 1699. In the sixteenth and seventeenth centuries, for example, the inhabitants of the Ottoman-Habsburg borderlands were doubly taxed and subjected to interminable raids and counter-raids launched from both sides.[21] Ottoman policymakers recognized the concept of maritime sovereignty or territoriality in certain circumstances. The Ottoman state jealously guarded its access to the Black Sea until the late eighteenth century and, as we have seen, it was not averse to temporarily asserting claims to broad swathes of the Mediterranean to keep out European privateers; it accepted Venetian claims to sovereignty in the Adriatic and even adopted the Venetians' styling of it as the "Gulf of Venice" (*Venedik körfezi*). Nevertheless, the idea of an observable, fixed boundary between the *darülislam* and the *darülharb* in the Mediterranean Sea was inconceivable in Islamic legal terms, as the *fetva*s themselves demonstrate.

So then what did these labels mean in Ottoman practice, when Islamic legal theory had such an enormous blind spot? How were *darülislam* and *darülharb* defined and understood at sea as useful ontological categories? Here again we look to the *fetva*s for an answer, returning to the example from Zekeriyyazade Yahya Efendi with which we opened the chapter:

Question: While Captain Zeyd is cruising towards the Mediterranean with his ship, he encounters the ships of enemy infidels. They seize Zeyd's ship. Afterwards, near the island of Cyprus, the ships of the Muslims happen upon the infidel ships and they prevail [in the ensuing conflict]. They take Zeyd's ship from their hands. If, after taking full possession of it, they sell it to Amr, and if Zeyd now finds his ship in Amr's possession, after providing proof [of his prior ownership], can he, according to the *şeriat*, take [it] from Amr's possession for free? **Answer:** Yes.[22]

This example, as noted above, is unusual because of its use of geographical place-names, artifacts from the original question submitted to the *fetvahane*. Ottoman *fetva* questions only rarely preserve superfluous details, so the reader must ask what role "the island of Cyprus" is playing in the affirmative decision. In terms of the legal reasoning involved, this *fetva* is identical to that of Minkarizade Yahya Efendi quoted earlier, in which Zeyd's ship, after capture, was not taken to the *darülharb* before sale and thus was reclaimed without cost to Zeyd, in spite of the fact that Bekr had purchased it in good faith. Here, the geographical details stand in for "*darülislam*," which does not appear in the text. When the ship is retaken by the Ottoman naval patrol within sight of Cyprus the ship is still within the *darülislam*. The classical Islamic position was that jurisdiction extends into coastal waters at least as far as one can see the top of a ship's mast from the shore, or about six miles, but proximity to the Ottoman coast was not the deciding factor here.[23] This was not a question of the geographical limits of *darülislam*, but rather of whether Zeyd's ship had "entered" the *darülharb*.

Most *fetva*s use only the *darülislam*/*darülharb* plus "import"/"export" formulae, either because the specific circumstances in the original query were unambiguous or because they were not germane to the decision, but the preservation of both the ship's original course and its specific point of re-capture in the preceding example is indicative of the confusion surrounding these issues and their importance for *fetva*-requesters, litigants, and judges. The mention of Cyprus here is not telling us that the ship is in the *darülislam* so much as it is confirming that it has not yet left it. Ottoman jurists did not recognize a transfer of ownership at the moment that a ship was seized and put under new command, but only after it was securely in their possession; entry into the *darülharb* occurred the moment the ship or property was brought into an enemy (*harbi*) port.[24] Similarly, Shaybani held that war spoils must be taken "to a place of security in the territory of Islam" before they could be divided.[25] Given the unending cycle of capture, re-capture, and sale of both ships and captives in the seventeenth-century Mediterranean, encapsulated in the *fetva*s and borne out by the historical record, this view was only logical. It also conformed precisely to Mediterranean-wide maritime legal custom; the rulings of the *şeyhülislam*s in this arena would not have looked out of place in the medieval western European compendium of maritime law, the *Consolato del Mare*.[26]

Even though Ottoman jurists deployed the full range of authoritative Hanafi jurisprudential texts to justify their opinions, evidenced in part by the Arabic proof-texts added after the fact to some *fetva* collections, the works they cited never directly confronted these issues. They dealt with analogous situations on land, but maritime law of this sort was in fact uncharted territory for the Hanafis. Despite the rigidity of Hanafi doctrine regarding the binary division of the world, Ottoman jurists displayed remarkable flexibility in finding applicable, real-world legal solutions in areas of the law that had not been adequately theorized. In the dynamic and increasingly dangerous maritime environment of the late sixteenth- and seventeenth-century Mediterranean, the Ottoman *şeyhülislam*s and their staffs met the challenge of defining the practical legal boundaries of the *darülislam* and the *darülharb* at sea when it was necessary, while preserving enough ambiguity to avoid the appearance of conflict with established Islamic legal theory when it was not.

CONTEXTUALIZING *FETVA*S AND *FETVA* COLLECTIONS IN THE OTTOMAN MEDITERRANEAN

The presence of a given *fetva* in a collection—whether selected from among the many thousands issued during an individual *şeyhülislam*'s tenure or fabricated afterward—can be explained by its ability to demonstrate the juridically correct ruling in an archetypical case that hinges on a specific point of law. Often, a number of similar or related *fetva*s would be strung together in a series to illustrate where variations in circumstance would lead to variations in outcome. *Fetva* collections were intended, first and foremost, to serve as searchable reference works. Written in simple Turkish, logically organized, and dealing with issues of contemporary relevance, they would have been easier to use and more accessible to native Turkish speakers than the complex Arabic jurisprudential works they often cited. As such, they likely served a critical role in both the education and daily practice of Ottoman legal professionals.[27] A *fetva* that merited inclusion showcased a juristic concept in a socially and legally relevant scenario with which the contemporary reader could identify and from which he could draw useful guidance, or had been issued in connection with a high-profile incident or controversy that was still part of the collective memory of the compilation's perceived audience and thus reflected the juristic legacy of the mufti and his head clerk–cum–compiler.

The head clerks/compilers of *fetva*s, as individuals involved in the original formulation of the questions, the giving of the answers, and the selection and arrangement of the *fetva*s into tightly organized collections, were much more than simple aggregators. They and their office were the true authors of the collections and their content, which constituted a legal genre that was particularly Ottoman in form and function.[28] The continuity of personnel and policy in the Ottoman *fetva*-granting institution, and the institutional authorship of the *fetva*s and *fetva* collections themselves, means that changes in the content of the collections over time reflect less the whims or peculiar interests of individual compilers, but changes in social and political realities and the needs of the publics that consumed these works.

The growing prominence of issues having to do with maritime raiding in the seventeenth- and eighteenth-century sections on *siyar* corresponds precisely with the dramatic rise in piratical violence during that period and reflects its powerful effect on law, imperial policy, and Ottoman society. Ebu Su'ud Efendi's *fetva* compilations, in contrast, the product of his nearly three decades as *şeyhülislam* (1545–1574), have comparatively little to say about these matters; they are far more vocal on questions relating to the conduct of *gaza* and jihad. Indeed, instead of a *kitab al-siyar* they have a *kitab al-jihad* covering the same field, and it is only in the context of questions concerning ransom and organized naval campaigns that ships and the sea appear.[29] Was the mufti receiving more questions concerning piracy and slave raiding in 1670 than in 1570? Probably. But Ebu Su'ud Efendi, author of untold thousands of *fetva*s, undoubtedly handled questions similar to those appearing in the seventeenth-century collections of Zekeriyyazade Yahya Efendi, Minkarizade Yahya Efendi, or Çatalcalı Ali Efendi. The compiler/clerks' inclusion of growing numbers of maritime-themed *fetva*s in the seventeenth- and early eighteenth-century collections—beginning in earnest with the collection of Sunullah Efendi (d. 1612), who served off and on between 1599 and 1608[30]—points to the fact that such examples would be both immediately relevant and genuinely useful for readers, and this was true whether a *fetva* in a collection originated from an actual questioner or a hypothetical one.

In contrast, the clerks who compiled Ebu Su'ud Efendi's collections were writing for a different time. The exhaustively detailed *fetva*s they preserved dealing with the division of spoils and the fates of those who jumped ship in battle to avoid certain death,[31] though they retained importance for later readers, were the product of a period when few could have anticipated that the 1571 Battle of Lepanto would have no sequel. For contemporary observers, the period of major naval disengagement in the Mediterranean that followed that encounter, confirmed in the 1581 truce with Habsburg Spain and persisting until the Ottoman invasion of Crete in 1645, was nowhere visible on the horizon. By the time Zekeriyyazade Yahya Efendi's collection appeared in the middle of the seventeenth century, several generations had come of age in the new Mediterranean, where massive armadas of war galleys had given way to a seemingly endless array of self-interested actors of often indeterminate origin and dubious allegiance, sailing in all manner of ships and engaging in raid and trade in equal measure. The bureaucrat-compilers behind his collection and those of his successors assembled manuals that, in their sections on *siyar*, confronted questions of very real significance that directly and indirectly affected the lives of numerous Ottoman and non-Ottoman subjects and had already had a marked impact on the conduct of government. Indeed, the *şeyhülislam*'s connection with the state played a key role in these developments; there was no corresponding appearance of maritime *siyar fetva*s in the collections of prominent provincial muftis' opinions, which had very different concerns and audiences.[32]

It is worth noting that the "protagonists" of the *fetva*s explicitly concerned with maritime raiding, usually Ottoman subjects or their slaves, are overwhelmingly the victims. A comparatively small number have Ottoman subjects filling the role of the original aggressor. Far more often they make an appearance *re*-taking ships or captives from enemy infidels. We should not assume that this is necessarily an accurate reflection of piracy in the Ottoman Mediterranean. Rather, it should drive us to ask who might request a *fetva* and under what circumstances and, on another level, what kinds of questions appealed to the compilers and helped contribute to their presumed goal of producing a comprehensive, usable volume.

Perhaps unsurprisingly, outside of the *fetva*s of Ebu Su'ud, whose tenure came on the heels of one war with Venice (that of 1537–1540) and culminated in another (that of 1570–1573), the next collection with a substantial number of *fetva*s originating from Ottoman-initiated acts of maritime raiding and captive-taking is that of Minkarizade Yahya Efendi, whose tenure included the last seven years of the long war with Venice for Crete (1645–1669).[33] Further examples appear in collections containing *fetva*s dating from the last quarter of the seventeenth century, such as that of Feyzullah Efendi (served 1688, 1695–1703), when the Ottomans were again battling the Venetians in the Mediterranean between 1684 and 1699. Although *fetva* collections followed a standardized format, they were, at least into the early eighteenth century, very much a product of their times, and their content reflected contemporary concerns.[34]

The *fetva*s do not provide a representative sample of the full range of experiences and legal conundrums at sea, nor do they address or give voice to all the actors. Women, for example, are conspicuously absent from the maritime *fetva*s. Women do appear frequently as victims and captives in land-based *siyar fetva*s, where the questions often revolve around the legality of their enslavement, the consequences of their conversion, or the limits of the sexual rights of their masters. Their total absence from the maritime *fetva*s might be explained with the twin assumptions that, one, the collections' land-*fetva*s say all that needs to be said about female captives and slaves that is distinct from the opinions concerning male captives and slaves—making the inclusion of *fetva*s about women in this arena superfluous—and, two, that female *müsteftis* with questions relating to conflict at sea were probably exceedingly rare.

One important group for the history of maritime raiding that was *not* requesting *şeyhülislam fetva*s can be easily identified. Although the rulers and subjects of the North African regencies could theoretically obtain *şeyhülislam fetva*s, they, the chief culprits of much early modern "Ottoman piracy," would find little reason to do so. Mostly Maliki in orientation, they had their own muftis they could turn to with questions. Moreover, in peacetime they would receive no support from the Hanafi *şeyhülislam* for their ventures, which flagrantly violated the anti-piracy clauses of the Ottomans' treaties with foreign powers. This was equally true for the naval irregulars operating out of bases more directly controlled by the Ottoman central government. In times of conflict, when privateering was actively encouraged, corsairs and their accomplices would likely only seek *fetva*s if there were an after-the-fact dispute over distribution of the spoils back on land and/or in court. This is borne out by the collection of the wartime *şeyhülislam* Minkarizade Yahya Efendi, whose collection does indeed contain *fetva*s of this sort.[35]

Outside of questions of faith and correct religious observance, most people requested *fetva*s to be brought into court to support their claims in a lawsuit. *Fetva*s were not "evidence" in the sense that witness statements were, but a positive *fetva* essentially assured victory for its bearer, for Ottoman judges were expected to rule in accordance with the *fetva*s of the *şeyhülislam*. Significant numbers of *fetva*s were also requested to strengthen petitions for imperial decrees—a practice enthusiastically adopted by Ottoman subjects of all confessions and the diplomatic representatives of foreign governments.[36] Finally, numerous *fetva*s were issued in response to internal requests from high-ranking administrators or the sultan to legitimate major decisions of state or to bolster decrees. All three types can be found in the *siyar* sections. Though the identity and motive of the original petitioner are rarely stated in the collections, close readings allow for informed speculation.[37] Most of the *fetva*s that concern us here were the product of litigation involving merchants disputing the ownership of ships and slaves after a pirate attack or of requests from government officials attempting to coax frontier naval auxiliary forces into obeying the peace treaties. Interrogating and contextualizing the *fetva*-text allows us to determine what mediating role it was intended to play in its original issue and what purpose its presence in the collection was meant to serve.

OF SHIPS SEIZED AT SEA

Of the *fetva*s dealing with seaborne raiding, the majority are concerned with whether and under what circumstances the original owner or owners can recover their lost ship, cargo, or slaves. While there are no such examples in the collections of Ebu Su'ud, they are present in all the collections examined from the seventeenth and eighteenth centuries. At their most basic, they resemble the examples discussed above, in which the original owner is able to reclaim his property if it has not been removed from the *darülislam* but cannot do so without cost if it has changed hands within the *darülharb* before being brought back into the *darülislam*. The collections typically contain *fetva*s illustrating both outcomes. But real-world business arrangements and political developments meant that property disputes were often considerably more complicated. The *fetva*s stemming from such cases can tell us a great deal about the developing "case law" surrounding the adjudication of these kinds of disputes and, more importantly, the changing economic and political climate from which they originated.

For example, the collection of Minkarizade Yahya Efendi contains a *fetva* that addresses the peculiar consequences of conquest and imperial expansion during wartime for the adjudication of such disputes:

> [**Question**]: Enemies (*harbiler*) take Zeyd's ship. After they import it to the *darülharb*, the Muslims conquer [that part of] the *darülharb* and take the ship by force. If they bring [it] to the *darülislam*, can Zeyd take the ship for free before the division [of the spoils]? **Answer:** Yes.[38]

As we have seen, under normal circumstances Zeyd would not be able to take back his ship for free. It was taken by force, brought into the *darülharb*, re-taken by force there, and then brought back into the *darülislam*. But because the territory where the enemy infidels brought the ship had been conquered in the interim—most likely a part of Crete or the Adriatic coast taken from the Venetians—and thus had become part of the *darülislam* before the ship was recaptured, it was legally as if the ship had never left *darülislam*. As a result, Zeyd's claim would be upheld. If the ship had been sold or given to another, Zeyd would have been able to take it back for free. The decision was thoroughly grounded in established Hanafi

Islamic legal theory—no qualified jurist would have ruled otherwise—and yet it was entirely a product of its time and reflected the peculiar conditions that the grinding midcentury conflict with Venice created for deciding such cases.[39] The *fetva*'s inclusion in the collection meant the establishment of an authoritative legal precedent that could be referred back to by future readers, muftis, and judges when faced with similar circumstances.

Other *fetvas* were distinguished by demonstrating how contemporary business arrangements on land could affect the outcome of cases originating at sea. Many ships were jointly owned with two or more partners, a fact which created a particular set of problems when such a ship was captured.[40] When one of the partners was also the ship captain, as was often the case, this could add another wrinkle to an already complex situation. Zekeriyyazade Yahya Efendi's collection is the first to address the issue:

> **Question**: Zeyd and Amr are *zimmis* whose jointly owned ship Zeyd is using with Amr's permission when enemy infidels take that ship from Zeyd's possession. After they import it into the *darülharb*, Zeyd, as a *müstemin* (i.e. with a safe-conduct) goes to that domain. When he requests the ship from the enemy infidels, those infidels do not give the ship to Zeyd. If, in exchange for it, they give Zeyd a quantity of goods, now when Zeyd imports those goods into the *darülislam*, can Amr take some of those goods from Zeyd? **Answer**: No.[41]

At first glance, this might seem extraordinary. How could Zeyd convince the enemy infidels to compensate him for the theft of his ship? In actuality, this *fetva*, issued between 1622 and 1644, indirectly hints at how Zeyd might have been successful in demanding restitution and provides us with an important clue in the first few words. Zeyd and his partner are *zimmis*, that is, non-Muslim Ottoman subjects, specifically Christians (Jews are nearly always identified as such, to the extent that *zimmi* in Ottoman usage is a byword for an Ottoman Christian). Although we can only speculate, the men behind the aliases were most likely Ottoman Greeks whose ship was captured by Maltese corsairs. In the seventeenth and eighteenth centuries, corsairs based in Malta frequently captured ships owned and operated by Ottoman Christians, disregarding their directive to only despoil Muslims under a variety of pretexts. After 1605, the Knights of Saint John maintained a court on Malta, the *Tribunale degli Armamenti*, for adjudicating claims of wrongful seizure, and numerous Ottoman Greeks went there to obtain redress and reclaim stolen property. Those who were stymied often appealed to Rome, which was more sympathetic and frequently ruled against the corsairs.[42]

This *fetva* collapses into a few lines proceedings that may have taken months or years, from the moment that Zeyd's ship was seized to the point when he arrived on Malta and initiated his suit. By this point, his ship might have changed hands too many times to be located or was unobtainable for some other reason, so Zeyd, victorious in his suit against the corsairs who robbed him, was compensated instead with a quantity of goods. The *fetva* itself undoubtedly emerged from the litigation that ensued when Zeyd returned home and denied his former business partner's claim to a share of the goods commensurate with his loss from their jointly owned ship. There is little question that the man behind the "Zeyd" alias requested the *fetva* to support his side in the suit; a businessman with the means to travel to and from Malta to pursue a claim must have been aware that Islamic law was on his side before denying his partner his erstwhile share.

Çatalcalı Ali Efendi's *fetva* collection returns to the issue of shared ownership, presenting a trio of parallel examples:

> [**Question**]: Enemy infidels seize Zeyd and Amr and Bekr's jointly owned ship by force. If, after they import it into the *darülharb*, Zeyd buys the ship from the enemies and exports it to the *dar-ı Islam*, can Amr and Bekr take formal possession of their shares of the ship for free? **Answer**: They cannot.

> [**Question**]: Enemy infidels seize Zeyd and Amr's equally jointly owned ship by force. After they import it into the *darülharb*, Zeyd arrives in the *darülharb* with a safe-conduct and the enemy infidels give the ship to Zeyd for free and surrender [it to him]. If Zeyd then exports [it] to the *dar-ı Islam*, when Zeyd says to Amr, "Give me half of the ship's value and take formal possession of half of the ship," can Amr say, "I'll take formal possession of half of the ship for free"? **Answer**: No.

> [**Question**]: Enemy infidels seize Zeyd and Amr's equally jointly owned ship by force. After they import it into the *darülharb*, Zeyd arrives in the *darülharb* with a safe-conduct and the enemy infidels give the ship to Zeyd for free and surrender [it to him]. If Zeyd then exports [it] to the *dar-ı Islam*, can Amr give half of the ship's value to Zeyd and take formal possession of half of the ship? **Answer**: Yes.[43]

These *fetva*s, issued between 1674 and 1686, expand on the legal logic of our preceding examples. In the first instance, Zeyd has ransomed back the ship that he owned in partnership with two others from the enemy infidels who captured it. Since Zeyd bought the vessel on his own initiative and with his own money, it might not surprise us that his former partners cannot reclaim their shares upon the ship's return to the *darülislam* without cost, but the subsequent examples reinforce the fact that their claims would have been vacated even if the ship had been returned to Zeyd for free.

The nearly identical phrasing and opposing answers of these *fetva*s suggest that at least one, if not all, was composed especially for the collection to illustrate how to decide these sorts of disputes. As in the previous cases, the circumstances surrounding Zeyd's reacquisition of the ship have deprived Amr of any right to claim his original share without cost. However, the final example makes it clear that the law does recognize Amr's prior stake in the property in question and affords him the right to reacquire his former share by giving Zeyd a sum equivalent to its value. The *fetva* demonstrates not only that the deal Zeyd offers Amr to buy back his share of the ship in the preceding example is lawful, but that Amr automatically possesses the right to repurchase his stake and thus reestablish the partnership more or less irrespective of Zeyd's wishes.

Çatalcalı Ali Efendi's *fetva*s on captured, (formerly) jointly owned vessels clarified the correct ruling in a rather delicate scenario, in which one or more partners would be legally stripped of his substantial investment even as his erstwhile ship lay safely moored in its home port. The decisions rewarded those who took the time and the risk to recover their stolen property in enemy territory. However, the legal right to buy back into a recovered ship that Ali Efendi's *fetva*s spelled out was no innovation; that legal principle was also at the center of many *fetva*s revolving around the return of captured ships and slaves that had been brought back into the *darülislam* by a third party. Nevertheless, a *fetva* and its follow-up from Minkarizade Yahya Efendi, Ali Efendi's predecessor in office, make it clear that the right to buy back one's stolen property could be easily derailed:

Question: Enemies take over Zeyd's ship, take a known quantity of goods, and bring [them] to the *darülharb*. Afterward, if Amr, a merchant with safe-conduct, buys those goods from the enemies in the *darülharb* and exports them to the *darülislam*, can Zeyd take those goods for free? **Answer:** No, he can take [them] with [their] price.

In that case: If Zeyd and Amr disagree on the price of the goods, who has the [last] word? **Answer:** Amr.[44]

This *fetva*, one among many similar *fetva*s from the collections, makes its real point in the follow-up question. Having already established that Zeyd cannot take back his goods (or his ship, or his slave) for free under such circumstances, it is reiterated that he can reclaim them for their price. If Amr had not purchased the goods, but had received them as a gift before importing them, the *fetva* would have indicated that they could be reclaimed for their *value*. In either case, if the two parties disagree on what the fair price should have been or what the value is, the law gives the benefit of the doubt to the person who actually possesses the property. As the original owner has no legal obligation to buy back his former property, this rule gives the new owner some leeway, despite the fact that he is obligated to sell it back if the original owner desires. Given the number of times that a ship or slave, once captured, could change hands, this type of ruling anticipates and short-circuits the potentially paralytic litigation that would arise if original owners of stolen property possessed an unconditional right to buy it back. Once an ownership dispute has been resolved in the new owner's favor, it is for him to set the price; he cannot be legally compelled to change it, and if the former owner rejects it, the matter is concluded. In this way, the muftis ensured a degree of stability and predictability in questions of ownership on land, in spite of the continuing chaos at sea.

OF SLAVES SEIZED AT SEA

At some point in the tense twenty years that preceded the 1645 Ottoman invasion of Crete, a Muslim merchant traveler (let us call him Zeyd) and his Christian slave (let us call him Amr) boarded a ship bound for the port cities of the North African littoral. The voyage passed without incident until the ship, hugging the coastline, was spotted by a Maltese flotilla loitering in the distance. As the corsairs' swift ships changed course to intercept the Ottoman vessel, the Muslim passengers on board convened to decide on a plan of action. Outnumbered and with little hope of outrunning or outmaneuvering the corsairs' agile frigates, the Muslims rapidly concluded that their only option was to abandon ship before the Maltese got within firing range. The reputations of the Maltese preceded them; every Muslim traveler knew of and feared the fate that awaited those who survived the initial onslaught and became captive on Malta, where the most fortunate might languish in the dungeons for years awaiting their ransoms and the least would likely die rowing on the galleys of the pope.[45] So the Muslims piled into the lifeboat and rowed for shore and safety as fast as they could, leaving their ship, their cargo, and even their slaves behind. After the Catholic corsairs finally drew up along the abandoned ship and boarded, they took stock of their newly acquired booty and captives, Amr among them, and then set course for Malta, ship in tow.

Once it became clear that Amr was a Christian slave, the corsairs released him. Left on Malta to do as he pleased, Amr determined to return to the homeland whence he had been abducted and sold into Ottoman slavery some time before. Amr slowly made his way back, by land and by sea, through Christian Europe until he reached the lands of "Rus," the Ukrainian steppe where he had been born. But Amr's extraordinary journey was not yet over, and it was about to take a terrible turn. A marauding party of Tatar raiders, on one of their habitual expeditions in the area, sacked Amr's settlement and seized Amr. Another successful raid concluded, the Tatars made their way back into Ottoman territory to sell their captives. There they sold Amr to Bekr and handed him over.

Sometime thereafter, Zeyd, who had eventually returned home safely after his close encounter with the damned Maltese, ran into Bekr with his former slave Amr. Although the sight of Amr again after so much time was a shock, their crossing paths once both were back in the city was less surprising. Zeyd and Bekr, as men of a certain class, moved in similar circles. Zeyd immediately tried to reclaim Amr from Bekr, but Bekr resisted having his new investment taken from him. Zeyd could legally prove his prior ownership of Amr in court, having registered his property after the initial purchase. However, a *fetva* was requested from the *şeyhülislam* that decided the case in Bekr's favor. Though the court and the mufti recognized Zeyd's prior ownership of Amr, the course of Amr's misadventures and the circumstances of his involuntary return to Ottoman territory meant that he unquestionably belonged to Bekr now. Zeyd could have Amr back, but he would have to pay for him. Amr was no longer the arbiter of his own fate, but property whose ownership was to be disputed in court and before the mufti.[46]

The preceding narrative, extrapolated from a particularly rich *fetva*, details an astonishingly tragic story, from which we learn about the origins and travails of one very unfortunate slave and about the remarkably small circles in which men of means traveled. If we assume that the city of Zeyd, Amr, and Bekr was Istanbul, a chance encounter in its slave market or in its port districts does not seem so unlikely. Indeed, contemporary court records reveal that such stories were, if not exactly common, far from extraordinary.[47] If nothing else, Amr's odyssey should drive home for us a sense of the incredible mobility of early modern travelers, the smallness of this world, and the cyclical, kinetic qualities of the stories encapsulated in the *siyar fetva*s.

A number of cases involving the capture of Ottoman-owned slaves at sea, like the one narrated above, appear in the seventeenth- and eighteenth-century *fetva* collections. The legal principles involved in the jurists' decisions will by now be familiar to the reader. But slaves, unlike ships, possess free will, self-propulsive capacity, and intrinsic, albeit mutable, legal identities. Though both can be bought, sold, stolen, used, owned, and inherited, only slaves can convert or be manumitted. Because a slave can cease to be a slave, but a ship can only ever be a ship, the moment of capture underpinning each *fetva* is always a potentially transformative event. Refracted through the *fetva*s generated from disputes over slaves seized at sea are precious, if blurry, glimpses of the experiences of and roles played by Ottoman-held slaves in the early modern maritime economy and their relations with their masters back on shore.

The presence of slaves on early modern ships is attested in numerous sources and in numerous capacities. Certainly the largest number served as oarsmen on the galleys, though contrary to popular conception, Ottoman war galleys were never rowed exclusively with slave or convict labor.[48] Slaves embarked on ships for rather less arduous purposes as well. Ottoman-owned slaves might travel with their masters in a general, personal service role, or they might travel independently of their masters and conduct business on their behalf. Even outside the realm of elite or palace slavery, it was not uncommon for slaves to be entrusted with substantial responsibility and a great deal of personal freedom.[49]

A *fetva* from the first half of the seventeenth century illustrates this latter sort of slavery:

Question: While Zeyd's wholly-owned slave Amr is trading by ship, enemy infidel[s] seize Amr. If Amr somehow escapes after a period of time from the *darülharb* and comes again to his master (*mevlası*) Zeyd's side, can Zeyd legally [re-]enslave Amr? **Answer:** No.[50]

Captured while engaged in maritime trade on his master's behalf, Amr returns to his master after his escape, but his voluntary entrance into the Abode of Islam makes Amr a free man. Nevertheless, the bond between them is not entirely broken. Zeyd cannot legally re-enslave Amr, but he is still his *mevla*, now in the sense of patron. This is the same legal relationship they would have if Zeyd had manumitted Amr. Because we do not know where Amr was originally from or how old he was when he was first abducted and enslaved, we can only assume that by the time he was captured by pirates, Zeyd's home had become the only home to which he would or could return. Though the *fetva* fixes Amr's changed legal status, his overall position in Zeyd's household would likely have remained relatively similar. And it is not hard to imagine that, once sailing weather returned, Amr would be back to conducting trade for Zeyd.

Another example, this one from Minkarizade Yahya Efendi (in office, 1662–1674), demonstrates again the inclination of at least some slaves, given a chance at a different fate, to return to their erstwhile masters:

Question: When Zeyd's slave Amr is going with the fleet with Zeyd's permission, [they] encounter enemy infidels. [They] seize Amr and, when the ships part, Amr is freed without entering the *darülharb*. If he comes to Istanbul, can Zeyd [re-] enslave Amr? **Answer:** Yes.[51]

Besides the fact that Amr, as in the previous example, returns to his master's service voluntarily after being captured independent of him at sea, this *fetva* is intriguing because of how Amr comes to be captured in the first place. Amr embarks with the fleet from Istanbul with Zeyd's permission. We do not know what Amr was supposed to be doing with it, but the fleet must have set out from the Imperial Arsenal during the final stages of the protracted conflict with Venice over Crete. Although the Ottomans were ultimately victorious, naval reversals were not infrequent. Our *fetva* must date from some point between 1662 and 1669 and details an unsuccessful engagement with the Venetians or their allies, who liberated the Christian slaves they found and put them ashore before sailing off. For whatever reason, Amr returned to Istanbul of his own accord and, because he had not been brought to the *darülharb*, to servitude as well.

If some slaves had grown sufficiently accustomed to their lives to return to their masters' side of their own volition, many others could be counted on to make common cause with those who had liberated them or to attempt to return to their former lives. If the stories of such men found their way into the *fetva* collections, however, it was because they had failed. Naturally, joining in hostilities against the Ottomans put one at risk of recapture. This *fetva*, in which the heirs of a deceased slave owner tried unsuccessfully to claim a liberated and subsequently recaptured slave, aptly illustrates that risk:

Question: Enemy infidels capture Zeyd the *zimmi*'s Christian slave Amr. After they import [him] to the *darülharb*, Zeyd dies. Afterward, Amr boards a ship with the enemy infidels and, while they are making war with the Muslims, the Muslims seize Amr. If, after the division of spoils, [he] is marked as Bekr's share, can Zeyd's heirs take Amr [from Bekr] for free? **Answer:** They cannot, they can take [him] for [his] value.[52]

It is impossible to tell here if Amr has joined up with the Venetians, since this *fetva* could date from the final years of the Cretan War, or if he is serving with a Christian corsairing outfit. From the religious-legal perspective, there was no difference. In any event, the encounter with the Ottoman naval force went poorly for Amr, who became part of the booty to be distributed among the victorious. Another *fetva*, this one from the early eighteenth century, tells a similar story in which the Christian slave of a frigate captain willingly joins the crew of the enemy vessel that captures his master's frigate. When that vessel is captured in turn by the Ottomans and the frigate captain is freed from captivity, his slave and erstwhile captor is returned to him.[53]

An initial encounter at sea was not necessary to introduce Ottoman-owned slaves into the maritime *siyar fetva*s. Some fugitive slaves who fled across Ottoman land borders later joined up with Christian pirating expeditions. The disputes over ownership that took place after they were recaptured brought them into our sources.

> [**Question:**] Zeyd's [Muslim] slave Amr runs away after apostatizing. When he enters the *darülharb*, the enemies (*harbiler*) do not seize or bind him. Afterwards, when Amr goes out corsairing with the enemies, if the Muslims seize Amr by force, and if Zeyd finds Amr in someone else's possession, can he take him for free? **Answer:** Yes, but Amr is required to [re-accept] Islam. If he does not accept, he is killed.[54]

The presence of *fetva*s like this one in the *siyar* sections amidst those concerning ships and slaves taken at sea requires additional comment. Ottoman *fetva* collections, like the *fiqh* manuals on which their organization was modeled, typically contained an entire section dealing with fugitive slaves, *kitab al-'ibak*. Such sections usually immediately followed the *kitab al-siyar* and dealt with related issues, but they were distinct. Whether or not the slave was recaptured inside or outside the *darülislam* (or had exited and reentered of his or her own accord), whether he or she was Christian, Muslim, or an apostate, the *fetva*s dealing with the disposition of such slaves belonged to the *kitab al-'ibak*. Why then would a case of a fugitive slave who joins the enemy and is recaptured by the Ottomans at sea be placed in the chapter of *siyar*? The answer, it seems, is the sea itself. The presence of this *fetva* in the *siyar* section should cement for us how cases that involved the sea and piracy were automatically understood as belonging to that legal realm in the seventeenth and eighteenth centuries.[55]

In the above example, taken from the collection of Çatalcalı Ali Efendi, the fugitive slave Amr repudiates Islam before fleeing the jurisdiction. He is not molested in any way by the Christians on the other side of the border but joins them willingly. Amr participates in a Christian pirating expedition and finds himself once again in Ottoman captivity after an unlucky encounter with the Ottomans. The reader might be surprised to see that here Zeyd is able to secure the return of Amr without cost, but this was the standard outcome for fugitive slaves who had fled the *darülislam* (or were recaptured within it) of their own accord and without compulsion, for, in the words of Abu Hanifa, "the runaway slave is unlike the prisoner of war or the property captured and taken to a place of security."[56] If the original owner can prove his prior ownership, the fugitive slave is returned to him. However, as an apostate Amr must first reaccept Islam or suffer the death penalty. Ultimately, the ruling here is no different than if the whole process had taken place on land.

Ottoman jurists of the seventeenth and early eighteenth centuries identified cases involving slaves and maritime violence as a *siyar* matter and one deserving of an increasingly prominent place in their *fetva* collections. As both the number and complexity of cases involving (re)captured Ottoman slaves and the sea ballooned, so too did their representation in the *şeyhülislam fetva* collections relative to more conventional, dry land–centered content. The muftis' answers to questions concerning the sea hewed closely to those involving land, and working by way of analogy, they invoked the same classic authorities in their proof-texts. Nevertheless, administrative disorder along the frontiers, unchecked piracy, and multiple protracted struggles with Venice and her allies meant that both muftis and *fetva*-compilers had to respond to the legal quandaries of the age with detailed guidance for readers unsure of how Islamic law would react to getting wet.

OTTOMAN CAPTORS, OTTOMAN CAPTIVES, AND THE QUESTION OF SUBJECTHOOD

The *fetva*s covered up to this point have been primarily concerned with property and questions of ownership, even as they have detailed the ordinary and extraordinary horrors of early modern seafaring in times of both war and peace. But ships, cargo, and Ottoman-owned slaves were certainly not the only casualties. Free Ottoman subjects—Christians, Jews, and Muslims—were frequent victims of piratical attacks on ships and shores. For most Ottoman Muslims and Jews captured by pirates or Catholic corsairs, to say nothing of those who lost their lives on the spot, their misfortune would have one of a few likely outcomes: they could be sold as slaves, they could be held for ransom, or they could be liberated if their captors were intercepted by an Ottoman patrol. Except in unusual cases, none of these outcomes would provide any occasion for requesting or issuing a *fetva*. The Ottomans' non-Muslim subjects, the *zimmi*s, on the other hand, were vulnerable to abuses that propelled them into our sources.

The illegal enslavement of Ottoman subjects by other Ottomans was discussed in Chapter 1 of this volume. Having examined how the administration responded to such complaints, we turn now to the *fetva* collections to see how Ottoman jurists confronted the problems posed by a Mediterranean maritime environment where subjecthood trumped confessional status in theory, but where mobility, absence of firm borders, and anarchy often frustrated the efforts of the Ottoman center to enforce Islamic and imperial law.

The legal tension between subjecthood and religious identity in Mediterranean space was manifested in the frequent victimization of Ottoman Greek Orthodox merchants by the corsairs of Malta, on the one hand, and of Ragusan and Venetian merchants—who were supposed to be protected—and Ottoman non-Muslims by Ottoman pirates and North African corsairs, on the other.[57] Jews, in all cases, were at risk. Nowhere was this tension greater than at sea, where the jurisdictional anchorage of land and the physical and legal security it provided were beyond reach. A Christian at sea could be, with a minimum of willful ignorance, construed as an "enemy infidel" and thus a legitimate target. Manifesting the same cyclical properties of many of the *siyar fetva*s remarked upon above, the capture of an "Ottoman" ship by "enemy infidels" followed by its recapture by Ottoman forces could have grave implications for the non-Muslim Ottomans aboard, whose identities and allegiances were immediately suspect.

How might an Ottoman Christian threatened with enslavement at sea prove his free origin? We have already seen how difficult this could be for the courts. Moreover, on a ship that might have violently changed possession several times over the course of the sailing season, how could a *zimmi* caught in the middle effectively demonstrate that he was not a willing participant in the preceding Christian takeover to men who, busy dividing the spoils, might be disinclined to listen? An opinion of Ebu Su'ud holds that it is the captor who must be able to prove the captive's unfree—that is, non-Ottoman—origin, and that in ambiguous circumstances, the potential captive who claims Ottoman subjecthood should be given the benefit of the doubt.[58] Nevertheless, it is clear that even when the law and the jurists favored a certain outcome, the man with the gun usually had his way.

Not only *zimmi*s were at risk in such circumstances. One might reasonably assume that the moment a "Christian" pirate ship was captured (or recaptured, or re-recaptured) and its Muslim prisoners liberated would be an unambiguously auspicious one. However, the sea power behind such clashes, whether operated independently or deployed on state orders, was not necessarily engaged in an altruistic humanitarian mission. Beyond the conflicts over the spoils, some liberators evidently thought themselves owed more than the Muslim prisoners' gratitude for their efforts:

Question: Enemies capture Zeyd the Muslim. Afterwards, they go out pirating. While they are using Zeyd on their ship [as an oarsman], a ship of the Muslims seizes the enemies' ship at sea by force and they export the ship and Zeyd into the *darülislam*. If Zeyd is freed from captivity, can Amr, captain of the aforementioned ship, say to Zeyd, "since [I] freed you from captivity, give me such-and-such amount of money," [and] force [him to do this]? **Answer:** No.[59]

In this early eighteenth-century *fetva*, the captive Zeyd was being employed as a galley slave when the enemy ship was intercepted and seized by an Ottoman patrol. Although he was freed and returned to Ottoman territory, he was still vulnerable to the captain's demands for payment. As long as he was on that ship, how could he refuse? Obviously, there is no way that a liberated galley slave could have paid on the spot. Rather, the captain was trying to force him to agree to pay what was in effect a ransom once back on land, and the *fetva* probably stems from Zeyd's attempt to extricate himself from that agreement.

In terms of Islamic law, the provision of bond and the securing of guarantors touched on a whole other side of legal theory which we shall not delve into here (such issues, in both *fiqh* manuals and *fetva* collections, appeared in the chapter on surety, or *kefalet*). It was, of course, perfectly acceptable for captive Muslims to make entreaties to friends, relatives, or profit-seeking merchants to front the money for their release. In the case of the aforementioned captain, the problem was not that he wanted money, but that no contract had been agreed upon prior to Zeyd's liberation. Another example, this one from Çatalcalı Ali Efendi, clarifies the problem:

> [**Question:**] After enemies capture Zeyd the Muslim, a Muslim merchant named Amr buys Zeyd from the enemies without Zeyd's permission for such-and-such amount of money (*akçe*). If Amr exports [Zeyd] into the *darülislam*, can he say to Zeyd, "give me that amount of money or I will enslave you"? **Answer:** No.[60]

Ali Efendi's *fetva* shows how a Muslim merchant traveling with a safe-conduct could redeem fellow Muslims from their Christian captors just as Christians could purchase the freedom of their coreligionists in Ottoman slave markets. Here again the problem with Amr's demand for payment is the absence of Zeyd's prior permission. If Zeyd had asked Amr to redeem him and had agreed to reimburse him for the expense, Amr would be justified in asking for payment and Zeyd would be liable to pay the agreed-upon sum. Amr's demand was both illegal and, in threatening to (re)enslave a fellow Muslim, outrageous, but assuming it emerged from a real-life query, the existence of the *fetva* would indicate that Zeyd acceded under duress. For Amr's threat to have had any weight behind it, the oral exchange preserved in the *fetva* must have taken place at sea. Only on a ship would one Muslim's threat to return another Muslim to slavery be plausible. And only once securely on land would Zeyd be able to safely renege on his coerced agreement with the merchant and petition the mufti to free him from any religious or legal obligation to pay.

"SULTAN OF THE HOLY WARRIORS": CENTRAL AUTHORITY AND THE MONOPOLY OF RELIGIOUS VIOLENCE

*Fetva*s dealing with incidents of maritime violence that resulted in property disputes or disputes over whether and in what circumstances a captive could or could not be legally (re)enslaved comprise the majority of the opinions contained in the *siyar* chapters of the seventeenth- and eighteenth-century collections that involve the sea. They represented a growing problem and a pressing need for up-to-date legal guidance. But the Ottoman *fetva* collections, starting with that of Ebu Su'ud Efendi, also confronted a far greater issue than property disposition: that of what constituted legitimate raiding. Through *fetva*s—and through *fetva* collections—the *şeyhülislam*s regulated the relationship between the government, raider, and potential booty. In particular, Ottoman jurists set out to define "holy war" in the Ottoman context, to delineate who was a "holy warrior," and to fix in law what he could or could not do and to whom in that capacity. In a Mediterranean world where piratical actors on both sides of the political-religious divide employed religious arguments to justify their actions, the *fetva*s demonstrate how the Ottoman state attempted to maintain its monopoly on religious violence and reassert its sovereignty in North Africa. The *şeyhülislam*s, as members of the Ottoman administration serving at the pleasure of the sultan and as the empire's chief jurisconsults, were given the task of reconciling the requirements of Islamic law with the provisions of the Ottomans' diplomatic agreements with foreign powers and the necessities of domestic politics.

The Ottoman state, which used the office of the *şeyhülislam* to make every conflict a "holy war," employed a rather loose definition of what it meant to be a *gazi*, or holy warrior. "The one who fights," according to Ebu Su'ud, "is truly a *gazi*."[61] Indeed, every Ottoman war from at least Ebu Su'ud's time onward was initiated by obtaining a *fetva* from the *şeyhülislam* to the effect that the war was required by the dictates of faith.[62] The impetus for such wars, at least with European powers, was never exclusively (or even primarily) religious, but obtaining religious sanction had numerous benefits, not the least of which could be justification for breaking a peace treaty that had not expired, as was the case with the 1570 invasion of Venetian Cyprus. Ebu Su'ud's statement defining the *gazi* as the one who fights for the Ottomans in an Ottoman war was not simply academic. It was imperial policy. The *fetva* containing that statement came at the behest of the Ottoman government during the latter stages of the 1570–1573 conflict with Venice. Describing how, in a recent naval engagement—undoubtedly the Battle of Lepanto in 1571—a number of Ottoman combatants had fled the fighting and drowned, Ebu Su'ud responded to the question of whether or not such men qualified as martyrs. The answer was that those *gazi*s who fought and died were martyrs, and that those who fled, whether they survived or perished, would suffer everlasting punishment for it.

The state's deployment of the vocabulary of holy war, with its promise of eternal reward for the brave, could be a powerful motivator. Conversely, the threat of damnation for cowardice was an important part of maintaining order on the battlefield. Ebu Su'ud's *fetva* was widely disseminated, and it was probably read aloud to the soldiers. In addition to appearing in all the major manuscript collections of Ebu Su'ud's *fetva*s, this particular *fetva* appears alone on the first page of a register compiled in the spring of 1572 listing the names of those who had distinguished themselves with their bravery on the battlefield in the previous year and the rewards, in pay and land, that they or their heirs received for their efforts.[63] The previous year's campaign season had concluded when the first orders were recorded in December 1571. Though Cyprus was fully secure by then, the war was not yet formally over and the defeat at Lepanto was still fresh, lending further urgency to Ebu Su'ud's words. The juxtaposition of Ebu Su'ud's *fetva* defining a *gazi* with the government's list of *gazi*s and the rewards owed to them for their service demonstrates the extent to which religious and imperial policy were intertwined and how the *şeyhülislam* and his *fetva*s could serve as a tool of the state, strategically deployed to support its goals.

While the state was generous with the language of *gaza*, that is, holy war, in times of conflict, it was equally assiduous in its withdrawal of it in peacetime.[64] The same piratical act could be holy war or criminal rebellion, with the only and crucial difference being the presence or absence of sultanic approval. It denied *gazi* status to men who engaged in attacks against the "enemy infidels" without the express permission of the state, condemning them as troublemakers or rebels. The Ottoman government's jealous protection of its sole right to initiate and engage in religious violence became increasingly important in the organized chaos of the seventeenth-century Mediterranean, when the freelance naval forces that had played such an important role in expanding Ottoman power across the sea in the sixteenth century became a diplomatic liability.

The treaties granted to friendly foreign powers were grounded in an understanding of reciprocity, and among the terms there was always an assurance that the subjects of the recipient would not be enslaved. Ottoman Muslims did not simply have license to enslave any and all non-Muslims who were not protected, *cizye*-paying subjects of a Muslim power, though it was only from this pool that captives might legally be obtained. The question of who could be legally enslaved was thus one that hinged on both subjecthood and religious identity, and the question of who had the right to determine which enemy infidels fell outside the protection of the state hinged on sovereignty.

Much modern scholarship has persisted in defining all "Ottoman" freebooters as corsairs (even when they acted against the state's wishes) and specifically as *deniz gazileri*, or holy warriors of the sea, whose commitment to the religious ideals of holy war compelled them to continue their attacks on Christian ships and shores (especially those belonging to Venice) in spite of orders from the imperial center to respect the terms of the peace treaties.[65] Setting aside the Ottoman Turkish semantic issues, this characterization is unhelpful for understanding the legal and political dynamics at work. Sea raiders operating out of North Africa in the seventeenth and eighteenth centuries were indeed corsairs in the eyes of the local administrations that financed their expeditions and depended on their profits, but they were seen as bandits and rebels in Istanbul when they failed to obey their sultan.

The "Ottoman" corsair attacks on Ottoman subjects and Ottoman institutions, not to mention the rather dubious religious credentials of many North African corsairs who were Christian renegades (or even unconverted Christians), call into question attempts to cast the phenomenon simply as a manifestation of perpetual religious conflict. That model, always rhetorically useful, hardly applied to the post-Lepanto Mediterranean.[66] The question of how such sea raiders conceived of themselves and their actions, though worth asking, is not our focus here. Of far greater importance to us is how the Ottomans' Islamic legal establishment understood and characterized the raiders' actions in the context of secular peace agreements. Through *fetva*s, Ottoman jurists employed Islamic legal arguments against the enslavement of specific "enemy infidels" in accordance with their treaties and underscored the Ottoman center's position that there could be no holy war, and no slaving, without the sultan's assent. In so doing, they reinforced Ottoman claims to authority in North Africa even as political, military, and diplomatic developments undermined it. Through *fetva*s, the sultan and his jurists attempted to bind the corsairing capitals to Istanbul's will.

A series of three connected *fetva*s from Zekeriyyazade Yahya Efendi, intended for a particular audience of Ottoman frontier raiders, contumacious corsairs, and their supporters, reveals the state's total claim to the banner of holy war, the rejection of the validity of retaliation for a prior attack if it would violate a preexisting treaty, and the absolute illegality of the enslavement of captives taken in unauthorized raids.

Question: The ruler and the infidels of a place of the *darülharb* reconcile and make a truce with his majesty, the Sultan of the *Gazis* and the *Mujahids*, may God almighty prolong his domain until the end of days. Without informing the center and when none of the necessary things were present, an expeditionary force from the Muslims went and, in contravention of the original order, raided and pillaged a number of the places in their territory. If they captured some of the infidels, can those captured infidels legally be enslaved and sold to another and owned and used? **Answer:** No.[67]

This initial *fetva* sets the stage: the sultan has already concluded a peace treaty with the infidels—in this case, the Venetians—when frontier raiders cross the border to pillage and take captives. In so doing, the raiders have contravened an imperial order to respect the truce, and they have committed the offense of acting without first consulting the central government and obtaining its permission. The contrast between the lofty language affirming the sultan's holy warrior credentials and the implicit condemnation of the raiders' actions reinforces the message that the initiation and prosecution of holy war is the exclusive domain of the sultan. The *fetva* is explicit about the captives, eschewing the standard "can he legally be enslaved?" in favor of an enumeration of each step of the process so that the anticipated "no" response encompasses not just the capture and enslavement, but also the sale, possession, and use of the captured infidels.

But the Adriatic-Ionian frontier, where this case originated, was remote and populated with hostile groups, like the Catholic Uskok raiders, who operated independently from Habsburg and Venetian territory and were unconcerned with treaties signed in Venice, Vienna, or Istanbul. What if the Ottoman expeditionary force was retaliating against the most convenient target following a raid on its own territory? The first follow-up question addresses this:

In that case: They are accustomed to overwhelming and raiding those places and capturing its infidels and when it was asked of the mufti, they merely responded that "previously some of the infidels of that place had taken a ship from among the ships of the Muslims, and that's why we did what we did." If solely in consequence of that action they captured them, can they legally enslave and own the captives? **Answer:** If the truce is ratified, they cannot.[68]

The *fetva* categorically rejects the validity of reprisal as a justification for initiating a raid against the territory of a power with which the sultan wishes to have peace. The infidels' capture of an Ottoman ship was not an adequate excuse; sultanic permission must still be obtained in order to raid. Relations along the Ottomans' Adriatic borders were characterized by a pattern of raids and counter-raids on land and sea.[69] The governments in Istanbul and Venice were largely powerless to stop this activity and indeed may have been willing to tolerate it at a low level, but not if it would threaten peace at an undesirable time.

These *fetva*s were issued at a time when pirates operating out of the Adriatic ports were extremely active, North African attacks on Venetian targets were on the rise, and the attentions of the Ottoman central government were directed toward quelling rebellions in Anatolia, managing conflicts in Poland and Iraq, and recovering from a series of debilitating upheavals in the palace.[70] They thus harnessed the moral and religious authority of the office of the *şeyhülislam* to the demands of the sultan's government, admonishing local officials, pirates, and slave raiders not to do what they were "accustomed" to doing.

Nevertheless, the raid had been carried out. Whether or not the raiders had believed that theirs was a legitimate reprisal, the fact remained that captives had been taken in contravention of both the sultan's treaty and his imperial decree. What was to be done about the captives, who would have been distributed and sold off as slaves upon the return of the raiders? The final *fetva* addresses this question:

> **In that case:** That party sold some of the infidels that they had captured to Zeyd and Amr. When the officials want to take [the slaves] from their possession and free them because their enslavement was not permissible, can Zeyd and Amr legally (*şer'en*) prevent [the slaves] being taken from their possession just by saying, "we bought [them] from the ones who captured [them] with our money (*akçemizle*)," and paying for the enslavement? **Answer:** They cannot.[71]

This *fetva* reflects Ottoman administrative practice. Following complaints that Venetian subjects had been illegally enslaved, orders would be sent to local officials to investigate, identify those responsible, and find and free the slaves. No ransom was to be demanded and no compensation given. The *fetva* makes it clear that just because the buyers are technically blameless in the matter, the enslavement and possession of the captives is no less illegal.

The ruling would have touched on a matter of very real significance to those living on the frontiers, for these sorts of situations were a regular occurrence. Given that slave raiding is only profitable if someone buys or ransoms the slaves, one might detect here a warning to buyers to thoroughly investigate captives' provenance. Zeyd and Amr bought theirs directly from the raiders; even if pleading ignorance of the captives' origin were a viable excuse, the mufti would be rightly incredulous of any protestations that the buyers were not aware of what they were getting. Regarding the illegally enslaved, the *şeyhülislam* toed the government line.

These *fetva*s simultaneously affirm the Sultan's claim to be a religious warrior, the "sultan of the *gazi*s"—a title first associated with Orhan in the 1330s[72]—and deny that label to those actors who would enslave the subjects of the Ottomans' treaty partners. The mufti emphasized that there could be no legal justification for engaging in a raid without the sultan's express permission, including retaliation, and he rejected borderland custom out of hand. Slave buyers, he implied, ought not to create demand for or buy illegally captured slaves, or else risk substantial loss.

Fetva series with an initial question and one or more follow-ups are not rare, but Zekeriyyazade Yahya Efendi's is uncommon in its length and specificity. Though the answers are characteristically short, the detail and length of the questions would suggest the mufti's personal involvement in their composition and a prompt from the highest levels of government. The fact that the concerns reflected in the series match those in numerous decrees dispatched to North Africa and the Adriatic-Ionian frontier demonstrates how the Ottoman administration used the *şeyhülislam*'s office, with all its prestige and moral authority, to bolster its political and diplomatic policies. We need not speculate on how this worked in this instance, because we know a great deal more about the origins and intended audience of these three *fetva*s than would otherwise be discernable from their reproduction in the *fetva* collections. This is because they are also preserved in the Venetian archival record.[73]

As a result, we know that these are the *fetva*s that were issued at the *kapudan pasha*'s request and at Venice's urging early in 1626, after the Venetian dragoman Giovanni Battista Salvago's mission to Algiers and Tunis to free hundreds of Venetian captives taken in 1624 from Perast and the Ionian Islands had failed. Before issuing his opinion, Zekeriyyazade Yahya Efendi heard arguments from the *kapudan pasha*, representing the position of both the Ottoman central administration and Venice, and from a Tunisian delegation, sent to Istanbul to defend Tunisian corsairing against Venice. Artifacts of these debates are clearly discernable in the *fetva* questions themselves. These *fetva*s were conveyed to Tunisian officials along with and subsequent to decrees relating to the specific incidents that the *fetva*s refer to in the abstract.[74] They were intended to be disseminated and read aloud to those the government thought needed to hear them. Other *fetva*s were generated in much the same way and were likewise later preserved in the *siyar* sections of *fetva* collections where they served to clarify law and policy for their readers, the second stage of the Ottoman *fetva* lifecycle. When "holy war" was indefinitely suspended by negotiated peace, it took the mufti of Istanbul to remind Ottomans what constituted real "holy war" and that the sultan's authorization was its sine qua non.

It was thus Istanbul, not Tunis, which made religious arguments, not in favor of unrestricted maritime holy war, but of peace. The center's orders to cease raiding and free captives would come as no surprise, but they would not be popular—not with those accustomed to raiding by land and sea, not with the local officials who took a cut of the booty, not with the slave dealers who turned large profits by buying fast and in bulk, not with the slave owners who would lose their slaves. In a period when the center's coercive power on the frontier was at a low and noncompliance was a persistent problem, *fetva*s served as an indispensable support for its policies and explained, in religious-legal terms, what was and was not permissible. In this, Zekeriyyazade Yahya Efendi was tapping into a strategy that had been in place for decades. *Şeyhülislam*s had been issuing anti-piracy *fetva*s of this sort at the request of French and Venetian diplomats since the 1590s.[75]

The Ottoman central government already had a long history of sending *şeyhülislam fetva*s in tandem with imperial decrees to governing officials in North Africa, especially when the subject of the order was likely to be difficult to enforce from Istanbul.[76] This should not be interpreted as a desperate strategy to increase the likelihood of compliance, but as further evidence of the power and reverence associated with the *şeyhülislam*ate throughout much of the empire and of the direct link between that office and the Ottoman administrative apparatus. This link, and the complicated nature of the relationship between the Ottoman center and the North African regencies in the first half of the seventeenth century, are manifested in another *fetva* from Zekeriyyazade Yahya Efendi, addressed to Tunis and Algiers at the sultan's instigation and ordering them to put an end to the war they were fighting with one another in 1628.[77] The scenario of the sultan effectively telling two of his nominal provinces to stop fighting by means of a *fetva* of the *şeyhülislam* is strange enough, but the *fetva* is instructive in the way it again deploys the language of holy war.

Once again the "sultan of the *gazi*s and the holy warriors" is invoked, this time before it is recalled that the "pious ones" of Algiers and Tunis were always distinguished by their commitment to holy war and their protection of pilgrims and merchants from the infidels who would enslave them. The appraisal does indeed reflect the duties of the "volunteer captains" to patrol the pilgrimage routes and convoy merchants, but the description is mobilized precisely because Tunis and Algiers are busy fighting one another, a state of affairs portrayed as contrary to both the dictates of the sultan and the faith. The *fetva* lauds the past holy warrior status of the two regencies, but in doing so it reasserts the position of the sultan as "caliph of Islam" and their religious and political obligation to obey him. Not only are they neglecting their duties by fighting one another, they are committing an egregious affront to their overlord.[78] Thus, the *fetva* reveals again the strategic deployment of the vocabulary of holy war, in this case to coax Tunis and Algiers into making peace and returning to the service of the sultan. The implication, however, is unmistakable: what Tunis and Algiers do at sea for the sultan is holy war, but what they do without his authorization is most certainly not.

This *fetva* accompanied efforts to mediate a peace between the two city-states in the capital, but the resolution achieved in that year was temporary.[79] Armed conflict between Algiers and Tunis continued to flare up periodically, and sieges of one city by the other took place in 1686, 1694, 1700, and 1705.[80] Whereas the archival record preserves a number of *fetva*s like these aimed at a North African audience, *şeyhülislam fetva*s that can be reliably traced to North African petitioners are virtually nonexistent. The North African regencies turned to their own chief muftis with questions when they had the need, and a mufti in Algiers would not take issue with the capture of, say, a Ragusan ship as the *şeyhülislam* would. Indeed, the muftis in Algiers, Tunis, and Tripoli were as much a part of the domestic political landscape as the *şeyhülislam* was in Istanbul and were thus typically enthusiastic supporters of corsairing.[81] In spite of Istanbul's efforts to export the authority and influence of the *şeyhülislam*, North Africa remained for the most part outside his purview, and his attempts to promote Ottoman diplomatic and political priorities there often fell flat. Unsurprisingly, that divide was mirrored in the reach of Ottoman maritime law more broadly and so reinforced the geographic limits, exclusive of North Africa, of the Ottoman Mediterranean.

But maritime raiding was not always an undesirable thing. Besides naval irregulars' support of the imperial fleet in battle, their raiding of enemy ships and shores (which provided its own reward) was a valuable and laudable contribution to any war effort. This too required regulation, and the *fetva* collections from times of war are not silent on the matter. Questions concerning fair distribution of booty and so forth were common and, as was often the case, many are represented in the collections with land-based or nonspecific *fetva*s. Nevertheless, the sea—and the way corsairing expeditions were financed—meant that the muftis were confronted with areas of the law that required clarification. A *fetva* from Minkarizade Yahya Efendi, dating from the time of the Cretan War, gives us a glimpse of corsair tactics and shows how the mufti tried to limit the illicit involvement of noncombatants in otherwise legal corsairing.

Question: Zeyd fills a frigate with *levend*s. When they are about to overtake an enemy infidel ship at sea, he says to Amr, "You wait on shore and if the enemy infidels disembark on the shore, fight [them], and if I capture infidels, I'll give you a share." Amr takes some men by his side and waits by the shore and Zeyd draws up along the enemy infidel [ship] with the frigate and fights [them]. If [they] seize a quantity of captives, can Amr give me a share of the captives? **Answer:** No.[82]

The *fetva* describes an organized corsairing mission and a coordinated assault. It would be understood that each member of the crew, fighters and sailors alike, would receive a share of the booty commensurate with their role and rank on the ship. Although the *fetva* does not identify the location of the engagement or the subject status of the enemy infidels, no legal objection to outfitting a ship for corsairing or attacking and enslaving the infidels is presented here: this is a legitimate raid carried out during a time of war and its targets are understood to be, in both the religious and political sense, fair game.

Like most Mediterranean engagements, the encounter takes place within sight of land. The Ottoman frigate captain has wisely anticipated the possibility that the crew of the target vessel, faced with the prospect of boarding by an adversary of superior strength, might abandon ship and make for the shore—much as the Muslim passengers did to escape capture when they spotted the Maltese flotilla in a *fetva* described earlier. As a result, he orders Amr to take some men and wait on land for just this eventuality. Amr and his men are promised their fair share of the captives even if they do not end up participating directly in the confrontation. And indeed, Zeyd's frigate successfully subdues the enemy ship before it can escape, rendering his precaution moot but Amr's contribution no less worthy of reward. The *fetva* makes it clear that even though Amr did not take any of the captives by his own sword, he was an integral part of the effort. At this point, the *fetva*'s central question is posed, and the jurist presents a contrast: Amr has received his share of the captives, even though he did not actually have to fight for them, but he cannot allot a share of the captives to "me," because "I" was not there to participate.[83]

The use of the first person here is extremely unusual, a rare artifact of the petitioner's original question preserved by the *fetvahane* clerk who framed the question. But why? Who is represented by this pronoun and why is it not permissible for Amr to give him a share of the captives? More importantly, why is this *fetva* worthy of reproduction in Minkarizade Yahya Efendi's *fetva* collection? The *fetva* is characteristically vague on the matter of the identity of the person behind the Turkish dative pronoun *bana*, but the fact that a first-person pronoun sits in a spot that could just as easily have been filled with the standard third alias "Bekr" is telling. While the ruler is due his share of the booty acquired through legitimate raiding, noncombatants are otherwise not allowed to share in the spoils. The *fetva* emphatically announces to the reader, no matter who "you" are, you absolutely cannot take a portion of the captives. This would include officials on land who might be accustomed to taking a cut from returning expeditions, as well as private individuals and business partners who provided funding and expected a percentage of the booty. Such men, who did not endanger their own persons in operations which most certainly qualified as *gaza* and jihad in wartime, were not entitled to receive a share of the captives. Amr earned his share of the captives, but it was not permissible for him to allocate a share (*hissa*) to anyone else.

This interpretation of the *fetva* might appear exaggerated, but for the presence of an extended Arabic proof-text citing two different Hanafi legal authorities. It is worth recalling at this point that the *şeyhülislam* was not obliged to provide citations for his opinions, and the original issue of the *fetva* would not have contained any references. Nevertheless, many *şeyhülislam fetva* collections contain Arabic proof-texts, added by the author-compilers, to improve their usability and increase their authority. The collection of Minkarizade Yahya Efendi, compiled in the early eighteenth century by his *fetva emini* and later *şeyhülislam* Mehmed Ataullah Efendi, is such a collection. In most cases, a proof-text would provide little more than the name of the authoritative work and the section referenced. In this instance, more lines are devoted to explaining the rationale than there are in the actual *fetva*, giving us a glimpse of how Ottoman *şeyhülislams* employed the classic texts of Hanafi jurisprudence to confront pressing, contemporary problems. Two works are cited, the *Hidaya* of al-Marghinani (d. 1197) and *Fath al-Qadir* of Ibn al-Humam (d. 1459).[84] Where the Ottoman Turkish *fetva* is vague, the Arabic proof-text is unequivocal: "Partnership in bride-acquisition and hunting is not permissible and whatever he hunted or married belongs entirely to him . . . partnership comprises the meaning of proxy and assigning proxy for the seizing of property (*al-mal*) is null and void."[85]

This declaration is attributed to the *Hidaya*'s section on partnership (*shirka*). The reader might note the resourcefulness of the *şeyhülislam*'s office in deploying a seemingly unrelated reference from the *shirka* chapter of the *Hidaya* to support a *siyar*-section *fetva*, but it was not uncommon for the authors to cast a wide interpretative net to find authoritative support for their opinions. It is followed by the clarification, based on the *Fath al-Qadir*, that this sort of sharing is permissible for a single owner, but the transference of war booty to nonparticipants prior to the general division of the spoils is forbidden. Relating a tradition in which some of the combatants at the Battle of Badr (fought in 624 between the early Muslim community and the Quraysh) who failed to take captives themselves were allocated a share by the Prophet—the parallel with the story in the *fetva* above is obvious—this part of the proof goes on to emphasize that they could not allocate further shares from the undivided booty to others. In other words, if Amr were inclined to give some of his own captives to someone else in his capacity as sole owner, that would be his prerogative, but no one waiting back on land can legally claim or receive a share from the total spoils. By harnessing two different, classic sources of Hanafi *fiqh*, the jurist has supported both parts of the argument encompassed in the *fetva*: that partnerships of the sort suggested in the question are invalid and that allocating shares of booty to absent partners is forbidden.

It is crucial to recognize that this ruling, if actually observed, would turn the whole maritime raiding industry on its head. The *fetva* and its proof-text expressly forbid partnerships that would entail *levend*s acting as proxies for their financial backers on land, who might claim a fixed percentage of the ship's haul. Such arrangements characterized pirating and corsairing operations, Muslim and Christian, practically everywhere in the early modern Mediterranean. Undoubtedly legal loopholes could be found to allow for some sort of profit sharing, but the *fetva* clearly meant to discourage the deep, symbiotic ties between sea raiders and port officials and businessmen that enabled much of the piracy of the age and made it so difficult for central governments to stop when it was no longer politically useful.

While we remain in the dark about who requested or consumed Minkarizade Yahya Efendi's original *fetva*, we can easily answer the question of why it was preserved in the *fetva* collection and why it received such a detailed explanation: the problem of illicit involvement in and profiting from maritime raiding—even in wartime—was a serious one of ongoing concern, and the *fetva emini*-cum-compiler-cum-*şeyhülislam* Mehmed Ataullah Efendi recognized the need for authoritative guidance among his far-flung readership. *Kadi*s in coastal districts, who were sometimes in on the action, might be expected to take note.

The preceding examples demonstrate how the issuance of *fetva*s and their inclusion in *fetva* collections helped to establish and clarify what did and did not constitute legally permissible raiding. Although some of this developed organically, the Ottoman government was responsible for shaping much of the discussion, in effect asking questions with predetermined answers. From the time of Ebu Su'ud Efendi in the second half of the sixteenth century onward, the *şeyhülislam* was expected to reconcile the requirements of Islamic law with Ottoman secular law (*kanun*) and, implicitly, with current Ottoman political, social, diplomatic, and military policies. This he did through *fetva*s, the only form of Islamic legal writing suited to the task. The *şeyhülislam* and the staff of his *fetvahane* crafted institutional opinions that rested on the accumulated scaffolding of centuries of Hanafi jurisprudence, but these jurists also responded to prompts from the sultan or his ministers and, as men who were first and foremost employees of the state, usually found ways to provide the desired answers.[86]

Through *fetva*s, Ebu Su'ud and his successors developed a pragmatic, particularly Ottoman understanding of holy war and of corsairing's relation to it that bent Hanafi legal theory to Ottoman political and diplomatic needs and emphasized its sole nature as a state enterprise. Holy war was defined as any conflict initiated by the Ottoman sultan, and the *şeyhülislam*s specifically excluded unauthorized attacks and reprisals against "enemy infidels" from the holy war rubric; they ruled that any prizes taken in such raids would have to be returned. Naturally, this dovetailed with Ottoman policy on the ground.

The Ottomans used *fetva*s as tools of internal and external diplomacy, attaching them to imperial decrees and letters to give them religious sanction and increase the likelihood of compliance, as well as to explain the religious-legal logic behind the orders. The provisions of the treaties the Ottoman government crafted with foreign powers had the force of law in Ottoman territory. When the situation demanded it, the *şeyhülislam*'s task was to give those treaties the force of Islamic law as well. These top-down *fetva*s, collected in the *siyar* chapters of widely disseminated *fetva* collections, reflected state policy in the realm of interstate and maritime law, and they were intended to guide judicial praxis on the local level.

CONCLUSION

In the early seventeenth century, as the sea became increasingly dangerous for Ottoman merchants and travelers, and as Ottoman naval mastery of it became an increasingly distant memory, Ottoman jurists responded with a novel body of legal opinions concerning maritime violence that developed progressively in complexity and specificity. United by a concern with the boundary between the *darülislam* and the *darülharb* and its crossing, the maritime *fetva*s helped to clarify what those terms meant for a sea without discernable borders. They compartmentalized acts of raiding and seizure that led to ownership disputes over ships and slaves into those where a previous owner could reclaim his property without payment and those where he could not; they reinforced the Ottoman

Islamic understanding of Ottoman subjecthood as inherently voluntary and contingent on obedience, but unaffected by involuntary or authorized travel by sea or to the *darülharb*; and they drew the line between acceptable and unacceptable raiding practices, underlining the necessity of sultanic approval and the sultan's role as the gatekeeper of holy war. In their original issue, the *fetva*s discussed above were often intended to support lawsuits or (requests for) sultanic edicts. In their collected form, this chapter has argued, the maritime *siyar fetva*s were meant to provide authoritative guidance.

While there is nothing like "case law" or the concept of *stare decisis* in Islamic law, *fetva*s, at least in the Ottoman context, cannot be dismissed as one-off opinions that were only of academic interest and had no impact on the development of later opinions or on judicial conduct. Rather, *şeyhülislam fetva*s fulfilled precisely this function.[87] The preceding analysis has traced the progressive development of maritime *fetva*s over the course of the seventeenth and early eighteenth centuries, an area of focus conspicuously absent in earlier collections. The institutional nature of the office of the *şeyhülislam* and of the authorship of both *fetva*s and *fetva* collections demonstrates not only their ties to the state, but the extent to which many *şeyhülislam*s had worked for their predecessors, catalogued their juristic legacies, and built on them in their own tenures. *Kadi*s did not dispense justice arbitrarily, but neither did they look to earlier rulings to guide their decisions. In contrast, muftis did reference their predecessors, built upon earlier opinions, and created usable reference works. They filled the role that superior court decisions did in common law jurisdictions, providing legal precedents of enduring value. The acknowledged legal expertise and prestige of the *şeyhülislam*s was one of the reasons that *fetva*s were such powerful tools in the courts, especially as the majority of the courts' business was either notarial or in the realm of family law.

For the new and inexperienced *kadi*, or one rotated to his first posting in a coastal district, adjudicating a complex ownership dispute over a ship formerly seized at sea by pirates might be a serious challenge. Unlike the English or the Maltese of the period, the Ottomans lacked specialized admiralty courts staffed with judges accustomed to hearing exclusively those sorts of cases and familiar with the relevant legal theory. It seems more than likely then that the sudden appearance of large numbers of *fetva*s concerned with maritime violence in the *siyar* chapters of seventeenth-century *fetva* collections came about in part as a response to the pressing need of law students and Ottoman judges in coastal districts for just this kind of guidance.

Although their opinions were rooted in the Hanafi legal tradition, the *şeyhülislam*s of the seventeenth century were dealing with a level of disorder in the Mediterranean unlike anything confronted by their Hanafi predecessors, and they responded to the challenge creatively. Much of the time, their role was not so much to create new solutions as to reframe in an acceptable Islamic form and give religious-legal sanction to secular state policies or ancient Mediterranean maritime customs. The *fetva* was the Islamic legal tool employed, in the tradition established by Ebu Su'ud, to harmonize Islamic and sultanic law, interstate and customary law. Jurists reached deep into the centuries-old Hanafi jurisprudential tradition to support the Ottoman government's attempts to control unruly independent actors on the frontiers and to bring order to all manner of maritime legal chaos. The *fetva*s of the seventeenth- and early eighteenth-century *şeyhülislam*s served as a bridge between state policies and Islamic law, on the one hand, and between individuals bringing questions to the *şeyhülislam* and to *kadi*s throughout the empire, on the other. Through *fetva*s, the *şeyhülislam*'s office managed the complex and fluid conjuncture of the state, Islamic law, the individual, and the sea.

CHAPTER SIX

Piracy in the Courts

A janissary from Salonica, Mahmud ibn Ahmed, came to court in June of 1594 because he wanted his ship back. A twenty-two-cubit *karamürsel*, it had been carrying a cargo of honey and salt from the village of Izdin, on the Greek mainland west of Euboea, to Istanbul when it was attacked by two pirate ships just outside the port of Sikinos in the Cyclades. Mahmud abandoned ship before he was overtaken, but the pirates did not get to savor their prize. They soon encountered an Ottoman naval patrol and fled, leaving Mahmud's *karamürsel* behind. The Ottoman naval commander, Tireli Hasan Reis, had the ship towed back to Istanbul, where it was claimed for the sultan's treasury by its chief clerk, Mehmed Çelebi. Now Mahmud was in Istanbul in the court of the military judge of the European half of the empire, the highest court in the land after the Imperial Council, suing the clerk for its return.[1]

After the pirates had sailed away, the task of sorting out the messes they left behind often fell to the Islamic courts of the Ottoman Empire. Ottoman judges, from the seaside districts most affected by maritime violence all the way to the imperial capital, had to weigh the competing claims of shipowners, merchants, representatives of local and central organs of government, and sometimes even the accused pirates themselves. The *kadi*'s court is where the macro and the micro meet in this study, where individual and communal dramas played out under the influence of imperial policies and legal, diplomatic, and military developments. The Ottoman courts applied Hanafi Islamic and Ottoman sultanic law, but they were open to all, whether female or male, free or slave, Muslim or non-Muslim, Ottoman subject or foreigner.

Although criminal prosecutions of suspected pirates did occur in some districts, the punishment of pirates, and of criminals generally, was the prerogative of the executive authorities and often took place outside the court system.[2] And yet pirates and those affected by them made frequent appearances in the courts. Seafarers and merchants, their heirs and creditors sued pirates if they could find them and, more often, those who had subsequently acquired their property, demanding restitution or compensation; local officials, paramilitaries, and shipowners contracted privateering arrangements in the courts and sometimes fought one another on the terms of the distribution of booty after returning to port; and, as we have already seen, the *kadi* courts were involved in every step of the ransom process.

This chapter explores the range of legal actions and lawsuits that emerged from maritime violence, asking how Ottoman judges handled piracy and the evidentiary and jurisdictional issues associated with it and how Ottoman Islamic legal doctrine was applied in practice. Reality in the courts did not always resemble the clean-cut questions posed in *fetva*s and their definitive, one-word answers. Litigants' legal strategies often took their cues from the opinions of the jurists and mirrored their language—the dominant question in the courts as in the *fetva*s was often whether "enemy infidels" had removed the property to the Abode of War before any transfer of possession—but securing admissible evidence to support their arguments bedeviled many litigants and led to court proceedings that were often inconclusive. With this in mind, the chapter continuously asks what brought plaintiffs to court and what they realistically hoped to achieve there, especially when outright victory was not a likely outcome.

Outside the Islamic courts, there was an extensive buffet of dispute resolution options available in the Ottoman Mediterranean, with the offerings available shifting depending on location and the juridical identities of the parties involved. Some of these, like arbitration, did not leave an institutional paper trail. Nevertheless, their gravitational distortions are often discernable in courts' records, since *kadi*s provided authentication, registration, and deposition services for the various venues orbiting them. In this way, too, court records provide a window into a much wider legal world.

Scholars who work with early modern Ottoman court records seldom have the opportunity to become well acquainted with the historical actors who populate their studies: they are typically encountered for the first and only time in a single entry, rarely longer than a folio page, in a court's register. That entry was usually a copy of the legal document (*hüccet*) issued to the principals, containing a terse summary of the proceedings, the names and origins of the parties involved, the basic claims presented, the evidence offered to support them, and sometimes a ruling. If the historians who work with early modern Tuscan or French court records could create feature-length movies from the reams of paper—depositions, affidavits, transcribed courtroom proceedings—documenting a single case, Ottomanists are usually limited to producing a solitary, faded and blurry Polaroid snapshot. Yet the stories they tell us are no less poignant, meaningful, or significant for being brief and sometimes inscrutable.[3] Stories reconstructed from Ottoman court records give us the closest possible glimpse of the individual experiences and local impact of piracy in the Ottoman Mediterranean.

Cases involving piracy also raise critical questions about legal procedure and jurisdiction in the early modern Ottoman Empire. Ottomanist historians have made use of court records to study social history for decades, drawn to the wealth of information they contain about quotidian life.[4] However, while some have examined legal procedure and how certain types of cases were handled across time and space, jurisdiction has rarely figured into the discussion, since most courts dealt primarily with matters taking place within their district (*kaza*).[5] Piracy, which by definition took place in interjurisdictional space, exposed a source of legal tension that litigants, judges, and jurists had to work together to resolve.

The Ottomans did not have a multitiered court system. There was a well-defined hierarchy of prestige to which judges' salaries were pegged, but there was no formal appellate process except to the Imperial Council, nor were there specialized courts like admiralty courts where maritime legal business could be funneled. Cases involving maritime violence, most of which involved the transfer of property or persons to a new location, could be heard anywhere, but suits were usually (though not always) filed wherever the defendant or contested property was located. The need for trustworthy witnesses to provide testimony and the often multiconfessional, multinational (in the early modern sense) nature of the parties involved complicated the quest for legal solutions. Questions of evidence and legal procedure ran up against jurisdictional issues when the sea separated the scene of the crime from principals who might be any permutation of Ottoman-subject or foreigner, Muslim, Christian, or Jewish.

The registers of Ottoman courts were traditionally kept in their jurisdictions and handed from one *kadi* to the next, though some were less than conscientious about this. Today, they are scattered across regional and national archives in the successor states of the Ottoman Empire. Most are uncatalogued. The ravages of war, worms, and water have destroyed many. This does not exempt some of those that would be of most interest to us: All of those from premodern Izmir were lost in the flames of 1922, while those from Salonica are only extant from 1697. Few complete registers survive from the Aegean archipelago, either from resident *kadi*s or those who worked an island circuit, though many *hüccet*s are preserved in monastic archives. The admiral was accompanied by a "sea judge" (*deniz kadisi*) on his flagship, but his registers too are lost.[6]

Nevertheless, hundreds of registers survive from some jurisdictions, sometimes with few obvious chronologic gaps for the period under study: it can be difficult to gauge how much may be missing because of the registers' opaque and inconsistent organization. Some courts kept multiple registers concurrently for different types of entries. Scribes often set aside chronological order in their record keeping, squeezing entries into an earlier page or an older book where there was just enough space. Individual *kadi*s and scribes had their preferred practices; the former rotated frequently, and each court might employ several of the latter simultaneously.

Investigating the impact of piracy in Ottoman courts requires us to work around these challenges by assembling a large sample of cases culled from dozens of registers from the late sixteenth and seventeenth centuries. Detailed case studies permit us to identify trends and common practices as well as focus in on the unique aspects of individual cases. The chapter draws principally on the records of three Ottoman courts: the court of Galata, the court of the Rumeli *kazasker* in Istanbul, and the court of Candia on Crete.

Although there is no question that courts throughout the Ottoman Mediterranean were touched by piracy—as were many of their unfortunate *kadi*s—the imperial capital and its environs were clearly a magnet for maritime litigation. Galata, the neighborhood across the Golden Horn from Constantinople and the maritime nerve center of the empire, was particularly notable in this respect. Mostly populated by Christians and Jews, it was home to a significant expatriate community of foreign merchants and diplomats, and it hosted a large population of seafarers, both residents and sojourners, and people involved in ancillary trades.

As a hub of maritime activity and commerce, Galata's court was staffed by local legal professionals who had a baseline level of knowledge of nautical affairs that exceeded the norm—the court's proceedings routinely include maritime vocabulary and details about ships elided elsewhere—and they could and did draw upon the expertise of the seafaring community in which they were situated when necessary. Consequently, the registers of its court are liberally seasoned with a wide variety of maritime cases besides those involving piracy.[7] A fair number of these cases could have been heard elsewhere but were brought by choice to Galata.

A reputation for probity and fairness undoubtedly played a role in this, but so too did the fact that commerce periodically brought most merchants and seamen worth their salt to Galata. Chance meetings on the quay or in the taverns reunited pirates and victims and current and former owners of stolen ships and pilfered cargo; they reopened old wounds for which redress might be sought before the *kadi*. The parade of people bringing suits and notarial business reflected the religious and ethnic diversity of the Ottoman Mediterranean, and the witnesses to the court's proceedings, though invariably Muslim, reflected the maritime character of the neighborhood, with sea captains frequently in attendance. But Galata was not the only option available to victims of piracy in great Istanbul.

The court that heard Mahmud ibn Ahmed's case in 1594 was the court of the military judge of Rumeli in Istanbul. The military judge, known as *kadiasker* or *kazasker*, was one of two (the other was the *kazasker* of Anatolia) with a seat on the Imperial Council. These men were the highest ranking judicial figures in the Ottoman religious-legal hierarchy, responsible for overseeing most judicial appointments in their respective halves of the empire, and their posts were often the final stepping stones on the career path that led to the office of the *şeyhülislam*.[8] In their capacity as judges, they presided over courts that primarily heard suits and registered business involving members of the *askeri*, or military class, which included all members of the military and government. But this was not the only avenue to a hearing before the *kazasker*.

The Imperial Council, the empire's chief governing body, was itself a court, open to any and all and presided over by the grand vizier. Aggrieved Ottoman subjects from throughout the empire brought petitions for justice, and foreigners were entitled to have their disputes with Ottoman subjects heard there according to the terms of the *ahdname*s. But the resolution of much of the legal business brought to the Imperial Council by Ottoman subjects, both Muslims and non-Muslims, was delegated on the spot to the *kazasker*, and on days when the Imperial Council was in session he heard cases at the Sublime Porte (otherwise he convened his *divan* at home).[9] Beginning in the late sixteenth century, the Rumeli *kazasker* heard large numbers of suits and his deputies registered significant numbers of transactions emanating from piratical violence.

Whether drawn by the *kazasker*'s prestige and reputation for expertise, or by the implicit promise of the Tower of Justice at Topkapı Palace, which dominated the city's sea and land approaches and telegraphed the location of the Imperial Council chambers below it, the Rumeli *kazasker*'s court was the chief venue for those with complex, interjurisdictional cases until Sultan Mehmed IV (r. 1648–1687) took much of the government with him to Edirne, where there was better hunting. The records of this court are little studied, perhaps because scholars interested in social history "from below" have assumed it to be the exclusive preserve of the Ottoman elite. In fact, there were frequently no Muslims involved in the cases heard by the *kazasker*, let alone anyone *askeri*. During this period, the *kazasker*'s court, partially as an adjunct to the Imperial Council, functioned in tandem with the court of Galata as the empire's de facto admiralty courts.

If Galata and the Rumeli *kazasker* reveal how the legal ripples of piracy eventually washed ashore in the imperial center, the court of Candia on Crete gives us a glimpse of its impact on the edge of the Ottomans' maritime frontier. Crete proved to be the Ottoman Empire's final enduring conquest, but the Ottomans were no more adept than their predecessors in defending the island from pirates after the surrender of Candia in 1669.[10] Cases from Crete thus show us not only how procedural and jurisdictional problems were handled on what the Ottomans self-consciously referred to as the "frontier of Islam," they also reveal how the piracy problem had changed by the late seventeenth century.[11]

Ottoman Crete was divided into three jurisdictions centered on the island's chief cities, all located on the northern coast: Chania (Hanya), Rethymnon (Resmo), and Candia (Kandiye, present-day Heraklion).[12] Although Chania became the principal port during Ottoman rule, Candia had the largest jurisdiction and was the seat of government, for which reason its court often dealt with administrative matters. Cases involving piracy routinely ended up there even if they had taken place in the jurisdiction of one of the other two main *kadi*s.[13]

The everyday dangers posed by piracy and the disconnect from the distant imperial center are especially apparent in this court's registers, and both intensified when war with Venice (and much of the rest of Christian Europe) resumed in 1684, dragging on until 1699. As in Galata, the religious and national diversity of the people who made use of the court stands out. Although there was significant conversion on Crete—the outstanding majority of Cretan Muslims (including Cretan janissaries) were born there—Muslims were still in the minority outside the cities.[14] If the examples from greater Istanbul show us how the highest court in the empire dealt with complex, interjurisdictional cases, those from Candia show us how the furthest Ottoman outpost in the Mediterranean handled them in an increasingly turbulent and hostile sea. On Crete, we see how piratical violence was both planned and combatted in war and peace, permitting comparison of the activities of its courts with those in the imperial capital. In so doing, the range of individual and communal experiences of piracy in the early modern Ottoman Mediterranean is brought into relief alongside the differing legal and administrative approaches of Ottoman courts to the problem.

HOW MAHMUD GOT HIS SHIP BACK

Ownership disputes originating in piratical seizures were among the most high-stakes types of maritime business handled by Ottoman courts. Ships and cargo snatched by pirates and corsairs changed hands rapidly and repeatedly, frequently leading to suits, as original owners sought to reclaim what had once been theirs and new owners, who may have been blameless in the previous owner's loss, sought to protect their investment. To succeed, plaintiffs had first to demonstrate that the disputed property had once been theirs. What happened next depended on who had taken the property. If the person who seized their ship or cargo was an Ottoman subject and the original owner could prove prior ownership, nothing more needed to be done for them to recover their property. But if their property had been stolen by "enemy infidels," as was most often the case in the seventeenth-century records, they had to demonstrate that it had not been removed from the Abode of Islam before it changed hands.

Locating the *darülharb/darülislam* divide and determining whether and how it had been crossed and by whom was the key to deciding ownership disputes in court, just as it was in the *fetva*s discussed in Chapter 5. The language of the court mirrored that used by the jurists, and like their counterparts in the *fetvahane*, court scribes traditionally did not bother to differentiate between enemy infidels who were not party to the proceedings. While the captains, merchants, and passengers who appeared in court very likely knew who had seized their belongings and probably had something to say about it, it was not the practice of the scribes to record information that was not germane to the judge's decision.

The specific political identity of "enemy infidel" sea raiders absolutely mattered in the diplomatic and administrative sphere, and executive authorities absorbed and acted on this information, excoriating English ambassadors for the piratical activities of their ship captains, accusing the Venetians of complicity with the Maltese, and chastising the French for the actions of their countrymen under Malta's banner. But efforts to obtain restitution and pursue claims for damages from the subjects of the Ottomans' treaty partners, whether initiated by Ottoman subjects or by representatives of the Ottoman state on their behalf, operated on a separate plane from legal actions taking place within Ottoman domains before Ottoman judges.

There it did not matter whether the *harbi kefere* in question were the subjects of actual enemies, like Malta or Spain, or of supposedly friendly powers like England or France, nor did their legal status, as fully licensed privateers versus pirates, make any difference to Ottoman courts implementing Ottoman Islamic law. There the question was deceptively simple: did enemy infidels take the property by force and bring it to a secure place—that is, a port—in the Abode of War before any further transfer took place? This latter fact was what set Ottoman practice apart from that of the Ottomans' European contemporaries, for whom the legality of the taking was a deciding factor in similar disputes, with fair prizes brought securely into port before sale belonging to their new owners and those taken by pirates or without license reverting to their original owners.[15]

The suit of Mahmud ibn Ahmed, a janissary engaged in trade and despoiled by pirates, against Mehmed Çelebi, the chief clerk of the privy treasury, shows us how some of the issues that were dealt with in theoretical terms by the *şeyhülislam*s in their *fetva* collections were handled in Ottoman courts, in this case by a judge, Sunullah Efendi, who would himself become *şeyhülislam* a few years later and whose *fetva* collection was the first to deal with maritime violence at any length.[16] It reveals some of the unique evidentiary problems piracy posed and the procedures the court adopted to work around them.

That Mahmud's case was brought before the Rumeli *kazasker* is not a surprise, as both defendant and plaintiff were members of the *askeri* class.[17] By the late sixteenth century, provincial janissaries were permitted to engage in trades in order to supplement their incomes; at the same time, many provincial tradesmen bought their way onto the janissary rolls in order to avail themselves of the social and economic benefits, including exemption from taxes, of janissary status.[18] It is difficult to say whether the prominence of janissary litigants reflects their growing participation in and share of maritime commerce, an increased willingness of that group to utilize the courts relative to others, or both, but merchants and tradesmen with janissary titles appear frequently in the litigation discussed below, though they did not patronize the *kazasker*'s court exclusively. Defendants had the right to select the venue, but because the defendant here was a high-ranking member of the government and Mahmud's ship was already in Istanbul, the *kazasker*'s court was the logical choice.[19] So, how did Mahmud get his ship back?

Mehmed disputed Mahmud's claim that the ship floating in the Istanbul harbor was his property. Was he denying that it had ever belonged to Mahmud, or was he implying that the pirates' seizure of the ship and Hasan Reis' subsequent capture of it meant that it was no longer his property? The record does not say. If Mehmed had argued the latter point, the question would have fallen to whether the ship had been brought securely into the *darülharb* before its recapture by the Ottoman naval force. Mahmud's account of the incident, which must have been corroborated by Tireli Hasan Reis, demonstrated unequivocally that the ship had not.

Thus, the judge's decision would turn on a very simple question: Was that ship the same salt and honey-laden *karamürsel* in which Mahmud had departed Izdin? Proof was required to answer this question to the satisfaction of the court. Even if Mahmud possessed documents affirming his ownership, supporting testimony from trustworthy, Muslim witnesses would be essential.[20] How would the court handle the evidentiary phase of the proceedings?

As the court scribe noted, "The aforementioned ship was not something that could be presented in the court," so the judge arranged for a hearing to take place shipside. Here the scribe and judge were following a well-established script, as contemporary judicial praxis manuals make clear. One, by a certain Sâni Efendi, provides an example for a dispute over a ship that mirrors precisely the language of the *kazasker*'s scribe and the procedures that the *kazasker* followed to decide Mahmud's suit. Sâni Efendi's sample entry had nothing to do with piracy, but neither did identifying a ship lying at anchor in the harbor, which was now the court's task.[21] A retired judge was deputized to go to the spot where the vessel was moored and hear the testimony of the witnesses Mahmud had designated. Assembled at the wharf, the five Muslim witnesses for the plaintiff—all men with seafaring or administrative/military backgrounds—indicated the ship in question and testified that "indeed this ship is the wholly-owned property of the aforementioned plaintiff Mahmud."[22] Because this testimony took place outside the court, however, there was another stage in the process.

Any action of an Islamic court had to be witnessed by at least two Muslim men who had no interest in the case at hand; the names of these witnesses to a case, the *şuhüdü'l-hal*, were always recorded in the registers below each entry. The hearing at the docks was no exception to this rule, and the two *şuhüdü'l-hal* there then became active witnesses back in the court of the Rumeli *kazasker*. They were witnesses to the witnessing, called upon to affirm in court that the five witnesses of the plaintiff had testified at the docks that the ship was Mahmud's property; the five were not called to testify again. This somewhat convoluted situation gives some indication of the crucial role of in-person witness testimony in adjudicating disputes; written depositions were not acceptable. Once the witnesses' bona fides were investigated and accepted by the court, their testimony was entered in the record and Mahmud's claim was upheld. He got his ship back.[23]

The entry was recorded on June 12, 1594, but the summary tells us nothing of the timeline of events leading up to the suit nor how much time elapsed before the final verdict. However Mahmud learned that his ship was in Istanbul and in Mehmed Çelebi's custody, he would have attempted to recover it personally before going to court. Did the clerk Mehmed refuse to return the ship because he doubted Mahmud's story, because he misunderstood the points of law that ultimately guaranteed the ship's return, or because he wanted to retain a valuable piece of property without regard to the law? Did Mahmud's witnesses have to travel from Salonica to fulfill their duties? And what was Tireli Hasan Reis' role in this affair? Under other circumstances, he might have had claim to the ship himself. Had he willingly acquiesced to its transfer to Mehmed Çelebi? Sadly, questions like these must go unanswered.

A similar case from Galata tells us a little bit more about how disputes over ships and cargo were framed and decided and how the Rumeli *kazasker* might delegate his authority to others. In July 1605, Marko, the dragoman of the Venetian *bailo* acting as the agent (*vekil*) of a Venetian businessman, "Ayobandid," and the Venetian's business partner, Nikola, a *zimmi* from Athens, sued Memi Reis. The plaintiffs claimed that their jointly owned ship, which had been loaded for trade in Izmir and captured at sea by enemy infidel pirates, was now in the possession of Memi Reis. As Mahmud ibn Ahmed had done ten years earlier, they demanded its return. The suit was initially brought to the Rumeli *kazasker*, perhaps via the Imperial Council, but because the disputed ship was moored in the Kürkçü Kapısı docks in the Galata district, the case was heard shipside "on behalf of" the Rumeli *kazasker*, Zekeriyyazade Yahya Efendi—who would later become one of the chief authors of maritime *fetva*s as *şeyhülislam*—by the *kadi* of Galata.[24]

The opening of the entry in the Galata registers notes specifically that the parties to the case met on the quay in front of the disputed ship—just like the shipside hearing conducted by the retired judge in Mahmud's case. Thus, even though Marko lived in Galata and the ship was there, the case had initially been brought to the Rumeli *kazasker*. There are a number of possible reasons for this. Memi Reis may have been a member of the *askeri* class and exercised his right, as the defendant, to select the venue, or the Venetian may have exercised his right, under the *ahdname*'s protections, to bring his legal business before the Imperial Council, which subsequently handed the case to the *kazasker* to decide. Or the rank and prestige of the *kazasker* himself may have made him the first choice for both parties.

The case is fascinating for what it reveals about what Ottomans and their foreign partners did and did not understand about Ottoman maritime law just as Ottoman jurists were beginning to reshape it. In making their appeal for the return of their ship, the plaintiffs understood well the importance of the *darülislam/darülharb* divide in their case. They therefore specifically claimed that the enemy infidel pirates had not removed the ship from the *darülislam* before its recapture which, if true, would have decided the suit in their favor. But the plaintiffs were unprepared for the evidentiary phase of the hearing, rendering their arguments moot.

The plaintiffs' claims were handled separately. Once it was determined that the dragoman Marko had been appointed agent by the Venetian *bailo* but that he had not been formally designated by the Venetian merchant whose interests he was representing, that is, Ayobandid, the court determined that Marko had no standing to sue on Ayobandid's behalf. His case was dismissed and he was excluded from the proceedings, though he would be able to try again if he could properly establish legal agency (*vekalet*). The court next turned to Nikola, who was suing for the return of his share of the ship and its cargo. Nikola claimed that the ship had departed Izmir, been captured by enemy infidel pirates, and ended up in the possession of Memi Reis without leaving the *darülislam*. Memi Reis countered that the ship had been captured by Algerian *gazi*s (that is, corsairs) in the *darülharb* who then sold it, after which it changed hands several times before being purchased by Hüsrevzade Mehmed Bey of Cairo. Hüsrevzade Mehmed Bey was subsequently killed, and Memi bought it from the deceased man's estate for 2,400 *filori*. Memi added that he did not know Nikola. The chain of possession from initial capture to court case was thus long and complicated—no account was given of how much time had passed—but the crux of the matter was that the ship had been brought to the *darülharb* by force before being retaken and sold in the *darülislam* and that Memi had bought it from a known source for a known sum.

To win, the plaintiffs would have to bring evidence that challenged this interpretation of events, but first they had to prove that the ship in question had once been theirs. To that end, the Athenian *zimmi* Nikola and his partner called three witnesses from the Ottoman Muslim elite of Athens: a *kadi*, a second-generation *çavuş*, and a high-ranking janissary. The three men testified that they had heard Nikola and the Venetian merchant say that they had jointly bought a ship and later had seen them in the ship that was now before them in Galata, wherefrom the plaintiffs had stated that they had bought the ship and were using it "like they owned it." But the judge, making rare reference to "books of jurisprudence (*fiqh*)" in the record, responded with an Arabic quote that the court could not accept testimony to the effect that "we saw him using it in the manner of one who owns it" as actual proof of ownership.[25] On these grounds alone he rejected their testimony, but even had he not, the witnesses could say nothing about what had happened to the ship after they saw it in Athens.

Mahmud ibn Ahmed's witnesses in the previous case had been able to establish that the contested ship had belonged to him—they were probably witnesses at its purchase, unlike Nikola's—but in that instance no one disputed that the ship had not left the *darülislam*. No such certainty existed here, and plaintiffs, defendant, and judge may have entertained differing interpretations of where the line with the *darülharb* was and how it was crossed. Despite the fact that Nikola and his partner clearly understood the importance of this distinction and had probably expended significant resources to bring their elite, Ottoman witnesses from Athens to Istanbul, these could neither definitively prove that Nikola was the previous co-owner of the ship in question nor that it had not left the *darülislam* after its initial capture. Their testimony being insufficient to establish prior ownership to the satisfaction of the court (the first reason) or counter Memi's claims (which would have been next), the Galata *kadi* asked Nikola to provide further witnesses. As Nikola was unable to do so, the hearing was adjourned and the ship left in the possession of Memi Reis.[26]

Nikola and Ayobandid knew they needed Muslim witnesses and summoned those they thought could support their case, even though in this regard they were to be disappointed. They may well have possessed ownership documents of some sort, and they may have known a number of non-Muslims who could have confirmed both their prior ownership of the ship and their account of what had happened to it, if only they were permitted to testify. But because uncorroborated documents were inadmissible and non-Muslims could not testify against Muslims (which Memi Reis was), whatever other evidence Nikola and Ayobandid may have had could not be considered by the court. The same factors that made the *kadi*s of Malta necessary for ransom brokers in the Ottoman Mediterranean also made the courts rather unwelcoming for litigants who had not contracted their business according to Ottoman norms at the outset.

Because foreigners in particular faced often insuperable challenges in establishing their property rights in Ottoman courts, many such victims of piracy likely chose to take their claims elsewhere or swallow their losses. Piracy suits with foreign plaintiffs appear comparatively infrequently in the registers. Nevertheless, we see in this 1605 property dispute occasioned by an act of Christian-on-Christian piracy in the Eastern Mediterranean that both the Christian (Ottoman and Venetian) plaintiffs and the Ottoman Muslim defendant understood how crucial locating the maritime *darülislam/darülharb* divide would be to the outcome of their case.

Being a Muslim by faith was neither a guarantee of nor a prerequisite for knowledge of Islamic law or of contemporary Ottoman legal understandings of how the sea divided the world. Court records confirm what the *fetva*s suggest: that litigants, including non-Muslims, often understood a great deal about the points of law that would decide their cases. This was no less true far from the capital. The suit of Aleksi the Armenian merchant in the court of Candia in 1684 illustrates both the growing sophistication of plaintiffs' arguments and their continuing struggles with securing evidence to support them. The entry is worth quoting in its entirety:

> The Armenian Aleksi veled Sekset, who is engaged in trade in the city of Candia, sued the Jew David veled Nazan in the court. He stated:
>
> "Previously, three bales of *astar* [coarse brown strips of cloth used for head wrapping], turban linen, twilled cotton, and unfinished striped cloth were loaded onto the frigate of a *zimmi* named Marko bin Yorgi in Izmir. When it was coming to Crete, it encountered enemy infidels. After they seized the aforementioned ship with the aforementioned goods, without entering the *darülharb*, they sold them on Milos. This David—who is now brought before the court—was among those who bought the goods. He is said to have bought 160 of my *astar*. Now I demand that David be questioned and that the aforementioned 160 of my *astar* be returned."
>
> After questioning, the aforementioned David responded, denying the claim: "I bought the aforementioned 160 *astar* in Rethymnon from a *zimmi* whose name is known for a known, recorded price, but legally. I had no knowledge that it was his property, loaded in Izmir on the aforementioned Marko bin Yorgi's frigate, seized by enemy infidels, and sold on the aforementioned Milos Island without entering the *darülharb*."
>
> When the aforementioned plaintiff Aleksi was asked to provide evidence for his claim, a continuance was requested in order to procure evidence and the case was postponed with a legal delay. If it is not possible to provide proof in some way, without proof they are ordered not to dispute the matter with each other. What happened was recorded as requested on 15 Receb, 1095 (=June 23, 1684).
>
> Witnesses: . . .[27]

If we accept Aleksi's account, this was a case of non-Ottoman Christian pirates seizing the goods of an Ottoman Christian merchant from an Ottoman Christian-captained vessel and selling them on an island, nominally subject to the Ottomans, to other Ottoman non-Muslims. As usual, the "enemy infidels" were not identified in the record, but Aleksi probably knew precisely who they were given that he knew where the booty had been sold. Milos was a true pirate entrepôt in this period, a spot where goods stolen by pirates and corsairs of every background were bought, sold, and traded by merchants of all stripes. Despite the total lack of Ottoman authority on the island, if the booty had been brought straight to Milos following its seizure, Aleksi absolutely had the right to reclaim his goods.

The defendant David's denial of Aleksi's claim put the burden of proof on the plaintiff. In order to win his case, Aleksi would have to provide witnesses who could affirm that the *astar* in David's possession had been sold on Milos without entering the *darülharb*. He did not have to prove that it was David who purchased them there, only that the stolen goods had never left the *darülislam*. The "I didn't know it was stolen" excuse did not suffice to retain possession. As a result, a plaintiff's success in court could create new victims once-removed of the same pirates. For defeated defendants, the loss of purchased goods to their original owners might be no less devastating for having taken place in a courtroom instead of at gunpoint on the high seas.

Although court scribes' rendering of plaintiffs' statements were not wholly faithful reproductions of what they actually said in court, the fact that Aleksi was recorded as having explicitly stated that the captured ship and stolen goods had not entered the *darülharb*—and that this phrase was repeated verbatim in David's denial—indicates that he actually framed his claim in this manner. As such, it provides convincing evidence for his savvy understanding of the grounds on which his case would be decided, for if the *astar* had been sold in, say, Messina, and David had bought them there before selling them in Crete, Aleksi would have no case.[28] It is unclear whether Aleksi had possessed this sort of knowledge all along or had consulted with Muslim legal experts before he appeared in court, but his legal positioning was entirely consonant with what had been appearing in contemporary *fetva* collections.

Indeed, evidence from both *fetva*s and court records suggests significant awareness among Ottoman seafarers, both Muslim and non-Muslim, of their rights under Ottoman Islamic law and a willingness to use Ottoman legal institutions and mores to their advantage. They were certainly well-informed. Time and again, these sources reveal how efficiently news was exchanged across the sea and how interconnected the various merchant networks were, both with each other and with the buyers and sellers of goods stolen by pirates. How else could an Armenian merchant sojourning in Candia learn that a local Jewish merchant had somehow acquired his stolen merchandise after its layover on Milos?[29]

But did Aleksi believe he could win without witnesses? Of the three examples of property disputes discussed above, two were inconclusive due to lack of evidence, but only Aleksi turned up in court completely empty-handed. Aleksi would have prevailed if David had not rejected his claim, but assuming that Aleksi had demanded the return of his merchandise before deciding to file suit, it seems unlikely that he would have expected such an outcome. Could Aleksi's suit have been the opening maneuver in an attempt to bring David to the negotiating table?

The strategy was particularly well suited to cases involving piracy, where circumstantial evidence abounded but securing the necessary in-person testimony was seldom possible. The original owner would sue over the disposition of plundered goods only to withdraw his suit and settle, returning to the court with the erstwhile defendant to register their agreement, which typically contained a promise not to pursue further litigation. Judges might specifically recommend this course of action, for amicable settlement (*sulh*) was always the preferred method of dispute resolution.[30] Sometimes disputants dispensed with the suing stage and the expense associated with it, agreeing to move immediately to mediation or arbitration. This they could arrange entirely on their own, or they could request that the court provide an impartial mediator, who would help disputants negotiate a resolution, or arbiter, who would render a decision. Guided by Islamic and customary law but not constrained by Islamic evidentiary rules, they might be able to offer more equitable outcomes than the law would otherwise allow.[31]

For example, in May 1633, a group of Ottoman Greek merchants from Naxos came to the court of the Rumeli *kazasker*. They had been traveling to Istanbul with a cargo of locally produced cloth when they were raided by enemy infidel pirates. All the merchants on the ship were *zimmis*—if the pirates in question were Catholic corsairs, they were not opposed to despoiling Greek Christians—but not all of them lost their shares of the cargo in the attack. The pirates had not been especially thorough in their plundering, so some of the merchants were unaffected by the raid, while others had their stores completely emptied. This led to disputes among the merchants, with those who had lost everything arguing that those who had not should share in the others' misfortune. After arriving safely in Istanbul, the Naxiotes arranged for a court appointed mediator, a deputy judge from the Rumeli *kazasker*'s court named Mustafa Efendi, to come aboard the ship and supervise the redistribution of the remaining goods so that everyone shared in the loss fairly, in proportion to what they had brought. In this way, none suffered disproportionately from the pirates' attack and each retained some quantity of cloth to trade. Once this was accomplished to their satisfaction, the merchants disembarked and registered their arrangement with the court, declaring that none of them had any outstanding claims or disputes and that they all had forfeited the right to future legal action. They were then issued a legal document certifying the settlement carrying Mustafa Efendi's signature.[32]

The fact that a party of Ottoman-subject Christian merchants turned to the court to mediate their dispute and register their settlement attests to the level of awareness, among a broad spectrum of Ottoman seafarers, that the courts generally and the *kazasker*'s court in particular could help supply legal solutions. Choose it they did, for there is no indication that the *kazasker* would have actively sought the business of petitioners like the Naxiote merchants. The court of Galata could also have provided them with the same service, and there were a variety of informal dispute-resolution mechanisms available as well. Merchants and mariners sometimes turned to communal leaders or local experts to decide their disputes. For instance, Nicolas Vatin has found evidence of a sort of bureau of Muslim maritime legal experts—sailors rather than *ulema*—in Galata, well known enough in the late sixteenth century to be sought out by Greek Orthodox merchants from Patmos engaged in business in Venice.[33] It was thus not unusual for Ottoman Christians to voluntarily submit their disagreements to either *kadi*s or Muslim seamen who were considered legal "experts," sometimes traveling long distances to have them decided according to the tenets of Hanafi Islamic law.[34] Whoever provided arbitration or mediation services and irrespective of whether those services were obtained through the offices of a *kadi* or independently, only the *kadi* courts could provide witnessed legal documentation formalizing the decision that would be acceptable throughout the Ottoman Mediterranean. The careful and the wise thus often chose to register both amicable settlements and arbitration decisions with the courts to forestall future lawsuits.[35]

While in most instances the *kadi*s required in-person witness testimony to corroborate documentary evidence in their courts, the documents the *kadi*s produced were admissible as standalone evidence in many other legal venues. In its role as the Ottoman supreme court, the Imperial Council considered a much broader range of evidence, including documents, in its deliberations. *Kadi*-produced *hüccet*s were often necessary to initiate proceedings there. Likewise, such documents were routinely deployed as evidence in the Greek communal courts on the islands.[36]

Although written witness depositions did not play a role in the proceedings of Ottoman Islamic courts, *kadi*s were entirely willing to produce them for use elsewhere. Ottoman customs agents in Iskenderun, troubled by the drop off in receipts following pirate attacks in 1624 and 1625, acquired them to forward to the capital to explain the revenue shortfall.[37] Greek monks on Andros, Patmos, and Mount Athos arranged for both local officials and the Muslims they had ransomed or rescued from pirates to appear in court and testify to their efforts, creating a paper trail demonstrating their loyalty to the dynasty.[38] European victims of pirates, including those who were their coreligionists, made a point of appearing before the nearest *kadi* as soon as they arrived on land to document their experiences. Laurent d'Arvieux, attacked by French corsairs off the Palestinian coast in 1660, noted that, once his party had arrived in Acre, "We were careful to make an official report to the *kadi* and to the French merchants of all that had happened to us."[39] And those despoiled by pirates who discovered their property in the possession of another might demand that they be questioned before the *kadi* without requesting restitution, generating documentation that could be used to support claims that could not be sustained under the rules of Ottoman Islamic law but might be pursued outside the court and even outside the Ottoman Mediterranean under the provisions of the *ahdname*.

In 1604 in the court of Galata, for example, the janissary Hızır Beşe requested that the Venetian Greek Manol Reis be questioned as to how he had come to be in possession of two cannons, one bronze, one iron, that had once been on Hızır Beşe's ship and had been stolen, along with the ship itself and its cargo of wheat, by enemy infidel pirates near the island of Thassos. Manol Reis stated that he had bought the cannon on Crete, then still Venetian territory, from a *zimmi* whose name he did not know hailing from Monemvasia in the Morea, which, as the scribe noted, was part of the Abode of Islam. The implication of the scribe's observation was that Hızır might still have a claim on his cannons, but untangling the chain of possession since the capture of his ship and the dispersal of his belongings would not be easy. On that day, Hızır requested only a copy of Manol's statement.[40] With this, he might pursue compensation out of court or launch an investigation into who had exported his cannon to Venetian territory. He might also have sought redress from the Venetian authorities had the "enemy infidels" brought his property straight to Crete; he would be on rather more shaky ground doing so here, but the sale of pirate booty on Venetian territory, stolen from an Ottoman janissary no less, still might have given him an actionable case in the Imperial Council, where treaty law and maritime custom would have informed any decision.[41] The *hüccet* Hızır Beşe acquired from the court of Galata thus would have formed an integral part of the evidentiary arsenal he would deploy there.

The ambiguity of cases like Hızır Beşe's was hardly unusual. Serendipity had led to the discovery of two of his cannons, but their new owner could only tell him part of the story of their circuitous path back to Galata and nothing of what had become of the rest of the ship's complement of cannon, let alone the ship itself. In both Ottoman and European courts, transfer of possession was not considered to have taken place until the property was brought securely into port, but the legitimacy of the taking was not decisive in Ottoman courts as it was in Europe.[42] With the burden of proof on the plaintiff, the Ottoman difference created serious obstacles to successful litigation in the Islamic courts. These were not necessarily insurmountable, but the need to prove a negative in many cases—that the ship or cargo had not been removed from the *darülislam*—was extremely challenging under the best of circumstances. The sources do not permit estimates, but the proportion of lawsuits brought to potentially actionable claims was probably quite small, both in relative and absolute terms. Most victims of piracy probably swallowed their losses, while many others, given the opportunity, pursued compensation through informal channels, which might cost less and permit a more equitable outcome. The courts were often closely involved in the process, however, providing impartial mediators and arbiters and documenting settlement agreements.

If an Ottoman subject were a victim of privateers or pirates who were subjects of the Ottomans' European treaty partners, he might submit his case to the Imperial Council. With sufficient evidence, including Ottoman court-issued documents, a hearing before the Imperial Council would be held in the presence of the relevant European diplomatic representatives. All this required a significant investment of time and money—court fees, travel, gifts to expedite the process, and, of course, opportunity cost. A positive ruling in the Imperial Council might be only the beginning of an Ottoman victim's attempt to obtain redress, which would then take on a more "political" cast, as Ottoman officials would lobby their European counterparts to offer an equitable settlement which would likely be resisted and lead, in turn, to more legal proceedings in the pirate's country of origin. This process could easily drag on for years without decision.[43]

Although any court could hear any kind of case, victims of pirate attacks sojourning in the imperial capital brought most of their business first to Galata or the Rumeli *kazasker*. Due to its centrality in maritime industry and its large population of local and transient merchants, mariners, and tradesmen, Galata was a logical choice. It was already home to many plaintiffs and defendants, their witnesses, and often the disputed property itself, which might be moored in the district's docks or stored in its warehouses. The *kadi*s of Galata and their scribes had experience with maritime cases and they could draw on a deep well of local expertise.

The Rumeli *kazasker* likewise dispatched a wide range of piracy-related suits brought by both Ottoman and non-Ottoman petitioners, either directly or via the Imperial Council on which he sat. Many *kazasker*s went on to serve as *şeyhülislam*s, and it was through their experience in this legal laboratory that these judges-cum-jurists formulated their approach to maritime law, which was later given form in their *fetva* collections. It may have been a coincidence that Sunullah Efendi, who decided Mahmud ibn Ahmed's case, was the author of the *fetva*s in the first collection to deal with piracy at any length, but the connection between this court, the *şeyhülislam* post, and the growing prominence of maritime *siyar*-section *fetva*s in the *fetva* collections starting in the early seventeenth century is noteworthy. By the time a *kazasker* became the mufti of Istanbul, he knew well the problems posed by piracy and the empire-wide need for guidance on the subject. But the *fetva*s do not anticipate every type of case that appeared before the courts. Most notable among these are the suits lodged by victims against pirates.

SUING PIRATES

This book began with the story of Ali bin Yusuf of Jerba, who sued a Venetian merchant named Nicolo in the court of Galata in 1614 for the murder of his son and five others in a piratical attack eight years earlier. Ali learned of his son Süleyman's fate from a crew member who had escaped the pirates, and they faced the alleged murderer together that day in Galata.[44] The case bore many of the hallmarks of Ottoman courtroom dramas emanating from piratical incidents: neither the plaintiff nor the defendant was from the court's jurisdiction, significant time had passed since the originating incident, and the proceedings were inconclusive owing to lack of evidence. And yet suing a pirate was a proposition entirely apart from the property disputes which often followed merchants ashore.

Victims of piracy could sue their attackers in Ottoman courts—if they could find them. With men, ships, and goods constantly in motion, opportunities to confront pirates in court might present themselves years after a violent encounter at sea or in a faraway port. That this actually happened is remarkable enough, further challenging any remaining inclination we may have to romanticize pirates as social outcasts who lived beyond, rather than on the edge of, the law. Like the Venetian Nicolo, many were men of commerce and would appear on land wherever and as often as their business interests required. But by the time a victim had his improbable day in court, the pilfered grain had been consumed, the stolen cloth cut and tailored, the ship sold, scrapped, or scuttled, and the onetime witnesses scattered among any of dozens of ports large and small across the Ottoman Mediterranean, or worse. As a result, these unlikely courtroom confrontations, which often took place before the *kadi* of Galata or the Rumeli *kazasker*, usually ended without resolution. The alleged victim had the satisfaction of having the accused pirate dragged before a judge, publicly airing his complaint before a bevy of the district's most distinguished residents, but in most instances he could hope for victory only in the court of public opinion.

Plaintiffs were hesitant to admit defeat, however. When chance brought them face-to-face with the men they held responsible for stealing their livelihood or the lives of their loved ones, they typically attempted to keep the suit open when they failed to secure adequate evidence, requesting a continuance to procure more. Nevertheless, the adjournment of such a case typically signified its effective conclusion, at least as far as the court was concerned; I have never found such a case resumed. In some instances, like the suit of Ali bin Yusuf against the Venetian pirate, it is hard to imagine that the defendant would wait around to see if chance would favor the plaintiff with the miraculous appearance of a long-lost witness. A grievance that had waited five, six, or eleven years to be aired might result in a sort of self-imposed exile for the defendant. Initiating a lawsuit could also serve as the opening salvo in negotiations for a compensatory settlement out of court. Parties would have a variety of reasons, not least the preservation of reputation and an end to harassment, to settle even unsubstantiated claims. This was no less true whether the defendant was an accused pirate or a trader in possession of stolen merchandise.

The suits victims lodged against accused pirates in Ottoman courts open a window onto the Ottoman Mediterranean maritime world that has otherwise been entirely closed to us, revealing in the process a far more diverse sea of pirates and victims than has been hitherto described. The salience of the labels of religion and subjecthood, let alone pirate and corsair, is far from clear in this space, complicating a received narrative in which Mediterranean maritime violence is largely the preserve of religiously motivated corsairs. They present us with stories of Ottoman-on-Ottoman piracy with every possible permutation of Christian and Muslim cast in the roles of pirate and victim, of religiously mixed crews, of Ottoman subjects taking on the corsairs of North Africa in Istanbul—and winning. They remind us that the Ottoman Mediterranean, for all its danger, disorder, and diversity, was united under the shadow of the Ottoman pavilion pitched in Istanbul.

These facts are exemplified in the suit of the Greek sea captain Manolaki veled Anton in 1617. Manolaki was a resident of the Bosphorus village of Yeniköy, which would be torched by Cossack raiders eight years later, in the jurisdiction of Galata. However, due to the interjurisdictional nature of his case and the international character of the seafaring litigants, his suit was brought before the Rumeli *kazasker*. Manolaki was suing Anton veled Isbanoli, a Greek Christian from Crete and thus a Venetian subject. The case is worth quoting in full in order to see how the claims and counterclaims of these men were transformed by the scribe, as the court contended with a complex case that had originated hundreds of miles away and, strikingly, fifteen years earlier:

A captain named Manolaki veled Anton who is a resident of Yeniköy in the district of Istinye, which is in the jurisdiction of well-protected Galata, sued Anton veled Isbanoli, who is a resident of the island of Crete, in the court, claiming: "In the year 1010 [i.e. July 1601–June 1602], I came with my ship to the port of Syros in the Mediterranean to unload wheat. When I dropped anchor, the aforementioned Anton came to the aforementioned port with his ship in the manner of a merchant vessel and drew alongside as if to buy wheat from me. While [my ship was] lying at anchor, he engaged in piracy (*korsanlık edüb*) and fired a cannonball, and my crewmembers and I escaped onto the shore. Once I fled, someone unloaded my 50,280 *kil* (bushels) of wheat that was inside my ship, took it, and left. Now I demand that the aforementioned [Anton] be questioned."

After questioning, the aforementioned Anton stated: "In fact, when I arrived at the aforementioned place to buy wheat, I purchased and took possession of 3,000 *kil* of wheat from the wheat on the aforementioned plaintiff Manolaki's ship which I paid for with money. I gave and turned over its price of 180,000 *akçe* to the aforementioned Manolaki. I did not take it by way of transgression and I did not take more than 3,000 *kil* of wheat."

After interrogation, the aforementioned Manolaki denied in the legal manner that he had sold the wheat and taken into possession the price. When the aforementioned Anton was asked to provide proof of his claim, he was unable to do so. Since they differed, after the aforementioned Manolaki, as requested, took an oath by God who sent the Gospels and on Jesus, peace be upon him, the aforementioned Manolaki was asked in the legal manner to provide proof that the aforementioned Anton had taken more than 3,000 *kil* of wheat by way of transgression, and he also was unable to do so. After he was invited to take an oath, the aforementioned Anton, as requested, swore upon God who sent the Gospels and on Jesus, peace be upon him. What happened was written as required. Recorded in the middle of Cemaziü'l-evvel in the year 1026 [=mid-May, 1617].

Witnesses of the case: . . .[45]

The case raises many questions. Chief among them is what chain of events brought both of these men before the highest ranking judicial figure in the Ottoman Empire, nearly fifteen years after the alleged theft occurred. The record hints at a drama of trade and betrayal knit together through trans-imperial networks of Greek merchants spanning the eastern half of the Mediterranean, from Venice to Istanbul by way of Crete and Syros. We have only a single page torn from a decades-long story. Evidently Manolaki had previously met Anton or at least recognized him after the encounter. Had they done business together before the incident in 1601–1602? Was it trade that brought Anton to Istanbul in 1617 and simple chance that led to a face-to-face encounter with his accuser on the quay? One way or another, Manolaki discovered that the man he held responsible for the disappearance of his wheat was in town and compelled him to appear in court to answer the charges against him.

The incident Manolaki described resembled countless run-ins with pirates in the early modern Mediterranean. Ships were at their most vulnerable when lying at anchor in port, when there was no cover and no space or time to maneuver. Just as with Mahmud ibn Ahmed several years earlier, Manolaki was calling in a small harbor when the pirate vessel approached. Whereas only Manolaki's attacker employed subterfuge to get in close, disguising himself as a friendly merchant and potential buyer—was he flying Venetian colors?—both sets of sea robbers announced their piratical intentions with a show of force once within striking range, driving the beset captains overboard to the safety of the shore.

Of course, Manolaki's attacker may not have been just assuming "the manner of a merchant vessel." The line between raid and trade was porous, and there is no reason to assume that the pirate here was not a merchant ship engaging in opportunistic raiding. But it is especially intriguing that in this incident of small-scale peacetime piracy perpetrated by and against Greek Christians, Manolaki was reported to have accused Anton of engaging in *korsanlık*—a reminder that the term cannot necessarily be understood to refer strictly to "corsairing" with all its religious and state-supported connotations. In any event, Manolaki might be considered lucky to have lost only his cargo and not his ship or his freedom.

Before turning to the question of what Manolaki hoped to achieve by suing Anton, let us examine how the case was handled. As usual, the entry begins by introducing the principals and their places of origin before fixing the type of case as a suit (*dava*) and transitioning into the plaintiff's opening statement. This statement and the defendant's rejoinder, though presented as quoted speech, should not necessarily be understood as such. For one thing, both men likely spoke before the court in Greek. They would have made their claims and counterclaims to the judge with the aid of an interpreter, who likewise would have translated the judge's questions from the Turkish and relayed their answers. Later, the court scribe composed an entry for the court's register in which their statements, having already passed through this intermediary from Greek into Turkish, were condensed and reformulated to fit the legal and stylistic idiom of the early modern Ottoman court.[46] As such, these "quotes" may bear only a passing resemblance to what they actually said, but they probably accurately represent the substance—or at least the court's perception—of the litigants' legal claims and the thrust of their strategies.

Manolaki, in describing the raid on his ship, identified Anton as the captain of the attacking ship and strongly implied that he was responsible for the theft of his wheat, but stopped short of accusing him of it. He may or may not have exhibited such restraint in his statement before the court, but the fact was that he had not seen his ship unloaded and could not state with certainty that Anton was the culprit, only that he had approached with hostile intent.[47] Thus, according to the record, Manolaki demanded that Anton be questioned in connection with the theft of his wheat, but he did not or was not allowed to demand restitution at this stage.

At this point, Anton was questioned by the judge and offered his own, sharply divergent account of events. Anton did not deny that he had visited the port or rendezvoused with Manolaki, only that he had taken any wheat by force. Anton asserted instead that he had come to purchase wheat and that he bought three thousand bushels for 180,000 *akçe*, which was promptly and properly handed over. Both men, of course, could not be telling the truth.

Following Anton's statement, a secondary phase of questioning occurred, and Manolaki denied (*inkar*) the veracity of Anton's counterclaim that he had bought and paid for a much smaller quantity of wheat. Manolaki's denial shifted the burden of proof to Anton, and the court asked him to provide evidence supporting his side of the story. Given that evidence in this case would have to be eyewitness testimony and that the incident took place fifteen years earlier in an island harbor hundreds of miles away, Anton was unable to do so. If Anton had categorically denied Manolaki's initial statement instead of offering his own—as Mehmed Çelebi had done vis-à-vis Mahmud ibn Ahmed—the burden of proof would have remained on Manolaki and he would have been asked then to provide evidence to substantiate his claims. As their accounts diverged so widely and Anton had failed to back up his story with evidence, the court now offered Manolaki the chance to take an oath.[48]

Oaths were a powerful tool in Islamic law; Manolaki would have won the case if Anton had not been willing to take the oath himself, even with his being unable to bring witnesses. Oaths were not undertaken lightly. Large-scale studies of Ottoman court records reveal many instances of litigants being unwilling to take the oath, even when failing to do so meant they would lose their case and the other party lacked any evidence.[49] Of course, swearing to tell the truth on holy books remains a hallmark of many modern legal systems. The fact that plaintiff and defendant were

Christians made no difference as far as the procedure of the court except for what they swore upon. When the judge asked Manolaki to take a solemn oath, upon Jesus and the Gospels, that he had not sold the wheat as Anton had claimed, Manolaki did so. Without evidence to the contrary from Anton, Manolaki's oath was legally admissible as evidence that he had not. But Anton's failure to substantiate his own version of the story did not mean that Manolaki had proven his case.

The court may not have accepted Anton's argument that he had bought the wheat, but without an admission of guilt from the defendant, the plaintiff would still have to prove that he had stolen it. Thus, Manolaki was next asked to provide evidence that Anton had taken the wheat by force. This, unsurprisingly, he could not do. Anton was then asked to swear an oath, likewise upon Jesus and the Gospels, that he had not committed the act of piracy of which he was accused. Once he did so, there was no more for the court to do. Neither man could meet the burden of proof. Both had taken solemn oaths that they had not done what the other man claimed. The case was dismissed and the proceedings were duly recorded.

Was Manolaki so ignorant of the Ottoman Islamic rules of evidence that he thought he could win a suit concerning a fifteen-year-old incident of piracy without a shred of proof? This seems unlikely. Desire for restitution alone is an unsatisfactory explanation for Manolaki's decision to go to court. As much as he might have desired to be recompensed for his alleged loss, it seems likely that suing Anton in the Ottoman court was not intended as a means to achieving this end, but was the end itself. There is no way to know for sure what compelled people to bring their problems to court, but the chance to make accusations publicly must have served as a powerful motivator, even if there was no chance of winning.[50]

The world of Greek merchants and sailors in the Ottoman Mediterranean was an intimately connected one. When Manolaki ran into Anton again in Istanbul in 1617, he seized the opportunity to get some small measure of satisfaction by dragging the man into court and accusing him of piracy in front of a group of powerful and influential men. Beyond the judge and court officers, this included the *şuhudü'l-hal*, the witnesses to the proceedings who were typically members of the Ottoman Muslim elite. Word of the allegations leveled against Anton would not have remained confined to the *kadi*'s chambers. In a world where reputation and trust were paramount to survival in networks of trade, by having his accusation heard in court, Manolaki may have already won.[51] And if Anton wanted Manolaki to stop spreading accusations about him wherever he went, he could settle with Manolaki while still maintaining his innocence, effectively paying for Manolaki's silence and his promise not to raise the issue again.[52]

Manolaki and Anton were both Greeks, but they were not both Ottoman subjects. The registers preserve ample evidence of intra-Ottoman piracy, however. For example, a little over two years earlier, in late February 1615, the same court heard the suit of el-Hac Ömer bin Mustafa Reis against a certain Mustafa Reis. Four years earlier, Ömer had been sailing from Payas in southern Anatolia to Damietta in Egypt when his ship was plundered by a *levend* frigate during a stopover at Cyprus. Ömer heard that Mustafa Reis was among the pirates on the frigate that stole his cargo and cash, on which basis he demanded that Mustafa be arrested and punished. Mustafa denied everything and the case was adjourned since Ömer had no specific evidence tying Mustafa to the events he described.[53]

Other, similar cases preserve evidence of ethno-religiously mixed Ottoman pirate ships and the difficulties associated with distinguishing pirates from their victims. For instance, Mustafa Beşe bin Abdallah, a janissary of the Porte, sued the Armenian Yorgi veled Anton of the island of Kos in the court of Galata in mid-April, 1616. Four years earlier Mustafa Beşe had been on a voyage in the Mediterranean, returning from a trading expedition to Egypt, when he dropped anchor for the night in a place known as Karabağlar along the coast near Kos. Mustafa Beşe and his crew had settled down for the night after dinner when, under cover of darkness, Yorgi and his compatriots fell upon Mustafa's ship, "because," Mustafa explained, "the aforementioned Yorgi is a frigateer (*firkateci*)." Mustafa was employing one of the standard Ottoman euphemisms for a true pirate, one who attacked opportunistically and without warning. Mustafa accused Yorgi of seizing him by force and despoiling his ship, stealing a quantity of cash which included his share of the profits from a *mudaraba* venture (in which another had invested the capital and he had provided the labor), and a variety of goods the values of which he provided the court. Mustafa now demanded the return of all that had been taken from him.

Yorgi responded that four years earlier he had been a prisoner of a pirate, a "frigateer" known as Ak Mehmed, and that it was Ak Mehmed who had directed the frigate's raiding vessel to Karabağlar by night to plunder Mustafa Beşe's ship. But Yorgi claimed that he was imprisoned on Ak Mehmed's frigate, chained hand and foot, at the time of the attack. Yorgi thus denied that he had played any role in the robbery, willing or otherwise, though there was no disputing that the men had encountered one another that night. When prompted to provide proof that Yorgi was responsible, Mustafa called a single witness who testified, presumably much to Mustafa's dismay, that he could not confirm Mustafa's account of events. Asked if he had any other witnesses, Mustafa requested a grace period to find more, which the court duly granted.[54]

Like Manolaki and Anton, Mustafa encountered Yorgi in Galata, recognized him from that fateful night near Kos, and sued him. Did Mustafa believe that Yorgi was the pirates' commander or simply one of their number? The ambiguity surrounding the events and the parties' roles in them is typical of these sorts of cases. Yorgi could have been a full, free member of Ak Mehmed's crew. Ethnically and religiously diverse ships crews were the norm in the early modern Mediterranean. Even when we write of an "English" or a "Tripolitan" ship, the colors it flew and the origins of its master tell us little about the composition of the crew. Yorgi's explanation, that he was an unwilling prisoner on Ak Mehmed's ship could just as easily be true. As we have seen, pirates routinely took prisoners to serve on their ships, both as oarsmen and in a variety of other roles. Those like Yorgi, who were from the area and had maritime experience, were especially valuable as guides and pilots. But he also could have been recruited from the island and paid for his services. The excuse that one was a prisoner of the pirates, or just a simple sailor who had no idea that piracy was on the agenda, was one reliably trotted out by crewmembers on trial for piracy across the Mediterranean.[55] Was Yorgi a fellow victim who, thanks to chance and a recognizable face, found himself standing before a judge? Or was he the arch pirate that Mustafa made him out to be? The truth might be somewhere in the middle, a man who, like the unhappy crews lured or pressed into service on some seventeenth-century Catholic corsairs, had little choice but to play the violent role fate had assigned him, attacking and plundering ships whenever ordered but enjoying none of the spoils.[56] The entry for the case cannot answer any of these questions, but it is a reminder of the existence and persistence of this sort of Ottoman-on-Ottoman piracy.

In this chapter so far we have considered disputes in which enemy infidels—including Catholic corsairs—seized ships and cargo as well as accusations of Ottoman-on-Ottoman piracy involving both Muslims and Christians. But the corsairs of North Africa also made appearances in the courts. An unusual case heard by the Rumeli *kazasker* reminds us that their piratical activities did not exempt Ottoman subjects but that their leadership, once returned to Istanbul, might be held to account for profiting from their crimes.

Manol veled Apostol, a Greek sailor from Mytilene, invested everything he had in leather. In Izmir, he purchased twenty thousand pieces of Morocco leather (*sahtiyan*) and ten thousand pieces of shoe leather (*köşele*) and loaded them onto his ship, intending to take them to Europe, where he could expect to make a tidy profit on their sale. The voyage did not go as planned. Although he successfully navigated the Aegean archipelagic obstacle course, dodging sandbars, Catholic corsairs, and local pirates, he was set up upon by Tripolitan corsairs as he sailed past. When the spoils were divided among the corsairs back in Tripoli, the *beylerbeyi* Kefelioğlu Süleyman Pasha, whose position was symbolic but lucrative, received a 10 percent share of the prize: 2,000 *sahtiyan* worth 1,500 *guruş* and 1,000 *köşele* worth 2,000 *guruş*.[57]

Manol was set free, his Ottoman subjecthood evidently sparing him from enslavement just as his Christian identity might have protected him from the same fate on Malta, but he left Tripoli with nothing. Süleyman Pasha's return to Istanbul after the conclusion of his term as *beylerbeyi* provided Manol with the opportunity to pursue some small measure of justice. In July 1633, Manol came to Istanbul and the "Saturn-like *divan* of the antechamber of the sultan"—the record's appropriately lofty description of the legal and administrative heart of the empire—to plead his case against the former governor of Tripoli. Before the Rumeli *kazasker*, who heard the case on behalf of the Imperial Council, Manol demanded that Süleyman Pasha return his stolen goods or provide compensation in cash equal to their value.

Süleyman Pasha denied Manol's account, but Manol was able to call two witnesses hailing from greater Istanbul, Hızır Bey bin Murad and Hızır bin Abdallah, who testified that Manol's ship was indeed seized by Memi Reis and brought to Tripoli, where in their presence the *beylerbeyi* did indeed take the quantities of leather Manol described. This was enough for the court. The pasha was ordered to pay up. There was no question here that the seizure of Manol's ship and his cargo could not be justified, that the corsairs had perpetrated a straightforward act of piracy. Having demonstrated that Süleyman had shared in the corsairs' ill-gotten gains, Manol had an absolute right to restitution.

It may have been a pyrrhic victory. Manol had sued a pasha and won, but at what cost? No doubt significant time and money had been expended in the effort, all for just 10 percent of his stolen cargo. There is no indication whether any satisfaction could be had as far as the other 90 percent, but Manol could not hold the pasha financially responsible for what the others around him had taken. He would have to bring claims against them as well, and it is difficult to imagine that Manol would be able to accomplish much against the corsairs of Tripoli in their home court. Things were different in the imperial capital. Were Memi Reis to appear in Istanbul, he could find himself facing the Rumeli *kazasker* and held to account for his crime.

If the former *beylerbeyi* had sanctioned Memi Reis' prize after the fact, it would have been in keeping with the non-interventionist line taken by most of the pashas sent from Istanbul after the 1580s. They had much to gain from their silence in the face of raids of questionable legality, whereas taking a principled stand would accomplish little besides endangering their position. Manol's case reminds us that the victims of the North African corsairs were not just the subjects of European powers; Ottoman subjects too suffered from their predations. But Manol would not find justice in Tripoli, where he was wronged with the full knowledge and participation of its governing elite. His case highlights the fact that North Africa occupied a position outside the borders of the Ottoman Mediterranean legal space and beyond the effective limits of its legal and administrative reach.

The cases above have shed light on manifestations of piracy in the Ottoman Mediterranean that have largely been missing from the scholarship. The court records make a broader spectrum of piracy visible and underscore the fact that the professional practitioners of maritime violence, the corsairs, were the most prominent but certainly not the only or necessarily even the most numerous perpetrators of piratical acts in the early modern Mediterranean. The violent but effective precautions taken by many engaged in true piracy account for why these kinds of pirates are not better represented in the sources. Of the pirates active in the Aegean archipelago around 1700, whom he referred to as "banditti" and clearly distinguished from the Catholic corsairs he so admired, the French traveler Tournefort wrote that, "these wretches, not content with plundering people, throw them overboard with a stone about their necks, for fear of being seized, upon the complaints of those they have ill used."[58] We have already seen that logic at work, and its undeniable effectiveness, in the case of the Venetian merchant-pirate Nicolo. Despite this, it was not unusual for victims and pirates to face one another in court, often years after the encounter that first brought them together. If plaintiffs could not necessarily arrange for the harsh punishment that pirates captured in the act might face, they could at least create suspicions that would follow them out of court and, perhaps, out to sea as well.

Farther from the capital, the accusations leveled against pirates were often fresher and the danger they posed more immediate. On Crete, for example, accused pirates were hauled before the *kadi*s and the communities they had attacked for criminal prosecution and, in the period of renewed warfare from 1684 to 1699, naval entrepreneurs arranged privateering expeditions and battled each other over the spoils. It was neither necessary nor practical to handle such business in Istanbul. Records from Crete also contain the more prosaic sorts of transactions brought about as a consequence of piracy, with merchant captains and accused pirates registering guarantors for their good behavior, victims despoiled of their property seeking debt relief, and relatives arranging ransoms for loved ones. These were examples of court business on the crossroads of the Mediterranean, on a predominantly Christian island engaged in trade in all directions and threatened by pirates from all sides.

PIRACY AND LAW ON THE "FRONTIER OF ISLAM"

The restoration of peace after the surrender of Candia in 1669 did not spell the end of piracy around Crete. While Venetian-sponsored privateering temporarily ceased, all manner of sea raiders still prowled Cretan and Aegean waters, including the dreaded Maltese whose predations had inspired the invasion of Crete a generation earlier. Undoubtedly the merchants of Venice still suffered, but Ottoman subjects—including Cretan Greeks who had only recently acquired this legal identity—bore the brunt of this activity. The impact of mostly Christian piracy on mostly Christian ship captains, Muslim passengers and others during the interwar years is well attested in the Cretan court records. Maritime violence had a disruptive effect on territorial economic life as well, for losses at sea often led to financial disputes on land.

Sea travel and finance were both unpredictable and sometimes treacherous pursuits, for which reason the Qur'an warned against the former and advised keeping a written record of the latter.[59] The story of two janissary-merchants despoiled by pirates captures the uncertain security situation in the years immediately following the completion of the Ottoman conquest of the island, the growing involvement of men with military titles in trade, and the kinds of disputes that washed ashore there. In 1673, Mehmed Beşe ibn Mahmud and Mehmed Beşe ibn Mustafa arranged to ship their goods, valued between the two of them at 510 *guruş*, from Istanbul to Chania on the frigate of Mihali veled Manol, an Ottoman Greek captain. The frigate hugged the Anatolian coast on its way south before stopping at Chios. There, Mihali Reis recommended that the janissaries disembark because of the danger from pirates during the particularly perilous trans-Aegean passage. Presumably they could wait on the island for an Ottoman naval convoy to transport them the rest of the way. Mihali said that he would sail under the Venetian flag he had in his possession and, the men later claimed, he reassured them that if pirates did strike, he would compensate them for any losses.

Mihali's prescience probably saved the janissaries' lives, but his Venetian flag provided scant protection against the corsairs who attacked during the voyage from Chios to Chania. While some sea raiders may have respected the banner of Saint Mark, most saw it as an invitation, the very temptation of a pirate, as Thomas Roe had put it some fifty years earlier.[60] Mihali escaped the encounter with his life and his ship, but the corsairs—who may have searched belowdecks specifically for the goods of "Turks" or may have had them helpfully pointed out by the terrified captain—made off with all the janissaries' goods. Sometime after both Captain Mihali and the two Mehmeds arrived safely in Crete, they sued him in the court of Candia for compensation for their losses. Mihali, they claimed, had reneged on his side of the bargain.

But the court disagreed. Whether or not Mihali had promised them that he would guarantee their goods, the plaintiffs had failed to establish a legally binding guarantee (*kefalet*) with him, which had to be "clearly recorded in the legal books"—that is, in court before a judge and witnesses.[61] And indeed, such guarantees do appear in the court's registers. The records from the years of renewed conflict with Venice (1684–1699) attest to the French consul posting bonds (*kefil*) guaranteeing the safe arrival of French ships contracted to carry Ottoman dignitaries or their goods through the treacherous Cycladic gauntlet to Istanbul.[62] In contrast, the janissaries' oral agreement with Mihali, if it had actually occurred, was not binding by Islamic legal standards. Thus, "from the evidentiary perspective," the judge concluded, "their suits were not correct." The case was dismissed and the janissaries were ordered not to trouble Mihali further.[63]

Here, the lack of documentary evidence, of a court-issued certificate of surety, resulted in the court terminating the proceedings. An oral contract for bond was neither verifiable nor binding by the standards of the court, and the janissaries would have to suffer their losses. The scribe's aside, that according to authoritative works of Islamic jurisprudence it is best to have a record of such things, might be taken as an admonition: the janissary plaintiffs should have known better.

The case is interesting for reasons beyond the legal. For one, it demonstrates how present the Ottoman fear of pirate attacks was in the 1670s, when the Ottoman Mediterranean was theoretically at peace once more. Mihali and the janissaries recognized the high risk of a run-in with pirates navigating between Chios and Crete and reckoned that the odds of making it through unscathed would be improved without the Ottoman Muslim military men on board. It also suggests once more the extent to which trust was crucial to shipping and passenger transport. Mihali may have been despoiled by corsairs, but he just as easily could have stopped off in Milos and sold the Mehmeds' goods for his own profit before concocting a story about a pirate raid. Incidents of Christian ship captains betraying their Muslim passengers to enemy slave traders were common enough to have entered the popular imagination in the later seventeenth century.[64] Yet trust remained crucial; even if it was breached in this instance, the janissaries had been willing to disembark at Chios with the understanding that their goods would be waiting for them whenever they arrived in Chania. Most journeys did not end in lawsuits, and merchants and passengers regularly put their fortunes and their lives in the hands of captains who were chimeras.

After all, who was Mihali? The Ottoman court in Candia described him as a *zimmi*, but he carried with him a Venetian flag. Ship captains—including pirates and corsairs—regularly carried and flew a kaleidoscopic array of flags to suit every situation, but let us assume for a moment that Mihali's possession of the banner of Saint Mark was more significant than just another embroidered rag in a mariner's bag of tricks. If Mihali was a Cretan Greek from Candia, then he had very likely been, until recently, a Venetian subject. Now nominally Ottoman, he still operated in a maritime world between these two poles, switching between Ottoman and Venetian juridical identities at will.

As far as defense against pirates, a heavily armed ship and the colors of Saint George might have served him better, but the example of Mihali and those like him gives some indication of the liminal position of seafaring Greeks in the seventeenth-century Ottoman Mediterranean, especially after the conquest of Crete. Although they often fell prey to Catholic corsairs, they usually survived the experience, and they could pass from the Abode of Islam to the Abode of War and back again through the increasingly dangerous legal vacuum of the sea in between. As for the corsairs in this case, they were, as usual, identified in the record only with the generic "enemy infidel" appellation. This changed with the renewal of war with Venice and much of the rest of Europe, however. Now Ottoman judges in Candia began to take a little more note of who these raiders were and whom, if anyone, they served.

Crete enjoyed fewer than fifteen years of peace between the surrender of Candia in 1669 and the start of the Morean War in 1684. The return of war to the seas around Crete made maritime raiding and amphibious violence a clear and present danger for the inhabitants of the island. The threat did not come just from the long-distance corsairs who had long targeted merchant traffic in the area. It came from just offshore—and from within. After the loss of Crete, the Venetians retained three heavily fortified islands located at strategic points just off the northern Cretan coast: Gramvousa to the west, Souda just to the east of Chania, and Spinalonga in the east. These were spots where the Abode of War was quite literally a stone's throw away. The situation on Crete is exemplary of the challenges posed by piracy and corsairing on the empire's maritime frontier and the local impact of efforts to combat them.

Gramvousa was betrayed by its Venetian commander to the Ottomans in 1691, but Venice retained Souda and Spinalonga until 1715. When Venice declared war on the Ottoman Empire in April 1684, these three islands became major centers for anti-Ottoman Venetian privateering.[65] Yet the main practitioners came not from Venice but from Crete itself. They were primarily Christian Cretan villagers who had, in Ottoman parlance, "rejected the pact" (*nakz-ı ahd*) and gone over to the enemy to raid by land and sea, pillaging villages, enslaving Muslims, and capturing boats and ships. They and those they attacked were mostly born and raised on Crete, for the Muslim-Christian divide on the island was primarily one between Orthodox Christians and converts and their descendants, not Muslim immigrants from elsewhere in the Ottoman world.[66] Because Spinalonga, Souda, and Gramvousa were formally *darülharb*, the Cretans who joined the Venetian enemy were considered "traitors" who, by crossing over, had renounced their Ottoman subjecthood and its protections.[67] In many village raids, the attackers knew their victims well. The damage this civil conflict caused to the social fabric on the island was significant. Its effects, along with the efforts of the Ottoman government on the island to combat the problem and prosecute the offenders, were manifested in the court of Candia.

Some of those who joined up with the corsairs at the Venetian fortresses and were subsequently captured by Ottoman forces received the opportunity to rejoin society and return to their homes. Surety (*kefalet*, *kefil*) as a form of bail contracted in the court provided the mechanism for this.[68] This was possible because much of the defense against the corsairs and "traitors" was locally organized, and captors had the freedom to choose what to do with their captives, including releasing them to their communities in exchange for payment, or the promise of a large one should the captured corsair fail to abide by the terms of his release.[69]

However, the redeemed sometimes skipped bail, leaving their guarantors in the lurch. An Ottoman naval captain named Hasan captured a certain Papa Georgi while he was corsairing with the "enemy infidels" from Spinalonga. As Papa Georgi had abandoned his village for Spinalonga, just offshore but formally in the *darülharb*, he was himself considered to be an "enemy infidel" and was thus Hasan's property to dispose of as he wished. Hasan sold Papa Georgi to a janissary from Candia named Sefer Beşe for 262 *guruş*, and Sefer imprisoned the captured corsair in his dungeon. At this point, Papa Georgi's mother, Zabeta, offered herself as her son's guarantor, promising to pay Sefer 400 *guruş* should her son run away or rejoin the enemy. The surety agreement was contracted in court with witnesses as the law required, and Zabeta's money and person became security for her son's freedom, with Zabeta promising to make her son appear in court whenever summoned.

But Papa Georgi soon fled, and Sefer called to collect his 400 *guruş* from Zabeta. When Zabeta refused, he sued her in the court of Candia in April 1694. Although she denied the agreement, Sefer's case was ironclad. Deploying the Muslim witnesses to the surety agreement, the sequence of events and legality of the arrangement were confirmed and Zabeta was ordered to surrender the money immediately.[70] The fact that Sefer agreed to parole his prisoner suggests that, like the present-day bail bondsman, there was potential for profit built into the arrangement whether Papa Georgi ran away or not—otherwise why would he pay 262 *guruş* and then free him?—but any form of interest or fees incorporated into such agreements (like those charged by ransom brokers) was an extralegal addition and consequently not mentioned in the records.

The flight of Papa Georgi notwithstanding, it is clear that Ottoman administrators considered the system of surety to be an effective method of social control. As the numbers of men going over to Souda, Spinalonga, and Gramvousa spiked and their attacks began to cause more serious damage toward the end of the 1680s, the Ottoman government on Crete was forced to step up its efforts to keep Cretans in their villages and prevent the economic devastation from causing greater flight to the bandits. The professional military forces on the island were spread thin and the local defense militias in many seaside villages, rather than performing their duties, were coordinating with (if not outright joining) the pirates and Venetian-sponsored corsairs operating in the vicinity.

Since Ottoman administrators lacked the manpower to augment their defense forces, they relied instead on the threat of collective punishment, linking villages together in a system of mutual guarantorship that ensured the economic ruin and potential execution of village notables if their neighbors, friends, and families did not do their part to keep the peace. This became a common Ottoman strategy to combat piracy and banditry throughout the empire.[71] Beginning in early April 1689 and continuing for over two weeks, a steady stream of villagers from coastal districts across the island were paraded before the judge in Candia and an assortment of some of the island's highest-ranked administrators to hear the sultan's decree.

The government had been made aware that the guards manning the coastal watch towers had been signaling the pirates to come ashore to raid instead of warning of their approach, for which they received a share of the booty. This kind of complicity would no longer be tolerated. Tower operators were now expected to signal the appearance of any ship in the distance, whether merchant or suspected pirate, by raising a red flag during the day and by lighting a fire at night. The names, descriptions, and worksites of all the locally appointed guards were to be provided to the Cretan administration so it would know whom to blame if pirates struck unopposed. The summoned notables were informed that they would henceforth be expected to organize a proper defense and that they would have to pay the ransom of any Muslims seized from their villages.[72]

Eleven groups of villagers passed through the court that April, each representing the most respected men in their districts, each of whom was required to stand surety for the others.[73] Although their oaths were framed as having been offered "most willingly," it requires little imagination to see the duress involved.[74] Henceforth, the system of surety registration served not just as a form of shipping insurance or bail for redeemed pirates but as a means for guaranteeing compliance with the Ottoman government's anti-piracy policies. It provided financial guarantees for the redemption of Muslim captives that placed the cost solely on their communities, holding them responsible for preventing their capture—much like the informal system in place in the Aegean in which local monasteries were expected to ransom and protect imperiled Muslims—and it specified the high price of failure to keep the pirates at bay. The notables' surety would be paid in both silver and blood.

The collective guarantorship strategy—arranged from a distance, orchestrated through the court, and involving an elaborate, faux-voluntary performance from the notables of nearly a dozen districts (*nahiye*) representing more than a hundred villages—helped establish collective responsibility for Crete's piracy problem. However, it was no substitute for a strong system of maritime defense organized around regular naval patrols, and, predictably, it did not spell the end of defections to the enemy either. Although the use of surety agreements for paroling suspected pirates was ongoing, law enforcement sometimes took a harsher stand.

On April 10, 1694—just four days after the court heard Sefer Beşe's suit against Papa Georgi's mother—a janissary commander, Mehmed Beşe, and his men brought five "traitors" before the *kadi* in Candia for trial. The men—one of whom, Mehmed ibn Mustafa, was a Muslim apostate—were all originally residents of the village of Bistagi who had long since defected to the Venetians at Souda. They, along with twenty-five others, had been part of a raiding party that had been looting and taking Muslim captives from the villages of Roufa and Vathiako when the Ottoman defense force led by Mehmed Beşe arrived on the scene. The raiders fled, but the five men were cornered at a mill in a nearby village and were arrested after a brief firefight. Now Mehmed Beşe asked the court to question the men and see to it that they be punished "according to the *şeriat*." After the prisoners offered an "unforced declaration and confession" to the janissaries' allegations, Muslim witnesses from the victimized villages testified that the defendants were habitual attackers, slaving and stealing in consort with the "traitors" on Souda. On the strength of this testimony and their own, supposedly uncoerced confessions, the defendants were convicted and sentenced to row for life on the imperial galleys.[75] Intriguingly, with the exception of the apostate, the men were referred to as "tax-payers," that is, as Ottoman subjects, suggesting that the court felt that they had not abjured their subjecthood even though they associated with the "traitors" and were "proved thieves." That being the case, death was an option, but sale into slavery was not.

A life sentence on the galleys was effectively a drawn-out death sentence, however, which might account for why the court did not call for the immediate execution of the apostate, Mehmed ibn Mustafa. It did so in other instances. But Yannis, aka Hüseyin, brought before the court in May 1695, was a repeat offender. Yannis had been working with the enemy at Spinalonga for more than seven years, serving as a guide for the Venetians and their Cretan allies in their amphibious assaults. Frigates regularly departed Spinalonga, hugged the coast, and then dispatched teams of thirty to forty men to raid villages and abduct Muslims, for which purpose the local knowledge of men like Yannis was essential. On one such raid, the attackers ran into an Ottoman patrol, and Yannis was captured in the resulting skirmish.

Brought before the court, Yannis confessed to the crimes of which he was accused. Stating that he had participated in multiple raids, that he "did *korsanlık*" and helped abduct Muslims, he pointed out Kara Mehmed, one of his kidnapping victims, since ransomed, who was present at the hearing. When he was previously arrested in connection with similar crimes, he said, he converted to Islam in the presence of the *kadi* of the Mirabello district and assumed the name of Hüseyin. Conversion had been the price of freedom, but he soon repudiated his new name and religion and rejoined the cohort on Spinalonga. Owing to the seriousness of his crimes and his apostasy, all present agreed that his execution was necessary. However, the court did not have the authority to order this punishment without executive approval; the record concludes by noting that the governor of Candia had given his permission for the prisoner to be hanged.[76] As a pirate, traitor, and apostate, there would be no mercy for a man like Yannis. If the confessions he and those like him gave really were freely offered—for Yannis did not shy away from any of the charges laid before him in his statement—it would seem they did not expect any.

Executive authorities sometimes chose to make a gruesome example of men like Yannis, which they were empowered to do without any input from the courts. For instance, in 1676, a Greek from Crete who converted to Islam during the Siege of Candia, married at Chios, and then abandoned his life as a Muslim to join the Maltese corsairs was captured during a raid on Euboea. Whereas his companions were condemned to the galleys, he, as a pirate and an apostate, was condemned to death. Eschewing the traditional hanging, the island's governor had him loaded into one of the shore battery's eighteen-inch guns and blasted therefrom.[77]

Apostates had to be executed unless they reaccepted Islam, but otherwise the execution of pirates was optional and, at least on Crete, infrequently applied. After all, men with physical strength and experience at sea were more useful as oarsmen or slaves. When, in June 1695, several armed men from an enemy infidel corsair galleon, the *Jerusalem,* were captured by an Ottoman patrol while searching for water in the Mirabello district, they were brought to the court in Candia and then, with the approval of the governor, sold as slaves for the benefit of the Ottoman soldiers who had apprehended them.[78] Likewise, when the *kapudan pasha* captured pirates, he might execute some, but most would be sent to the oars.[79]

In short, the possible outcomes of capture in the act of piracy and banditry were conditional release, release with bond, imprisonment, service as an oarsman, enslavement, or death. These penalties were inconsistently applied, though most of the cases described up to this point involved defendants who were participants in but not leaders of pirating expeditions. Nevertheless, it is evident from the surviving record that, at least in the mid-1690s, there was a spike in prosecutions on Crete of those involved in piracy and amphibious raiding. This may have been the result of more effective patrolling by land and sea. So what happened when the Ottoman defenders of Crete caught a "big fish"?

The pirate admiral Stratis veled Manolis was a shark. The number of military officers—over twenty—filing charges against him in the court of Candia in June 1695 bore witness to his successful career and to the many challenges that frustrated attempts to eradicate piracy in the area. The captains of three Ottoman frigates based out of Chania had captured

Stratis along with seven others a few weeks earlier while he was corsairing (*korsanlık edüb*) near the island of Kythera (off the southeastern tip of the Morea) with the four ships under his command. In so doing, they put a stop to a rash of attacks that could easily have been prevented.

In 1691, the fortress of Gramvousa was betrayed by its Venetian commander, Loukas Delarokas, to the Ottomans and Stratis was among the five high-ranking Venetian captives transferred to Ottoman custody in the process. Delarokas knew who Stratis was and warned the local Ottoman officials to keep him imprisoned and not to give him over to anyone unless they had an imperial decree from the sultan; the governor of Chania, Ahmed Pasha, made arrangements with the French consul to have the five transferred to Istanbul.[80] However, once Delarokas, his co-conspirator, and Ahmed Pasha were en route to Istanbul, the then-governor of Crete, Mehmed Pasha, freed all five men, including Stratis, in exchange for a 6,000-*guruş* ransom.

It was a fateful mistake, for Stratis quickly became more dangerous than he had been before. Assembling four frigates, he began attacking villages between Candia and Rethymnon, carrying off forty to fifty Muslims at a time from each. Soon he was sailing all around Crete, descending on remote stretches of coast from his base on Kythera, killing men, abducting women and children, and looting their belongings. He ransomed many of his captives and sold others. It was rumored that many of those he snatched had been shipped off to Venice to work in the cannon foundries. At the time of his arraignment, he was thought to still have some sixty to seventy prisoners on Kythera.

Stratis was enough of a threat that the court scribe allowed what sounds like the actual words of the plaintiffs to enter the record when they said: "Thank God that, thanks to the aforementioned Derviş Reis in the service of the Faith and the Dynasty, this thief (*harami*) Stratis has been arrested, something that has freed the poor people of the island of Crete from his evil and brigandage." They asked the court to sentence him to death and to inform the Imperial Council of its decision. After this, two military officers offered testimony confirming the allegations.[81] No statement from Stratis was recorded. Because of the suffering caused by this man, the judge declared, his execution was both necessary and "urgently required."

However urgent it was, it would have to wait. Informed of the court's ruling, the Porte decreed that a hanging in the provinces would not do for a man like Stratis. In late December 1695, six months after his conviction, the sultan ordered the governors of Crete and the Candia district to "board him on a galley . . . and send him safe and sound to Istanbul" for punishment, "because his transfer here is necessary."[82] With language reminiscent of the *ahdname*'s provision that Ottoman pirates captured by the Venetians be sent "safe and sound" to Istanbul so that they might be made into an example for others, the Ottoman center exercised its authority to punish prominent pirates itself.

Yet Crete was not simply ravaged by pirates and visited by unlucky travelers who already had been. It also supported its own anti-corsair privateers. The line between a system of naval defense, which had been lacking since before the start of the war, and privateering was blurry. Semiprivate concerns were, just as they had been over a century earlier during the Cyprus campaign, a cost effective means of ensuring a modicum of defense.

PRIVATEERING AND DISPUTES ORIGINATING THEREFROM

Ottoman privateering in the seventeenth century was not the exclusive purview of North Africa and Adriatic-based irregulars. Consortia of military officials, local administrators, foreign and Ottoman shipowners, and fighting men formed up from Istanbul to Crete to bring the fight to the enemy's shipping for fixed periods of time or even to pursue specific targets. This activity, often explicitly authorized by the central or local government, was contracted in the courts before witnesses to minimize later disagreements, and the arrangements, including the division of the spoils, were typically specified in detail. Disputes did occur, however, and it is in those instances that the privateering organized outside the regions most associated with it becomes most visible in the historical record.

War created all sorts of opportunities for piratical entrepreneurship. In June 1696, the central government ordered the governor of Candia to allow a certain Mustafa Reis from Monemvasia in the Morea access to three old frigates lying in the port of Candia. Mustafa had notified the Porte of the frigates' inactive presence and requested the right to operate them. Mustafa would repair, man, and employ the vessels to patrol the island and protect the sea lanes summer and winter.[83] Implicit was that Mustafa, who was given access to the ships for free but would outfit them at his own expense, would keep whatever prizes and booty he took in the process of defending Crete.

The situation was somewhat more complicated when military men arranged to lease—or commandeered—a private vessel for a corsairing expedition. Some shipowners came to regret such arrangements and on occasion reneged on their agreements. Such was the case with Mustafa bin Sanasi, who provided his ship for *levendlik*, or corsairing, to Halil Bey, one of the navy's "Lords of the Sea." In 1693, he rented his ship to the *levends* for six full months, that is, the entirety of the sea season from March/April to September/October, for a fee of twenty-two *guruş* paid in advance; he would probably receive a predetermined share of the spoils as well. Halil Bey and his legal agent were formal members of the military rather than private entrepreneurs, but the bulk of their crew may have been irregulars contracted for the season. Mustafa, as owner-operator, accompanied his ship on its cruise. Whether it was lack of confidence in the expedition's military commander, fear of damage to his ship, or growing discomfort with the comportment of its unruly *levend* crew, after three months at sea Mustafa had had enough. Halfway through the cruise, he fled and took his ship with him.

Halil Bey and his men had been sailing with consorts and continued their mission without Mustafa, but they eventually caught up with him after the end of the sea season. In February 1694, Halil Bey's agent, one of the *levends* serving on his flagship, sued Mustafa in the court of Galata, demanding repayment for the three months of service remaining in the contract. This Mustafa agreed to do, handing over eleven *guruş* before the *kadi*.[84]

A dispute from Crete over the spoils from a privateering expedition that same year gives us another rare look into the organization of piratical ventures in the late seventeenth-century Ottoman Mediterranean and the pragmatic concerns of those involved, which transcended religious affiliation. French participation, already noted in ransoming and the provision of local and long-distance transport, extended into this arena as well. It all started when a French merchant and ship captain named "Ranav" sued Hasan Reis, one of the Ottoman frigate captains active in the area and probably the same Hasan Reis who captured and sold the fugitive Papa Georgi to Sefer Beşe some months earlier. In the court of Candia, Ranav testified:

> Four months ago (i.e., late June 1694), according to the agreement (*temessük*) in the aforementioned Hasan Reis' possession, we agreed that he would man my saettia (*şayta*—a fast, small to medium-sized vessel well-suited for coastal trading and raiding) and his two frigates with *levends* and we would sail to the Siteia coast to attack and fight the Mallorcan saettia that was pirating there. According to the agreement, if any damage were done to my saettia, he would give me 500 *guruş*, and if we captured the aforementioned Mallorcan saettia or his prize (a recently captured Ottoman saettia) or his frigate or whatever other booty, half of whatever was taken would go to my saettia and half would go to his frigate and the *levends*. After this was said and decided and a group of Muslims witnessed it,

we sailed to the aforementioned place where the Mallorcan pirate (*harami*) saettia was. With a big battle and much slaughter, the Mallorcan abandoned the prize saettia and fled with his frigate. Thus, Hasan Reis took the prize saettia with eight enemy captives into his possession and after he brought them to Candia port, he sold the booty at auction for 1,800 *guruş*. Of that 1,800 *guruş*, the aforementioned Hasan Reis gave me only 170 *guruş*, sharing out the rest with his *levends* despite our agreement. I request that he be questioned and that justice be served in accordance with the document (*temessük*) in his possession.[85]

During questioning, Hasan Reis responded that Ranav had accurately described their agreement and was correct that the sale of the prize ship, its cargo, and the slaves had totaled 1,850 *guruş*, adding that they had done their accounting "in the presence of a group of Muslims and experts and together with the French consul." However, he reminded Ranav that transfer costs and port fees had to be deducted from this total, leaving only 1,300 *guruş*. He claimed he had given half of that sum—650 *guruş*—to Ranav in that very courtroom. Ranav denied this, but Hasan Reis provided witnesses who testified that the Frenchman had received his promised cut. Ranav was told to drop the matter, and the case was closed on October 20, 1694.[86]

In fact, the case was not quite so simple, for the cargo on the Mallorcan's prize had belonged to a party of six Cretan janissary-merchants. Ranav may have agreed to lend his ship with the promise of easy money, but for Hasan Reis and his compatriots, the motivation was more complex, a combination of the desire for profit and the need to rid the area of a specific threat. As Ranav's statement makes clear, Hasan had specific intelligence that the Mallorcan pirate was off the coast of Siteia and had a prize in tow. He probably knew whose ship it was too. At the very least, he was clearly aware that the two frigates under his command were not adequate to the task of taking on the Mallorcan captain and his associates.

After the success of the expedition, the janissary-merchants demanded the return of their cargo of olive oil. It took some time to work out a solution, but in mid-September—three months after the recapture of the prize from the Mallorcan and a little over a month before Ranav's case was recorded—the janissaries came to the court of Candia to register the settlement of their dispute with Captain Hasan. They noted that, "after the Mallorcan saettia fled . . . when [Hasan] brought the [prize ship] to the port of Candia, each of us sued since our goods onboard had not entered the *darülharb*."[87] As we have seen, proving that a ship had or had not entered the *darülharb* was hardly straightforward, but since the Mallorcan pirate ship was still in Cretan waters when his prize was recaptured and there was no indication that it had been brought into any enemy port, the janissaries were well within their rights to demand its return. This of course would have rendered the privateering expedition with Ranav financially pointless except for the value of the slaves, and the janissaries had to acknowledge that, if not for Hasan Reis and his partners, they would have nothing at all.

Since the division of the shares had been previously arranged between Hasan, Ranav, and their men, it was determined through local arbitration that, in lieu of the return of their cargo, the janissary-merchants would share the proceeds from the sale of two of the Mallorcan slaves, totaling 350 *guruş*. In exchange, they agreed not to pursue any further claim against Captain Hasan.[88] They probably suffered some loss in doing so, but, like the merchants from Naxos who had endured a pirate raid en route to Istanbul and relied on a court-appointed mediator to distribute the burden equally among them, this was a pragmatic solution to the problem. The letter of Islamic law gave them some leverage over Hasan—because the ship had not left the *darülislam*, they could reclaim their goods without cost—but actually proving their case would have been difficult.[89] Settling the dispute amicably—something the judge had doubtless encouraged the parties to do—made an accommodation possible that could not have been achieved in the court itself (the janissaries would either prove their case and get their goods back or fail and get nothing) and acknowledged the perilous efforts of those the janissaries called "Muslim *gazis*." Nevertheless, if the accounting presented in the documents was accurate and Hasan really did hand over 650 *guruş* to Ranav, then he and the *levend*s he commanded had to make do with only 300 *guruş* split between them.

Setting aside the question of whether Ranav was being swindled or greedy, the story raises a number of key points. One is the international character of piracy in the Ottoman Mediterranean. Although the court records normally refer to such characters only as "enemy infidels," the entries relating to this expedition against the Balearic pirates tell us they were Mallorcan because the Ottoman-French privateering concern had this specific target in mind, which was mentioned repeatedly in the principals' statements. This brings us to a second point: whether privateers or pirates, sea raiding was not necessarily random or haphazard. Here the division of spoils and goals of the expedition were predetermined and based on fresh intelligence concerning the location, course, and armament of specific quarry.

The case of Ranav and Hasan Reis reflects both the deep involvement of the French in all aspects of late seventeenth-century Cretan commerce and the willingness of the resident French to cooperate in small-scale privateering ventures, even directed against their coreligionists. Ranav, it is worth noting, objected to not being paid enough but not to the sale of captured Catholic seamen in the slave market of Candia. Perhaps Ranav would offer his services as a ransom broker to the enslaved Mallorcan pirates. After all, the French in Candia were already loaning money to Cretan Muslims to help liberate their own.[90] Regardless, the venture is intriguing, for Ranav provided the means for Cretan Ottomans to hunt down a lurking pirate ship, which made the triumphant Muslim *levend*s holy warriors, *gazi*s in the parlance of the janissary-merchants and the court's scribe. All benefited from the effort, both from the profits gained from the booty and from the temporarily reduced threat to merchant traffic and to the population resident in the area, unquestionably an ecumenical concern.

Piracy had taken a severe toll on remote, poorly defended areas like Siteia, where the Mallorcan had been prowling: by this time, almost thirty years after the completion of the conquest, tax revenue from the district had dropped by 43 percent and large plots of land lay fallow.[91] The Ottomans, like the Venetians before them, lacked the resources to keep close watch over the vast stretches of Cretan coastline beyond the principal cities, but local government, paramilitary forces, and private investors could cooperate to mount an effective response to specific threats—especially when there was money to be made in the process. The Nine Years' War (1688–1697) was ongoing and France and Spain were on opposing sides, so Ranav could presumably legally engage in anti-Spanish privateering, but the cross-confessional dimension to this act of corsairing remains noteworthy, supplying further evidence that, at least in the Ottoman Mediterranean, the vocabulary of intractable holy war is insufficiently nuanced for the phenomenon.

CONCLUSION

Ottoman court records provide us with our only source to retrieve the everyday experiences of Ottoman subjects and seaside communities affected by piracy. That the stories they tell are inevitably and inextricably bound up with the courts means that they also tell us a great deal about how piracy and law collided in the early modern Ottoman Mediterranean. They tell us how questions of jurisdiction were managed, how victims of piracy articulated their claims, and how the experience of and response to piracy varied over time and space.

The consequences of piracy frequently washed up on the shores of the Marmara. Istanbul, as imperial capital and bustling port city, hosted more than its fair share of victims of pirate attacks. As we have already seen, rising maritime violence in the seventeenth century led many to request *fetva*s from the *şeyhülislam* for guidance regarding their situations and the disposition of contested cargoes, ships, or slaves—*fetva*s that in their collected form helped provide guidance for others.

Nevertheless, examining the adjudication of piracy-related cases in Ottoman courts exposes the gap between doctrine as espoused in the *fetva* collections and actual practice. The evidentiary requirements of Islamic law frequently frustrated the efforts of plaintiffs affected by piracy who, time and again, found it difficult to substantiate their claims in Ottoman courts. However, the rationale for going to court could be more complex than the wish to win back one's ship or cargo through litigation, as the example of Manolaki veled Anton, who probably filed suit in 1617 to tarnish the reputation of a rival, makes clear. In other instances, the courts were the first stop on a longer legal journey. The next step might be arbitration, in which the courts often played a supporting role, or a hearing before the Imperial Council, and from there on to courts in Venice, England, or the Netherlands.

The legal, financial, and human impact of piracy in the seventeenth century appears most starkly in the registers of Ottoman Crete. Victims and practitioners of maritime violence appear alongside the local officials tasked with coastal defense and the villagers caught in between the two. In addition to the disputes over stolen cargo that have their counterparts in the Istanbul courts, the Cretan registers reveal how the experience of sea raiding changed between periods of war and peace and how the local government's struggles to control the island's population, deter potential pirates, and punish others played out in the courts. They open a window onto the densely connected networks of merchants and ransom agents in the eastern half of the Mediterranean and Crete's key strategic position therein. They show how the concerns of foreigners and locals coincided and clashed on the island and the great diversity of both pirates and victims in the region. Furthermore, they demonstrate how a great deal of the response to piracy and privateering was handled locally and without interference from the center, but that in prominent cases, like that of Stratis in 1695, the sultan could and did exercise his prerogative to punish pirates in the imperial capital.

The records of Ottoman court encounters with piracy demonstrate convincingly that in the Ottoman Mediterranean, those who made use of the courts, whether Muslims, Christians, or Jews, often had access to significant knowledge of Islamic legal procedure and of the key questions—exemplified in the seventeenth-century *şeyhülislam fetva* collections—that would decide their cases. They thus positioned themselves strategically and made sophisticated arguments about *darülislam* and *darülharb* and the place of ships, cargo, and themselves in it. Although Muslims, especially janissaries, make frequent appearances as plaintiffs in the cases described above—evidence of the fact that Muslims were still very much involved in maritime trade—being Muslim did not guarantee victory, nor did it ensure greater legal knowledge.

The number of suits and registrations lodged by and contracted between non-Muslims, who in some circumstances had other venues open to them, underscores the fact that the *kadi*s' courts, despite their frequent inability to provide definitive decisions, were integral to and unavoidable for the smooth functioning of both interconfessional and international trade in the Ottoman Mediterranean. Ottoman political and military control of the Mediterranean maritime world was shaky and uncertain throughout the seventeenth century. What made this the Ottoman Mediterranean was not the once fabled, now faded prowess of the Ottoman navy that patrolled it nor the faith of its inhabitants, but the fact that it was a unified, Ottoman legal space.

Conclusion

On March 11, 1751, a lengthy imperial decree arrived in Crete. Addressed to all the governors, *kadi*s, and fortress commanders on the island, it told a familiar story of piracy and law transgressed in the Ottoman Mediterranean. At the start of the 1750 sea season, two ships captained by Cretan Muslims had departed Chania for Tripoli. Their aim was to acquire Tripolitan flags and license to practice the *corso* under Tripoli's banner, and then to recruit fighting men. In Tripoli, both ships embarked three hundred *levend*s and joined forces with two Tripolitan vessels, carrying 150 men apiece. The already formidable flotilla then rendezvoused with a formerly Venetian galleon that had been captured the previous year by Tripolitan corsairs in the waters of Lefkada, the once-dreaded Ottoman pirate stronghold in the Ionian Sea that had been, since 1684, a Venetian possession. The five fully manned ships flying Tripolitan colors sailed north, passing Crete to prowl the waters below the Morea in search of Venetian traffic coming and going from Cyprus and the Arab provinces "in the waters of my well-protected domains."[1]

The story of the Cretans in Tripolitan colors ties together the issues raised in this book and their afterlives. After repeated bombardments beginning in the second half of the seventeenth century, the North African port cities' respective raiding activities had been severely curtailed.[2] The navies of France, Great Britain, and the Netherlands were strong enough to enforce the peace treaties that they imposed on the ports, and although they were sometimes breached, by 1750 Tripolitan corsairs were generally disinclined to pick a fight with any of these powers, content instead to accept the annual disbursements that these and other European states paid to keep the peace. But Venice still had no agreement with Tripoli and lacked the military strength to shell it into compliance with the sultan's *ahdname*, which neither the sultan nor the rest of Europe expected Tripoli to respect.[3]

For a seafaring entrepreneur from Crete wishing to toe the line between *guerre de course* and outright piracy, sailing under Tripolitan colors made sense. The outstanding majority of maritime raiders of any faith or subjecthood looked for ways to position their activities within established legal norms, and the Cretan Muslims hoped the association with Tripoli, which thought of itself as at war with Venice, would provide legal cover. Ottoman subjects and statesmen alike thought of Tripoli as independent, rather than as a full-fledged province of the Ottoman sultan bound by his laws and treaties.

During their joint cruise in the Ottoman Mediterranean, one of the Tripoli-flagged Cretan vessels, captained by Hanyalı ("from Chania") Ismail, captured a Salonica-bound Venetian ship off the Morea. This Venetian prize he brought back to Crete, sharing out the booty with the *levends* and his partners on land.[4] A little more than a century after Maltese corsairs stopped in Venetian-held Crete to divvy up the loot from a rich Ottoman galleon, provoking the Ottoman invasion of the island, Cretan Ottomans–cum–North African corsairs had done much the same thing with a Venetian prize on the same island.

Sultan Ibrahim and his advisers had held Venetian authorities responsible for their failure to prevent the corsairs from landing on the Cretan coast, and it was widely believed in Istanbul that Venetian officials had colluded with them. Now Venice could level similar accusations against the Porte for its subjects' breach of the *ahdname* in Crete.

Once informed of the Cretans' predations, the Venetian *bailo* followed the procedure that had been established for well over two hundred years. He submitted a formal petition to the Ottoman government recounting what had happened in Ottoman waters in violation of the peace and "in contravention of the imperial *ahdname* and the conditions of the noble *nişan*," that is, the 1670 edict that had constituted the last major development in Ottoman anti-piracy law. The result was the Ottoman decree to the entirety of Cretan officialdom, ordering them to resolve the problem and respect the provisions of the *ahdname* and anti-piracy decrees, the substance of which it recapitulated at length.

In spite of two wars (1684–1699 and 1714–1718, the last ever fought between the Ottoman Empire and Venice) and the passage of eighty years, Ottoman-Venetian maritime law had hardly changed. Neither side was to do damage to the other. Both sides' merchants and ships were to be able to travel freely, in accordance with "ancient custom." Long-established provisions were repeated, promising that when corsairs came to Ottoman ports, they would do no harm to Venice and would be required to post bonds to ensure their good behavior; violators would be severely punished. Venice's right to pursue and destroy North African corsairs was reiterated.[5]

Istanbul did not directly address the legality of Tripoli's war, but it deplored the attempts of Ottoman subjects, the Cretans, to join it. The recipients were ordered to seize those Cretans who dared to venture out to sea to attack Venetian subjects and to ensure henceforth that the requirements of the *ahdname* be fully upheld. Hanyalı Ismail was just one in a recent upsurge of Cretans taking advantage of Tripoli's war to engage in anti-Venetian raiding. Another captain, Giridli ("Cretan") Hüseyin, had commissioned a forty-four-gun galleon and manned it with a complement of three hundred local *levend*s. His plan was to intercept Venetian ships coming from and going to Ottoman domains and, ominously, make them "disappear."[6]

Warships could not be built without Istanbul's permission. In the late sixteenth and seventeenth centuries, pirates on the Adriatic and Ionian coasts had frequently flouted these rules and built small frigates with which to raid. After 1670, the central administration had ordered all shipowners on the Adriatic to register their craft with the government and provide bonds to prevent them from engaging in unauthorized raiding. But here, in 1750, a Cretan captain was overseeing the launch of a man-of-war in the harbor of Chania, not a small, hastily constructed coastal cruiser. Sultan Mahmud I ordered the destruction or, if at sea, confiscation of the ship and the arrest of the captain "who dared to build it."[7]

Given that it was open season on Venice in Tripoli, the Sublime Porte ordered thorough inspections for Venetian property of all ships from the North African port. More importantly, the Porte ordered that no Ottoman subject be permitted to travel with his ship to Tripoli in order to obtain a flag, lest he take up arms against Venice and damage the "friendship" that existed between the two states. The Porte dispatched a decree to the same effect to the *beylerbeyi* of Tripoli, ordering him not to give privateering licenses to Ottoman subjects who arrived in Tripoli desiring to raid, but no attempt was made to dissuade Tripoli from pursuing its war as Ottoman administrators once would have.[8] The once vexing question of the legal status of the North African ports—rebellious dependencies or independent sovereign entities?—had long since been resolved. The Porte wrote of when "one of the subjects of my exalted state" went to Tripoli, the implication being that Tripoli's people were not the sultan's subjects.[9]

The words of the sultanic decree were quite deliberate, referring more than once to the "waters of my well-protected domains" when referencing the location of the pirate attacks, and making mention only of the prize taken by the Cretan, and thus indisputably Ottoman, captain. If any prizes were taken by the Tripolitan component of the flotilla, they were not mentioned. This reflected the consequences of the diplomatic divergence of the seventeenth century, which led to the European recognition and Ottoman acceptance of North Africa's independence in matters both foreign and domestic. Since the mid-seventeenth century, Ottoman-European treaty law effectively absolved the Ottoman sultan of responsibility for the corsairs' actions except when they brought prizes taken from protected nations into Ottoman—but not North African—ports. Corsairs who did so were to be punished, captives from friendly states freed, and wrongfully taken goods returned, but it was the Europeans' right and responsibility to defend themselves on the high seas.

Whereas the Cretan, Ottoman-subject mariners' participation in Tripoli's *corso* was considered a crime punishable by the Ottoman government, and the Cretan authorities were responsible for ensuring that the Venetian prize brought there be returned, the Tripolitan corsairs' violation of Ottoman territorial waters by seizing Venetian ships there—rather than the seizure itself—was viewed as the corsairs' primary offense. Whereas Ottoman protests in the past had been generated by attacks in the immediate vicinity of Ottoman ports, like Digby at Iskenderun in 1628 and Duquesne at Chios in 1681, developments vis-à-vis North Africa and the expansion of intra-European privateering in the Mediterranean led Ottoman administrators to declare ever larger zones of the Ottoman Mediterranean off-limits to privateers and corsairs in times of war. By the mid-eighteenth century, the limits of that zone corresponded closely with the borders of the Ottoman Mediterranean this book has proposed, stretching diagonally from the Ionian Sea and the western Morea to the western reaches of Egypt.[10]

But by then the "golden age" of Mediterranean piracy was long over. In the first decades of the eighteenth century, while the corsairs of North Africa scaled back their attacks and expanded their diplomatic networks, Maltese corsairing in the Levant went into steep decline. It was partially a victim of the commercial success of the French, who had achieved dominance in Levantine shipping toward the end of the seventeenth century, aided in no small part by the corsairs who attacked their competition. When the Ottomans threatened to hold them responsible for the predations of their countrymen under Maltese banners, the French demanded that the Maltese cease their activities. Indeed, because the Ottomans had spun off responsibility for the North African corsairs and abandoned them to their erstwhile European victims, the Ottoman government could more effectively apply political and economic pressure on others to restrain their own piratically inclined subjects. At the same time, the

Ottoman Greeks who carried much of the Ottoman Mediterranean trade not in European hands had become more adept at taking their appeals to Rome, meaning that booty was increasingly tied up in years of litigation.[11] Between Paris and Rome, Malta found itself kicked out of the Levant and largely limited to battling the neighboring North African corsairs in the central Mediterranean. These developments were reflected in the Maltese *bagno*, where the numbers of *kadi*s and other Ottoman functionaries held captive on Malta steeply declined. In the decades leading up to Napoleon's seizure of the island, the "slaves' *kadi*" might not even be a *kadi* by profession. In 1787, for example, a multilingual ship captain with some legal education from the Adriatic port of Ülgün, by then nine years a slave, was nominated for the position.[12]

Although piracy persisted, the Ottoman navy had also played a role in the restoration of a modicum of security to the Ottoman Mediterranean. The modernization of the fleet that had begun in the last quarter of the seventeenth century accelerated in the mid-1690s with a new and dynamic admiral. Mezzomorto ("Half-Dead") Hüseyin Pasha (d. 1701) was a former *dey* of Algiers and the most talented admiral the fleet had had in living memory, but unlike Uluc Ali or Hayreddin Barbarossa before him, he had not been recruited from Algiers for the post. Rather, Mezzomorto Hüseyin, who seized power during the 1683 French bombardment, found refuge and a career with the Ottomans when he was himself overthrown in 1689 and forced to flee for his life. It was neither career advancement nor invitation but instability in Algiers that propelled him into the sultan's navy. He spent six years proving himself in various commands before he was entrusted with the admiralty in 1695.[13]

The contrast in these careers says much about the changed relationship between Istanbul and North Africa. And yet the words of Mustafa Ali and Katib Çelebi regarding the wisdom of appointing a corsair as admiral continued to ring true.[14] Mezzomorto Hüseyin brought the Ottomans repeated victories over the Venetians, reconquering Chios in 1696 just months after Venetian forces took it during the 1684–1699 war. He wrote a code of naval conduct for the Ottoman navy and oversaw major improvements to the fleet and the training of its men, bringing the navy closer to standards prevailing elsewhere in the Mediterranean and Atlantic. It was not a fleet for grand conquests, but by the second decade of the eighteenth century, the Ottomans were no longer reliant on Adriatic and North African irregulars for their security and were far more capable of defending against the pirates and corsairs who had plagued the Ottoman Mediterranean for 150 years.[15] During the comparatively peaceful and prosperous decades of the mid-eighteenth century, the Ottomans combined significant investments in new ships and patrols with an ambitious program of fortification-building on the islands and coasts in an effort to reassert themselves in their maritime dominions and restore security.[16] Nevertheless, such defensive measures could never fully eliminate piracy and did nothing to resolve the diplomatic imbroglios and courtroom battles that emerged when pirates inevitably struck. As the events of 1750 demonstrated, the legal and administrative response remained key.

This book opened in Tripoli, with a doomed dictator's desperate warning of renewed holy war, of the imminent return to the days of "Ottomans imposing ransoms on ships." The story narrated above, of eighteenth-century Ottoman Cretans setting sail for Tripoli to become corsairs precisely because they could not legally raid the Venetians as Ottoman subjects, gives lie to the uncritical association of Mediterranean piracy generally and North African corsairing specifically with the Ottomans and Islam. Explanations of the phenomenon that point exclusively, or even primarily, to religious motivations or divisions are wholly unsatisfactory. Religion could provide targets, justification, and even inspiration, but Tripoli's war against Venice and the Cretan captains' decision to join it were grounded in political, economic, and legal concerns—concerns that were not shared by the Ottoman government.

An unusual quasi-epistolary Ottoman pirate novella is suggestive of the choices facing those navigating piratical careers in the early modern Mediterranean and the fluidity of political and religious identities. Composed in the late seventeenth century and set in the 1670s, *The Story of the Jailor-Captain Mahmud and His Victories over the Damned Hell-Dwelling Maltese* purports to be an account of the experiences of a manumitted slave from Egypt named Yusuf, who embarks on a trading voyage from Alexandria on a French ship and is wrecked on a deserted island in a violent storm.[17] He and the other surviving passengers are picked up by a passing French galleon, which turns out to be a corsair, and the Muslims among them are chained up in the hold. Fortunately for them, the galleon's jailor nurses a grudge against the captain and plots a mutiny in which he enlists his Muslim prisoners. When the captain and most of the crew go ashore to raid Cyprus, the jailor, a small group of French co-conspirators, and the Muslim captives violently seize control of the ship.

The motley crew is now faced with a pivotal decision: which outfit should they join? Convening a council, the mutinous jailor-cum-captain explains, "We must join and take the flag of some power or an *ocak* [lit. "hearth," term used for the governments in North Africa]; it is not reasonable for us to continue alone like this." Having immediately ruled out the possibility of being independent pirates—even fictional sea raiders desired the legitimacy and access to port infrastructure and markets that association with a sovereign entity provided—they run through the options:

> If we go to Istanbul and fall into the clutches of the Ottomans: it is known that they would take our galleon and our goods from us, and afterward they would take us captive as well, and so long as we lived we would never be free. And if we were to go to Algiers: that *ocak* is truly zealous, but because it is a greedy *ocak*, in all likelihood they would confiscate our ship for the *ocak*, since right now there is not in Algiers a ship as sleek or as swift as our ship. . . . And if we went to Tripoli: that is a destitute *ocak* and also not accommodating enough. But the *ocak* of Tunis is a rich *ocak* compared to the others and, aside from that, we ran up a flag of Tunis at the beginning [of the mutiny] because it happened to be at hand—God-willing this flag is a good sign. This flag originally belonged to the previously captured ship of a Tunisian vice-admiral. What do you say?[18]

The men agreed, deferring to the wisdom of their French Christian captain, and just like that the galleon went from being a French corsair to a Tunisian corsair. Switching allegiances was as simple as swapping flags. Despite the fact that most of this newly constituted corsair crew were Ottoman Muslims, the Ottoman capital, portrayed as fundamentally hostile to piratical entrepreneurs, is the first option to be dismissed, and the men are equally suspicious of the Ottoman governor of Cyprus, whose invitation to come ashore following the mutiny they reject.

Having abandoned the Catholic side of the corsairing industry and spurned the Ottomans, the remaining options for this mixed crew of maritime mercenaries are restricted to North Africa. Religious or political convictions play little obvious role in their decision. Nevertheless, later in the story, the French jailor-captain—a man who had formerly made his living selling Muslims into slavery—swaps faiths as he had flags. In the heat of a battle with a Maltese galleon near Damietta, he spontaneously converts to Islam, declaring to the men, "Brothers! My name is Mahmud!"[19] In so doing, he comes to resemble the archetypical North African corsair, an opportunistic European renegade commanding an ethnically, religiously, and linguistically diverse crew and taking advantage of a permissive regime to pursue profit under the protection of its flag. At the end of the tale, Mahmud and his crew switch allegiances again when they learn that the new *dey* of Tunis is plotting against them, and they sail with their wealth to Algiers and make it their new homeland (*vatan*) and base.[20] The Ottomans, once rejected, never reenter the picture. So it was for many Ottoman and European adventurers who made their livings under North African banners in the seventeenth and eighteenth centuries.

But these men would have taken umbrage at being labeled pirates: theirs was an honorable profession. The true pirates were the amphibious bandits of the coasts, the Scyllas and Charybdises of the narrow straits, for whom neither religious identity nor subjecthood factored into the decision to attack. Their numbers, their names, their stories, and their motives remain stubbornly difficult to retrieve, but Ottoman sources leave little doubt as to their presence and impact, as well as their connections with the wider piratical ecosystem. Turning to the Ottoman Mediterranean and exploring it with Ottoman sources reminds us that piratical practice existed on a multiplanar spectrum of professionalization, legality, and scale.

Individuals might occupy multiple places on that spectrum over the course of their careers, swinging from local to long-distance raiding, from illegal pillage to licensed plundering. While we can isolate different practitioners, the Muslim and Catholic corsairs from the English merchant-pirates, the Albanian *levend*s from the Greek sea bandits, the fact of the matter was that the Ottomans (and the Venetians) had to deal with them all simultaneously. They needed a relatively uniform set of political, diplomatic, and legal policies to resolve the problems sea raiders, licensed or not, created. These were given expression in the *ahdname*s and in the opinions of the *şeyhülislam*s. Ottoman Islamic and sultanic law remained formally separate—the *şeriat* as holy law was immiscible with the laws of men—but the Ottoman triad of *kadi*, *şeyhülislam*, and sultan formed them into a durable emulsion that covered the whole Ottoman Mediterranean.

The challenges inherent in enforcing Ottoman policies were great indeed in a Mediterranean world in which the enslaveable enemy and the protected subject often worshipped the same way and spoke the same language and neither carried identity cards; in which the identities and allegiances of pirates themselves were fluid; and in which prizes taken at sea might change hands multiple times before entering port. The results of the Ottomans' efforts defy simple divisions of the early modern Mediterranean into opposing Muslim and Christian spheres just as they call into question attempts to characterize it as essentially unified. Ottoman Mediterranean space was bounded by a semi-permeable legal membrane through which only some laws and traditions might enter, despite the fact that ships, goods, and people could often pass freely.

The history of piracy and law, both in the Mediterranean and beyond, has typically been told from the viewpoint of Europeans and on the basis of European sources. This book has endeavored to introduce the Ottoman perspective to the political, military, economic, and legal developments that transformed the Mediterranean and the globe in the sixteenth and seventeenth centuries, of which piracy was but one consequence. It has provided the context necessary to understand why piracy flared beginning in the late sixteenth century, why legal and diplomatic responses took precedence for the Ottomans, and how local and long-distance manifestations of maritime violence coexisted and reinforced one another. Putting the Ottomans back into the picture does more than fill a lacuna in our understanding of the nature and impact of piracy in the early modern Mediterranean; it forms an integral part of the broader history of piracy, law, and empire in a globalizing age.

Notes

PREFACE

1. Laurent Valdiguié, "Kadhafi: 'J'en appelle à la France,'" *Le Journal du Dimanche*, March 6, 2011, www.lejdd.fr/International/Afrique/Actualite/Exclusif-L-interview-integrale-accordee-par-Mouammar-Kadhafi-au-JDD-278745/.

2. Hastings, "Understanding Maritime Piracy."

3. See, for example, Tinniswood, *Pirates of Barbary*; Matar, *Britain and Barbary*; Bono, *Lumi e corsari*; Bono, *I corsari barbareschi*; Fisher, *Barbary Legend*; Lane-Poole, *Barbary Corsairs*; Tenenti, *Piracy and the Decline of Venice*; Fontenay, *La Méditerranée entre la croix et le croissant*; Earle, *Corsairs of Malta and Barbary*.

4. For example, Weiss, *Captives and Corsairs*; Friedman, *Spanish Captives*; for Ottoman Greek victims of the Maltese, see Greene, *Catholic Pirates and Greek Merchants*.

INTRODUCTION

1. Galata 36, 163v (8/Ş/1023).

2. Grotius, *De Jure Pradae*, 325–326.

3. Galata 36, 163v (8/Ş/1023).

4. Greene, *Shared World*, 11.

5. Largueche, "Origins of Beylical Sovereignty," 111; in Tunis, the pre-Ottoman practice of having four muftis representing the four schools of Sunni Islamic jurisprudence persisted through the Ottoman period, with the muftis and judge attending the meetings of the ruling council. See Abun-Nasr, "Beylicate," 72.

6. Hess, *Forgotten Frontier*; on the origins of the Barbarossa brothers, see Vatin, "Comment êtes-vous apparus, toi et ton frère?"

7. Soucek, "Rise of the Barbarossas"; Gürkan, "Centre and the Frontier."

8. Gürkan, "Centre and the Frontier"; for Barbarossa's memoirs, see Düzdağ, *Hayreddin Paşa'nın Hatıraları*; on the Nice expedition, see Isom-Verhaaren, "Ottoman and French Views."

9. Vatin, *L'ordre de Saint-Jean-de-Jérusalem*; Mallia-Milanes, *Hospitaller Malta*; Earle, *Corsairs*; Cavaliero, *Last of the Crusaders*.

10. This in the estimation of Norwich, *History of Venice*, 487. Guilmartin, *Gunpowder and Galleys.*

11. Guilmartin, *Gunpowder and Galleys.*

12. See, for example, Hopkins, *Confrontation at Lepanto.*

13. Guilmartin, *Gunpowder and Galleys*; on oarsmen, see also Williams, *Empire and Holy War.*

14. This is the scenario proposed by Hess, *Forgotten Frontier*; cf. Williams, *Empire and Holy War.*

15. Braudel, *Mediterranean*, 1:615–642. The "Northern Invasion" paradigm has since undergone some recalibration, first in a critique by Greene, "Beyond the Northern Invasion"; and most recently in a response by Heywood, "The English in the Mediterranean"; Tenenti, *Piracy and the Decline of Venice*, 56–86.

16. See Tenenti, *Piracy and the Decline of Venice*; Braudel, *Mediterranean*; Bono, *Corsari nel Mediterraneo.*

17. De Groot, "Ottoman North Africa and the Dutch Republic." On the 1627 Iceland raid, see Lewis, "Corsairs in Iceland"; on the 1631 sack of an Irish village in Cork, see Barnby, "Algerian Attack on Baltimore."

18. See Chapter 2, this volume.

19. Hastings, "Understanding Maritime Piracy Syndicate Operations"; López Nadal, "Corsairing as a Commercial System"; Prange, "A Trade of No Dishonor"; Prange, "Outlaw Economics."

20. Rapp, "Unmaking of the Mediterranean Trade Hegemony"; Wood, *Levant Company*; Agoston, "Merces Prohibitae"; Bulut, "Role of the Ottomans and Dutch"; Masson, *Histoire du commerce français*; Masters, *Origins of Western Economic Dominance*; Goffman, *Izmir and the Levantine World.*

21. Hanna, *Making Big Money in 1600*; Faroqhi, "Coffee and Spices"; Ginio, "When Coffee Brought about Wealth"; Greene, "Beyond the Northern Invasion."

22. Brummett, "The Ottomans as a World Power."

23. Fodor, "Between Two Continental Wars"; on failed efforts to reorient the Ottomans toward the Mediterranean in the 1580s, see Gürkan, "Fooling the Sultan."

24. Inalcik, "Military and Fiscal Transformation"; Barkan and McCarthy, "Price Revolution"; Pamuk, *Monetary History*; Darling, *Revenue-Raising and Legitimacy*; Murphey, *Ottoman Warfare.*

25. White, *Climate of Rebellion.*

26. Adanır, "Heiduckentum und osmanische Herrschaft"; there has been a tendency to read nationalist motivations into bandit activity in the Balkans, for example, Cvetkova, "Bulgarian Haiduk Movement"; Vasdravellis, *Klephts, Armatoles, and Pirates.*

27. See Chapter 4, this volume; on the Cossacks, see Ostapchuk, "Human Landscape of the Ottoman Black Sea."

28. Finkel, *Osman's Dream*, 197.

29. See Tezcan, *Second Ottoman Empire.*

30. Finkel, *Osman's Dream*, 197–228.

31. Venetian ambassadors to the English court reported on James I's hatred of English pirates and the spate of executions he had ordered, *CSP*, 11:480 (February 25, 1610).

32. *CSP*, 10:211 (January 20, 1605). On the *bailo*, see Dursteler, "Bailo."

33. *CSP*, 18:397 (July 20, 1624).

34. Nadal, "Corsairing as a Commercial System," 125–136; Fodor, "Piracy, Ransom Slavery and Trade," 120–121.

35. *CSP*, 20:221 (May 15, 1627).

36. *CSP*, 12:309 (March 10, 1612). On renegades, see Bennassar, *Chrétiens d'Allah*; Graf, "Half-Lives."

37. This is one of the primary arguments in Guilmartin, *Gunpowder and Galleys*; Mahan, *Influence of Sea Power*.

38. On Ottoman naval organization in the sixteenth century, see Imber, "Navy of Süleyman"; for institutions and structures, see Uzunçarşılı, *Merkez ve Bahriye Teşkilâti*; for the navy and shipbuilding in the seventeenth century, see Bostan, *Osmanlı bahriye teskilâtı.*

39. Kâtib Çelebi, *Gift*, 144, 149.

40. Murphey, "Ottoman Resurgence," 189–190.

41. On French galleys and their manpower needs, see Weiss, "Infidels at the Oar."

42. Imber, *Ebu Su'ud*; Gerber, "Kanun, Sharia and Custom"; Inalcık, "Imtiyazat."

43. Azuni, *Maritime Law of Europe*, 414.

44. Kermeli, "Right to Choice"; van den Boogert, "Consular Jurisdiction."

45. On "legal pluralism" and overlapping legal cultures, see Benton, *Law and Colonial Cultures*, 8.

46. See Chapters 5 and 6, this volume; the former point is documented in Greene, *Catholic Pirates and Greek Merchants*.

CHAPTER 1

1. Mustafa Ali, *Mevā'idü'n-Nefāis*, 288–290; Mustafa Ali, *Ottoman Gentleman*, 33–37. I have adapted the translations below from Brookes.

2. Noted previously by Laiou, "Levends of the Sea."

3. Mustafa Ali, *Mevā'idü'n-Nefāis*, 288; Brookes, *Ottoman Gentleman*, 33–34.

4. Ibid.; ibid., 34.

5. Ibid.

6. For examples, see Bostan, *Adriyatik'te Korsanlık*.

7. Mustafa Ali, *Mevā'idü'n-Nefāis*, 288; Brookes, *Ottoman Gentleman*, 35.

8. Fleischer, *Bureaucrat and Intellectual*. On piracy during the reign of Süleyman, see Vatin, "L'Empire ottoman."

9. For Kemal Reis, see Hess, "Evolution of the Ottoman Seaborne Empire"; Brummet, *Ottoman Seapower*, 94–108. For the latter period, see Gürkan, "Centre and the Frontier," 128–139. Turgud Reis was never *kapudan pasha*, but he was the most powerful and respected naval commander from Barbarossa's retirement until his death at the siege of Malta.

10. Gürkan, "Centre and the Frontier," 139–140.

11. Kâtib Çelebi, *Gift*, 148. It is worth noting that seventeenth- and eighteenth-century European navies often recruited from the Knights of Malta—successful corsairing enterprises were the ideal farm teams for professional naval commanders.

12. Mustafa Ali, *Mevā'idü'n-Nefāis*, 289; Brookes, *Ottoman Gentleman*, 35—"If he says he doesn't know about it, then he is not a corsair (*korsan*), and the one who is not a corsair is not an admiral worthy of that high post."

13. The issue of fleet captains and errant naval irregulars engaging in piracy was confronted in Ottoman-Venetian treaty law from 1482, on which see Chapter 3 of this volume.

14. Mustafa Ali, *Mevā'idü'n-Nefāis*, 290; Brookes, *Ottoman Gentleman*, 37.

15. Ibid.; ibid., 36.

16. Shuval, "Cezayir-i Garp," 93–96.

17. Mustafa Ali, *Mevā'idü'n-Nefāis*, Brookes, *Ottoman Gentleman*, 35.

18. See Chapter 5 of this volume and Imber, *Ebu's-su'ud*, 65–88.

19. In a late seventeenth-century Ottoman pirate novella, a Maltese galleon recruits "levend kefere," i.e., Greek "infidel pirates," from the Aegean islands to replenish its crew; see İz, "Makale-i Zindancı Mahmud Kapudan," 139. In Algiers, according to Sosa, all "soldiers of the sea—whether renegades, janissaries who go privateering . . . or Turks . . . are commonly called *levends*" (Sosa, *Topography*, 154).

20. Laiou, "Levends of the Sea"; Cezar, *Osmanlı Tarihinde Levendler*; Vatin, "Une affaire interne," 155.

21. Pellat, Imber, and Kelly, "Ḳurṣān," 5:502; Bostan, *Adriyatik'te Korsanlık*, 17–19.

22. Idris Bostan has argued that the Ottoman Turkish for true, unaffiliated, indiscriminate piracy is *deniz haydutluğu*, "sea banditry" (*Adriyatik'te Korsanlık*, 17–19), but this term appears infrequently in the sources and seemingly only when the identity of the culprits was utterly unknown—e.g., BOA MD 58: 540/228 (28/R/994). *Harami levend* and its derivatives, as well as *firkateci*, were more common terms for Ottoman-subject pirates. The word *şaki* (plural, *eşkiya*) can be translated as "bandit" or "brigand," but it also carries the meaning of "rebel" or "outlaw." Both meanings applied when describing those who attacked the sultan's subjects or those with whom he wished peace.

23. See Chapter 3 of this volume.

24. See Chapter 6 of this volume.

25. Thomas Dallam, master organ builder, had been commissioned to construct a combination clock and mechanical organ with numerous complications to serve as Queen Elizabeth's (by then quite late) accession gift to the sultan. Dallam was required to accompany the gift to Istanbul to reassemble it. His account of the voyage was reproduced in "Dallam's Travels." Dallam seems to have taken a dim view of the unnamed English captain's piratical activities.

26. BOA MD 14: 1261/ 863 (18/N/978).

27. For example, BOA MD 67: 244/92, 245/93. On the sea season, see Imber, "Navy of Süleyman," 216; on the squadron bases and their organization, see ibid., 252–260.

28. Ibid., 247.

29. Tenenti, *Piracy and the Decline of Venice,* 17–21; Bostan, *Adriyatik'te Korsanlık*, 36.

30. BOA MD 14: 361/255 (14/RA/978); MD 16: 633/ 358 (9/RA/979).

31. BOA MD 15: 693/ 81 (17/RA/979).

32. As in BOA MD 40: 61/30 (25/Z/986), and below.

33. BOA MD 16: 633/358 (9/RA/979).

34. Gürkan, "Centre and the Frontier," 146n38.

35. BOA MD 14: 544/388; Soucek, "Naval Aspects," 238–249.

36. Fisher, "Sale of Slaves."

37. BOA MD 14: 799/565.

38. Guilmartin, *Gunpowder and Galleys*, 262–264.

39. BOA MD 9: 392/ 254 (18/B/979).

40. Laiou, "Levends of the Sea," 241.

41. BOA MD 16: 360/188.

42. BOA MD 16: 558/315.

43. Kiel, "Smaller Aegean Islands"; Kermeli, "Central Administration"; Slot, *Archipelagus Turbatus*, 98–109.

44. Slot, *Archipelagus Turbatus*, 73–86; Vatin, "L'Empire ottoman et la piraterie en 1559–1560."

45. The "Ottoman"-ness of the Aegean islands is a central concern in Vatin, "Iles grecques? Iles ottomans?"; see also Heywood, "Ottoman Territoriality."

46. BOA MD 16: 214/109.

47. BOA MD 16: 305/156, 655/373 (Lemnos); MD 19: 5/2 (Naxos).

48. BOA MD 16: 305/156; MD 19: 5/2.

49. BOA MD 19: 196/90.

50. On Ottoman subjecthood, see White, "Slave Laundering."

51. BOA MD 19: 211/99.

52. BOA MD 21: 434/179.

53. BOA MD 21: 624/261.

54. BOA MD 23: 367/174.

55. BOA MD 52: 285/115.

56. BOA MD 24: 744/277 (3/S/982); MD 26: 132/51 (5/RA/982), 133/52 (8/RA/982), 697/243 (13/C982), 713/248 (13/C/982); BOA MZD 2: 52/21 (28/Ş/982).

57. BOA MD 24: 744/277 (3/S/982).

58. BOA MD 26: 697/243 (13/C982), 713/248 (13/C/982).

59. Ibid.

60. BOA MD 26: 135/53 (8/RA/982).

61. Copies of the decree were sent to the *beylerbeyi*s of these three provinces, suggesting that the center believed that some of the captives may have ended up

in those ports and/or that the pirate quartet was splitting its time between North Africa and the Albanian coast.

62. BOA MD 36: 722/274 (21/RA/987).

63. The estimate was Grand Vizier Koca Sinan Pasha's; see Fodor, "Between Two Continental Wars," 175.

64. BOA MZD 5: 30/14 (Evail/S,/999).

65. BOA MD 21: 763/324 (981).

66. BOA MD 21: 315/ 130 (20/L/980); Kara Hoca was involved in the efforts to arrange an exchange of his Venetian captive, the "Körfus Baylosu," for the release of several Ottomans including his brother, Kadri Reis.

67. Kolovos, *Οθωμανικές πηγές για τη νεώτερη ιστορία της Λευκάδας*.

68. Evliya Çelebi, *Seyahatnâmesi*, 8:282 (343v). On lingua franca, see Dakhlia, *Lingua franca*; Kahane and Tietze, *Lingua Franca in the Levant*; Panzac, "Lingua franca."

69. Evliya Çelebi, *Seyahatnâmesi*, 8:282 (343v).

70. Ibid.

71. Kolovos, "Ottoman Frontiers and their Historiography."

72. Evliya Çelebi, *Seyahatnâmesi*, 8:282 (343v).

73. Contreras, *Adventures*, passim; Evliya Çelebi, *Seyahatnâmesi*, 8:282 (343v).

74. ASVe BAC, Carte turche 252/10, 28r (undated); BAC, Carte turche 252/10, 35r (Evahir/M/1084).

75. The 1675 expedition is mentioned in Wheler, *Journey into Greece*, 37; on continuing attacks, see ASVe BAC, Carte turche 252/12 (Evail/R/1093).

76. BOA MD 22: 30/12 (21/M/981).

77. BOA MD 22: 332/172 (26/RA/981).

78. BOA MD 4: 750/74 (24/Ş/967).

79. For example, BOA MD 26: 180/68 (17/RA/982); MD 31: 184/75 (12/CA/985); MD 34: 550/261 (986); MD 35 520/206 (986); MD 470/252 (12/Ş/988).

80. BOA MZD 4: 403/186 (20/ZA/999).

81. Ottoman intragovernmental correspondence does not survive, so we have little direct evidence for how governors worked with one another independently of the center, but there is no question that they did so.

82. Kolovos, "Ottoman Frontiers and Their Historiography."

83. BOA MD 82: 114/57 (9/L/1026); White, "Slave Laundering."

84. ASVe BAC, Carte turche 250/1, 13r (Evasit/C/998).

85. Bostan, *Adriyatik'te Korsanlık*, 36; for a brief overview of the history of Albania's coastal towns between Venetian and Ottoman rule in the fifteenth and sixteenth centuries, see Malcolm, *Agents of Empire*, 1–22.

86. Bracewell, *Uskoks of Senj*, 108–109.

87. Fodor, "Maltese Pirates, Ottoman Captives," 223.

88. Suraiya Faroqhi, "Venetian Presence," 362; Tenenti, *Piracy and the Decline of Venice*, 19–21, 24, 56–57, 81–82; Bostan, *Adriyatik'te Korsanlık*, 36.

89. BOA ED 13, 493–5/99 (1021).

90. Evliya Çelebi, *Seyahatnâmesi*, 8:314 (362v).
91. BOA MD 53: 41/18 (7/CA/992).
92. BOA MD 29: 476/202 (Selh/ZA/984).
93. For example, BOA MD 26: 180/68 (17/RA/982); MD 46: 602/267 (2/Z/989); MD 53: 41/18 (7/CA/992); BOA *Ecnebi Defteri* (ED) 13: 101–2/27 (6/C/1014); ED 13: 493–4/ 99 (8/M/1022); see also Bostan, *Adriyatik'te Korsanlık*, 36–42; Faroqhi, "Venetian Presence," 346–348, 361–363.
94. For example, BOA MD 24: 596/ 224 (20/M/982); MD 26: 135/53 (8/RA/982); MD 26: 180/ 68 (17/RA/982).
95. BOA MD 82: 137/68 (26/L/1026).
96. *Celali* is the umbrella term used to describe the participants in a series of desultory revolts and widespread brigandage in Anatolia that began in the 1590s and continued through the first quarter of the seventeenth century; although the Balkans experienced similar disorders, the brigandage there is not usually called *celali*. See Adanır, "Heiduckentum und osmanische Herrschaft"; cf. Barkey, *Bandits and Bureaucrats*.
97. BOA MD 76: 371/143 (3/CA/1013).
98. BOA MD 76: 371/143 (3/CA/1013).
99. Panzac, *Barbary Corsairs*, 21–22; Bostan, *Adriyatik'te Korsanlık*,18–9; Faroqhi, "Venetian Presence," 383; cf. Gürkan, "Batı Akdeniz'de Osmanlı Korsanlığı ve Gaza Meselesi."
100. BOA MD 82: 233/113 (7/C/1027).
101. BOA MD 85: 115/ (11/C/1040).
102. BOA MD 85: 115/ (11/C/1040)—*asla eman u zaman virmeyüb*.

CHAPTER 2

1. Macuncuzade, *Malta Esirleri*, 21–22; İz, "Macuncuzade," for the untransliterated Ottoman Turkish text. Godfrey Wettinger located Mustafa Efendi's safe-conduct in the Maltese archives, in which he is said to be about forty-six; see Wettinger, *Slavery*, 87n6.
2. Macuncuzade, *Malta Esirleri*, 21–22.
3. Fontenay, "L'Empire ottoman et le risque corsaire," 194.
4. Macuncuzade, *Malta Esirleri*, 23.
5. Uzunçarşılı, *Ilmiye Teşkilâti*, 87–99.
6. Quoted in Soucek, "Navals Aspects," 233.
7. This failure leads Soucek to doubt the primacy of the piracy justification for conquest (ibid., 235–237, 247–249).
8. *Târih-i Na'îmâ*, 2:388.
9. Roberts, "Adventures," 8–9.
10. Chardin, *Travels*, 3. In addition to Malta and Livorno, some of the corsairs were based out of Mallorca and Villefranche (Savoy).
11. Roberts, "Adventures," 10.
12. Thévenot, *Travels*, 228; Roberts, "Adventures," 9.
13. Dankoff, *Ottoman Mentality*, 141.
14. For example, Contreras, *Adventures*, 37–42, 51–53.

15. Roberts, "Adventures," 11.
16. Bono, *Schiavi musulmani*; Fontenay, "L'esclave galérien"; Weiss, "Infidels at the Oar."
17. Brogini, "L'esclavage," 137–8.
18. Fontenay, "Mercato," 397.
19. Angiolini, "Slaves," 74; on the order, see Guarnieri, *I cavalieri.*
20. Calafat and Santus, "Les avatars du 'Turc.'"
21. Fontenay, "L'Empire ottoman et le risque corsaire," 194–196.
22. Fischer, "Bagno"; Nadalo, "Negotiating Slavery"; Brogini, "Une activité sous contrôle."
23. Especially in comparison to the voluminous scholarship on the redemption of European Christians in the western Mediterranean; for an overview, see Kaiser and Calafat, "Economy of Ransoming"; see also Kaiser, *Commerce des captifs.*
24. Fontenay, "L'Empire ottoman et le risque corsaire," 204.
25. *Târih-i Na'îmâ*, 3:1011–1012.
26. D'Arvieux, *Memoires*, 5:20.
27. *Târih-i Na'îmâ*, 2:388, 3:972; informally organized convoys were also common. In late 1656, for example, Jean Thévenot joined a convoy of thirty saïques with a galleon consort that formed at Chios for the journey to Alexandria; see *Travels*, 114–119.
28. *Bu sularda yalnız kalyon gezmez meğerki korsan ola*—so remarks the title character of a seventeenth-century pirate novella upon sighting a solitary sail north of Damietta; see İz, "Zindancı Mahmud," 138.
29. Roberts, "Adventures," 3.
30. RSM 60, 4r (29/B/1045). On *mudaraba* generally, see Udovitch, *Partnership and Profit*, 170–248; on the Ottoman *mudaraba*, see Çizakça, *Comparative Evolution*, 66–76.
31. TAH 3, 174 (2/M/1083).
32. RSM 36, 20r (Evahir/S/1027). Entries like this are especially common. For another example, see Galata 40, 21r (Evail/M/1025).
33. RSM 68, 12v (8/B/1054).
34. Slot, *Archipelagus Turbatus*, 168; Roberts, "Adventures," 25.
35. Slot, *Archipelagus Turbatus*, 170.
36. Randolph, *Present State*, 14; Slot, *Archipelagus Turbatus*, 170.
37. Tournefort, *Voyage*, 1:267.
38. BOA MD 84: 18/10 (17/N/1038).
39. Cohen, "Ottoman Rule and the Re-Emergence of the Coast of Palestine," 163–175, esp. 163–167; on piracy off Jaffa, see Ze'evi, *Ottoman Century*, 101, 163–164.
40. Thévenot, *Travels*, 227; on using captives as sources of intelligence and guides, see Contreras, *Adventures*, 58–59, İz, "Zindancı Mahmud."
41. Thévenot, *Travels*, 229.
42. Zecevic, "Missing Husbands."
43. For Salonica, see Ginio, "Piracy and Redemption"; for Izmir, see Fodor, "Piracy, Ransom Slavery and Trade."
44. For example, TAH 4, 256 (Evahir/S/1084).

45. RSM 117, 18r (Evahir/B/1078).

46. Eyüb 37, 64r (20/L/1047); *İstanbul kadı sicilleri*, 40:317. For another example, in which a man tried to recover a debt after fourteen years of captivity, see Istanbul Bab 46, 84r (14/Ş/1097); *İstanbul kadı sicilleri*, 19:438.

47. BOA MD 89, 12 (26/M/1052).

48. Neumann, "Hızır, der Kadi und der Kryptomuslim von Malta," 210.

49. On which, see Petersen, *Medieval and Ottoman Hajj Route*.

50. Randolph, *Present State*, 54; Tournefort, *Voyage*, 2:2.

51. Macuncuzade, *Malta Esirleri*, 32.

52. Ibid.

53. Ibid., 21.

54. BOA MD 61: 223/92 (29/ZA/994), 312/129–30 (20/S/995).

55. There are at least half a dozen references to *Esiri*s or *Esirizade*s in the *Sicill-i Osmani*; for literary artifacts of other *Esiri*s, not mentioned there, see Kut, "Esîrî, His 'Sergüẕeşt' and His Other Works." Note that this *Sergüẕeşt* is not that of Macuncuzade Mustafa Efendi. On Esiri Mehmed Efendi, see *Sicill-i Osmani*, 3:995.

56. There are references to similar, earlier works, now lost; see Meredith-Owens, "Traces."

57. Nabil Matar makes a similar observation regarding early modern Arabic authors, for whom the self-narration of captivity was no more popular, in "Piracy and Captivity in the Early Modern Mediterranean."

58. On such collections, see Riedlmayer, "Ottoman Copybooks"; Quinn, "Making Sense of Miscellanies."

59. Hindi Mahmud, the author of a lost work on his captivity in Rome in the 1570s, described his eight-thousand-verse book (titled *Hediye*, "The Gift") as written for his friends "by way of advice"; see Meredith-Owens, "Traces," 462.

60. See Vitkus and Matar, *Piracy, Slavery, and Redemption*; Matar, "English Accounts."

61. Macuncuzade, *Malta Esirleri*, 22.

62. Bono, "Achat d'esclaves"; Weiss, "Infidels at the Oar."

63. Wettinger, *Slavery*, 65–66.

64. Ibid., 494.

65. For one example, see the case of Fatima bint Ali, ransomed from Malta for 400 *guruş* by a *zimmi* from Paros in 1663 and settled in two different courts: Istanbul 12, 47r (29/ZA/1073) and Galata 90, 77r (11/M/1074).

66. Macuncuzade, *Malta Esirleri*, 82.

67. Ibid., 29, 57.

68. Ibid., 48.

69. Ibid., 24.

70. Ibid., 27. Within a few years of Mustafa's illness, a separate prison hospital would be built to treat sick captives and the Hospital of Saint John would be reserved for Christians; see Wettinger, *Slavery*, 508–509.

71. Macuncuzade, *Malta Esirleri*, 29.

72. Dankoff, *Ottoman Mentality*, 139–140.

73. Wettinger, *Slavery*, 59–61.

74. Nadalo, "Negotiating Slavery," 302; Calafat and Santus, "Les avatars du 'Turc,'" 492–493.

75. Wettinger, *Slavery*, 59.

76. Captives were paroled along the Ottoman-Habsburg land frontier, as well; see Palffy, "Ransom Slavery" and the other contributions in Dávid and Fodor, *Ransom Slavery*. For examples from Malta, Wettinger, *Slavery*, 205–8.

77. Galata 36, 93v (16/R/1023).

78. Macuncuzade, *Malta Esirleri*, 30–33.

79. Ibid., 34–41.

80. Naima recounts an episode from the siege of Candia in 1650 in which the Venetians proposed to swap the captives each side held and fix a price for all those subsequently caught: 100 *guruş* for Ottoman captives and 200 for Venetians; funds for this purpose had been established in Venice and in Malta. The Ottomans refused, declaring that they would not pay for their captured comrades—the captives' and martyrs' recompense would come from God; see *Târih-i Na'îmâ*, 3:1269.

81. BnF Supplement Turc 119, 11r; Calafat and Santus, "Les avatars du 'Turc,'" 472.

82. BOA MD 58: 60/20 (R/993), 78/26 (19/R/993), 79/26 (19/R/993).

83. Ginio, "Piracy and Redemption"; Fodor, "Piracy, Ransom Slavery, and Trade."

84. Dankoff, *Ottoman Mentality*, 142.

85. BOA MD 67: 73/30 (12/M/999); MD 69: 280/140 (3/CA/1000), 292/146 (3/CA/1000), 297/149 (3/CA/1000), 373/186 (20/R/1000).

86. On the western Mediterranean, see Kaiser, *Commerce des captifs*; on Jewish ransoming activities and captivity, see Orfali, "Ragusa and Ragusan Jews"; Bashan, *Shivyah u-fedut*.

87. Galata 36, 93v (16/R/1023).

88. Galata 36, 163r (27/Ş/1023). The later entry notes that Gaspar's value as a slave, converted from *akçe* to gold florins, was 30 *filori* versus his ransom value of 300 *filori*. On these concepts, see Fontenay, "Esclaves et/ou captifs." Note, however, that Fontenay, as well as Kaiser and Calafat in "Economy of Ransoming," insist on boundaries between "captive" and "slave" statuses which are perhaps too firm, in both practical and legal terms, for the early modern Ottoman Mediterranean. The semantic distinctions between the two in Ottoman Turkish usage are not so clear cut, and men like Gaspar could easily inhabit both statuses, being employed as slaves in every sense of the word until such time as they might be ransomed or exchanged.

89. Galata 36, 93v (16/R/1023).

90. Galata 36, 163r (27/Ş/1023).

91. Galata 90, 23v (2/L/1073); *İstanbul kadı sicilleri*, 40:169.

92. Macuncuzade, *Malta Esirleri*, 44–45. On royal women and architectural patronage, see Peirce, *Imperial Harem*; Singer, *Constructing Ottoman Beneficence*.

93. Macuncuzade, *Malta Esirleri*, 57.

94. Ibid., 60.

95. Ibid., 58.
96. Ibid., 66–69.
97. Ibid., 70–77.
98. Ibid., 92; İz, "Macuncuzade," 116.
99. Wettinger, *Slavery*, 87n6.
100. Macuncuzade, *Malta Esirleri*, 96.
101. Ibid., 98.
102. Galata 160, 26r (19/RA/1105)—*eğer mezbur Mehmed Kapudan'ın Malta kadisi tahlis olunduğunu hüccet edüb.*
103. Macuncuzade, *Malta Esirleri*, 93.
104. Cf. Kaiser and Calafat, "Economy of Ransoming," in which they argue for the reciprocal acceptance of documents produced by Islamic and Christian courts in the Mediterranean. This may well have been the case in the western Mediterranean between southern Europe and North Africa, but whereas Ottoman documents appear to have had some limited evidentiary value in courts outside the Ottoman Mediterranean, the reverse was not true. The consequences of this fact for litigants are discussed in greater detail in Chapter 6 of this volume.
105. BnF, MS Turc 37. The manuscript serves as the primary source for Fodor, "Piracy, Ransom Slavery and Trade," cited therein according to its former classification, "BnF manuscrit orientaux, fonds turc 1234."
106. BnF, MS Turc 37, 11.
107. BnF, MS Turc 37, 8 (first instance).
108. BnF, MS Turc 37, 1 (first instance).
109. For example, BnF, MS Turc 37, 20; self-referential use by *kadi*s of "this poor one" (*fakir*) was standard in *hüccet*s produced throughout the empire, but the rest of the quoted formulation was not.
110. There was overlapping production in Depuy's volume. The six *hüccet*s produced by Halil bin Zülfikar stretch over the longest period—late November 1624 through mid-June 1627—during which time a *kadi* named Hamza produced fifteen between early June 1625 and late August 1626. The numbers reflect only those ransoms in which Jean Depuy played a role, but these *kadi*s probably worked with other brokers and many more captives.
111. Galata 110, 92v (17/ZA/1082).
112. Garasko appears again in Galata 110, 109r (20/M/1083). For a ransom agent from Mytilene, contracted to free a *kadi* from the Anatolian *sancak* of Hamid, see RSM 68, 35v (4/Ş/1054).
113. Galata 90, 42v (3/ZA/1073); *İstanbul kadı sicilleri*, 40:256.
114. Wettinger, *Slavery*, 194–196.
115. Kaiser and Calafat have made a similar observation for the ransoming of Christians in the central/western Mediterranean, between southern Europe and the Maghreb, in "Economy of Ransoming," 125–130.
116. Galata 90, 42v (3/ZA/1073); *İstanbul kadı sicilleri*, 40:255.
117. Galata 36, 109v (10/CA/1023); the ambassador is described as *França elçisi olan fahir-i emasıl Akila veled Thrlis.* On Harlay-Sancy's embassy, see Tongas, *Relations*, 9–13.

118. Galata 36, 129r (Evahir/C/1023); the ambassador is described as *Ingiliz balyozu olan Pavlu veled Bender*.

119. Randolph, *Present State*, 3; Covel, *Early Voyages*, 137.

120. Ginio, "Piracy and Redemption," 145.

121. Galata 41, 25v (8/M/1026).

122. On fees at Malta, see Wettinger, *Slavery*, 183–189; on the broker's percentage, see Fodor, "Piracy, Ransom Slavery, and Trade," 127ff.

123. Wettinger, *Slavery*, 237–238.

124. Galata 110, 37v–38r (Selh/C/1082).

125. See Chapter 5, this volume.

126. Tournefort, *Voyage*, 1:298.

127. Little is known about this post or its occupants, see Veinstein, "Documents emis par le kapudan"; Ursinus, "Local Patmians." On the *kapudan pasha*'s role as justice-provider and criminal-punisher on the islands, see Kermeli, "Right to Choice," 187.

128. Slot, *Archipelagus Turbatus*, 193–194.

129. Ibid., 237–238; Cavaliero, "Decline of the Maltese Corso."

130. Tournefort, *Voyage*, 1:154.

131. On which see Kermeli, "Right to Choice," 185–187.

132. Contreras, *Adventures*, 41–42; Tournefort, *Voyage*, 1:187–188.

133. See Chapter 6, this volume; Vatin, "Ces Messieurs de Galata."

134. Tournefort, *Voyage*, 2:137.

135. TAH 2, 247 (Evahir/CA/1126).

136. Tournefort, *Voyage*, 1:187–188.

137. For a brief overview of the relationship between the monasteries and the Ottoman center, see Zachariadou, "Monks and Sailors"; Kermeli, "Central Administration."

138. For Andros, see Kolovos, "Insularity and Island Society"; for Patmos, see Vatin and Veinstein, "Une bonté unique au monde." Elias Kolovos has published the Ottoman documents of the Kaireios Library on Andros, most from the Hagia Monastery, at http://androsdocs.ims.forth.gr/.

139. Kaireios Library, No. 134 (1/B/1060), http://androsdocs.ims.forth.gr/documentsview.php?l=1&id=146.

140. TAH 2, 247 (Evahir/CA/1126).

141. Ghobrial, *Whispers of Cities*, 81.

142. For the Ottoman Turkish text, see Neumann, "Hızır, der Kadi und der Kryptomuslim von Malta," 210–219.

143. al-Zayani, *Al-Tarjumanah al-Kubra*, 192–193, translated in Matar, *Europe through Arab Eyes*, 242; al-Zayani traveled through Ottoman domains on multiple occasions as part of Moroccan embassies to the Ottoman court.

CHAPTER 3

1. ASVe BAC, Carte turche 251/6, 7 (C/1036).

2. ASVe BAC, Carte turche 251/6, 8 (undated, probably C/1036).

3. See Brummett, *Ottoman Seapower*; Hess, *Forgotten Frontier*; Hess, "Evolution of the Ottoman Seaborne Empire."

4. Thomson, *Mercenaries, Pirates, and Sovereigns*; Benton, *Search for Sovereignty*, which refines many of the ideas presented first in "Legal Spaces of Empire"; Kempe, "'Even in the Remotest Corners of the World.'"

5. See Gentili, *De iure belli*. Gentili's ideas about piracy in particular are elaborated in greater detail in *Hispanicae advocationis*, published posthumously in 1612 on the basis of his work in the English admiralty courts between 1605 and 1608. Hugo Grotius' thoughts on piracy were first presented in *De iure praedae commentarius* (Commentary on the Law of Prize), but this work was not published until the nineteenth century. It provided the basis, however, for his *Mare Liberum* (1609) and for the sections concerning piracy in his *De iure belli ac pacis* (1625). As for Cicero's actual words and their context, see Souza, *Piracy*, 149–78; Heller-Roazen, *Enemy of All*, 13–22.

6. Benton, "Legalities of the Sea"; Calafat, "Ottoman North Africa." See also Rubin, *Law of Piracy*, 29–35; Heller-Roazen, *Enemy of All*, 105–112.

7. Malcolm, "Alberico Gentili and the Ottomans."

8. Bülent Arı notes that the *ahdname*s were the primary locus for the exposition of Ottoman maritime law, but while he discusses the parallel development of "Western" maritime law, he does not explicitly link the two in "Akdeniz'de Korsanlık ve Osmanlı Deniz Hukuku."

9. A brief overview of the parallel development of these instruments is de Groot, "Historical Development."

10. There is an expansive literature on the *ahdname*s, written mostly from the angle of diplomatics; see Kołodziejczyk, *Ottoman-Polish Diplomatic Relations*. On the Venetian *ahdname*s, see Theunissen, "Ottoman-Venetian Diplomatics"; Gökbilgin, "Venedik devlet arşivindeki Türkçe belgeleri." For the English and Dutch cases, see Skilliter, *William Harborne*; de Groot, *Ottoman Empire and the Dutch Republic*. A case-study-based analysis of the interpretation and implementation of the *ahdname*s in the eighteenth century is van den Boogert, *Capitulations and the Ottoman Legal System*.

11. Theunissen, "Ottoman-Venetian Diplomatics," 218.

12. For background, see Eldem, "Capitulations and Western Trade"; de Groot, "Historical Development"; on the question of extraterritoriality, see van den Boogert, *Capitulations and the Ottoman Legal System*; cf. Inalcık, "Status of the Greek Orthodox Patriarch." It is crucial not to confuse the later history of these texts with their earlier status.

13. For more on the concept of land and sea borders between the Ottoman Empire and Venice and its evolution, see Pedani, "Beyond the Frontier."

14. Theunissen, "Ottoman-Venetian Diplomatics," 240.

15. de Groot, "Historical Development," 579; see also Panaite, *Ottoman Law of War and Peace*.

16. de Groot, "Historical Development," 579; for an example of how the Ottomans invoked similar language in their relations with the Habsburgs, see BOA MD 31: 373/161 (2/C/985).

17. de Groot, "Historical Development," 582–584.

18. Biegman, *Turco-Ragusan Relationship*.
19. de Groot, "Historical Development," 582.
20. Theunissen, "Ottoman-Venetian Diplomatics," 186, 210.
21. Ashtor, *Levant Trade*; Christ, *Trading Conflicts*; Meloy, "Imperial Strategy."
22. Fuess, "Rotting Ships."
23. Wansbrough, "Venice and Florence," 490.
24. Ibid., 491–492, 517.
25. Ibid., 521–522.
26. On the treaty itself, see Mackay and Wright, "When the Serenissima and the Gran Turco Made Love."
27. For the Ottoman Turkish texts of the Venetian *ahdname*s, I have relied throughout this chapter on the authoritative critical editions in Theunissen, "Ottoman-Venetian Diplomatics"; translations are mine. For the clause releasing the Venetian slaves, see ibid., 374–375. In later treaties, Venetian slaves taken during wartime did not have to be freed, in contrast with those illegally taken before and after the war. On the naval developments of this period, see Hess, "Evolution of the Ottoman Seaborne Empire."
28. Theunissen, "Ottoman-Venetian Diplomatics," 375.
29. Hess, "Evolution of the Ottoman Seaborne Empire"; Brummett, "Foreign Policy."
30. Vatin, *L'Ordre de Saint-Jean-de Jérusalem*; Brummett, "Overrated Adversary."
31. Theunissen, "Ottoman-Venetian Diplomatics," 381–382.
32. Souza, *Piracy*, 108–114.
33. Theunissen, "Ottoman-Venetian Diplomatics," 384.
34. Ibid., 396–398, 403–405.
35. Ibid., 396.
36. Hess, "Ottoman Conquest of Egypt"; Casale, "Ottoman Administration of the Spice Trade"; Brummett, *Ottoman Seapower*.
37. Theunissen, "Ottoman-Venetian Diplomatics," 420–421.
38. Copies of Ottoman documents resulting from Venetian petitions are preserved in both Venetian and Ottoman archival sources, especially the ASVe DT and BAC, "Carte turche" series and the BOA MD and ED fonds.
39. Theunissen, "Ottoman-Venetian Diplomatics," 422.
40. A number of seventeenth-century European travelers mentioned having witnessed such executions, including Ottavio Bon in 1605 (*CSP*, 10:211), Robert Bargrave in 1647 (*Travel Diary*, 70), and Bernard Randolph in 1676 (*Present State*, 2).
41. Theunissen, "Ottoman-Venetian Diplomatics," 423–424.
42. Ibid., 378–379.
43. Ibid., 427–428.
44. The irrevocability of conversion was successfully challenged by the Russians in the late eighteenth century; see Smiley, "Meanings of Conversion."
45. Chapter 1, this volume.
46. Cezar, *Osmanlı Tarihinde Levendler*, passim.

47. The 1521 version read: "They shall come and go whenever they wish by land and sea with galleys and *köke*s (i.e., cogs, single-masted, square-rigged ships with a high freeboard) and other small ships to my well-protected domains . . . and to all the places that are connected with my well-protected domains" (Theunissen, "Ottoman-Venetian Diplomatics," 419–420).

48. Ibid., 454–455.

49. ASVe BAC, Carte turche 251/7, 8–9 (B/1039).

50. Theunissen, "Ottoman-Venetian Diplomatics," 445.

51. The 1573 *ahdname* renewed without relisting the previous provisions. The Ottomans dictated the terms of the agreement to the Venetians, who then had to present them to the Porte as if they were their own (ibid., 210–211).

52. BOA MD 2: 1929/213 (15/R/964).

53. BOA MD 4: 459/43 (6/B/967).

54. BOA MD 4: 750/74 (24/Ş/967).

55. BOA MD 4: 1593/153 (23/S/968).

56. Soucek, "Navals Aspects," 219–261; for Ebu Su'ud's *fetva*, see Imber, *Ebu Su'ud*, 84–85.

57. Theunissen, "Ottoman-Venetian Diplomatics," 493–495.

58. Faroqhi suggests this explanation for their disobedience in "Venetian Presence," 383.

59. BOA MD 24: 596/ 224 (20/M/982).

60. BOA MD 24: 745/ 278 (3/S/982).

61. Ibid. The preceding decree had also expressed Ottoman desires to keep the border quiet.

62. BOA MD 26: 400/152 (22/R/982).

63. BOA MD 26: 180/68 (17/RA/982).

64. Theunissen, "Ottoman-Venetian Diplomatics," 529.

65. BOA MD 31: 549–550/261 (16/RA/986).

66. BOA MD 48: 638/229 (9/Z/990).

67. The affair is the subject of Fabris, "Un caso di pirateria veneziana." Decrees concerning the final resolution of the story—the handing over of the captured galley at Preveza and the return of the remaining captives and goods—are found in BOA MD 58: 14/3 (R/993), 20/5 (R/993), 33/11 (8/R/993), 49/16 (8/R/993), 50/16 (8/R/993), 273/ 97 (17/CA/993), and 314/116 (17/CA/993). The sheer number of decrees preserved in the registers gives some indication of how seriously the Ottomans took the matter. On its afterlife in Tunis, see Chapter 4, this volume.

68. For example, BOA MD 48: 646/232 (18/Z/990). See also Bostan, *Adriyatik'te Korsanlık*, 97–112; Bracewell, *Uskoks of Senj*, passim.

69. ASVe BAC, Carte turche 250/1, 50–51.

70. ASVe BAC, Carte turche 250/2, 22–23.

71. Isom-Verhaaren, *Allies with the Infidel*, 114–140.

72. de Groot, "Historical Development," 596–597; Skilliter, *William Harborne*, 86–90.

73. Skilliter, *William Harborne*; de Groot, *Ottoman Empire*; Agoston, "Merces Prohibitae."

74. Braudel, *Mediterranean*, 1:615–642.
75. Tenenti, *Piracy and the Decline of Venice*, 56–86.
76. *CSP*, 9:535–540 (February 22, 1603). On the trade in currants, see Wood, *Levant Company*, 24–5, 66–71.
77. For two sultanic letters to England complaining about the depredations of English pirates, see BnF Supplement Turc 119, 12v–13v.
78. For the Ottoman draft document, see BnF Supplement Turc 119, 11r.
79. See, for example, *CSP*, 9:547–548 (February 1603); *CSP*, 10:320–321 (February 10, 1606).
80. BOA MD 28: 663/270.
81. BOA MD 43: 214/117–9 (27/CA/988).
82. BOA MD 47: 105/41 (7/RA/990).
83. BOA MD 62: 43/14 (14/RA/994).
84. BOA MD 67: 218/84, 362/137 (7/N/999).
85. BOA MD 62: 428/190 (11/RA/996).
86. *CSP*, 8:51; de Groot, "Historical Development," 597; on French consulates, see Poumarède, "Naissance d'une instiution royale."
87. Theunissen, "Ottoman-Venetian Diplomatics," 569–570.
88. Ibid., 570.
89. For the Ottoman text of the 1597 *ahdname*, see BnF Turc 130, 17v–27v; Anon., *Translation of the Chapters*.
90. Calafat, "Ottoman North Africa," 173.
91. Poumarède, "La France et Les Barbaresques," 124.
92. For parallel Ottoman and French texts of the 1604 *ahdname*, see Savary de Brèves, *Articles du traicte*.
93. The anti-piracy law was updated and simplified in 1670, but the 1595 version was the platform on which this and every other power's *ahdname* was founded. See below.
94. For the Turkish texts of these *ahdname*s, see Theunissen, "Ottoman-Venetian Diplomatics," 579–591, 592–615, 616–625, and 626–636.
95. For the case-specific decrees, see ASVe BAC, Carte turche 252/13, 63 (Z/1003), 59–62.
96. See Chapter 5, this volume; contemporary Ottoman jurists rejected the "I bought it with my own money" justification using much the same language.
97. ASVe BAC, Carte turche 250/2, 22–23 (L/1013). It also contained a significant change in policy, absolving Venice of responsibility for the predations of the Uskoks.
98. ASVe BAC, Carte turche 252/13, 55r-57r (Evasıt/M/1003).
99. ASVe BAC, Carte turche 250/2, 57v-62v (Evasit/CA-Evail/C/1014); BOA ED 13: 101–2/27 (6/C/1014); the incident is also mentioned in Bostan, *Adriyatik'te Korsanlık*, 41–42.
100. ASVe BAC, Carte turche 250/2, 46 (S/1014).
101. For example, ASVe BAC, Carte turche 250/3, 8 (RA/1021); 250/3, 25 (C/1021).
102. ASVe BAC, Carte turche 250/2, 112–3 (C/1016).
103. *CSP*, 9:454–456, 459.

104. *CSP*, 10:6–7, 13, 39, 60, 173, 181.

105. For an overview of the Dutch privateer-to-North African corsair connection, see de Groot, "Ottoman North Africa"; Gelder, "Republic's Renegades."

CHAPTER 4

1. ASVe BAC, Carte turche 251/4, 121–123, 126–131; 251/5, 27, 55–61; and from Salvago, *Africa overo Barbaria*. On irregular violence along the Adriatic frontier, see Faroqhi, "Ottoman Views"; Bostan, *Adriyatik'te Korsanlık*; Bracewell, *Uskoks of Senj*.

2. Salvago, *Africa overo Barbaria*, 47.

3. ASVe BAC, Carte turche 251/4, 121–123, 126–131; 251/5, 27, 55–61; for his services as a spy and guide for the expedition, a certain "Ali of Castelnuovo" received thirteen of the Perastini captives; see Salvago, *Africa overo Barbaria*, 96.

4. ASVe BAC, Carte turche 251/4, 121–3, 126–131; 251/5, 27, 55–61.

5. Salvago, *Africa overo Barbaria*, 96.

6. White, "Shifting Winds."

7. BOA ED 13: 61/273 (L/1018), 62/281 (L/1018), 96/476, 478 (N/1021); White, "Shifting Winds."

8. TSMA.d 1306.03—*hikmeti Allahın geçen sene magreb korsanları gelüb.*

9. White, "Shifting Winds."

10. Twenty foreign vessels called in Iskenderun during the 1624–1625 financial year, TSMA.d 1306.01, 10v; by way of comparison, a register from 1660–1661, another troubled time, records eighteen; see Faroqhi, *Making a Living*, 230.

11. TSMA.d 1306.03–6.

12. Roe, *Negotiations*, 243 (May 15/25, 1624). The Roman traveler Pietro della Valle surveyed the destruction in person in late August 1625 and said much the same, noting that the "corsairs showed no respect to the sultan, their lord, and spared none of their religion or any other" (*Viaggi*, 1:877).

13. Ibid. On the Cossacks, see Ostapchuk, "Human Landscape."

14. Kâtib Çelebi, *Gift*, 122–123.

15. TNA SP 97/10, 261r (April 30/May 10, 1625).

16. *CSP*, 18:321 (May 27, 1624).

17. Lewis, "Corsairs in Iceland"; Tinniswood, *Pirates of Barbary*; *CSP*, 12:309 (March 10, 1612).

18. *CSP*, 18:358 (June 22, 1624).

19. *CSP*, 18:378 (July 6, 1624).

20. Roe, *Negotiations*, 270 (August 20/30, 1624).

21. Ibid., 4 (September 9, 1621); Louis XIII ordered the French ambassador de Césy to complain once more about losses to Algiers and Tunis in March 1623; see Poumarède, "France et les Barbaresques," 122–123.

22. For the orders to protest once more, see Roe, *Negotiations*, 52 (May 22, 1622); for his advocacy for blockade, bombardment, or invasion and frustration with the ineffectiveness of dealing with the Porte, see *Negotiations*, 6 (September 9, 1621); 57–58 (June 17/27, 1622); 118 (January 25, 1623).

23. This was not a formal peace treaty like those concluded in later years; in most of the English copies, it is referred to simply as an "agreement"; see TNA SP 103 (March 1622).

24. de Groot, "Ottoman North Africa," 135–137; the 1617 agreement was rapidly abrogated and a new round of direct negotiations with both Algiers and Tunis began in 1622.

25. Tongas, *Relations*, 162–163.

26. Roe, *Negotiations*, 118 (January 25, 1623).

27. Ibid., 57–58 (June 17/27, 1622), 112 (December 14/24, 1622).

28. TNA SP 103, multiple unnumbered copies (March 1622).

29. Roe, *Negotiations*, 260–261 (July 24, 1624 OS).

30. de Groot, "Historical Development," 596–597.

31. Roe, *Negotiations*, 271 (August 20/30, 1624); 276 (September 4/14, 1624); 278–280 (September 4/14, 1624); 311–312 (November 14/24, 1624). For the report that peace had been proclaimed and the captives freed, see *Negotiations*, 346 (February 5/15, 1625).

32. Ibid., 376 (April 15/25, 1625); Naima briefly describes the negotiations and the dispatch of a *kapıcı* from Istanbul to solemnize the agreement, which he called an *akd-ı musalaha*, or "peace pact" (*Târih-i Na'îmâ*, 2:608); for a narrative of the negotiations between 1622 and 1625 and the decrees dispatched from Istanbul in support of them, see TNA SP 103/72–72, 62v–77r.

33. *CSP*, 18:396 (July 20, 1624).

34. *Târih-i Na'îmâ*, 2:407–408; on the shifting political organization of the Maghreb during the centuries of Ottoman overlordship, see Abun-Nasr, *History of the Maghrib*, 144–205.

35. *Târih-i Na'îmâ*, 3:994–995.

36. Kâtib Çelebi, *Gift*, 118–123.

37. *CSP*, 18:397 (July 20, 1624).

38. Grandchamp, "Une mission délicate," 303.

39. White, "Fetva Diplomacy."

40. ASVe BAC, Carte turche 251/4, 121–123 (M/1034).

41. ASVe BAC, Carte turche 251/4, 126–131 (no date).

42. Grandchamp, "Une mission délicate," 304.

43. ASVe BAC, Carte turche 251/4, 126 (no date).

44. ASVe BAC, Carte turche 251/4, 121v; White, "It Is Not Halal to Raid Them."

45. On Salvago, see Rothman, "Self-Fashioning"; see also Sacerdoti's introduction in *Africa overo Barbaria*, i–xiv.

46. Salvago, *Africa overo Barbaria*, 4–5.

47. Ibid.

48. Ibid., 10.

49. Pedani Fabris, *Relazioni*, 348, 677–678.

50. Salvago, *Africa overo Barbaria*, 21–22.

51. Ibid., 22.

52. ASVe BAC, Carte turche 251/5, 27 (B/1034).

53. Salvago, *Africa overo Barbaria*, 40.

54. Gürkan, *Centre*, passim; for contemporary descriptions of Algiers and Tunis and their governments, see Sosa, *Topography*; Salvago, *Africa overo Barbaria*, 53–90; for Yusuf Dey's reign, see Ibn Abi Dinar, *al-Mu'nis*, 191–200.

55. Salvago, *Africa overo Barbaria*, 41–42.

56. Ibid., 41–43; Salvago lists the North Africans' chief objections on pages 34–46.

57. Benton, "Legal Spaces of Empire," passim.

58. Salvago, *Africa overo Barbaria*, 34.

59. Ibid., 25.

60. Ibid., 47.

61. Ibid., 38.

62. Grandchamp, "Une mission délicate," 306.

63. Salvago, *Africa overo Barbaria*, 40.

64. See Chapter 3, this volume.

65. Salvago, *Africa overo Barbaria*, 35.

66. Ibid., 46–47.

67. Ibid., 36.

68. Ibid., 46. The capture of the two Maltese vessels, a cause of great celebration, was of sufficient import to merit a mention in Ibn Abi Dinar's history of Tunis, *al-Mu'nis*, 196.

69. White, "Shifting Winds."

70. Salvago, *Africa overo Barbaria*, 47.

71. *CSP*, 19:23 (April 27, 1625).

72. TNA SP 97/10, 83v (July 12/22, 1624), 85r-v (July 14/24, 1624).

73. TSMA.d 1341.04.

74. *CSP*, 19:262 (December 28, 1625).

75. ASVe SDC 101, 179r-184v (January 1625 m.v.), 207r-211r (January 24, 1625 m.v.), 225r-229v (Feb. 7, 1625 m.v.), 239r-243v (Feb. 7, 1625 m.v.), 264r-283r (Feb. 21, 1625 m.v.); BAC, Carte turche 251/5, 55–61.

76. ASVe SDC 101, 179r-180r.

77. ASVe SDC 101, 181r.

78. ASVe SDC 101, 207r.

79. Ibid.

80. ASVe BAC, Carte turche 251/5, 55–6 (CA/1035).

81. Poumarède, "France et Les Barbaresques," 131.

82. Panzac, *Barbary Corsairs*, 31. There were no new treaties between 1628 and 1658.

83. Weiss, *Captives and Corsairs*, passim.

84. TNA SP 103 (1662).

85. Ibid.; Pennell, "Treaty Law."

86. TNA SP 103 (1662).

87. Ibid.

88. *CSP*, 20:221.

89. On Ottoman finances in this period, see Inalcık, "Military and Fiscal Transformation."

90. White, "Shifting Winds," 50–51.

91. Roe, *Negotiations*, 346 (February 5/15, 1625); 376 (April 15/25, 1625).

92. Ibid., 449 (November 2/12, 1625). Alberto Tenenti has argued that the impact of piracy—especially English piracy—on Venice's marine insurance rates starting in the late sixteenth century was among the principal causes for the decline of her shipping; see *Piracy and the Decline of Venice*, especially 100–104.

93. *CSP*, 20:392 (September 24, 1627); the corsairs entered the harbor on June 5 and captured two French vessels, which they ransomed back on the spot.

94. TNA SP 97/13, 235r (1627).

95. Kenelm Digby's privateering venture is the subject of his *Journal of a Voyage into the Mediterranean*; after the engagement with the Venetians, Digby wrote a letter aboard his flagship to the English ambassador to explain, TNA SP 97/14, 153r–155r (June 13/23, 1628). For a fawning portrait of Digby and more on this incident, see Bligh, *Sir Kenelm Digby*, 136–146.

96. TNA SP 97/14, 164r–165r (June 25, O.S., 1628).

97. TNA SP 97/14, 192–193 (July 12, O.S., 1628); translated copies of the Porte's decrees on the affair are in the same bundle, 185r–88r (July 10, 1628), 216r–219r (August 20, 1628).

98. Molloy, *De Jure Maritimo*, 45–46.

99. Talbot, "Ottoman Seas and British Privateers," 54–70; Heywood, "Ottoman Territoriality," 145–173.

100. TNA SP 97/11, 113r (October 8/18, 1625).

101. TSMA.d 7687 (1048).

102. ASVe BAC, Carte turche 251/5, 104 (CA/1034).

103. For some indication of the bracing uncertainty preceding every encounter at sea, see Wheler, *Journey*, 29, 46.

104. For dozens of documents relating to the affair, see ASVe DT 1334; Querini's report of the encounter is 4r–5v (March 5, 1626). For the letters, see ASVe BAC, Carte turche 251/6, 1 (CA/1036), 3 (no date); DT 1347 (CA/1036), DT 1349 (no date).

105. TSMA.d 7687 (1048).

106. ASVe BAC, Carte turche 252/8, 5–6 (ZA/1046).

107. For the navy's activities in the summer of 1638, see *Târih-i Na îmâ*, 2:905–907.

108. Mallia-Milanes, "From Valona to Crete," 160–162.

109. *Peçevi Tarihi*, 2:428.

110. *Târih-i Na'îmâ*, 2:934–935; see also Rycaut, *History of the Turkish Empire*, 72–6, 85–6.

111. Mallia-Milanes, "From Valona to Crete," 164.

112. ASVe BAC, Carte turche 252/8, 40 (RA/1049).

113. The *nişan* is preserved in translation in Rycaut, *History of the Turkish Empire*, 86–7.

114. TSMA.d 7687 (1048).

115. ASVe BAC, Carte turche 252/8, 51; 54; 70 (1049–1050).

116. Theunissen, "Ottoman-Venetian Diplomatics," 635.

117. *Târih-i Na'îmâ*, 3:994–995.

118. Ibid., 3:1023.

119. Abun-Nasr, "Beylicate."

120. On the diverse origins of Algiers' soldiers, administrators, and corsairs, see Sosa, *Topography*, 119–134; on the fleet, see ibid., 151–159.

121. *Târih-i Na'îmâ*, 3:1029–1030.

122. Ibid., 3:1030.

123. For the naval conflict, see Setton, *Venice, Austria, and the Turks*, 137–205; Anderson, *Naval Wars*, 121–184.

124. *Târih-i Na'îmâ*, 3:1130, 1237; TNA SP 97/17, 135r (1657).

125. Quoted in Shuval, "Cezair-i Garp," 104.

126. *Solak-zâde tarihi*, 2:563–564.

127. Setton, *Venice, Austria, and the Turks*, 236.

128. de Groot, "Historical Development," 594.

129. BOA ED 16/4: 1–2 (R/1081).

130. Ibid.

131. The Ottomans had been using this sort of language in their discussions with European ambassadors for decades. Regarding the corsairs who afflicted both the Ottoman Empire and Venice, the *kaymakam* was said to have declared to the *bailo* in 1639 that "it would be necessary for the good of the World that such violences were prevented in all places and that men of such wicked profession should be esteemed for universal Enemies and to have no other Quarter nor Articles granted them than what we give to wild and hurtful beasts," Rycaut, *History of the Turkish Empire*, 85.

132. Chardin, *Travels*, 3–4.

133. Slot, *Archipelagus Turbatus*, 193–195.

134. ASVe BAC, Carte turche 252/10, 35–6 (M/1084).

135. ASVe BAC, Carte turche 252/10, 59; 92–97; 252/12, 24; 26.

136. Panzac, *Barbary Corsairs*, 31–35. European observers of the period were well aware of the widening gulf separating Istanbul and North Africa. For example, in the 1670 edition of his oft-updated and reprinted book on contemporary Ottoman politics and society, Paul Rycaut explained that he excluded Algiers, Tunis, and Tripoli from his discussion because they had "much fallen off from the Turks obedience, and become almost independent of themselves," and "because of late years the mutual Treaties with Barbary, and interchanges of War and Peace with those Countries" had made them so familiar to his audience that there was no need to include them; see Rycaut, *Present State*, 56.

137. On French commerce in this period, see Masson, *Histoire du commerce français*.

138. See Pennell, "Ottoman Empire in North Africa."

139. Argenti, *Diplomatic Archive*, 164.

140. Ibid., 166.

141. Sarı Mehmed Paşa, *Zübde-i Vekayiât*, 122; *Târih-i Râşid*, 1:220; for Duquesne's own after action report, see Argenti, *Diplomatic Archive*, 171–178.

142. Sarı Mehmed Paşa, *Zübde-i Vekayiât*, 122; *Târih-i Râşid*, 1:220; for untranslated French, English, Dutch, and Venetian documents concerning the events at Chios and their aftermath, see Argenti, *Diplomatic Archive*, 158–353.

143. Argenti, *Diplomatic Archive*, 202.

144. The parallel was not lost on contemporary observers, such as in the English account purporting to have been written by an "Officer of the Grand Vizir," *An Account*, 26.

145. Baker, *Journal*, 131–132.

146. Molloy, *De Jure Maritimo*, 12.

147. Poumarède, "France et les Barbaresques," 139–140.

148. Sarı Mehmed Paşa, *Zübde-i Vekayiât*, 127–129; *Târih-i Râşid*, 1:224–226; Argenti, *Diplomatic Archive*, 180–183.

149. Argenti, *Diplomatic Archive*, 204.

150. Sarı Mehmed Paşa, *Zübde-i Vekayiât*, 127–129; *Târih-i Râşid*, 1:225–226.

151. Argenti, *Diplomatic Archive*, 204.

152. "Officer of the Grand Vizir," *An Account*, 7–15; Poumarède, "France et les Barbaresques," 141.

153. Argenti, *Diplomatic Archive*; 214–218, 232–238; Pennell, "Ottoman Empire in North Africa."

154. *Târih-i Râşid*, 1:229; for the French description of the gifts and their values, see Poumarède, "France et les Barbaresques," 141–142; the elaborate ceremony is described, possibly on the basis of ambassadorial reports and local informants, in "Officer of the Grand Vizir," *An Account*, 33–38.

155. Pennell, "Ottoman Empire in North Africa"; Baker, *Journal*, 134–136.

156. Weiss, *Captives and Corsairs*, 72–75.

157. Poumarède, "France et les Barbaresques," 144.

158. Sarı Mehmed Paşa, *Zübde-i Vekayiât*, 137; *Târih-i Râşid*, 1:232. Slot argues that it was in fact a reprisal for the events at Chios in *Archipelagus Turbatus*, 209.

159. In Finch's opinion, Duquesne's fleet was "more than doubly able to fight all the force the Ottoman Empire is able to make appear at Sea"; see Argenti, *Diplomatic Archive*, 202.

160. Murphey, "Ottoman Resurgence," 198–199.

161. On European gunboat diplomacy of this sort, see Panzac, *Barbary Corsairs*, 31–41.

162. Gédoyn, *Journal*, 69–70. Copies of these *fetva*s survive in BnF MS Turc 130, a manuscript assembled by the ambassador who requested them, François Savary de Brèves; see Panaite, "French Commerce."

163. Molloy, *De Jure Maritimo*, 54–55; Calafat, "Ottoman North Africa," 171–188.

164. BOA AE.SMHD.I 66 4268 (29/M/1155).

165. Heywood, "Ottoman Territoriality"; Talbot, "Ottoman Seas and British Privateers."

166. Talbot, "Ottoman Seas and British Privateers," 65.

167. Calafat, "Ottoman North Africa," 174–182; for a broader range of European views on the position of North Africa vis-à-vis the Ottoman Empire, see Thomson, *Barbary and Enlightenment*, 51–55.

168. Folayan, *Tripoli.*

169. Abun-Nasr, *History of the Maghrib*, 144–205.

CHAPTER 5

1. SK MS Amcazade Hüseyin 254, 107r.

2. They are the *Fetava* of Ebu Su'ud Efendi (d. 1574), *Fetava-yı Sunullah Efendi* of Sunullah Efendi (d. 1612), *Fetava-yı Muntehabe* of Hocazade Esad Efendi (d. 1625), *Fetava-yı Yahya Efendi* of Zekeriyyazade Yahya Efendi (d. 1644), the *Fetava* of Karaçelebizade Abdülaziz Efendi (d. 1657), the *Fetava* of Minkarizade Yahya Efendi (d. 1678), *Fetava-yı Ali Efendi* of Çatalcalı Ali Efendi (d. 1692), *Fetava-yı Feyziye* of Feyzullah Efendi (d. 1703), *Behçetü'l-Fetava* of Yenişehirli Abdullah Efendi (d.1743), and *Neticetü'l-Fetava*, compiled by Dürrizade Mehmed Arif Efendi (d.1810).

3. Majid Khadduri observed that "few subjects has the juristic literature of Islam treated so inadequately as salt-water warfare" (*War and Peace*, 109). To the extent that jurists confronted the issue, they did so by means of analogy or on the basis of prevailing custom (ibid., 112). The Ottomans were no different.

4. Repp, *Mufti of Istanbul*, 196, passim; Imber, *Ebu's-Su'ud*, 13–14; for background on fatwas and muftis generally, see Masud, Messick, and Powers, "Muftis, Fatwas, and Islamic Legal Interpretation," 3–32.

5. Imber, *Ebu's-Su'ud*, 12–15; for brief biographical sketches of the Ottoman *şeyhülislams*, see Altunsu, *Osmanlı Şeyhülislamları*.

6. Imber, *Ebu's-Su'ud*, 51.

7. The Ottoman *fetva* and the Ottoman *fetva*-granting institution were first described in detail by Heyd, "Some Aspects of the Ottoman Fetva," 35–56; for Ebu Su'ud's claim, see ibid., 46.

8. Ibid., 48.

9. For example, Esiri Mehmed Efendi, Mehmed Ataullah Efendi, Yenişehirli Abdullah Efendi, and Vassaf Abdullah Efendi. Heyd, "Some Aspects of the Ottoman Fetva," 48.

10. For example, Mehmed Ataullah Efendi (d. 1715), whose collection, titled in some manuscripts *Fetava-yı Ataiye*, is actually a collection of the *fetvas* of Minkarizade Yahya Efendi. Miscataloging of manuscripts has led to some confusion among scholars, who have mistaken the *fetvas* for his own.

11. Some manuscripts have additional proof-texts and supplementary *fetvas* written in the margins by later users. Regarding their dissemination, the libraries of Bosnia alone preserve more than twenty manuscript copies of the *Fetava-yi Alı Efendi* of Çatalcalı Ali Efendi (d. 1692); see Zecevic, "On the Margin of Text," 196.

12. Özen, "Osmanlı Döneminde Fetva Literatürü," 252–253; Imber, *Ebu's-Su'ud*, 57; Tuşalp, "Treating Outlaws," 17–18. For a brief introduction to Ottoman *fetva* production and compilation in the post-Ebu Su'ud era, see Imber, "Eleven Fetvas," 141–149.

13. Kruger, *Fetva und Siyar*, 31–33. Kruger's work is the only analysis of the Ottoman approach to *siyar*, but it is based on the published Ottoman collections of the late seventeenth and eighteenth centuries alone; it does not comment on the peculiar development of the maritime corpus of *fetvas*.

14. Hamidullah, *Muslim Conduct of State*, 186; Imber, *Ebu's-Su'ud*, 89–91.

15. Khadduri, *Shaybani's Siyar*, 39.

16. SK MS Amcazade Hüseyin 254, 106v–107r.

17. SK MS Pertevniyal 341, 25r.

18. For the rationale behind this, see Khadduri, *Shaybani's Siyar*, 130–133, 152, 160–168.

19. Biegman, *Turco-Ragusan Relationship*, 30–31. For more on the concept of *dar al-ahd*, see Inalcık, "Dar al-'Ahd," *EI2*.

20. Biegman, *Turco-Ragusan Relationship*, 30–31.

21. See Dávid and Fodor, *Ransom Slavery*. On boundaries between the Ottoman Empire and Venice and problems caused by pirates and slaves, see Pedani, "Beyond the Frontier," 45–60.

22. SK MS Amcazade Hüseyin 254, 107r.

23. Khalilieh, *Islamic Maritime Law*, 138.

24. For an example, see SK MS Amcazade Hüseyin 254, 105v; MS Kasidecizade 276, 104v–105r.

25. Khadduri, *Shaybani's Siyar*, 108–109.

26. See *Consolato Del Mare Relating to Prize Law*, esp. 6–7.

27. Imber, "Eleven Fetvas," 142.

28. Tuşalp makes a similar argument ("Treating Outlaws," 19–23); see also Imber, "Eleven Fetvas," 141–142.

29. See SK MSS Ismihan Sultan 223, 96r–99v and Ismihan Sultan 226, 148r–153v.

30. Sunullah Efendi (d.1612) followed a typical post-Ebu Su'ud career path. He was appointed Anadolu *kazasker* (military judge of Anatolia) in 1591, Rumeli *kazasker* (military judge of Europe) in 1592, and *şeyhülislam* for the first time in 1599, holding the position on and off for a total of five years, seven months, and two days. See İpşirli, "Şeyhülislam Sun'ullah Efendi," 209–256. His is the first collection that shows appreciable numbers of maritime *fetva*s. His was also only the second collection to appear after those of Ebu Su'ud (the collection of Hoca Sadeddin Efendi, who held the office immediately before Sunullah, came first, but it does not reflect the developments of the late sixteenth and early seventeenth centuries like those of Sunullah and his successors, perhaps because he only held the post for a year). The two decades after Ebu Su'ud's death were marked by significant turnover in the *şeyhülislam* slot and were otherwise dominated by his protégés, including two of his former *fetva* clerks. From Sunullah Efendi on, there are always maritime *fetva*s in the *siyar* sections.

31. On the clerks behind Ebu Su'ud's collection, see Imber, *Ebu's-Su'ud*, 20.

32. On such collections, see Zecevic, "On the Margin of Text"; Tucker, *In the House of the Law*; Semerdjian, *Off the Straight Path*.

33. See SK MSS Pertevniyal 341, Esad Efendi 1095.

34. By the later eighteenth century, most "new" *fetva* collections were compilations of *fetva*s from multiple earlier *şeyhülislam*s. *Neticetü'l-Fetava* (by 1800) is one of the most prominent examples.

35. SK MSS Pertevniyal 341, 24r–27r; Esad Efendi 1095, 22r–27r.

36. On the connection between *kadi* and mufti in the Ottoman context, see Gerber, *State, Society, and Law*, 79–83; on foreigners' use of *fetva*s to support petitions, see White, "Fetva Diplomacy."

37. A number of Ebu Su'ud's *fetva*s are followed by a line naming the questioner and the year of the request; the same is true for a small number of eighteenth-century *fetva*s.

38. SK MS Pertevniyal 341, 24r.

39. In this instance, the Arabic proof-text references the *siyar* chapter of the famed *Hidaya* of al-Marghinani (d. 1197).

40. On partnerships in Ottoman Islamic law generally, see Gerber, "Muslim Law of Partnerships."

41. SK MS Amcazade Hüseyin 254, 107r.

42. See Greene, *Catholic Pirates and Greek Merchants.*

43. Çatalcalı Ali Efendi, *Fetava-yı Ali Efendi*, 213. The usage of the Persian *izafet* construction *dar-ı Islam* instead of *darülislam*, as above, was not uncommon.

44. SK MS Pertevniyal 341, 24r.

45. See Chapter 2, this volume.

46. This *fetva* appears in slightly different form in two manuscripts, though without any effect on meaning. SK MS Amcazade Hüseyin 254, 105v (H. 1092) is the older of the two; cf. MS Kasidecizade 276, 104v–105r (H. 1135).

47. See, for example, RSM 35, 9r (15/CA/1026), for the case of a Vlach slave who escaped and whose former owner ran into him in Istanbul nine years later in the possession of another master.

48. See Thermopoulou, "Kurekci de la flotte ottomane"; İpşirli, "Kürek Cezası."

49. Because manumission was common, often after a predetermined period of time that had been legally contracted (*mukatebe*) between master and slave, the incentive to serve faithfully could be very strong. Manumitted slaves typically continued to serve their former masters in a patron-client relationship. See Khan, *Slaves without Shackles.*

50. SK MS Amcazade Hüseyin 254, 106r.

51. SK MS Pertevniyal 341, 24v.

52. SK MS Pertevniyal 341, 25r.

53. In *Neticetü'l-Fetava*, SK MS Kasidecizade 278, 87r.

54. Çatalcalı Ali Efendi, *Fetava-yı Ali Efendi*, 211–212.

55. The only exception to this rule is ransoming, which usually appears in the *kefalet* (surety) section.

56. Khadduri, *Shaybani's Siyar*, 259.

57. This "legal tension" is a major focus in Greene, *Catholic Pirates and Greek Merchants.*

58. SK MS Ismihan Sultan 226, 152r.

59. SK MS Kasidecizade 278, 88v.

60. Çatalcalı Ali Efendi, *Fetava-yı Ali Efendi*, 207.

61. SK MS Ismihan Sultan 223, 97r.

62. Panaite, *Ottoman Law of War and Peace*, 284–291.

63. BOA A.NŞT.D 1066, 1r. The scribal notation is dated 12/ZA/979—March 27, 1572. The entries on the following pages begin with orders dated several months earlier, at the start of Şaban 979 (mid-December 1571).

64. The meaning of *gaza* (or *ghaza*) is more complex than "holy war." Although it was often used synonymously with jihad in the Ottoman context, its original Arabic meaning is more closely tied to frontier raiding. On the question of what it meant to whom and when, see Imber, "What Does Ghazi Actually Mean?"; Darling, "Contested Territory."

65. For example, see Bostan, *Adriyatik'te Korsanlık*; Panzac, *Barbary Corsairs*; and to some extent Faroqhi, "Venetian Presence."

66. Consider the English and Dutch raiders who set up shop in North Africa and then returned home following the promise of amnesty; see Tinniswood, *Pirates of Barbary*, passim.

67. SK MS Amcazade Hüseyin 254, 106v; MS Kasidecizade 276, 102r.

68. Ibid.

69. Bracewell, *Uskoks of Senj*, passim; Bostan, *Adriyatik'te Korsanlık*, 97–112.

70. For a chronology, see Finkel, *Osman's Dream*, 200–223.

71. SK MS Amcazade Hüseyin 254, 106v; MS Kasidecizade 276, 102r-v.

72. Darling, "Contested Territory," 130.

73. ASVe BAC, Carte turche 251/5, 60.

74. For more on this episode, see Chapter 4, this volume; White, "Fetva Diplomacy."

75. ASVe BAC b. 364; Panaite, "French Commerce, North African Piracy, and Ottoman Law"; White, "Fetva Diplomacy."

76. BOA MD 30: 844/358 (21/R/985).

77. The *fetva* is undated, but the war is that of 1628; see *Târih-i Na'îmâ*, 2:567; Ibn Abi Dinar, *al-Mu'nis*, 196; Abun-Nasr, "Beylicate," 74.

78. SK MS Kasidecizade 276, 102v.

79. *Târih-i Na'îmâ*, 2:567.

80. Abun-Nasr, "Beylicate," 70–93.

81. On the relationship between political leaders and the Hanafi and Maliki ulama in Tunis, see Abun-Nasr, "Tunisian State in the Eighteenth Century," 38–42.

82. SK MS Pertevniyal 341, 25v.

83. In this somewhat confusing *fetva*, we know that "I" was not there to participate in the raid because the *fetva* does not specifically say otherwise, as well as from the content of the extended proof-text, discussed below. The *fetva* conforms completely to Shaybani's views on the distribution of spoils; see Khadduri, *Shaybani's Siyar*, 108–111.

84. The latter is in fact a commentary on the former.

85. SK MS Pertevniyal 341, 25v.

86. Sherman Jackson argues that though jurists in the post-formative period could innovate and respond to new problems with new solutions, they were not exercising *ijtihad*, since they were not turning to *usul al-fiqh* in support of their opinions but to the rulings of distinguished predecessors from within their *madhhab*. See Jackson, "Taqlid."

87. Masud, Messick, and Powers describe *fetva*s as "the closest equivalent to the familiar Anglo-American legal mechanism of case-law precedent" in, "Muftis,

Fatwas, and Islamic Legal Interpretation," 4; see also Hallaq, "From Fatwas to Furu."

CHAPTER 6

1. RSM 21, 35r (23/N/1002); *İstanbul Kadı Sicilleri*, 12:152–153.

2. Criminal cases were not a significant part of the *kadi*'s caseload. When Islamic courts did order extreme punishment or execution, the sentence usually had to be approved by the local governor or the Imperial Council. See Ginio, "Administration of Criminal Justice."

3. For an overview of Ottomanists' methodological approaches, see Ze'evi, "Use of Ottoman Sharīʿa Court Records."

4. Some examples among many include Jennings, *Christians and Muslims*; Jennings, *Studies on Ottoman Social History*; Ergene, *Local Court*; Peirce, *Morality Tales*.

5. See, for example, Jennings, "Kadi, Court, and Legal Procedure"; Ergene, "Why Did Ummu Gulsum Go to Court?; Ergene, "Pursuing Justice"; Gerber, *State, Society, and Law*; Semerdjian, *Off the Straight Path*; on selecting a *kadi*, see Atcil, "Procedure in the Ottoman Court," 42–49.

6. For a list of extant registers, see Akgündüz, *Şer'iye sicilleri*; on the loss of the Izmir records, see Goffman, *Izmir and the Levantine World*; on the "sea judge," see Veinstein, "Les Documens emis par le kapudan paşa"; Ursinus, "Local Patmians."

7. White, "Litigating Disputes."

8. On the *kazasker*, see Uzunçarşılı, *Merkez ve Bahriye Teşkilâtı*, 228–241; for the judicial appointments he made, see Inalcik, "*Ruznamce* Registers." For the aristocratification of the Ottoman *ulema*, see Tezcan, "Ottoman Mevali."

9. Uzunçarşılı, *Merkez ve Bahriye Teşkilâtı*, 236. On the growing importance of the Imperial Council from the second half of the sixteenth century, see Fodor, "Sultan, Imperial Council, Grand Vizier."

10. See Greene, "Ruling an Island."

11. Formulae declaring that Crete was on the *serhad-i islamiyye* and within the *darüljihad* appear frequently in the Candia registers, especially in the early eighteenth century (i.e., following the 1684–1699 war), for example, TAH 13, 45 (1118).

12. On the post-conquest administrative division of the island, see Gülsoy, *Girit'in Fethi*, 223–239.

13. Greene, *A Shared World*, 23. Adiyeke, "Kadi Registers," 447–448, holds that the *kadi* of Chania was considered Crete's chief *kadi*, but Candia's court seemingly vied for it in importance.

14. On Cretan janissaries and the conversion question, see Greene, *A Shared World*, 36–44.

15. Benton, "Legalities of the Sea," 269–82; Benton, "Toward a New Legal History."

16. See Chapter 5, this volume.

17. RSM 21, 35r (23/N/1002); *İstanbul Kadı Sicilleri*, 12:152–153.

18. On which, see Raymond, "Soldiers in Trade."

19. Atcil, "Procedure in the Ottoman Court," 42–49.

20. Aḥmad ibn Muḥammad and Wakin, *Function of Documents*; Ergene qualifies Wakin's interpretation in "Document Use"; Ergene, "Evidence in Ottoman Courts."

21. Mehmed b. Derviş Mehmed es-Sâni el-Edirnevi, *Sukuk-i Sâni Efendi*, BnF MS Supplement Turc 66, 60v–61v.

22. RSM 21, 35r (23/N/1002); *İstanbul Kadı Sicilleri*, 12:152–153.

23. Ibid. Written communications between judges of evidentiary findings were more acceptable to other legal schools, Hallaq, "Qadis Communicating."

24. Galata 27, 83r (Evahir/S/1014); Kuran, *Social and Economic Life*, 806–809. The English/Modern Turkish summaries in Kuran omit the involvement of the *kazasker*, the fact that the pirates were "enemy infidels," and the competing *darülislam/darülharb* claims that were crucial to the case.

25. Ibid.

26. Ibid.

27. TAH 4, 339 (15/B/1095).

28. Although it is hard to imagine there being much of a market in Messina for coarse brown turban cloth.

29. Molly Greene has noted the same about news and information in "Victims of Piracy?," 197–200; cf. Braude, "Venture and Faith." On Milos, see Slot, *Archipelagus Turbatus*, 169–170; d'Arvieux, *Memoires*, 4:327–335; Roberts, "Adventures," 25, who wrote that Milos "is a place of great Rendevouz for Crusals [i.e., pirates], and thither they bring their Prizes, which causes a considerable Trade."

30. Othman, "Amicable Settlement Is Best."

31. On the relationship between the court and mediation, and the decision to go to the former before agreeing to the latter, see Ergene, "Why Did Ummu Gulsum Go to Court?"

32. RSM 56, 8r (Evail/ZA/1042); *İstanbul Kadı Sicilleri*, 14:66–67.

33. Vatin, "Ces Messieurs de Galata"; in Vatin, "Errata," he states that the sources actually date to 1596.

34. Suits and settlement registrations brought by Christians from Naxos, Mytilene, and other islands involving business confined to their home islands are common in Galata's seventeenth-century records.

35. Tamdoğan, "*Sulh* and the 18th-Century Ottoman Courts."

36. Stefini, "Ottoman Merchants"; van den Boogert, "Redress for Ottoman Victims"; Kermeli, "Right to Choice."

37. White, "Shifting Winds."

38. Kolovos, "Insularity and Island Society," 58–59; Vatin and Veinstein, "Une bonté unique au monde"; Kermeli, "Central Administration."

39. D'Arvieux, *Memoires*, 2:92.

40. Galata 25, 50r (1013); Kuran, *Social and Economic Life*, 784–785.

41. Stefini, "Ottoman Merchants"; van den Boogert, "Redress for Ottoman Victims."

42. See Chapters 3 and 5, this volume.

43. Van den Boogert, "Redress for Ottoman Victims."
44. Galata 36, 163v (8/Ş/1023).
45. RSM 35, 9r-v (Evasit/CA/1026).
46. Many have taken note of the seemingly standardized language of Ottoman courts; see, for example, Peirce, *Morality Tales*, passim.
47. Given the stated size of the cargo, a little skepticism regarding Manolaki's account might be in order. Where did he go after he fled? It would have taken some time to unload 50,280 bushels of wheat and a large ship to carry it off. What prevented Anton from simply taking Manolaki's ship, cargo and all?
48. On the burden of proof and oaths, see Ergene, "Evidence in Ottoman Courts," 474. On oaths and swearing (of the other sort) in another Ottoman context, see Grehan, "The Mysterious Power of Words."
49. Gerber, *State, Society, and Islam*, 49–50.
50. Leslie Peirce makes a similar argument in *Morality Tales*, and Daniel Lord Smail has observed the same phenomenon in medieval Marseilles in *Consumption of Justice*.
51. On trade and trust, see Braude, "Venture and Faith"; Trivellato, *The Familiarity of Strangers*; Aslanian, "Social Capital."
52. This is *inkardan sulh*; see Othman, "Amicable Settlement Is Best."
53. RSM 34, 13r–v (c. 29/M/1024).
54. Galata 40, 67v (Evail/R/1025).
55. See, for example, the Venetian trial record of a diverse crew of accused pirates, commanded by an English renegade and based out of North Africa, captured off Candia in CSP, 12:559–563 (January 3–6, 1610). Sailors in general were highly mobile maritime mercenaries who routinely hopped from ship to ship, often without completing a voyage. The example of Edward Coxere, who served (both by choice and by force) on English, Dutch, Spanish, and Tunisian vessels in short succession in the mid-seventeenth century, was hardly unusual; see Coxere, *Adventures*, 37.
56. Roberts, "Adventures," 8–9.
57. RSM 56, 44r (Evahir/M/1043); *İstanbul Kadı Sicilleri*, 14:220.
58. Tournefort, *Voyage*, 1:268.
59. Qur'an 10:22, 17:66–9, 2:282; see also Jennings, "Loans."
60. See Chapter 4, this volume.
61. TAH 5, 30 (5/C/1084).
62. Greene, *A Shared World*, 76.
63. TAH 5, 30 (5/C/1084).
64. Tietze, "Die Geschichte von Kerkermeister-Kapitän," 152–210.
65. Greene, *A Shared World*, 70–71.
66. Ibid., 38–44.
67. The Cretan registers referred to these islands as being "in *darülharb*" every time they were mentioned.
68. For more on this type of practice, see Canbakal, "Vows as Contract."
69. TAH 4, 382 (19/RA/1097).
70. TAH 8, 2 (11/Ş/1105).

71. See Faroqhi, "Räuber, Rebellen und Obrigkeit"; Canbakal, "Vows as Contract," 88–94.
72. TAH 5, 299–300 (17/C/1100).
73. TAH 5, 237–41, 299–301 (C/1100). Most entries have large numbers of witnesses listed, often more than fourteen, most of whom held high-ranking military/administrative positions.
74. Or, as Canbakal ("Vows as Contact," 94) puts it, "There is good reason to suspect that vows that involved the state did not really depend on the freewill of the communities in question."
75. TAH 8, 132 (15/Ş/1105).
76. TAH 8, 51 (Evahir/N/1105).
77. Randolph, *Present State*, 2.
78. TAH 8, 55 (15/ZA/1106).
79. Randolph, *Present State*, 15–20.
80. The story is recounted in TAH 8, 56 (ZA/1106); see also TAH 8, 7 (L/1104).
81. TAH 8, 56 (ZA/1106).
82. TAH 11, 28–29 (15/CA/1107).
83. TAH 11, 41 (8/ZA/1107).
84. Galata 160, 53v (17/C/1105).
85. TAH 8, 20 (Evail/RA/1106).
86. Ibid.
87. TAH 8, 16 (Evahir/M/1106).
88. Ibid.
89. See Chapter 5, this volume.
90. TAH 8, 123 (15/N/1105).
91. Greene, *A Shared World*, 68.

CONCLUSION

1. TAH 3, 332–5 (Dispatched Evahir/M/1164; received 13/R/1164).
2. Panzac, *Barbary Corsairs*, 31–42; Weiss, *Captives and Corsairs*, 72–91.
3. On eighteenth-century Tripoli, see Folayan, *Tripoli*. In 1751, Tripoli's incursions into the Adriatic led to armed (but mostly diplomatic) conflict between Venice and Dubrovnik; Istanbul had to mediate between all three, see Miović-Perić, "Conflict between Dubrovnik and Venice."
4. TAH 3, 333.
5. Ibid., 333–334.
6. Ibid.
7. Ibid., 334.
8. Ibid.
9. Ibid.—*devlet-i aliyyeme tabi'lerinden biri.*
10. See Chapter 4 of this volume.
11. Cavaliero, "The Decline of the Maltese Corso," 224–238; Poumarède, *Pour en finir.*

12. Wettinger, *Slavery*, 62.
13. On his career with the Ottoman navy, see Safvet, *Mezemorta Hüseyin Paşa*.
14. See Chapter 1 of this volume.
15. Bostan, "Kadirga'dan Kalyon'a," 82–86.
16. Talbot, "Protecting the Mediterranean"; Aydın, "Ottoman Security Parameters."
17. The work was first described in Tietze, "Geschichte von Kerkermeister-Kapitän"; the transcribed Ottoman text was published in İz, "Makale-i Zindancı Mahmud." See also Sariyannis, "Images of the Mediterranean."
18. İz, "Makale-i Zindancı Mahmud," 129.
19. Ibid., 140.
20. Ibid., 147.

Bibliography

Archival Sources

Archivio di Stato di Venezia (ASVe), State Archives of Venice
Bailo a Costantinopoli (BAC)
Documenti Turchi (DT)
Senato, Dispacci Costantinopoli (SDC)

Başbakanlık Osmanlı Arşivi (BOA), Prime Ministry's Ottoman Archives, Istanbul
Ecnebi Defterleri (ED)
Mühimme Defterleri (MD)
Mühimme Zeyli Defterleri (MZD)

Bibliothèque nationale de France (BnF), National Library of France, Paris

İslam Araştırmaları Merkezi (İSAM), Islamic Research Center, Istanbul
Galata Mahkemesi
Rumeli Sadareti Mahkemesi (RSM)

Süleymaniye Kütüphanesi (SK), Süleymaniye Library, Istanbul

The [UK] National Archives (TNA), Kew (London)
State Papers, Foreign (SP)

Topkapı Sarayı Müzesi Arşivi (TSMA), Topkapı Palace Museum Archives, Istanbul

Vikelaia Municipal Library, Heraklion, Crete
Kandiye Mahkemesi, Turkish Archive of Heraklion (TAH)

Published Primary Sources

3 Numaralı Mühimme Defteri (966–968/1558–1560). Edited by İsmet Binark and Nezihi Aykut. Ankara: T. C. Başbakanlık Devlet Arşivleri Genel Müdürlüğü, 1993.

5 Numaralı Mühimme Defteri (973/1565–1566). Edited by Hacı Osman Yıldırım. 2 vols. Ankara: T. C. Başbakanlık Devlet Arşivleri Genel Müdürlüğü, 1994.

6 Numaralı Mühimme Defteri (972/1564–1565). Edited by Hacı Osman Yıldırım. 3 vols. Ankara: T. C. Başbakanlık Devlet Arşivleri Genel Müdürlüğü, 1995.

7 Numaralı Mühimme Defteri (975–976/1567–1569). Edited by Murat Şener. 4 vols. Ankara: T. C. Başbakanlık Devlet Arşivleri Genel Müdürlüğü, 1998.

12 Numaralı Mühimme Defteri (978–979/1570–1572). Edited by İsmet Binark and Hacı Osman Yıldırım. 2 vols. Ankara: T. C. Başbakanlık Devlet Arşivleri Genel Müdürlüğü, 1996.

82 Numaralı Mühimme Defteri (1026–1027/1617–1618). Edited by Murat Şener and Hacı Osman Yıldırım. Ankara: T. C. Başbakanlık Devlet Arşivleri Genel Müdürlüğü, 2000.

83 Numaralı Mühimme Defteri (1036–1037/1626–1628). Edited by Hacı Osman Yıldırım. Ankara: T. C. Başbakanlık Devlet Arşivleri Genel Müdürlüğü, 2001.

85 Numaralı Mühimme Defteri (1040–1041 (1042)/1630–1631 (1632)). Edited by Murat Şener. Ankara: T. C. Başbakanlık Devlet Arşivleri Genel Müdürlüğü, 2002.

91 Numaralı Mühimme Defteri (H. 1056/M. 1646–1647). Edited by Uğur Ünal and Murat Cebecioğlu. Istanbul: T. C. Başbakanlık Devlet Arşivleri Genel Müdürlüğü, 2015.

Alberti, Tommaso. *Viaggio a Costantinopoli (1609–1621)*. Bologna: Commissione per i testi di lingua, 1969.

Âli, Mustafa bin Ahmet. *Gelibolulu Mustafa ʿÂlî ve Mevâʿıdüʾn-nefâis Fî ḳavâʿıdiʾl-mecâlis*. Edited by Mehmet Şeker. Ankara: Türk Tarih Kurumu Basımevi, 1997.

———. *The Ottoman Gentleman of the Sixteenth Century: Ali's Mevaʾiduʾn-nafaʾis Fi Kavaʾidiʾl-mecalis*. Translated by Douglas S. Brookes. Cambridge, MA: Department of Near Eastern Languages and Civilizations, Harvard University, 2003.

Anonymous. *A Translation of the Chapters CCLXXIII and CCLXXXVII of the Consolato Del Mare Relating to Prize Law*. London: W. Wilson, 1800.

Anonymous ("An Officer of the Grand Vizir"). *An Account of Monsieur De Quesne's Late Expedition at Chio: Together with the Negotiation of Monsieur Guilleragues, the French Ambassadour at the Port*. London: Richard Tonson and Jacob Tonson, 1683.

Argenti, Philip, ed. *Diplomatic Archive of Chios, 1577–1841*. Cambridge: Cambridge University Press, 1954.

Arvieux, Laurent d'. *Mémoires du Chevalier d'Arvieux . . . Contenant ses Voyages à Constantinople, dans l'Asie, La Syrie, La Palestine, l'Egypte, & Le Barbarie . . . recüeillis de ses Mémoires originaux, & mis en Ordre avec des refléxions*. Edited by Jean Baptiste Labat. 6 vols. Paris: C. J. B. Delespine, 1735.

Atsız, Buğra, ed.. *Das osmanische Reich um die Mitte des 17. Jahrhunderts: nach den Chroniken des Vecihi (1637–1660) und des Mehmed Halifa (1663–1660)*. Munich: R. Trofenik, 1977.

Aydın, M. Âkif., and Coşkun Yılmaz, eds. *İstanbul Kadı Sicilleri*. 40 vols. Istanbul: İSAM Yayınları, 2008–2011.

Azuni, Domenico Alberto. *The Maritime Law of Europe*. New York: G. Forman, 1806.
Baker, Thomas. *Piracy and Diplomacy in Seventeenth-Century North Africa: The Journal of Thomas Baker, English Consul in Tripoli, 1677–1685*. Edited by C. R. Pennell. Rutherford: Fairleigh Dickinson University Press, 1989.
Bargrave, Robert. *The Travel Diary of Robert Bargrave, 1647–1656*. Edited by Michael G. Brennan. London: Hakluyt Society, 1999.
Belin, François Alphonse. *Des capitulations et des traités de la France en Orient*. Paris: Challamel Ainé, 1870.
Bonnac, Jean Louis d'Usson marquis de. *Mémoire historique sur l'ambassade de France à Constantinople*. Paris: Societe d'histoire diplomat, 1894.
Brèves, François Savary de. *Articles du traicte faict en l'annee mil six cens quatre, entre Henri le Grand Roy de France, et de Navarre, et Sultan Amat Empereur des Turcs*. Paris: Paulin, 1615.
Calendar of State Papers and Manuscripts Relating to English Affairs, Existing in the Archives and Collections of Venice, and in Other Libraries of Northern Italy (abbreviated *CSP*). Vols. 8–38. London: H. M. Stationery Office, 1894–1940.
Çatalcalı Ali Efendi. *Fetava-yı Ali Efendi ma'an-Nükûl*. Istanbul: Matbaat el-Hac Muharrem Efendi el-Bosnavi, H. 1289 [1872].
Chalmers, George. *A Collection of Treaties between Great Britain and Other Powers*. London: J. Stockdale, 1790.
Chardin, Jean. *The Travels of Sir John Chardin into Persia and the East Indies*. London: Christopher Batemen, 1691.
Charrière, Ernest. *Négociations de la France dans le Levant; ou, Correspondances, mémoires et actes diplomatiques des ambassadeurs de France à Constantinople . . . à Venise, Raguse, Rome, Malte et Jérusalem, en Turquie, Perse, Géorgie, Crimée, Syrie, Égypte, etc., et dans les États de Tunis, d'Alger et de Maroc*. Paris: Imprimerie Nationale, 1860.
Contreras, Alonso de. *The Adventures of Captain Alonso de Contreras: A 17th-Century Journey*. Translated by Philip Dallas. New York: Paragon House, 1989.
Coxere, Edward. *Adventures by Sea of Edward Coxere: A Relation of the Several Adventures by Sea with the Dangers, Difficulties and Hardships I Met for Several Years*. Edited by E. H. W. Meyerstein. London: Oxford University Press, 1946.
Dallam, Thomas, and John Covel. *Early Voyages and Travels in the Levant: With Some Account of the Levant Company of Turkey Merchants*. London: Hakluyt Society, 1893.
Della Valle, Pietro. *Viaggi di Pietro della Valle, Il Pellegrino*. 3 vols. Brighton: G. Gancia, 1843.
Düzdağ, M. Ertuğrul, ed. *Barbaros Hayreddin Paşa'nın Hatıraları: Gazavat-ı Hayreddin*. Istanbul: Kaynak Yayınları, 1995.
———. *Seyhülislâm Ebussuud Efendi Fetvaları Işığında 16. Asır Türk Hayat*. Istanbul: Enderun Kitabevi, 1972.
Evliya Çelebi. *Evliya Çelebi Seyahatnâmesi: Topkapı Sarayı Kütüphanesi Bağdat 308 Numaralı Yazmanın Transkripsiyonu*. 10 vols. Istanbul: Yapı Kredi Yayınları, 1996–2007.

———. *Evliya Çelebi in Albania and Adjacent Regions: Kossovo, Montenegro, Ohrid*. Edited by Robert Dankoff and Robert Elsie. Leiden: Brill, 1999.

Evliya Çelebi, Robert Dankoff, and Sooyong Kim. *An Ottoman Traveller: Selections from the Book of Travels of Evliya Çelebi*. London: Eland, 2010.

Gédoyn, Louis. *Journal et correspondance de Gédoyn "Le turc," consul de France à Alep 1623–1625*. Edited by Auguste Boppe. Paris: Typographie Plon-Nourrit, 1909.

Gentili, Alberico. *De iure belli libri tres*. Edited and translated by John Carew Rolfe and Coleman Phillipson. Oxford: Clarendon, 1933.

———. *Hispanicae advocationis, libri dvo*. New York: Oxford University Press, 1921.

Grotius, Hugo. *De jure praedae commentarius. Commentary on the Law of Prize and Booty*. Oxford: Clarendon, 1950.

Guilleragues, Gabriel Joseph de Lavergne. *Correspondance*. Paris: Droz, 1976.

Ibn Abi Dinār, Muḥammad ibn Abi al-Qāsim. *al-Mu'nis fī akhbār Ifrīqīyah wa-Tūnis*. Tunis: Maṭba'at al-Dawlah al-Tūnisiyah, 1869.

İz, Fahir. "Macuncuzade Mustafa'nın Malta Anıları: Sergüzeşt-i Esir-i Malta." In *Türk Dili Araştırmaları Yıllığı*, 69–121. Ankara: Türk Dil Kurumu, 1971.

———. "Makale-i Zindancı Mahmud Kapudan." *Türkiyat Mecmuası* 14 (1965): 111–150.

Kâtib Çelebi. *Deniz savaşları hakkında büyüklere armağan/Tuhfetü'l-kibar fi esfari'l-bihar*. Istanbul: Kabalcı Yayınevi, 2007.

———. *Fezleketü Akvâli'l-Ahyâr Fî Ilmi't-Târîh Ve'l-Ahbâr (Fezleketü't-Tevârîh): Târîhu Mülûki Âli 'Osmân*. Ankara: Türk Tarih Kurumu Basımevi, 2009.

———. *The Gift to the Great Ones on Naval Campaigns (Tuhfetü'l-kibar fi esfari'l-bihar)*. Edited by İdris Bostan. Ankara: Prime Ministry Undersecretariat for Maritime Affairs, 2008.

Kolovos, Elias, ed. *A Database of the Ottoman Documents in the Kaireios Library of the Island of Andros: Short Summaries, Transliterations, Facsimiles*. http://androsdocs.ims.forth.gr/

Kuran, Timur, ed. *Mahkeme Kayıtları Işığında 17. Yüzyıl İstanbul'unda Sosyo-ekonomik Yaşam (Social and Economic Life in Seventeenth-Century Istanbul: Glimpses from Court Records)*. Istanbul: Türkiye İş Bankası, 2010.

Lello, Henry. *The Report of Lello Third English Ambassador to the Sublime Porte*. Ankara: Türk Tarih Kurumu Basımevi, 1952.

Macuncuzade, Mustafa Efendi. *Malta Esirleri: Baz Keşt-i Hakiri-i Malta, Sergüzeşt-i Esir-i Malta*. Edited by Cemil Çiftçi. Istanbul: Kitabevi, 1996.

Molloy, Charles. *De Jure Maritimo et Navali or a Treatise of Affaires Maritime and of Commerce: In Three Books*. London: John Bellinger, 1682.

Naima, Mustafa. *Târih-i Na'îmâ: Ravzatü'l-Hüseyn Fî Hulâsati Ahbâri'l-Hâfikayn*. Edited by Mehmet İpşirli. 4 vols. Ankara: Türk Tarih Kurumu Basımevi, 2007.

Peçevî İbrahim Efendi. *Peçevi Tarihi*. Edited by Bekir Sıtkı Baykal. 3 vols. Ankara: Kültür Bakanlığı Yayınları, 1999.

Pedani Fabris, Maria Pia, ed. *Relazioni di ambasciatori veneti al Senato, vol. XIV: Costantinopoli relazioni inedite (1512–1789)*. Padua: Ausilio, 1996.

Randolph, Bernard. *The Present State of the Islands in the Archipelago, or Arches, Seas of Constantinople and Gulph of Smyrna with the Islands of Candia and Rhodes*. Oxford: Theater, 1687.

Raşid Mehmed Efendi. *Târih-i Râşid ve Zeyli*. Edited by Abdülkadir Özcan, Yunus Oğur, Baki Çakır, and Ahmet Zeki İzgöer. 5 vols. Istanbul: Vefa, 2013.

Roberts, Mr. "Mr. Roberts's Adventures among the Corsairs of the Levant; His Account of Their Way of Living; Description of the Archipelago Islands, Taking of Scio, &c." In *A Collection of Original Voyages (1699): A Facsimile Reproduction*, edited by William Hacke. Delmar, NY: Facsimiles & Reprints, 1993.

Roe, Thomas. *The Negotiations of Sir Thomas Roe in His Embassy to the Ottoman Porte, from the Year 1621 to 1628 Inclusive*. London: Samuel Richardson, 1740.

Rycaut, Paul. *The History of the Turkish Empire from the Year 1623 to the Year 1677*. London: J.D., 1680.

———. *The Present State of the Ottoman Empire*. London: John Starkey and Henry Brome, 1670.

Salvago, Giovanni Battista. *"Africa overo Barbaria": relazione al doge di Venezia sulle reggenze di Algeri e di Tunisi del dragomanno Gio. Batta Salvago, 1625*. Edited by Alberto Sacerdoti. Padua: A. Milani, 1937.

Sanderson, John. *The Travels of John Sanderson in the Levant, 1584–1602*. Edited by William Foster. London: Hakluyt Society, 1931.

Sarı Mehmed Paşa. *Zübde-i Vekayiât: Tahlil ve Metin (1066–1116/1656–1704)*. Edited by Abdülkadir Özcan. Ankara: Türk Tarih Kurumu Basımevi, 1995.

Selânikî Mustafa Efendi. *Tarih-i Selânikî*. Edited by Mehmet İpşirli. 2 vols. Ankara: Türk Tarih Kurumu Basımevi, 1999.

Selden, John. *Of the Dominion or Ownership of the Sea*. London: William Du-Gard, 1652.

Solakzade, Mehmed Hemdemî Çelebi. *Solak-zâde Tarihi*. Edited by Vahid Çabuk. 2 vols. Ankara: Kültür Bakanlığı Yayınları, 1989.

Sosa, Antonio de, María Antonia Garcés, and Diana de Armas Wilson. *An Early Modern Dialogue with Islam: Antonio de Sosa's Topography of Algiers (1612)*. South Bend, IN: University of Notre Dame Press, 2011.

Testa, Baron I. de. *Recueil des traités de la Porte ottomane avec les puissances étrangères depuis le premier traité conclu, en 1536, entre Suléyman I et François I jusqu'à nos jours*. Paris: Amyot, 1864.

Thévenot, Jean de. *The Travels of Monsieur De Thevenot into the Levant: In Three Parts. Turkey*. Translated by Archibald Lovell. London: Faithorne, 1687.

Tournefort, Joseph Pitton de. *A Voyage into the Levant . . . Containing the Ancient and Modern State of the Islands of the Archipelago; as Also of Constantinople, the Coasts of the Black Sea, Armenia, Georgia, the Frontiers of Persia, and Asia Minor*. 2 vols. London: D. Midwinter, 1741.

Visé, Jean Donneau de. *Ambassades de M. le Comte de Guilleragues et de M. Girardin auprès du Grand Seigneur. Avec plusieurs pièces curieuses, tirées de Mémoires de tous les Ambassadeurs de France à la Porte*. Paris: Thomas Amaulry, 1688.

Wansleben, Johann Michael. *The Present State of Egypt, or a New Relation of a Late Voyage into That Kingdom Performed in the Years 1672 and 1673 by F. Vansleb*. London: R.E., 1678.
Webbe, Edward. *Edward Webbe, Chief Master Gunner, His Trauailes (1590)*. Edited by Edward Arber. London: A. Constable, 1895.
Wheler, George. *Journey into Greece in Six Books*. London: Cademan, 1682.
Zayānī, Abū al-Qāsim ibn Aḥmad, and ʻAbd al-Karīm Fīlālī. *al-Tarjumānah al-kubrā fī akhbār al-maʻmūr barran wa-baḥran*. Rabāṭ: Dār Nashr al-Maʻrifah, 1991.

Secondary Sources

Abun-Nasr, Jamil M. "The Beylicate in Seventeenth-Century Tunisia." *International Journal of Middle East Studies* 6, no. 1 (1975): 70–93.
———. *A History of the Maghrib in the Islamic Period*. Cambridge: Cambridge University Press, 1987.
———. "The Tunisian State in the Eighteenth Century." *Revue de l'Occident musulman et de la Méditerranée* 33, no. 1 (1982): 33–66.
Adanır, Fikret. "Heiduckentum und osmanische Herrschaft: Sozialgeschichtliche Aspekte der Diskussion um das frühneuzeitliche Räuberwesen in Südosteuropa." *Südost-Forschungen* 41 (1982): 43–116.
Adiyeke, Nükhet, and Nuri Adiyeke. "Newly Discovered in Turkish Archives: Kadi Registers and Other Documents on Crete." *Turcica* 32 (2000): 447–463.
Akgündüz, Ahmet. *Şer'iye Sicilleri: Mahiyeti, Toplu Kataloğu ve Seçme Hükümler*. Istanbul: Türk Dünyası Araştırmaları Vakfı, 1988.
al-Qattan, Najwa. "Dhimmīs in the Muslim Court: Legal Autonomy and Religious Discrimination." *International Journal of Middle East Studies* 31, no. 3 (1999): 429–444.
———. "Litigants and Neighbors: The Communal Topography of Ottoman Damascus." *Comparative Studies in Society and History* 44, no. 3 (2002): 511–533.
Altunsu, Abdülkadir. *Osmanli Şeyhülislâmlari*. Ankara: Ayyıldız Matbaası, 1972.
Amirell, Stefan Eklöf, and Leos Müller, eds. *Persistent Piracy: Maritime Violence and State-Formation in Global Historical Perspective*. Houndsmill: Palgrave Macmillan, 2014.
Anderson, R. C. *Naval Wars in the Levant, 1559–1853*. Princeton, NJ: Princeton University Press, 1952.
Anderson, Sonia P. *An English Consul in Turkey: Paul Rycaut at Smyrna, 1667–1678*. Oxford: Clarendon, 1989.
Angiolini, Franco. *I cavalieri e il principe: l'ordine di Santo Stefano e la società toscana in età moderna*. Florence: Edifir, 1996.
———. "Slaves and Slavery in Early Modern Tuscany (1500–1700)." *Italian History and Culture* 3 (1997): 66–88.
Arbel, Benjamin. "Maritime Trade and International Relations in the Sixteenth-Century Mediterranean: The Case of the Ship Girarda (1575–1581)." In *Living in the Ottoman Ecumenical Community*, edited by Markus Koller and Vera Costantini, 389–408. Leiden: Brill, 2008.

Arı, Bülent. "Akdeniz'de Korsanlık ve Osmanlı Deniz Hukuku." In *Türkler ve Deniz*, edited by Özlem Kumrular, 265–318. Istanbul: Kitabevi, 2007.

———. "Early Ottoman-Dutch Political and Commercial Relations after 1612 Capitulations." *Bulgarian Historical Review* 3–4 (2004): 116–144.

Ashtor, Eliyahu. *Levant Trade in the Later Middle Ages*. Princeton, NJ: Princeton University Press, 1983.

Aslanian, Sebouh. "Social Capital, Trust and the Role of Networks in Julfan Trade: Informal and Semi-Formal Institutions at Work." *Journal of Global History* 1, no. 3 (2006): 383–402.

Atcil, Abdurrahman. "Procedure in the Ottoman Court and the Duties of the Kadis." MA thesis, Bilkent University, 2002.

———. "The Route to the Top in the Ottoman Ilmiye Hierarchy of the Sixteenth Century." *Bulletin of the School of Oriental and African Studies* 72, no. 3 (2009): 489–512.

Aydın, Yusuf Alperen. "The Ottoman Security Parameters for the Aegean Sea (Archipelago) and the Levant in the 18th Century." *Osmanlı Araştırmaları/Journal of Ottoman Studies* 45 (2015): 161–184.

Bachrouch, Taoufik. *Formation social barbaresque et pouvoir à Tunis au XVIIe siècle*. Tunis: Université de Tunis, 1977.

Bamford, Paul Walden. *Fighting Ships and Prisons: The Mediterranean Galleys of France in the Age of Louis XIV*. Minneapolis: University of Minnesota Press, 1973.

Barkan, Ömer Lutfi. "La 'Méditerranée' de Fernand Braudel vue d'Istamboul." *Annales. Histoire, Sciences Sociales* 9, no. 2 (1954): 189–200.

Barkan, Ömer Lutfi, and Justin McCarthy. "The Price Revolution of the Sixteenth Century: A Turning Point in the Economic History of the Near East." *International Journal of Middle East Studies* 6, no. 1 (1975): 3–28.

Barkey, Karen. *Bandits and Bureaucrats: The Ottoman Route to State Centralization*. Ithaca, NY: Cornell University Press, 1994.

Barnby, H. "The Algerian Attack on Baltimore 1631." *Mariner's Mirror* 56 (1970): 27–31.

Bayraktutan, Lütfi. *Şeyhülislâm Yahya: Hayatı, Edebî Kişiliği, Sanatı, Eserleri ve Divanından Seçmeler*. Ankara: Kültür Bakanlığı Yayınları, 1990.

Ben-Naeh, Yaron. "Blond, Tall, with Honey Colored Eyes: Jewish Ownership of Slaves in the Ottoman Empire." *Jewish History* 20, no. 3 (2006): 315–332.

Bennassar, Bartolomé, and Lucile Bennassar. *Les chrétiens d'Allah: L'histoire extraordinaire des renégats, XVIe et XVIIe siècles*. Paris: Perrin, 1989.

Benton, Lauren. "Beyond Legal Pluralism: Towards a New Approach to Law in the Informal Sector." *Social & Legal Studies* 3, no. 2 (1994): 223–242.

———. "Historical Perspectives on Legal Pluralism." *Hague Journal on the Rule of Law* 3, no. 1 (2011): 57–69.

———. *Law and Colonial Cultures: Legal Regimes in World History, 1400–1900*. New York: Cambridge University Press, 2002.

———. "Legal Spaces of Empire: Piracy and the Origins of Ocean Regionalism." *Comparative Studies in Society and History* 47, no. 4 (2005): 700–724.

———. "Legalities of the Sea in Gentili's Hispanica Advocatio." In *The Roman Foundations of the Law of Nations: Alberico Gentili and the Justice of Empire*, edited by Benedict Kingsbury and Benjamin Straumann, 269–282. New York: Oxford University Press, 2010.

———. *A Search for Sovereignty: Law and Geography in European Empires, 1400–1900*. New York: Cambridge University Press, 2010.

———. "Toward a New Legal History of Piracy: Maritime Legalities and the Myth of Universal Jurisdiction." *International Journal of Maritime History* 23, no. 1 (2011): 225–240.

Berckman, Evelyn. *Victims of Piracy: The Admiralty Court, 1575–1678*. London: Hamilton, 1979.

Berridge, Geoff R. *Notes on the Origins of the Diplomatic Corps: Constantinople in the 1620s*. Clingendael: Netherlands Institute of International Relations, 2004.

Biegman, Nicolaas H. *The Turco-Ragusan Relationship. According to the Firmāns of Murād III (1575–1595) Extant in the State Archives of Dubrovnik*. The Hague: Mouton, 1967.

Bligh, E. W. *Sir Kenelm Digby and His Venetia*. London: S. Low, Marston, 1932.

Blondy, Alain. "L'ordre de Saint-Jean et l'essor economique de Malte (1530–1798)." *Revue du monde musulman et de la Méditerranée* 71, no. 1 (1994): 75–90.

Bono, Salvatore. "Achat d'esclaves turcs pour les galères pontificales (XVIe–XVIIe siècles)." *Revue de l'Occident musulman et de la Méditerranée* 39, no. 2 (1985): 79–92.

———. *Corsari nel Mediterraneo: cristiani e musulmani fra guerra, schiavitù e commercio*. Milan: A. Mondadori, 1993.

———. *I corsari barbareschi*. Turin: Edizion RAI Radiotelevisione Italiana, 1964.

———. *Lumi e corsari: Europa e Maghreb nel Settecento*. Perugia: Morlacchi, 2005.

———. *Schiavi musulmani nell'Italia moderna: galeotti, vu' Cumpra,' domestici*. Naples: Edizioni scientifiche italiane, 1999.

Borromeo, Elisabetta. *Voyageurs occidentaux dans l'Empire ottoman (1600–1644)*. 2 vols. Paris: Maisonneuve & Larose, 2007.

Bostan, İdris. *Adriyatik'te Korsanlık: Osmanlılar, Uskoklar, Venedikliler, 1575–1620*. Istanbul: Timaş, 2009.

———. *Beylikten Imparatorluğa Osmanlı Denizciliği*. Istanbul: Kitap Yayınevi, 2006.

———. "Kadırga'dan Kalyon'a (XVII. Yüzyılın İkinci Yarısında Osmanlı Gemi Teknolojisi'nin Değişimi)." *Osmanlı Araştırmaları/Journal of Ottoman Studies*, no. 24 (2004): 65–86.

———. *Osmanlı Bahriye Teskilâtı: XVII. Yüzyılda Tersâne-i Âmire*. Ankara: Türk Tarih Kurumu Basımevi, 1992.

Bosworth, C. E. *An Intrepid Scot: William Lithgow of Lanark's Travels in the Ottoman Lands, North Africa and Central Europe, 1609–21*. London: Ashgate, 2006.

Bracewell, Catherine Wendy. *The Uskoks of Senj: Piracy, Banditry, and Holy War in the Sixteenth-Century Adriatic*. Ithaca, NY: Cornell University Press, 1992.

Braude, Benjamin. "Venture and Faith in the Commercial Life of the Ottoman Balkans, 1500–1650." *International History Review* 7, no. 4 (1985): 519–542.

Braudel, Fernand. *The Mediterranean and the Mediterranean World in the Age of Philip II*. Translated by Sian Reynolds. 2 vols. New York: Harper, 1972.

Brogini, Anne. "L'esclavage au quotidien à Malte au XVIe siècle." *Cahiers de la Méditerranée* 65 (2002): 137–158.

———. "Une activité sous contrôle: l'esclavage à Malte à l'époque modern." *Cahiers de la Méditerranée* 87 (2013): 49–61.

———. *Malte, frontière de chrétienté (1530–1670)*. Rome: École française de Rome, 2005.

Brummett, Palmira. "Competition and Coincidence: Venetian Trading Interests and Ottoman Expansion in the Early Sixteenth-Century Levant." *New Perspectives on Turkey* 6 (1991): 29–52.

———. "Foreign Policy, Naval Strategy, and the Defence of the Ottoman Empire in the Early Sixteenth Century." *International History Review* 11, no. 4 (1989): 613–627.

———. *Mapping the Ottomans: Sovereignty, Territory, and Identity in the Early Modern Mediterranean*. New York: Cambridge University Press, 2015.

———. *Ottoman Seapower and Levantine Diplomacy in the Age of Discovery*. Albany: State University of New York Press, 1994.

———. "The Ottomans as a World Power: What We Don't Know about Ottoman Sea-Power." *Oriente Moderno* 20, no. 1 (2001): 1–21.

———. "The Overrated Adversary: Rhodes and Ottoman Naval Power." *Historical Journal* 36, no. 3 (1993): 517–541.

Burak, Guy. *The Second Formation of Islamic Law: The Hanafi School in the Early Modern Ottoman Empire*. New York: Cambridge University Press, 2015.

Calafat, Guillaume. "Les interprètes de la diplomatie en Méditerranée. Traiter à Alger (1670–1680)." In *Les musulmans dans l'histoire de l'Europe, Tome II. Passages et contacts en Méditerranée*, edited by Wolfgang Kaiser and Jocelyne Dakhlia, 371–410. Paris: Albin Michel, 2011.

———. "Ottoman North Africa and Ius Publicum Europaeum: The Case of the Treaties of Peace and Trade (1600–1750)." In *War, Trade and Neutrality: Europe and the Mediterranean in the Seventeenth and Eighteenth Centuries*, edited by Antonella Alimento, 171–188. Milan: Franco Angeli, 2011.

Calafat, Guillaume, and Cesare Santus. "Les avatars du 'Turc.' Esclaves et commerçants musulmans à Livourne (1600–1750)." In *Les musulmans dans l'histoire de l'Europe, Tome I: Une intégration invisible*, edited by Wolfgang Kaiser and Jocelyne Dakhlia, 471–522. Paris: Albin Michel, 2011.

Canbakal, Hülya. "Vows as Contract in Ottoman Public Life (17th–18th Centuries)." *Islamic Law and Society* 18, no. 1 (2011): 85–115.

Casale, Giancarlo. "The Ottoman Administration of the Spice Trade in the Sixteenth-Century Red Sea and Persian Gulf." *Journal of the Economic and Social History of the Orient* 49, no. 2 (2006): 170–198.

Cassar, Paul. "The Maltese Corsairs and the Order of St. John of Jerusalem." *Catholic Historical Review* 46, no. 2 (1960): 137–156.

Cavaliero, Roderick. "The Decline of the Maltese Corso in the XVIIIth Century." *Melita Historica* 2, no. 4 (1959): 224–238.

———. *The Last of the Crusaders: The Knights of St. John and Malta in the Eighteenth Century*. London: I. B. Tauris, 2009.

Cezar, Mustafa. *Osmanlı Tarihinde Levendler*. Istanbul: Çelikcilt Matbaası, 1965.

Christ, Georg. *Masked Cooperation with the Infidel? The Venetian Commercial Privileges, Political Power, and Legal Culture in Mamlûk Egypt*. Leiden: Brill, 2006.

———. *Trading Conflicts: Venetian Merchants and Mamluk Officials in Late Medieval Alexandria*. Leiden: Brill, 2012.

Çizakça, Murat. *A Comparative Evolution of Business Partnerships: The Islamic World and Europe, with Specific Reference to the Ottoman Archives*. Leiden: Brill, 1996.

Cohen, Amnon. "Ottoman Rule and the Re-Emergence of the Coast of Palestine (17th–18th Centuries)." *Revue de l'Occident musulman et de la Méditerranée* 39, no. 1 (1985): 163–175.

Colley, Linda. *Captives: Britain, Empire and the World, 1600–1850*. London: Jonathan Cape, 2002.

Cvetkova, Bistra. "The Bulgarian Haiduk Movement in the 15th–18th Centuries." In *East Central European Society and War in the Pre-Revolutionary Eighteenth Century*, edited by Gunther Rothenberg, 301–338. Boulder: University of Colorado Press, 1982.

Dakhlia, Jocelyne. *Lingua franca*. Arles: Actes sud, 2008.

Dankoff, Robert. *An Ottoman Mentality: The World of Evliya Çelebi*. Leiden: Brill, 2004.

Darling, Linda. "Contested Territory: Ottoman Holy War in Comparative Context." *Studia Islamica* 91 (2000): 133–163.

———. "The Mediterranean as a Borderland." *Review of Middle East Studies* 46, no. 1 (2012): 54–63.

———. *Revenue-Raising and Legitimacy: Tax Collection and Finance Administration in the Ottoman Empire, 1560–1660*. Leiden: Brill, 1996.

Dávid, Geza. "The Muhimme Defteri as a Source for Ottoman-Habsburg Rivalry in the Sixteenth Century." *Archivum Ottomanicum* 20 (2002): 167–209.

Dávid, Geza, and Pál Fodor, eds. *Ransom Slavery along the Ottoman Borders: Early Fifteenth-Early Eighteenth Centuries*. Leiden: Brill, 2007.

Davis, Robert C. *Christian Slaves, Muslim Masters: White Slavery in the Mediterranean, the Barbary Coast, and Italy, 1500–1800*. Houndmills, UK: Palgrave Macmillan, 2003.

———. "Counting European Slaves on the Barbary Coast." *Past and Present* 172 (2001): 87–124.

———. "The Geography of Slaving in the Early Modern Mediterranean, 1500–1800." *Journal of Medieval and Early Modern Studies* 37, no. 1 (2007): 57–74.

———. *Holy War and Human Bondage: Tales of Christian-Muslim Slavery in the Early-Modern Mediterranean.* Santa Barbara, CA: Praeger/ABC-CLIO, 2009.

de Groot, Alexander.H. "The Historical Development of the Capitulatory Regime in the Ottoman Middle East from the Fifteenth to the Nineteenth Centuries." In *The Ottoman Capitulations: Text and Context*, edited by Maurits van den Boogert and Kate Fleet, 575–604. Rome: Istituto per l'Oriente C. A. Nallino, 2003.

———. *The Ottoman Empire and the Dutch Republic: A History of the Earliest Diplomatic Relations, 1610–1630.* Leiden: Nederlands Historisch-Archaeologisch Instituut, 1978.

———. "Ottoman North Africa and the Dutch Republic in the Seventeenth and Eighteenth Centuries." *Revue de l'Occident musulman et de la Méditerranée* 39, no. 1 (1985): 131–147.

———. "A Seventeenth Century Ottoman Statesman 'Kayseriyeli' Khalil Pasha (1565–1629) and His Policy towards European Powers." *Islam* 54 (1977): 305–308.

Demetriades, Vassilis. "Piracy and Mount Athos." In *The Kapudan Pasha: His Office and His Domain: Halcyon Days in Crete IV, a Symposium Held in Rethymnon, 7–9 January 2000*, edited by Elizabeth Zachariadou, 356. Rethymnon: University of Crete Press, 2002.

Dursteler, Eric. "The Bailo in Constantinople: Crisis and Career in Venice's Early Modern Diplomatic Corps." *Mediterranean Historical Review* 16, no. 2 (2001): 1–30.

———. "Commerce and Coexistence: Veneto-Ottoman Trade in the Early Modern Era." *Turcica* 34 (2002): 105–133.

———. *Renegade Women: Gender, Identity, and Boundaries in the Early Modern Mediterranean.* Baltimore, MD: Johns Hopkins University Press, 2011.

———. "Speaking in Tongues: Language and Communication in the Early Modern Mediterranean." *Past and Present* 217, no. 1 (2012): 47–77.

———. *Venetians in Constantinople: Nation, Identity and Coexistence in the Early Modern Mediterranean.* Baltimore, MD: Johns Hopkins University Press, 2006.

Earle, Peter. *Corsairs of Malta and Barbary.* London: Sidgwick & Jackson, 1970.

Ekin, D. *The Stolen Village: Baltimore and the Barbary Pirates.* Dublin: O'Brien Dublin, 2006.

Eldem, Edhem. "Capitulations and Western Trade." In *The Cambridge History of Turkey. Vol. 3: The Later Ottoman Empire, 1603–1839*, edited by Suraiya Faroqhi, 283–335. Cambridge: Cambridge University Press, 2006.

———. "Strangers in Their Own Seas? The Ottomans in the Eastern Mediterranean Basin in the Second Half of the Eighteenth Century." *Studi Settecenteschi* 29–30 (2014): 25–58.

Eldem, Edhem, Daniel Goffman, and Bruce Masters. *The Ottoman City between East and West: Aleppo, Izmir, and Istanbul.* Cambridge: Cambridge University Press, 2005.

Engels, Marie-Christine. *Merchants, Interlopers, Seamen and Corsairs: The "Flemish" Community in Livorno and Genoa (1615–1635)*. Hilversum: Uitgeverij Verloren, 1997.

Erdbrink, G. R. Bosscha. *At the Threshold of Felicity: Ottoman-Dutch Relations during the Embassy of Cornelis Calkoen at the Sublime Porte, 1726–1744*. Ankara: Türk Tarih Kurumu Basemevi, 1975.

Erdem, Hakan. *Slavery in the Ottoman Empire and Its Demise, 1800–1909*. New York: Macmillan, 1996.

Ergene, Boğaç A. "Document Use in Ottoman Courts of Law: Observations from the Sicils of Çankiri and Kastamonu." *Turcica* 37 (2005): 83–111.

———. "Evidence in Ottoman Courts: Oral and Written Documentation in Early-Modern Courts of Islamic Law." *Journal of the American Oriental Society* 124, no. 3 (2004): 471–491.

———. *Local Court, Provincial Society and Justice in the Ottoman Empire: Legal Practice and Dispute Resolution in Çankırı and Kastamonu (1652–1744)*. Leiden: Brill, 2003.

———. "On Ottoman Justice: Interpretations in Conflict (1600–1800)." *Islamic Law and Society* 8 (2001): 52–87.

———. "Pursuing Justice in an Islamic Context: Dispute Resolution in Ottoman Courts of Law." *Political and Legal Anthropology Review* 27 (2004): 51–71.

———. "Why Did Ummu Gulsum Go to Court? Ottoman Legal Practice between History and Anthropology." *Islamic Law and Society* 17 (2010): 215–244.

Ezzahidi, Malika. "Le rachat des captifs musulmans à Malte en 1782, d'après le récit de voyage d'Ibn Uthmân Al-Meknassî." *Cahiers de la Méditerranée* 87 (2013): 221–228.

Fabris, Antonio. "Un caso di pirateria veneziana: La cattura della galea del bey di Gerba (21 Ottobre 1584)." *Quaderni di Studi Arabi* 8 (1990): 91–112.

Faroqhi, Suraiya. "Coffee and Spices: Official Ottoman Reactions to Egyptian Trade in the Later Sixteenth Century." *Wiener Zeitschrift für die Kunde des Morgenlandes* 76 (1986): 87–93.

———. *Making a Living in the Ottoman Lands 1480 to 1820*. Istanbul: Gorgias Press, 1995.

———. *The Ottoman Empire and the World around It*. London: I. B. Tauris, 2004.

———. "Ottoman Views on Corsairs and Piracy in the Adriatic." In *The Kapudan Pasha: His Office and His Domain: Halcyon Days in Crete IV, a Symposium Held in Rethymnon, 7–9 January 2000*, edited by Elizabeth Zachariadou, 357–371. Rethymnon: University of Crete Press, 2002.

———. "Räuber, Rebellen und Obrigkeit im osmanischen Anatolien." *Periplus* 3 (1993): 31–46.

———. "Social Mobility among the Ottoman Ulema in the Late Sixteenth Century." *International Journal of Middle East Studies* 4, no. 2 (1973): 204–218.

———. *Towns and Townsmen in Ottoman Anatolia: Trade, Crafts, and Food Production in an Urban Setting, 1520–1650*. Cambridge: Cambridge University Press, 1984.

———. "The Venetian Presence in the Ottoman Empire (1600–1630)." *Journal of European Economic History* 22 (1986): 345–384.

Finkel, Caroline. *Osman's Dream*. New York: Basic Books, 2006.

Fischer, Lucia Frattarelli. "Il bagno delle galere in 'terra cristiana.' Schiavi a Livorno fra Cinque e Seicento." *Nuovi Studi Livornesi* 8 (2000): 69–94.

Fisher, Alan. "Chattel Slavery in the Ottoman Empire." *Slavery & Abolition* 1, no. 1 (1980): 25–45.

———. "The Sale of Slaves in the Ottoman Empire: Markets and State Taxes on Slave Sales." *Bogazici Universitesi Dergisi* 6 (1978): 149–174.

———. "Studies in Ottoman Slavery and Slave Trade, II: Manumission." *Journal of Turkish Studies* 4 (1980): 49–56.

Fisher, Godfrey. *Barbary Legend: War, Trade, and Piracy in North Africa, 1415–1830*. Oxford: Clarendon, 1957.

Fleischer, Cornell H. *Bureaucrat and Intellectual in the Ottoman Empire: The Historian Mustafa Ali (1541–1600)*. Princeton, NJ: Princeton University Press, 1986.

Fodor, Pál. "Between Two Continental Wars: The Ottoman Naval Preparations in 1590–1592." In *In Quest of the Golden Apple: Imperial Ideology, Politics, and Military Administration in the Ottoman Empire*, 171–190. Istanbul: Isis Press, 2000.

———. "The Grand Vizieral *Telhis* a Study in the Ottoman Central Administration 1566–1656." *Archivum Ottomanicum* 15 (1997): 137–188.

———. "Piracy, Ransom Slavery and Trade: French Participation in the Liberation of Ottoman Slaves from Malta during the 1620s." *Turcica* 33 (2001): 119–134.

———. "Sultan, Imperial Council, Grand Vizier: Changes in the Ottoman Ruling Elite and the Formation of the Grand Vizieral *Telhis*." *Acta Orientalia Academiae Scientiarum Hungaricae* 47 (1994): 67–85.

Folayan, Kola. *Tripoli during the Reign of Yusuf Pasha Qaramanli*. Ile-Ife, Nigeria: University of Ife Press, 1979.

Fontenay, Michel. "Corsaires de la foi ou rentiers du sol? Les chevaliers de Malte dans le 'corso' méditerranéen au XVIIe siècle." *Revue d'histoire moderne et contemporaine (1954–)* 35, no. 3 (1988): 361–384.

———. "Esclaves et/ou captifs: Préciser les concepts." In *Le commerce des captifs: Les intermédiaires dans l'échange et le rachat des prisonniers en Méditerranée, XVe-XVIIIe siècle*, edited by Wolfgang Kaiser, 15–24. Rome: École française de Rome, 2008.

———. "Il mercato maltese degli schiavi al tempo dei Cavalieri di San Giovanni (1530–1798)." *Quaderni Storici* 36, no. 2 (2001): 391–414.

———. "Interlope et violence dans l'économie d'échanges: L'exemple des eaux grecques de l'Empire ottoman aux XVIe et XVIIe siècle." In *El Comerç alternatiu: corsarisme i contraban: SS. XV–XVIII*, edited by Gonçal López Nadal, 279–289. Palma de Mallorca: Institut d'Estudis Baleàrics, 1990.

———. *La Méditerranée entre la croix et le croissant: Navigation, commerce, course et piraterie, XVIe–XIXe siècle*. Paris: Classiques Garnier, 2010.

———. "La place de la course dans l'économie portuaire: L'exemple de Malte et des ports barbaresques." *Annales. Économies, Sociétés, Civilisations* 43, no. 6 (1988): 1321–1347.

———. "L'Empire ottoman et le risque corsaire au XVIIe siècle." *Revue d'histoire moderne et contemporaine (1954–)* 32, no. 2 (1985): 185–208.

———. "Les missions des galères de Malte 1530–1798." In *Guerre et commerce en Méditerranée, IXe–XIXe siècles (Colloque De Toulon, 1987)*, edited by Michel Vergé-Franceschi, 103–122. Paris: Veyrier, 1991.

———. "Routes et modalités du commerce des esclaves dans la Méditerranée des temps modernes (XVIe, XVIIe et XVIIIe Siècles)." *Revue historique* 4 (2006): 813–830.

Freller, T. "'Adversus Infideles': Some Notes on the Cavalier's Tour, the Fleet of the Order of St. John, and the Maltese Corsairs." *Journal of Early Modern History* 3, no. 4 (2000): 405–430.

Friedman, Ellen G. "Christian Captives at 'Hard Labor' in Algiers, 16th–18th Centuries." *International Journal of African Historical Studies* 13, no. 4 (1980): 616–632.

———. "North African Piracy on the Coasts of Spain in the Seventeenth Century: A New Perspective on the Expulsion of the Moriscos." *International History Review* 1, no. 1 (1979): 1–16.

———. *Spanish Captives in North Africa in the Early Modern Age*. Madison: University of Wisconsin Press, 1983.

Fuchs, Barbara. "Faithless Empires: Pirates, Renegadoes, and the English Nation." *ELH* 67, no. 1 (2000): 45–69.

Fuess, Albrecht. "Rotting Ships and Razed Harbors: The Naval Policy of the Mamluks." *Mamluk Studies Review* 5 (2001): 45–71.

Fusaro, Maria. "After Braudel: A Reassessment of Mediterranean History between the Northern Invasion and the Caravane Maritime." In *Trade and Cultural Exchange in the Early Modern Mediterranean: Braudel's Maritime Legacy*, edited by Maria Fusaro, Colin Heywood, and Mohamed-Salah Omri, 1–22. London: I. B. Tauris, 2010.

———. "Coping with Transition: Greek Merchants and Shipowners between Venice and England in the Late Sixteenth Century." In *Diaspora Entrepreneurial Networks. Four Centuries of History*, edited by Ina Baghdiantz McCabe, Gelina Harlaftis, and Ioanna Pepelasis Minoglou, 95–123. New York: Berg, 2005.

García-Arenal, Mercedes. *A Man of Three Worlds: Samuel Pallache, a Moroccan Jew in Catholic and Protestant Europe*. Baltimore, MD: Johns Hopkins University Press, 2003.

Gelder, Maartje van. "The Republic's Renegades: Dutch Converts to Islam in Seventeenth-Century Diplomatic Relations with North Africa." *Journal of Early Modern History* 19, nos. 2–3 (2015): 175–198.

Gerber, Ḥaim. *Islamic Law and Culture: 1600–1840*. Leiden: Brill, 1999.

———. "The Muslim Law of Partnerships in Ottoman Court Records." *Studia Islamica* 53 (1981): 109–119.

———. "Sharia, Kanun and Custom in the Ottoman Law: The Court Records of 17th-Century Bursa." *International Journal of Turkish Studies* 2, no. 1 (1981): 131–147.

———. *State, Society, and Law in Islam: Ottoman Law in Comparative Perspective.* Albany: State University of New York Press, 1994.

Ghobrial, John-Paul. *The Whispers of Cities: Information Flows in Istanbul, London, and Paris in the Age of William Trumbull.* Oxford: Oxford University Press, 2014.

Ginio, Eyal. "The Administration of Criminal Justice in Ottoman Selânik (Salonica) during the Eighteenth Century." *Turcica* 30 (1998): 185–209.

———. "Perceiving French Presence in the Levant: French Subjects in the Sicil of 18th Century Ottoman Salonica." *Südost-Forschungen* 65–66 (2006): 137–164.

———. "Piracy and Redemption in the Aegean Sea during the First Half of the Eighteenth Century." *Turcica* 33 (2001): 135–147.

———. "When Coffee Brought about Wealth and Prestige: The Impact of Egyptian Trade on Salonica." *Oriente Moderno* 86, no. 1 (2006): 93–107.

Goffman, Daniel. *Britons in the Ottoman Empire during the English Civil Wars, 1642–1660.* Seattle: University of Washington Press, 1998.

———. *Izmir and the Levantine World, 1550–1650.* Seattle: University of Washington Press, 1990.

———. "Negotiating with the Renaissance State: The Ottoman Empire and the New Diplomacy." In *The Early Modern Ottomans: Remapping the Empire,* edited by Virginia Aksan and Daniel Goffman, 15–58. Cambridge: Cambridge University Press, 2007.

Gökbilgin, M. Tayyip. "Venedik devlet arşivindeki Türkçe belgeleri koleksiyonu ve bizimle ilgile diğer belgeler." *Belgeler* 5–8 (1968–1971): 1–152.

Gradeva, Rossitsa. "Orthodox Christians in the Kadı Courts: The Practice of the Sofia Sheriat Court, Seventeenth Century." *Islamic Law and Society* 4, no. 1 (1997): 37–69.

Graf, Tobias. "Of Half-Lives and Double-Lives: 'Renegades' in the Ottoman Empire and Their Pre-Conversion Ties, ca. 1580–1610." In *Well-Connected Domains,* edited by Tobias Graf, Christian Roth, Gülay Tulasoğlu, and Pascal Firges, 131–149. Leiden: Brill, 2014.

Grammont, Henri Delmas de. *Histoire d'Alger sous la domination turque (1515–1830).* Paris: E. Leroux, 1887.

———. *Relations entre la France & la Régence d'Alger au XVIIe siècle.* Paris: Adolphe Jourdan, libraire-éditeur, 1880.

Grandchamp, Pierre. "Une mission délicate en Barbarie au XVIIe siècle: Jean-Baptiste Salvago, drogman vénitien à Alger et à Tunis (1625)." *Revue tunisienne* 8 (1937): 299–322.

Greene, Molly. "Beyond the Northern Invasion: The Mediterranean in the Seventeenth Century." *Past and Present* 174, no. 1 (2002): 42–71.

———. *Catholic Pirates and Greek Merchants: A Maritime History of the Mediterranean.* Princeton, NJ: Princeton University Press, 2010.

———. "Ruling an Island without a Navy: A Comparative View of Venetian and Ottoman Crete." *Oriente Moderno* 20, no. 1 (2001): 193–207.
———. *A Shared World: Christians and Muslims in the Early Modern Mediterranean*. Princeton, NJ: Princeton University Press, 2002.
———. "'Victims of Piracy?': Ottoman Lawsuits in Malta (1602–1687) and the Changing Course of Mediterranean Maritime History." In *Trade and Cultural Exchange in the Early Modern Mediterranean: Braudel's Maritime Legacy*, edited by Maria Fusaro, Colin Heywood, and Mohamed-Salah Omri, 177–201. London: I. B. Tauris, 2010.
Grehan, James. "The Mysterious Power of Words: Language, Law, and Culture in Ottoman Damascus (17th–18th Centuries)." *Journal of Social History* 37, no. 4 (2004): 991–1015.
Guarnieri, Gino. *I cavalieri di Santo Stefano: nella storia della marina italiana, 1562–1859*. Pisa: Nistri-Lischi, 1960.
Gugliuzzo, Elina. "Être esclave à Malte à l'époque moderne." *Cahiers de la Méditerranée* 87 (2013): 63–75.
Guilmartin, John Francis. *Gunpowder and Galleys. Changing Technology and Mediterranean Warfare at Sea in the Sixteenth Century*. London: Cambridge University Press, 1974.
———. "The Military Revolution in Warfare at Sea during the Early Modern Era: Technological Origins, Operational Outcomes and Strategic Consequences." *Journal for Maritime Research* 13, no. 2 (2011): 129–137.
Gülsoy, Ersin. *Girit'in Fethi ve Osmanlı Idaresinin Kurulması (1645–1670)*. Istanbul: TATAV, 2004.
Gürkan, Emrah Safa. "Batı Akdeniz'de Osmanlı Korsanlığı ve Gaza Meselesi." *Kebikeç: İnsan Bilimleri İçin Kaynak Araştırmaları Dergisi* 33 (2012): 173–204.
———. "The Centre and the Frontier: Ottoman Cooperation with the North African Corsairs in the Sixteenth Century." *Turkish Historical Review* 1, no. 2 (2010): 125–163.
———. "The Efficacy of Ottoman Counter-Intelligence in the 16th Century." *Acta Orientalia* 65, no. 1 (2012): 1–38.
———. "Fooling the Sultan: Information, Decision-Making and the 'Mediterranean Faction' (1585–1587)." *Osmanlı Araştırmaları/Journal of Ottoman Studies* 45 (2015): 57–96.
———. "Mediating Boundaries: Mediterranean Go-Betweens and Cross-Confessional Diplomacy in Constantinople, 1560–1600." *Journal of Early Modern History* 19, nos. 2–3 (2015): 107–128.
Hagen, Gottfried. Afterword to *An Ottoman Mentality: The World of Evliya Çelebi*, by Robert Dankoff, 215–256. Leiden: Brill, 2004.
———. *Ein osmanischer Geograph bei der Arbeit: Entstehung und Gedankenwelt von Kātib Čelebis Ǧihānnümā*. Berlin: Klaus Schwarz Verlag, 2003.
Haggenmacher, Peter. "Grotius and Gentili: A Reassessment of Thomas E. Holland's Inaugural Lecture." In *Hugo Grotius and International Relations*, edited by Hedley Bull, Benedict Kingsbury, and Adam Roberts, 133–176. Oxford: Clarendon, 1990.

Hallaq, Wael. B. "From Fatwas to Furu: Growth and Change in Islamic Substantive Law." *Islamic Law and Society* 1, no. 1 (1994): 29–65.

———. "Model Shurūṭ Works and the Dialectic of Doctrine and Practice." *Islamic Law and Society* 2, no. 2 (1995): 109–134.

———. "Qadis Communicating: Legal Change and the Law of Documentary Evidence." *Al-Qantara* 20, no. 2 (1999): 437–466.

———. "Was the Gate of Ijtihad Closed?" *International Journal of Middle East Studies* 16, no. 1 (1984): 3–41.

Hamidullah, Muhammad. *Muslim Conduct of State, Being a Treatise on Siyar*. Lahore: Sh. M. Ashraf, 1961.

Hanna, Mark. *Pirate Nests and the Rise of the British Empire, 1570–1740*. Chapel Hill: University of North Carolina Press, 2015.

Hanna, Nelly. *Making Big Money in 1600: The Life and Times of Isma'il Abu Taqiyya, Egyptian Merchant*. Syracuse: Syracuse University Press, 1998

Hastings, Justin V. "Understanding Maritime Piracy Syndicate Operations." *Security Studies* 21, no. 4 (2012): 683–721.

Heller-Roazen, Daniel. *The Enemy of All*. New York: Zone Books, 2009.

Hershenzon, Daniel. "The Political Economy of Ransom in the Early Modern Mediterranean." *Past and Present* 231, no. 1 (2016): 61–95.

Hess, Andrew C. "The Battle of Lepanto and Its Place in Mediterranean History." *Past and Present* (1972): 53–73.

———. "The Evolution of the Ottoman Seaborne Empire in the Age of the Oceanic Discoveries, 1453–1525." *American Historical Review* 75 (1970): 1892–1919.

———. *The Forgotten Frontier: A History of the Sixteenth Century Ibero-African Frontier*. Chicago: University of Chicago Press, 1978.

Heyd, Uriel. "Some Aspects of the Ottoman Fetvā." *Bulletin of the School of Oriental and African Studies* 32, no. 1 (1969): 35–56.

Heyd, Uriel, and V. L Ménage. *Studies in Old Ottoman Criminal Law*. Oxford: Clarendon, 1973.

Heywood, Colin. "The English in the Mediterranean, 1600–1630: A Post-Braudelian Perspective on the 'Northern Invasion.'" In *Trade and Cultural Exchange in the Early Modern Mediterranean: Braudel's Maritime Legacy*, edited by Maria Fusaro, Colin Heywood, and Mohamed-Salah Omri, 23–44. London: I. B. Tauris, 2010.

———. "Fernand Braudel and the Ottomans: The Emergence of an Involvement (1928–50)." *Mediterranean Historical Review* 23, no. 2 (2008): 165–184.

———. "A Frontier without Archaeology? The Ottoman Maritime Frontier in the Western Mediterranean, 1660–1760." In *The Frontiers of the Ottoman World*, edited by A. C. S. Peacock, 493–508. London: British Academy, 2009.

———. "The Kapudan Pasha, the English Ambassador and the Blackham Galley: An Episode in Anglo-Ottoman Maritime Relations (1697)." In *The Kapudan Pasha: His Office and His Domain: Halcyon Days in Crete IV, a Symposium Held in Rethymnon, 7–9 January 2000*, edited by Elizabeth Zachariadou, 410–438. Rethymnon: University of Crete Press, 2002.

———. "Ottoman Territoriality versus Maritime Usage." In *Insularités Ottomanes*, edited by Nicolas Vatin and Gilles Veinstein, 145–173. Paris: Maisonneuve & Larose, 2004.

Horniker, Arthur Leon. "Anglo-French Rivalry in the Levant from 1583 to 1612." *Journal of Modern History* 18, no. 4 (1946): 289–305.

———. "William Harborne and the Beginning of Anglo-Turkish Diplomatic and Commercial Relations." *Journal of Modern History* 14, no. 3 (1942): 289–316.

İlter, Aziz Samih. *Şimalî Afrikada Türkler*. Istanbul: Vakıt, 1934.

Imber, Colin. *Ebu's-su'ud: The Islamic Legal Tradition*. Stanford, CA: Stanford University Press, 1997.

———. "Eleven Fetvas of the Ottoman Sheikh ul-Islam 'Abdurrahim." In *Islamic Legal Interpretation. Muftis and Their Fatwas*, edited by Muhammad Khalid Masud, Brinkley Messick, and David Powers, 141–149. Cambridge, MA: Harvard University Press, 1996.

———. "The Navy of Süleyman the Magnificent." *Archivum Ottomanicum* 6 (1980): 211–282.

———. "What Does Ghazi Actually Mean?" In *The Balance of Truth: Essays in Honour of Professor Geoffrey Lewis*, edited by Çiğdem Balım-Harding and Colin Imber, 165–178. Istanbul: Isis Press, 2000.

İnalcık, Halil. *An Economic and Social History of the Ottoman Empire: Volume One, 1300–1600*. Cambridge: Cambridge University Press, 1994.

———. "Imtiyazat." In *Encyclopedia of Islam, Second Edition*, edited by P. Bearman, Th. Bianquis, C. E. Bosworth, E. van Donzel, W. P. Heinrichs, 1179–1189. Leiden: Brill, 1971.

———. "Military and Fiscal Transformation of the Ottoman Empire, 1600–1700." *Archivum Ottomanicum* 6 (1980): 283–337.

———. "Ottoman Methods of Conquest." *Studia Islamica* 2 (1954): 103–129.

———. "The *Rūznāmče* Registers of the *Kadıasker* of Rumeli as Preserved in the Istanbul *Müftülük* Archives." *Turcica* 20 (1988): 251–275.

———. "The Status of the Greek Orthodox Patriarch under the Ottomans." *Turcica* 21–23 (1991): 407–436.

İpşirli, Mehmet. "Şeyhülislam Sun'ullah Efendi." *Tarih Enstitüsü Dergisi* 13 (1987): 209–256.

———. "XVI. Asrın İkinci Yarısında kürek cezası ile ilgili hükümler." *Tarih Enstitütüsü Dergisi* 12 (1982): 204–248.

Isom-Verhaaren, Christine. *Allies with the Infidel: The Ottoman and French Alliance in the Sixteenth Century*. London: I. B. Tauris, 2011.

Jackson, Sherman A. "Taqlīd, Legal Scaffolding and the Scope of Legal Injunctions in Post-Formative Theory Muṭlaq and 'Āmm in the Jurisprudence of Shihāb al-Dīn al-Qarāfī." *Islamic Law and Society* 3, no. 2 (1996): 165–192.

Jaspert, Nikolas, and Sebastian Kolditz. *Seeraub im Mittelmeerraum: Piraterie, Korsarentum und maritime Gewalt von der Antike bis zur Neuzeit*. Schöningh: Fink Wilhelm GmbH, 2013.

Jennings, Ronald. *Christians and Muslims in Ottoman Cyprus and the Mediterranean World, 1571–1640*. New York: New York University Press, 1993.

———. "Kadi, Court, and Legal Procedure in 17th C. Ottoman Kayseri: The Kadi and the Legal System." *Studia Islamica* 48 (1978): 133–172.

———. "Limitations of the Judicial Powers of the Kadi in 17th C. Ottoman Kayseri." *Studia Islamica* 50 (1979): 151–184.

———. "Loans and Credit in Early 17th Century Ottoman Judicial Records: The Sharia Court of Anatolian Kayseri." *Journal of the Economic and Social History of the Orient* 16, nos. 2–3 (1973): 168–216.

———. "The Office of Vekil (Wakil) in 17th-Century Ottoman Sharia Courts." *Studia Islamica* (1975): 147–169.

———. "Zimmis (Non-Muslims) in Early 17th Century Ottoman Judicial Records: The Sharia Court of Anatolian Kayseri." *Journal of the Economic and Social History of the Orient* 21, no. 3 (1978): 225–293.

Johansen, Baber. "Formes de langage et fonctions publiques: Stéréotypes, témoins et offices dans la preuve par l'écrit en droit musulman." *Arabica* 44 (1997): 333–376.

Kafadar, Cemal. "A Death in Venice (1575): Anatolian Muslim Merchants Trading in the Serenissima." *Journal of Turkish Studies* 10 (1986): 191–218.

———. "Self and Others: The Diary of a Dervish in Seventeenth Century Istanbul and First-Person Narratives in Ottoman Literature." *Studia Islamica* 69 (1989): 121–150.

Kahane, Henry, and Andreas Tietze. *The Lingua Franca in the Levant: Turkish Nautical Terms of Italian and Greek Origin*. Urbana: University of Illinois, 1958.

Kaiser, Wolfgang. "L'économie de la rançon en Méditerranée occidentale (XVIe–XVIIe siècle)." *Hypotheses* 10, no. 1 (2007): 359–368.

———, ed. *Le commerce des captifs: Les intermédiaires dans l'échange et le rachat des prisonniers en Méditerraneé, XVe–XVIIIe siècle*. Rome: École française de Rome, 2008.

———. "Négocier la liberté. Missions françaises pour l'échange et le rachat de captifs au Maghreb (XVIIe siècle)." In *La mobilité des personnes en Méditerranée de l'antiquité à l'époque moderne*, edited by Claude Moatti, 1000–1036. Rome: École française de Rome, 2004.

Kaiser, Wolfgang, and Guillaume Calafat. "The Economy of Ransoming in the Early Modern Mediterranean: A Form of Cross-Cultural Trade between Southern Europe and the Maghreb (Sixteenth to Eighteenth Centuries)." In *Religion and Trade: Cross-Cultural Exchanges in World History, 1000–1900*, edited by Francesca Trivellato, Lior Halevi, and Catia Antunes, 108–130. Oxford: Oxford University Press, 2014.

Kaya, Süleyman. "Mahkeme Kayıtlarının Kılavuzu: Sakk Mecmuaları." *Türkiye Araştırmaları Literatür Dergisi* 3, no. 5 (2005): 379–416.

Kempe, Michael. "Beyond the Law. The Image of Piracy in the Legal Writings of Hugo Grotius." *Grotiana* 26, no. 1 (2007): 379–395.

———. "'Even in the Remotest Corners of the World': Globalized Piracy and International Law, 1500–1900." *Journal of Global History* 5, no. 3 (2010): 353–372.

Kermeli, Eugenia. "Central Administration versus Provincial Arbitrary Governance: Patmos and Mount Athos Monasteries in the 16th Century." *Byzantine and Modern Greek Studies* 32, no. 2 (2008): 189–202.

———. "The Right to Choice: Ottoman Justice vis-à-vis Ecclesiastical and Communal Justice in the Balkans, Seventeenth-Nineteenth Centuries." In *Studies in Islamic Law: A Festschrift for Colin Imber*, edited by Andreas Christmann and Robert Gleave, 165–210. Oxford: Oxford University Press, 2007.

Khiari, Farid. *Vivre et mourir en Alger: l'Algérie ottomane aux XVIe–XVIIe siècles: Un destin confisqué*. Paris: Harmattan, 2002.

Khadduri, Majid. *The Law of War and Peace in Islam; a Study in Muslim International Law*. London: Luzac, 1940.

———. *War and Peace in the Law of Islam*. Baltimore, MD: Johns Hopkins University Press, 1955.

Khalilieh, Hassan S. *Admiralty and Maritime Laws in the Mediterranean Sea (ca. 800–1050): The Kitāb Akriyat al-Sufun vis-à-vis the Nomos Rhodion Nautikos*. Leiden: Brill, 2006.

———. *Islamic Maritime Law: An Introduction*. Leiden: Brill, 1998.

Kizilov, Mikhail. "Slave Trade in the Early Modern Crimea from the Perspective of Christian, Muslim, and Jewish Sources." *Journal of Early Modern History* 11, nos. 1–2 (2007): 1–31.

Kołodziejczyk, Dariusz. *Ottoman-Polish Diplomatic Relations (15th–18th Century): An Annotated Edition of ʿahdnames and Other Documents*. Leiden: Brill, 2000.

Kolovos, Elias. "Insularity and Island Society in the Ottoman Context: The Case of the Aegean Island of Andros (Sixteenth to Eighteenth Centuries)." *Turcica* 39 (2007): 49–122.

———. "Les documents ottomans de la bibliothèque Kaïreios d'Andros (Grèce)." *Turcica* 35 (2003): 317–321.

———. "Ottoman Frontiers and their Historiography in the Mediterranean: The Case of the Ottoman Aya Mavra as a Frontier in the Ionian Sea (Late Fifteenth to Late Seventeenth Century)." Unpublished manuscript.

———. *Οθωμανικές πηγές για τη νεώτερη ιστορία της Λευκάδας* [Ottoman Sources Concerning the Early Modern History of Lefkada]. Herakleio: Πανεπιστημιακές Εκδόσεις Κρήτης, 2013.

———. "A Town for the Besiegers: Social Life and Marriage in Ottoman Candia outside Candia (1650–1669)." In *The Eastern Mediterranean under Ottoman Rule: Crete, 1645–1840: Halcyon Days in Crete VI: A Symposium Held in Rethymno, 13–15 January 2006*, edited by Antonis Anastasopoulos, 103–175. Rethymnon: University of Crete Press, 2008.

Krstić, Tijana. *Contested Conversions to Islam: Narratives of Religious Change in the Early Modern Ottoman Empire*. Stanford, CA: Stanford University Press, 2011.

———. "Contesting Subjecthood and Sovereignty in Ottoman Galata in the Age of Confessionalization: The Carazo Affair, 1613–1617." *Oriente Moderno* 93, no. 2 (2013): 422–453.

Krüger, Hilmar. *Fetwa und Siyar: zur internationalrechtlichen Gutachtenpraxis der osmanischen Şeyh ül-Islâm vom 17. Bis 19. Jahrhundert besonderer Berücksichtigung Des "Behcet ül-Fetâva."* Wiesbaden: Harrossowitz, 1978.

Kut, Günay. "Esîrî, His 'Sergüzeşt' and His Other Works." *Journal of Turkish Studies* 10 (1986): 235–244.

Laiou, Sophia. "The Levends of the Sea in the Second Half of the 16th Century: Some Considerations." *Archivum Ottomanicum* 23 (2005–2006): 233–247.

Lane, Frederic Chapin. *Venice, a Maritime Republic.* Baltimore, MD: Johns Hopkins University Press, 1973.

Lane-Poole, Stanley. *The Barbary Corsairs.* London: T. Fischer Unwin, 1890.

Largueche, Delenda, J. Clancy-Smith, and C. Audet. "The Mahalla: The Origins of Beylical Sovereignty in Ottoman Tunisia during the Early Modern Period." *Journal of North African Studies* 6, no. 1 (2001): 105–116.

Lewis, Bernard. "Corsairs in Iceland." *Revue de l'Occident musulman et de la Méditerranée* 15, no. 1 (1973): 139–144.

Libson, Gideon. "On the Development of Custom as a Source of Law in Islamic Law." *Islamic Law and Society* 4, no. 2 (1997): 131–155.

Lindner, Rudi Paul. *Explorations in Ottoman Prehistory.* Ann Arbor: University of Michigan Press, 2007.

Lloyd, Christopher. *English Corsairs on the Barbary Coast.* London: Collins, 1981.

Longino, Michèle. *French Travel Writing in the Ottoman Empire: Marseilles to Constantinople, 1650–1700.* New York: Routledge, 2015.

López Nadal, Gonçal. "Corsairing as a Commercial System: The Edges of Legitimate Trade." In *Bandits at Sea: A Pirates Reader*, edited by C. R. Pennell, 125–136. New York: New York University Press, 2001.

Loualich, Fatiha. "In the Regency of Algiers: The Human Side of the Algerine Corso." In *Trade and Cultural Exchange in the Early Modern Mediterranean: Braudel's Maritime Legacy*, edited by Maria Fusaro, Colin Heywood, and Mohamed-Salah Omri, 69–96. London: I. B. Tauris, 2010.

Mahan, Alfred Thayer. *The Influence of Sea Power upon History, 1660–1783.* Boston: Little, Brown, 1918.

Malcolm, Noel. *Agents of Empire: Knights, Corsairs, Jesuits and Spies in the Sixteenth-Century Mediterranean World.* Oxford: Oxford University Press, 2015.

———. "Alberico Gentili and the Ottomans." In *The Roman Foundations of the Law of Nations: Alberico Gentili and the Justice of Empire*, edited by Benedict Kingsbury and Benjamin Straumann, 127–145. Oxford: Oxford University Press, 2010.

Mallia-Milanes, Victor. "From Valona to Crete: Veneto-Maltese Relations from the Late 1630s to the Outbreak of the Cretan War." In *Malta: A Case Study in International Cross Currents: Proceedings of the First International Colloquium on the History of the Central Mediterranean Held at the University of Malta, 13–17 December 1989*, edited by Victor Mallia-Milanes and S. Fiorini, 159–173. Malta: Malta University Publications, 1991.

———. *Hospitaller Malta, 1530–1798: Studies on Early Modern Malta and the Order of St. John of Jerusalem*. Malta: Mireva Publications, 1993.

———. *Venice and Hospitaller Malta, 1530–1798: Aspects of a Relationship*. Malta: Publishers Enterprise Group, 1992.

Mantran, Robert. "Monsieur de Guilleragues, ambassadeur de France à Constantinople, et le commerce français au Levant (1679–1685). Documents et notes." In *L'Empire ottoman, la République de Turquie et la France*, edited by Hâmit Batu and Jean-Louis Bacqué-Grammont, 59–72. Paris: Association pour le développement des études turques, 1986.

Masson, Paul. *Histoire du commerce français dans le Levant au XVIIe siècle*. Paris: Hachette, 1896.

Masters, Bruce Alan. *The Origins of Western Economic Dominance in the Middle East: Mercantilism and the Islamic Economy in Aleppo, 1600–1750*. New York: New York University Press, 1988.

Masud, Muhammad Khalid, Brinkley Messick, and David Powers. "Muftis, Fatwas, and Islamic Legal Interpretation." In *Islamic Legal Interpretation. Muftis and Their Fatwas*, edited by Muhammad Khalid Masud, Brinkley Messick, and David Powers, 3–32. Cambridge: Harvard University Press, 1996.

Masud, Muhammad Khalid, Rudolph Peters, and David Powers. *Dispensing Justice in Islam: Qadis and Their Judgements*. Leiden: Brill, 2006.

Matar, Nabil. "The Barbary Corsairs, King Charles I and the Civil War." *Seventeenth Century* 16, no. 2 (2001): 239–258.

———. *Britain and Barbary, 1589–1689*. Gainesville: University Press of Florida, 2005.

———. "English Accounts of Captivity in North Africa and the Middle East: 1577–1625." *Renaissance Quarterly* 54, no. 2 (2001): 553–572.

———. *Europe through Arab Eyes, 1578–1727*. New York: Columbia University Press, 2013.

———. "Piracy and Captivity in the Early Modern Mediterranean: The Perspective from Barbary." In *Pirates?: The Politics of Plunder, 1550–1650*, edited by Claire Jowitt, 56–73. Basingstoke: Palgrave Macmillan, 2007.

McGowan, Bruce. *Economic Life in Ottoman Europe: Taxation, Trade, and the Struggle for Land, 1600–1800*. Cambridge: Cambridge University Press, 1981.

Meloy, John. "Imperial Strategy and Political Exigency: The Red Sea Spice Trade and the Mamluk Sultanate in the Fifteenth Century." *Journal of the American Oriental Society* 123, no. 1 (2003): 1–19.

Menage, V. L. "The English Capitulation of 1580: A Review Article." *International Journal of Middle East Studies* 12, no. 3 (1980): 373–383.

Meredith-Owens, G. M. "Traces of a Lost Autobiographical Work by a Courtier of Selim II." *Bulletin of the School of Oriental and African Studies* 23, no. 3 (1960): 456–463.

Miović-Perić, Vesna. "The Conflict between Dubrovnik and Venice 1751–1754." *Dubrovnik Annals* 1 (1997): 71–96.

Mumcu, Serap. *Venedik Baylosu'nun Defterleri. The Venetian Baylo's Registers (1589–1684)*. Venice: Edizioni Ca' Foscari, 2014.

Murphey, Rhoads. "The Ottoman Resurgence in the Seventeenth-Century Mediterranean: The Gamble and Its Results." *Mediterranean Historical Review* 8, no. 2 (1993): 186–200.

———. *Ottoman Warfare, 1500–1700.* New Brunswick, NJ: Rutgers University Press, 1999.

———. "Provisioning Istanbul: The State and Subsistence in the Early Modern Middle East." *Food and Foodways* 2, no. 1 (1987): 217–263.

Nadalo, Stephanie. "Negotiating Slavery in a Tolerant Frontier: Livorno's Turkish Bagno (1547–1747)." *Mediaevalia* 1, no. 1 (2011): 275–324.

Neumann, Christoph K. "Hizir, der Kadi und der Kryptomuslim von Malta. Zum Text Národní Knihovna v Praze XVIII A 126, fols. 11v-12r." *Archiv Orientální* 69, no. 2 (2001): 207–224.

Nutku, Özdemir. *Meddahlık ve Meddah Hikâyeleri.* Istanbul: Türkiye İş Bankası, 1976.

Olson, Robert W. "The Ottoman-French Treaty of 1740: A Year to Be Remembered?" *Turkish Studies Association Bulletin* 15, no. 2 (1991): 347–355.

Oral, Özgür. "17. yüzyılda Akdeniz'de Osmanlı Korsanlığı." MA thesis, Istanbul University, 2004.

Orfali, Moisés. "Ragusa and Ragusan Jews in the Effort to Ransom Captives." *Mediterranean Historical Review* 17, no. 2 (2002): 14–31.

Ostapchuk, Victor. "The Human Landscape of the Ottoman Black Sea in the Face of the Cossack Naval Raids." *Oriente Moderno* 20 (2001): 23–95.

Othman, Aida. "'And Amicable Settlement Is Best': Sulh and Dispute Resolution in Islamic Law." *Arab Law Quarterly* 21, no. 1 (2007): 64–90.

Özen, Şükrü. "Osmanlı Döneminde Fetva Literatürü." *Türkiye Araştırmaları Literatür Dergisi* 3, no. 5 (2005): 249–378.

Palffy, Geza. "Ransom Slavery along the Ottoman-Hungarian Frontier in the Sixteenth and Seventeenth Centuries." In *Ransom Slavery along the Ottoman Borders: Early Fifteenth–Early Eighteenth Centuries*, edited by Geza Dávid and Pal Fodor, 35–84. Leiden: Brill, 2007.

Pamuk, Şevket. *A Monetary History of the Ottoman Empire.* New York: Cambridge University Press, 2000.

———. "The Ottoman Monetary System and Frontier Territories in Europe, 1500–1700." *International Journal of Turkish Studies* 9, nos. 1–2 (2003): 175–182.

Panaite, Viorel. "A French Ambassador in Istanbul, and His Turkish Manuscript on Western Merchants in the Ottoman Mediterranean (Late 16th and Early 17th Centuries)." *Revue des études sud-est européennes* 42, nos. 1–4 (2004): 117–132.

———. "French Commerce, North African Piracy, and Ottoman Law in the Mediterranean (Close-Sixteenth and Early-Seventeenth Century)." *Revue roumaine d'histoire* 46 (2007): 69–81.

———. *The Ottoman Law of War and Peace: The Ottoman Empire and Tribute Payers.* Boulder, CO: East European Monographs, 2000.

———. "Western Merchants and Ottoman Law. The Legal Section of the Turkish Manuscript No. 130 from the Bibliothèque Nationale in Paris." *Revue des études sud-est européennes* 45 (2007): 45–62.

Panzac, Daniel. *Barbary Corsairs: The End of a Legend, 1800–1820*. Leiden: Brill, 2005.

———. "International and Domestic Maritime Trade in the Ottoman Empire during the 18th Century." *International Journal of Middle East Studies* 24, no. 2 (1992): 189–206.

———. *La caravane maritime: Marins européens et marchands ottomans en Méditerranée, 1680–1830*. Paris: CNRS, 2004.

———. *La marine ottomane: de l'apogée à la chute de l'empire, 1572–1923*. Paris: CNRS, 2009.

———. "La lingua franca: Un outil de communication." In *Living in the Ottoman Ecumenical Community*, edited by Markus Koller and Vera Costantini, 409–422. Leiden: Brill, 2008.

Parmaksızoğlu, İsmet. "Bir Türk Kadısının Esâret Hâtıraları." *Tarih Dergisi* 5, no. 8 (1953): 77–84.

Pearson, Michael. "'Tremendous Damage' or 'Mere Pinpricks': The Costs of Piracy." *Journal of Early Modern History* 16, no. 6 (2012): 463–480.

Pedani, Maria Pia. "Beyond the Frontier: The Ottoman-Venetian Border in the Adriatic Context from the Sixteenth to the Eighteenth Centuries." In *Zones of Fracture in Modern Europe: The Baltic Countries, the Balkans, and Northern Italy*, edited by Almut Bues, 45–60. Wiesbaden: Harrassowitz, 2005.

———. *In nome del Gran Signore: Inviati ottomani a Venezia dalla caduta di Costantinopoli alla guerra di Candia*. Venice: Deputazione editrice, 1994.

Pedani Fabris, Maria Pia, and Alessio Bombaci. *I "documenti turchi" dell'Archivio di Stato di Venezia: inventario della miscellanea a cura di Maria Pia Pedani Fabris*. Rome: Ministero per i Beni Culturali e Ambientali, Ufficio Centrale per i Beni Archivistici, 1994.

———. *Inventory of the Lettere e Scritture Turchesche in the Venetian State Archives*. Leiden: Brill, 2010.

Peirce, Leslie. "Abduction with (Dis)honor: Sovereigns, Brigands, and Heroes in the Ottoman World." *Journal of Early Modern History* 15, no. 4 (2011): 311–329.

———. *The Imperial Harem: Women and Sovereignty in the Ottoman Empire*. New York: Oxford University Press, 1993.

———. *Morality Tales: Law and Gender in the Ottoman Court of Aintab*. Berkeley: University of California Press, 2003.

Pellat, Charles, Colin Imber, and J.B. Kelly. "Ḳurṣān." In *Encyclopaedia of Islam, Second Edtion*, edited by P. Bearman, Th. Bianquis, C.E. Bosworth, E. van Donzel, and W.P. Heinrichs. Leiden: Brill, 2009. Brill Online. Accessed November 12, 2009. http://www.brillonline.nl/subscriber/entry?entry=islam_COM-0546

Pennell, C. R. "The Ottoman Empire in North Africa: A Question of Degree—Tripoli in the Seventeenth Century." *Studies on Ottoman Diplomatic History* 5 (1990): 35–55.

———."Treaty Law: The Extent of Consular Jurisdiction in North Africa from the Middle of the Seventeenth to the Middle of the Nineteenth Century." *Journal of North African Studies* 14 (2009): 235–256.

Petersen, Andrew. *The Medieval and Ottoman Hajj Route in Jordan: An Archaeological and Historical Study*. Oxford: Oxford University Press, 2012.

Pixley, M. M. "The Development and Role of the Şeyhülislam in Early Ottoman History." *Journal of the American Oriental Society* (1976): 89–96.

Poumarède, Géraud. "La France et les Barbaresques: Police des mers et relations internationales en Méditerranée (XVIe–XVIIe Siècles)." *Revue d'histoire maritime* 4 (2005): 117–146.

———. "Naissance d'une instiution royale: Les consuls de la nation francaise en Levant et en Barbarie aux XVIe et XVIIe siècles." *Annuaire-Bulletin de la société de l'histoire de France* 1 (2001): 65–128.

———. "Négocier près la Sublime Porte: Jalons pour une nouvelle histoire des capitulations franco-ottomanes." In *L'invention de la diplomatie*, edited by Lucien Bély, 71–85. Paris: Presses Universitaires de France, 1998.

———. *Pour en finir avec la Croisade*. Paris: Presses Universitaires de France, 2009.

———. "Venise et la défense de ses territoires d'outre-Mer, XVIe–XVIIe siècles." *Dix-septième siècle* 4 (2005): 613–626.

Powers, David S. "Fatwas as Sources for Legal and Social History: A Dispute over Endowment Revenues from Fourteenth-Century Fez." *al-Qantara* 11, no. 2 (1990): 295–340.

———. "On Judicial Review in Islamic Law." *Law and Society Review* 26, no. 2 (1992): 315–341.

Prange, Sebastian R. "Outlaw Economics: Doing Business on the Fringes of the State. A Review Essay." *Comparative Studies in Society and History* 53, no. 02 (2011): 426–436.

———. "A Trade of No Dishonor: Piracy, Commerce, and Community in the Western Indian Ocean, Twelfth to Sixteenth Century." *American Historical Review* 116, no. 5 (2011): 1269–1293.

Quinn, Meredith M. "Making Sense of Miscellanies: Houghton Library MS Turk 11, an Ottoman Mecmua." *Harvard Library Bulletin* 24, no. 1 (2013): 27–44.

Raymond, André. "Soldiers in Trade: The Case of Ottoman Cairo." *British Society for Middle Eastern Studies. Bulletin* 18, no. 1 (1991): 16–37.

Repp, R. C. *The Müfti of Istanbul: A Study in the Development of the Ottoman Learned Hierarchy*. London: Ithaca Press, 1986.

Ressel, Magnus. "Conflicts between Early Modern European States about Rescuing Their Own Subjects from Barbary Captivity." *Scandinavian Journal of History* 36, no. 1 (2011): 1–22.

———. *Zwischen Sklavenkassen und Türkenpässen: Nordeuropa und die Barbaresken in der frühen Neuzeit*. Berlin: Walter de Gruyter, 2012.

Riedlmayer, András. "Ottoman Copybooks of Correspondence and Miscellanies as a Source for Political and Cultural History." *Acta Orientalia* 61, nos. 1–2 (2008): 201–214.

Rothman, E. Natalie. *Brokering Empire: Trans-Imperial Subjects between Venice and Istanbul*. Ithaca, NY: Cornell University Press, 2012.

———. "Conversion and Convergence in the Venetian-Ottoman Borderlands." *Journal of Medieval and Early Modern Studies* 41, no. 3 (2011): 601–633.

———. "Self-Fashioning in the Mediterranean Contact Zone: Giovanni Battista Salvago and His *Africa Overo Barbaria* (1625)." In *Renaissance Medievalisms*, edited by Konrad Eisenbichler, 123–143. Toronto: Centre for Reformation and Renaissance Studies, 2009.

Rubin, Alfred P. *The Law of Piracy*. Irvington-on-Hudson, NY: Transnational, 1988.

Sabev, Orlin. "The First Ottoman Turkish Printing Enterprise: Success or Failure?" In *Ottoman Tulips, Ottoman Coffee: Leisure and Lifestyle in the Eighteenth Century*, edited by Dana Sajdi, 63–89. London: I. B. Tauris, 2007.

Sadok, Boubaker. *La Régence de Tunis au XVIIe siècle: ses relations commerciales avec les ports de l'Europe méditerranéenne, Marseille et Livourne*. Zaghouan: Ceroma, 1987.

Safvet. *Mezemorta Hüseyin Paşa: Divân-ı Hümayun Kayıtlarından Çıkarılmıştır*. Istanbul: Deniz Kuvvetleri Komutanlığı Basımevi, 1994.

———. "Nakşa (Naksos) Dukalığı, Kiklad Ataları." *Tarih-i Osmani Encumeni Mecmuası* 23 (1913): 1444–1457.

———. "Yusuf Nasi." *Tarih-i Osmani Encumeni Mecmuası* 16 (1912): 982–993.

Sahillioğlu, Halil. "Akdeniz'de Korsanlara Esir Düşen Abdi Çelebi Mektubu." *Tarih Dergisi* 17–18 (1963): 241–256.

Salzmann, Ariel. "Migrants in Chains: On the Enslavement of Muslims in Renaissance and Enlightenment Europe." *Religions* 4, no. 3 (2013): 391–411.

Sariyannis, Marinos. "Images of the Mediterranean in an Ottoman Pirate Novel from the Late Seventeenth Century." *Osmanlı Araştırmaları/Journal of Ottoman Studies* 39 (2012): 189–204.

Schmidt, Jan. "First-Person Narratives in Ottoman Miscellaneous Manuscripts." In *Many Ways of Speaking about the Self: Middle Eastern Ego-Documents in Arabic, Persian, and Turkish (14th–20th Century)*, edited by Ralf Elger and Yavuz Köse, 159–170. Wiesbaden: Otto Harrassowitz Verlag, 2010.

Schmucker, W. "Die maltesischen Gefangenschaftserinnerungen eines türkischen Kadi von 1599." *Archivum Ottomanicum* 2 (1970): 191–251.

Semerdjian, Elyse. *"Off the Straight Path": Illicit Sex, Law, and Community in Ottoman Aleppo*. Syracuse: Syracuse University Press, 2008.

Seng, Yvonne J. "Fugitives and Factotums: Slaves in Early Sixteenth-Century Istanbul." *Journal of the Economic and Social History of the Orient* 39, no. 2 (1996): 136–169.

Setton, Kenneth M. *Venice, Austria, and the Turks in the Seventeenth Century*. Philadelphia: American Philosophical Society, 1991.

Shahar, Ido. "Legal Pluralism and the Study of Sharia Courts." *Islamic Law and Society* 15, no. 1 (2008): 112–141.

Shaybānī, Muḥammad ibn al-Ḥasan, and Majid Khadduri. *The Islamic Law of Nations: Shaybānī's Siyar*. Baltimore, MD: Johns Hopkins University Press, 1966.

Shuval, Tal. "Cezayir-i Garp: Bringing Algeria Back into Ottoman History." *New Perspectives on Turkey* 22 (2000): 85–116.

———. "The Ottoman Algerian Elite and Its Ideology." *International Journal of Middle East Studies* 32, no. 3 (2000): 323–344.

Sicking, Louis. "The Dichotomy of Insularity: Islands between Isolation and Connectivity in Medieval and Early Modern Europe, and Beyond." *International Journal of Maritime History* 26, no. 3 (2014): 494–511.

Singer, Amy. *Constructing Ottoman Beneficence: An Imperial Soup Kitchen in Jerusalem*. Binghamton: SUNY Press, 2012.

Skilliter, Susan. A. *William Harborne and the Trade with Turkey 1578–1582: A Documentary Study of the First Anglo-Ottoman Relations*. Oxford: Oxford University Press, 1977.

Slot, Benjamin. *Archipelagus Turbatus: Les Cylades entre colonisation latine et occupation ottomane c. 1500–1718*. Istanbul: Nederlands Historisch-Archaeologisch Instituut, 1982.

Smail, Daniel Lord. *The Consumption of Justice: Emotions, Publicity, and Legal Culture in Marseille, 1264–1423*. Ithaca, NY: Cornell University Press, 2003.

Smiley, Will. "'After Being So Long Prisoners, They Will Not Return to Slavery in Russia': An Aegean Network of Violence between Empires and Identities." *Osmanlı Araştırmaları/Journal of Ottoman Studies* 44 (2014): 221–234.

———. "The Burdens of Subjecthood: The Ottoman State, Russian Fugitives, and Interimperial Law, 1774–1869." *International Journal of Middle East Studies* 46, no. 1 (2014): 73–93.

———. "The Meanings of Conversion: Treaty Law, State Knowledge, and Religious Identity among Russian Captives in the Eighteenth-Century Ottoman Empire." *International History Review* 34, no. 3 (2012): 1–22.

———. "'When Peace Is Made, You Will Again Be Free': Islamic and Treaty Law, Black Sea Conflict, and the Emergence of 'Prisoners of War' in the Ottoman Empire, 1739–1830." PhD dissertation, Cambridge University, 2012.

Smith, Logan Pearsall, and Sir Henry Wotton. *The Life and Letters of Sir Henry Wotton*. Oxford: Clarendon, 1907.

Sobers-Khan, Nur. *Slaves without Shackles: Forced Labour and Manumission in the Galata Court Registers, 1560–1572*. Berlin: Klaus Schwarz Verlag, 2014.

Soucek, Svat. "Certain Types of Ships in Ottoman-Turkish Terminology." *Turcica* 7 (1975): 233–249.

———. "Navals Aspects of the Ottoman Conquests of Rhodes, Cyprus and Crete." *Studia Islamica* 98–99 (2004): 219–261.

———. "Review Essay: The Ottoman Empire and the Sea." *Journal of the Ottoman and Turkish Studies Association* 1, nos. 1–2 (2014): 207–228.

———. "The Rise of the Barbarossas in North Africa." *Archivum Ottomanicum* 3 (1971): 238–250.

Souza, Philip de. *Piracy in the Graeco-Roman World*. Cambridge: Cambridge University Press, 2002.

Steensgaard, Niels. *The Asian Trade Revolution of the Seventeenth Century: The East India Companies and the Decline of the Caravan Trade*. Chicago: University of Chicago Press, 1974.

Stefini, Tommaso. "Ottoman Merchants in Dispute with the Republic of Venice at the End of the 16th Century: Some Glances on the Contested Regime of the Capitulations." *Turcica* 46 (2015): 153–176.

Strachan, Michael. *Sir Thomas Roe, 1581–1644: A Life*. Salisbury, Wiltshire: M. Russell, 1989.

Süreyya, Mehmed. *Sicill-i Osmanī*. 6 vols. Istanbul: Sebil, 1996.

Sugar, Peter. "The Ottoman 'Professional Prisoner' on the Western Borders of the Empire in the Sixteenth and Seventeenth Centuries." *Etudes Balkaniques* 1 (1971): 82–91.

Tabak, Faruk. *The Waning of the Mediterranean, 1550–1870: A Geohistorical Approach*. Baltimore, MD: Johns Hopkins University Press, 2008.

Ṭaḥāwī, Aḥmad ibn Muḥammad, and Jeanette A. Wakin. *The Function of Documents in Islamic Law: The Chapters on Sales from Ṭaḥāwī's Kitāb al-shurūṭ al-kabīrc*. Albany: State University of New York Press, 1972.

Talbot, Michael. "Ottoman Seas and British Privateers: Defining Maritime Territoriality in the Eighteenth-Century Levant." In *Well-Connected Domains*, edited by Tobias Graf, Christian Roth, Gülay Tulasoğlu, and Pascal Firges, 54–70. Leiden: Brill, 2014.

———. "Protecting the Mediterranean: Ottoman Responses to Maritime Violence, 1718–1770." *Journal of Early Modern History* 21, no. 3 (2017): 1–35.

———. "When Proof Is Not Enough: An Ottoman Merchant in the Gibraltar Vice-Admiralty Court in the 1760s." *Quaderni Storici* 51, no. 3 (2016): 753–775.

Tamdoğan, Işık. "Sulh and the 18th Century Ottoman Courts of Üsküdar and Adana." *Islamic Law and Society* 15, no. 1 (2008): 55–83.

Tenenti, Alberto. *Piracy and the Decline of Venice, 1580–1615*. Berkeley: University of California Press, 1967.

Tezcan, Baki. "The Ottoman Mevali as 'Lords of the Law.'" *Journal of Islamic Studies* 20, no. 3 (2009): 383–407.

———. "The Ottoman Monetary Crisis of 1585 Revisited." *Journal of the Economic and Social History of the Orient* 52, no. 3 (2009): 460–504.

———. *The Second Ottoman Empire: Political and Social Transformation in the Early Modern World*. New York: Cambridge University Press, 2010.

Thermopoulou, Emilie. "Les kurekci de la flotte ottomane au XVIIe siècle." In *The Kapudan Pasha: His Office and His Domain: Halcyon Days in Crete IV, a Symposium Held in Rethymnon, 7–9 January 2000*, edited by Elizabeth Zachariadou, 165–180. Rethymnon: University of Crete Press, 2002.

Theunissen, Hans. "Ottoman-Venetian Diplomatics: The Ahd-names. The Historical Background and the Development of a Category of Political-Commercial Instruments Together with an Annotated Edition of a Corpus of Relevant Documents." *Electronic Journal of Oriental Studies* 1, no. 2 (1998): 1–698.

Thomson, Ann. *Barbary and Enlightenment: European Attitudes towards the Maghreb in the 18th Century*. Leiden: Brill, 1987.

Thomson, Janice E. *Mercenaries, Pirates, and Sovereigns: State-Building and Extraterritorial Violence in Early Modern Europe*. Princeton, NJ: Princeton University Press, 1996.

Tietze, Andreas. "Die Geschichte von Kerkermeister-Kapitän, ein türkischer Seeräuberromane aus dem 17. Jahrhundert." *Acta Orientalia* 19 (1942): 152–210.

Tinniswood, Adrian. *Pirates of Barbary: Corsairs, Conquests and Captivity in the 17th-Century Mediterranean*. London: Random House UK, 2011.

Tongas, Gérard. *Les relations de la France avec l'Empire ottoman: durant la première moitié du XVIIe siècle et l'ambassade à Constantinople de Philippe de Harlay, Comte de Césy, 1619–1640*. Toulouse: Impr. F. Boisseau, 1942.

Trivellato, Francesca. *The Familiarity of Strangers: The Sephardic Diaspora, Livorno, and Cross-Cultural Trade in the Early Modern Period*. New Haven, CT: Yale University Press, 2009.

Tucker, Judith. *In the House of the Law: Gender and Islamic Law in Ottoman Syria and Palestine*. Berkeley: University of California Press, 1998.

———. "She Would Rather Perish: Piracy and Gendered Violence in the Mediterranean." *Journal of Middle East Women's Studies* 10, no. 3 (2014): 8–39.

Tuşalp, Emine Ekin. "Treating Outlaws and Registering Miscreants in Early Modern Ottoman Society: A Study on the Legal Diagnosis of Deviance in *şeyhülislam* Fatwas." MA thesis, Sabanci University, 2005.

Udovitch, Abraham L. "An Eleventh Century Islamic Treatise on the Law of the Sea." *Annales Islamologiques* 27 (1993): 37–54.

———. *Partnership and Profit in Medieval Islam*. Princeton, NJ: Princeton University Press, 1970.

Ursinus, Michael. "Local Patmians in Their Quest for Justice: Eighteenth-Century Examples of Petitions Submitted to the Kapudan Paşa." *Documents de travail du CETOBAC* 1 (January 2010): 20–23.

Uzunçarşılı, İsmail Hakkı. *Osmanli Devletinin Ilmiye Teşkilâti*. Ankara: Türk Tarih Kurumu Basımevi, 1965.

———. *Osmanli Devletinin Merkez ve Bahriye Teşkilâti*. Ankara: Türk Tarih Kurumu Basımevi, 1948.

van den Boogert, Maurits H. *The Capitulations and the Ottoman Legal System Qadis, Consuls, and Beratlıs in the 18th Century*. Leiden: Brill, 2005.

———. "Consular Jurisdiction in the Ottoman Legal System in the Eighteenth Century." *Oriente Moderno* 83, no. 3 (2003): 613–634.

———. "Redress for Ottoman Victims of European Privateering: A Case against the Dutch in the Divan-ı Hümayun (1708–1715)." *Turcica* 33 (2001): 91–118.

Vasdravellis, John. *Klephts, Armatoles and Pirates in Macedonia during the Rule of the Turks 1627–1821*. Thessaloniki: Hetaireia Makedonikōn Spoudōn, 1970.

Vatin, Nicolas. "Ces Messieurs de Galata. Note sur deux rapports d'expertise en droit maritime rédigés en août 1640 à Galata au profit d'un capitaine patmiote." *Journal of the Economic and Social History of the Orient* 49, no. 1 (2006): 48–67.

———. "Errata: Ces Messieurs de Galata." *Journal of the Economic and Social History of the Orient* 49, no. 3 (2006): 280–284.

———. "Iles grecques? Iles ottomans?" In *Insularités ottomanes*, edited by Nicolas Vatin and Gilles Veinstein, 71–89. Paris: Maisonneuve & Larose, 2004.

———. "L'Empire ottoman et la piraterie en 1559–1560." In *The Kapudan Pasha: His Office and His Domain: Halcyon Days in Crete IV, a Symposium*

Held in Rethymnon, 7–9 January 2000, edited by Elizabeth Zachariadou, 371–408. Rethymnon, 2002.

———. *L'ordre de Saint-Jean-de Jérusalem, l'Empire ottoman et la Méditerranée orientale entre les deux sièges de Rhodes, 1480–1522*. Leuven: Peeters, 1994.

———. "Note sur l'attitude des sultans ottomans et de leurs sujets face à la captivité des leurs en terre chrétienne (fin XVe-XVIe siècle)." *Wiener Zeitschrift für die Kunde des Morgenlandes* 82 (1992): 375–395.

———. "Note sur l'entrée d'Alger sous la souveraineté ottomane (1519–1521)." *Turcica* 44 (2013): 131–166.

———. "Une affaire interne: Le sort et la libération des personnes de condition libre illégalement retenues en esclavage sur le territoire ottoman (XVIe siècle)." *Turcica* 33 (2001): 149–190.

Vatin, Nicolas, and Gilles Veinstein. "'Une bonté unique au monde': Patmos et son monastère, havre des musulmans en péril (1625–1636)." *Turcica* 35 (2003): 9–79.

Veinstein, Gilles. "Le Sheikh ul-Islâm et l'ambassadeur: de l'autorité religieuse à la diplomatie." In *L'autorité religieuse et ses limites en terres d'islam*, edited by Alexandre Papas, Nathalie Clayer, and Benoit Fliche, 55–68. Leiden: Brill, 2013.

———. "Les documents emis par le *kapudan paşa* dans le fonds ottoman de Patmos." *Documents de travail du CETOBAC* 1 (January 2010): 13–19.

———. "Les fondements juridiques de la diplomatie ottoman en Europe." *Oriente Moderno* 88, no. 2 (2008): 509–522.

———. "L'oralité dans les documents d'archives ottomans: Paroles rapportées ou imaginées?" *Revue du monde musulman et de la Méditerranée* 75, no. 1 (1995): 133–142.

Vitkus, Daniel J., and Nabil I. Matar. *Piracy, Slavery, and Redemption: Barbary Captivity Narratives from Early Modern England*. New York: Columbia University Press, 2001.

Wansbrough, John. "Venice and Florence in the Mamluk Commercial Privileges." *Bulletin of the School of Oriental and African Studies* 28, no. 3 (1965): 483–523.

Weiss, Gillian. *Captives and Corsairs: France and Slavery in the Early Modern Mediterranean*. Stanford, CA: Stanford University Press, 2011.

———. "Infidels at the Oar: A Mediterranean Exception to France's Free Soil Principle." *Slavery & Abolition* 32, no. 3 (2011): 397–412.

Wettinger, Godfrey. *Slavery in the Islands of Malta and Gozo Ca. 1000–1812*. Malta: Publishers Enterprise Group, 2002.

White, Joshua M. "Fetva Diplomacy: The Ottoman Şeyhülislam as Trans-Imperial Intermediary." *Journal of Early Modern History* 19, nos. 2–3 (2015): 199–221.

———. "'It Is Not Halal to Raid Them': Piracy and Law in the Seventeenth-Century Ottoman Mediterranean." In *Corsairs and Pirates in the Eastern Mediterranean, 15th–19th Centuries*, edited by Gelina Harlaftis and David Starkey, 77–94. Athens: Sylvia Ioannou Foundation, 2016.

———. "Litigating Disputes over Ships and Cargo in Early Modern Ottoman Courts." *Quaderni Storici* 51, no. 3 (2016): 701–725.

———. "Shifting Winds: Piracy, Diplomacy, and Trade in the Ottoman Mediterranean, 1624–1626." In *Well-Connected Domains*, edited by Tobias Graf, Christian Roth, Gülay Tulasoğlu, and Pascal Firges, 37–53. Leiden: Brill, 2014.

———. "Slave Laundering: Piracy, Subjecthood, and the Illegal Captive Trade in the Ottoman Mediterranean." In *The Mediterranean Re-Imagined*, edited by Judith Tucker. Forthcoming.

Williams, Phillip. *Empire and Holy War in the Mediterranean: The Galley and Maritime Conflict between the Habsburgs and Ottomans*. London: I. B.Tauris, 2014.

Wood, Alfred Cecil. *A History of the Levant Company*. New York: Barnes & Noble, 1964.

Wright, Diana, and Pierre MacKay. "When the Serenissima and the Gran Turco Made Love: The Peace Treaty of 1478." *Studi Veneziani* 53 (2007): 261–277.

Zachariadou, Elizabeth. "Changing Masters in the Aegean." In *The Greek Islands and the Sea; Proceedings of the First International Colloquium Held at the Hellenic Institute, Royal Holloway, University of London*, edited by Julian Chrysostomides, Charalambos Dendrinos, and Jonathan Harris, 199–212. Camberly: Porphyrogenitus, 2004.

———. "Holy War in the Aegean during the Fourteenth Century." *Mediterranean Historical Review* 4, no. 1 (1989): 212–225.

———. "Monks and Sailors under the Ottoman Sultans." *Oriente Moderno* 20 (2001): 139–151.

———. "The Sandjak of Naxos in 1641." In *Osmanistik, Turkologie, Diplomatic; Festgabe an Josef Matuz*, edited by Christa Fragner and Klaus Schwarz, 329–342. Berlin: Klaus Schwarz Verlag, 1992.

Zecevic, Selma. "On the Margin of Text, On the Margin of Empire: Geography, Identity and Fatwa-Text in Ottoman Bosnia." PhD dissertation, Columbia University, 2007.

———. "Translating Ottoman Justice: Ragusan Dragomans as Interpreters of Ottoman Law." *Islamic Law and Society* 21, no. 4 (2014): 388–418.

Ze'evi, Dror. *An Ottoman Century: The District of Jerusalem in the 1600s*. Albany: State University of New York Press, 1996.

———. "The Use of Ottoman Sharīʿa Court Records as a Source for Middle Eastern Social History: A Reappraisal." *Islamic Law and Society* 5, no. 1 (1998): 35–56.

Zilfi, Madeline. *The Politics of Piety: The Ottoman Ulema in the Postclassical Age (1600–1800)*. Minneapolis: Bibliotheca Islamica, 1988.

———. *Women and Slavery in the Late Ottoman Empire: The Design of Difference*. Cambridge: Cambridge University Press, 2010.

Index

FSC
www.fsc.org
MIX
Papier | Fördert gute Waldnutzung
FSC® C083411

Kolibri 360 GmbH
Ferdinand-Jühlke-Straße 7
99095 Erfurt, Deutschland
produktsicherheit@kolibri360.de